LEVITICUS

Brazos Theological Commentary on the Bible

LEVITICUS

LEVITICUS

EPHRAIM RADNER

Brazos Press

a division of Baker Publishing Group
Grand Rapids, Michigan

Published by Brazos Press
a division of Baker Publishing Group
P.O. Box 6287, Grand Rapids, MI 49516–6287
www.brazospress.com

Printed in the United States of America

Library of Congress Cataloging-in-Publication Data

Radner, Ephraim, 1956–
    Leviticus / Ephraim Radner.
        p.   cm. — (Brazos theological commentary on the Bible)
    Includes bibliographical references and indexes.
    ISBN 978-1-58743-099-2 (pbk.)
    1. Bible. O.T. Leviticus—Commentaries. I. Title. II. Series.
BS1255.53.R33 2007
222′.1307—dc22   2007052336

To my father,
Roy Radner,
in thanksgiving for the sharing of his faith and love,

and for his parents,
Samuel and Ella

CONTENTS

SERIES PREFACE

Near the beginning of his treatise against Gnostic interpretations of the Bible, *Against the Heresies*, Irenaeus observes that Scripture is like a great mosaic depicting a handsome king. It is as if we were owners of a villa in Gaul who had ordered a mosaic from Rome. It arrives, and the beautifully colored tiles need to be taken out of their packaging and put into proper order according to the plan of the artist. The difficulty, of course, is that Scripture provides us with the individual pieces, but the order and sequence of various elements are not obvious. The Bible does not come with instructions that would allow interpreters to simply place verses, episodes, images, and parables in order as a worker might follow a schematic drawing in assembling the pieces to depict the handsome king. The mosaic must be puzzled out. This is precisely the work of scriptural interpretation.

Origen has his own image to express the difficulty of working out the proper approach to reading the Bible. When preparing to offer a commentary on the Psalms he tells of a tradition handed down to him by his Hebrew teacher:

> The Hebrew said that the whole divinely inspired Scripture may be likened, because of its obscurity, to many locked rooms in our house. By each room is placed a key, but not the one that corresponds to it, so that the keys are scattered about beside the rooms, none of them matching the room by which it is placed. It is a difficult task to find the keys and match them to the rooms that they can open. We therefore know the Scriptures that are obscure only by taking the points of departure for understanding them from another place because they have their interpretive principle scattered among them.[1]

As is the case for Irenaeus, scriptural interpretation is not purely local. The key in Genesis may best fit the door of Isaiah, which in turn opens up the meaning of Matthew. The mosaic must be put together with an eye toward the overall plan.

---

1. Fragment from the preface to *Commentary on Psalms 1–25*, preserved in the *Philokalia* (trans. Joseph W. Trigg; London: Routledge, 1998), 70–71.

Irenaeus, Origen, and the great cloud of premodern biblical interpreters assumed that puzzling out the mosaic of Scripture must be a communal project. The Bible is vast, heterogeneous, full of confusing passages and obscure words, and difficult to understand. Only a fool would imagine that he or she could work out solutions alone. The way forward must rely upon a tradition of reading that Irenaeus reports has been passed on as the rule or canon of truth that functions as a confession of faith. "Anyone," he says, "who keeps unchangeable in himself the rule of truth received through baptism will recognize the names and sayings and parables of the scriptures."[2] Modern scholars debate the content of the rule on which Irenaeus relies and commends, not the least because the terms and formulations Irenaeus himself uses shift and slide. Nonetheless, Irenaeus assumes that there is a body of apostolic doctrine sustained by a tradition of teaching in the church. This doctrine provides the clarifying principles that guide exegetical judgment toward a coherent overall reading of Scripture as a unified witness. Doctrine, then, is the schematic drawing that will allow the reader to organize the vast heterogeneity of the words, images, and stories of the Bible into a readable, coherent whole. It is the rule that guides us toward the proper matching of keys to doors.

If self-consciousness about the role of history in shaping human consciousness makes modern historical-critical study critical, then what makes modern study of the Bible modern is the consensus that classical Christian doctrine distorts interpretive understanding. Benjamin Jowett, the influential nineteenth-century English classical scholar, is representative. In his programmatic essay "On the Interpretation of Scripture," he exhorts the biblical reader to disengage from doctrine and break its hold over the interpretive imagination. "The simple words of that book," writes Jowett of the modern reader, "he tries to preserve absolutely pure from the refinements or distinctions of later times." The modern interpreter wishes to "clear away the remains of dogmas, systems, controversies, which are encrusted upon" the words of Scripture. The disciplines of close philological analysis "would enable us to separate the elements of doctrine and tradition with which the meaning of Scripture is encumbered in our own day."[3] The lens of understanding must be wiped clear of the hazy and distorting film of doctrine.

Postmodernity, in turn, has encouraged us to criticize the critics. Jowett imagined that when he wiped away doctrine he would encounter the biblical text in its purity and uncover what he called "the original spirit and intention of the authors."[4] We are not now so sanguine, and the postmodern mind thinks interpretive frameworks inevitable. Nonetheless, we tend to remain modern in at least one sense. We read Athanasius and think him stage-managing the diversity of Scripture to support his positions against the Arians. We read Bernard of Clairvaux and

2. *Against the Heretics* 9.4.
3. Benjamin Jowett, "On the Interpretation of Scripture," in *Essays and Reviews* (London: Parker, 1860), 338–39.
4. Ibid., 340.

assume that his monastic ideals structure his reading of the Song of Songs. In the wake of the Reformation, we can see how the doctrinal divisions of the time shaped biblical interpretation. Luther famously described the Epistle of James as a "strawy letter," for, as he said, "it has nothing of the nature of the Gospel about it."[5] In these and many other instances, often written in the heat of ecclesiastical controversy or out of the passion of ascetic commitment, we tend to think Jowett correct: doctrine is a distorting film on the lens of understanding.

However, is what we commonly think actually the case? Are readers naturally perceptive? Do we have an unblemished, reliable aptitude for the divine? Have we no need for disciplines of vision? Do our attention and judgment need to be trained, especially as we seek to read Scripture as the living word of God? According to Augustine, we all struggle to journey toward God, who is our rest and peace. Yet our vision is darkened and the fetters of worldly habit corrupt our judgment. We need training and instruction in order to cleanse our minds so that we might find our way toward God.[6] To this end, "the whole temporal dispensation was made by divine Providence for our salvation."[7] The covenant with Israel, the coming of Christ, the gathering of the nations into the church—all these things are gathered up into the rule of faith, and they guide the vision and form of the soul toward the end of fellowship with God. In Augustine's view, the reading of Scripture both contributes to and benefits from this divine pedagogy. With countless variations in both exegetical conclusions and theological frameworks, the same pedagogy of a doctrinally ruled reading of Scripture characterizes the broad sweep of the Christian tradition from Gregory the Great through Bernard and Bonaventure, continuing across Reformation differences in both John Calvin and Cornelius Lapide, Patrick Henry and Bishop Bossuet, and on to more recent figures such as Karl Barth and Hans Urs von Balthasar.

Is doctrine, then, not a moldering scrim of antique prejudice obscuring the Bible, but instead a clarifying agent, an enduring tradition of theological judgments that amplifies the living voice of Scripture? And what of the scholarly dispassion advocated by Jowett? Is a noncommitted reading, an interpretation unprejudiced, the way toward objectivity, or does it simply invite the languid intellectual apathy that stands aside to make room for the false truism and easy answers of the age?

This series of biblical commentaries was born out of the conviction that dogma clarifies rather than obscures. The Brazos Theological Commentary on the Bible advances upon the assumption that the Nicene tradition, in all its diversity and controversy, provides the proper basis for the interpretation of the Bible as Christian Scripture. God the Father Almighty, who sends his only begotten Son to die for us and for our salvation and who raises the crucified Son in the power of the Holy

---

5. *Luther's Works*, vol. 35 (ed. E. Theodore Bachmann; Philadelphia: Fortress, 1959), 362.

6. *On Christian Doctrine* 1.10.

7. *On Christian Doctrine* 1.35.

Spirit so that the baptized may be joined in one body—faith in *this* God with *this* vocation of love for the world is the lens through which to view the heterogeneity and particularity of the biblical texts. Doctrine, then, is not a moldering scrim of antique prejudice obscuring the meaning of the Bible. It is a crucial aspect of the divine pedagogy, a clarifying agent for our minds fogged by self-deceptions, a challenge to our languid intellectual apathy that will too often rest in false truisms and the easy spiritual nostrums of the present age rather than search more deeply and widely for the dispersed keys to the many doors of Scripture.

For this reason, the commentators in this series have not been chosen because of their historical or philological expertise. In the main, they are not biblical scholars in the conventional, modern sense of the term. Instead, the commentators were chosen because of their knowledge of and expertise in using the Christian doctrinal tradition. They are qualified by virtue of the doctrinal formation of their mental habits, for it is the conceit of this series of biblical commentaries that theological training in the Nicene tradition prepares one for biblical interpretation, and thus it is to theologians and not biblical scholars that we have turned. "War is too important," it has been said, "to leave to the generals."

We do hope, however, that readers do not draw the wrong impression. The Nicene tradition does not provide a set formula for the solution of exegetical problems. The great tradition of Christian doctrine was not transcribed, bound in folio, and issued in an official, critical edition. We have the Niceno-Constantinopolitan Creed, used for centuries in many traditions of Christian worship. We have ancient baptismal affirmations of faith. The Chalcedonian definition and the creeds and canons of other church councils have their places in official church documents. Yet the rule of faith cannot be limited to a specific set of words, sentences, and creeds. It is instead a pervasive habit of thought, the animating culture of the church in its intellectual aspect. As Augustine observed, commenting on Jeremiah 31:33, "The creed is learned by listening; it is written, not on stone tablets nor on any material, but on the heart."[8] This is why Irenaeus is able to appeal to the rule of faith more than a century before the first ecumenical council, and this is why we need not itemize the contents of the Nicene tradition in order to appeal to its potency and role in the work of interpretation.

Because doctrine is intrinsically fluid on the margins and most powerful as a habit of mind rather than a list of propositions, this commentary series cannot settle difficult questions of method and content at the outset. The editors of the series impose no particular method of doctrinal interpretation. We cannot say in advance how doctrine helps the Christian reader assemble the mosaic of Scripture. We have no clear answer to the question of whether exegesis guided by doctrine is antithetical to or compatible with the now-old modern methods of historical-critical inquiry. Truth—historical, mathematical, or doctrinal—knows no contradiction. But method is a discipline of vision and judgment, and we

8. *Sermon* 212.2.

cannot know in advance what aspects of historical-critical inquiry are functions of modernism that shape the soul to be at odds with Christian discipline. Still further, the editors do not hold the commentators to any particular hermeneutical theory that specifies how to define the plain sense of Scripture—or the role this plain sense should play in interpretation. Here the commentary series is tentative and exploratory.

Can we proceed in any other way? European and North American intellectual culture has been de-Christianized. The effect has not been a cessation of Christian activity. Theological work continues. Sermons are preached. Biblical scholars turn out monographs. Church leaders have meetings. But each dimension of a formerly unified Christian practice now tends to function independently. It is as if a weakened army had been fragmented, and various corps had retreated to isolated fortresses in order to survive. Theology has lost its competence in exegesis. Scripture scholars function with minimal theological training. Each decade finds new theories of preaching to cover the nakedness of seminary training that provides theology without exegesis and exegesis without theology.

Not the least of the causes of the fragmentation of Christian intellectual practice has been the divisions of the church. Since the Reformation, the role of the rule of faith in interpretation has been obscured by polemics and counterpolemics about *sola scriptura* and the necessity of a magisterial teaching authority. The Brazos Theological Commentary on the Bible series is deliberately ecumenical in scope, because the editors are convinced that early church fathers were correct: church doctrine does not compete with Scripture in a limited economy of epistemic authority. We wish to encourage unashamedly dogmatic interpretation of Scripture, confident that the concrete consequences of such a reading will cast far more light on the great divisive questions of the Reformation than either reengaging in old theological polemics or chasing the fantasy of a pure exegesis that will somehow adjudicate between competing theological positions. You shall know the truth of doctrine by its interpretive fruits, and therefore in hopes of contributing to the unity of the church, we have deliberately chosen a wide range of theologians whose commitment to doctrine will allow readers to see real interpretive consequences rather than the shadowboxing of theological concepts.

Brazos Theological Commentary on the Bible has no dog in the current translation fights, and we endorse a textual ecumenism that parallels our diversity of ecclesial backgrounds. We do not impose the thankfully modest inclusive-language agenda of the New Revised Standard Version, nor do we insist upon the glories of the Authorized Version, nor do we require our commentators to create a new translation. In our communal worship, in our private devotions, in our theological scholarship, we use a range of scriptural translations. Precisely as Scripture—a living, functioning text in the present life of faith—the Bible is not semantically fixed. Only a modernist, literalist hermeneutic could imagine that this modest fluidity is a liability. Philological precision and stability is a consequence of, not a basis for, exegesis. Judgments about the meaning of a text fix its literal sense, not the other way around. As a result, readers should expect an eclectic use of biblical translations, both across the different volumes of the series and within individual commentaries.

We cannot speak for contemporary biblical scholars, but as theologians we know that we have long been trained to defend our fortresses of theological concepts and formulations. And we have forgotten the skills of interpretation. Like stroke victims, we must rehabilitate our exegetical imaginations, and there are likely to be different strategies of recovery. Readers should expect this reconstructive—not reactionary—series to provide them with experiments in postcritical doctrinal interpretation, not commentaries written according to the settled principles of a well-functioning tradition. Some commentators will follow classical typological and allegorical readings from the premodern tradition; others will draw on contemporary historical study. Some will comment verse by verse; others will highlight passages, even single words that trigger theological analysis of Scripture. No reading strategies are proscribed, no interpretive methods foresworn. The central premise in this commentary series is that doctrine provides structure and cogency to scriptural interpretation. We trust in this premise with the hope that the Nicene tradition can guide us, however imperfectly, diversely, and haltingly, toward a reading of Scripture in which the right keys open the right doors.

R. R. Reno

PREFACE

I would like to thank Rusty Reno for his invitation, encouragement, and critical engagement with this commentary—he remains a true friend in Christ and brother in the church's devotion to the word of God; Christopher Seitz, for his tireless, rigorous, and intellectually challenging advocacy of Scripture's integrity and coherence, which he shared with me; the Church of the Ascension (Pueblo) and its people and the parish of Grace Episcopal Church (Colorado Springs) and its rector, the Rev. Donald Armstrong, for their support of my work in 2006 and their always eager and excited engagement with the Scriptures; my family, Annette, Hannah, and Isaac, for their openness to discussion, their patience with reflection, their support of labor, and their love. May the Lord bless them all.

ABBREVIATIONS

Acts	Acts	Jas.	James	Neh.	Nehemiah
Amos	Amos	Jer.	Jeremiah	Num.	Numbers
1 Chr.	1 Chronicles	Job	Job	Obad.	Obadiah
2 Chr.	2 Chronicles	Joel	Joel	1 Pet.	1 Peter
Col.	Colossians	John	John	2 Pet.	2 Peter
1 Cor.	1 Corinthians	1 John	1 John	Phil.	Philippians
2 Cor.	2 Corinthians	2 John	2 John	Phlm.	Philemon
Dan.	Daniel	3 John	3 John	Prov.	Proverbs
Deut.	Deuteronomy	Jonah	Jonah	Ps.	Psalms
Eccl.	Ecclesiastes	Josh.	Joshua	Rev.	Revelation
Eph.	Ephesians	Jude	Jude	Rom.	Romans
Esth.	Esther	Judg.	Judges	Ruth	Ruth
Exod.	Exodus	1 Kgs.	1 Kings	1 Sam.	1 Samuel
Ezek.	Ezekiel	2 Kgs.	2 Kings	2 Sam.	2 Samuel
Ezra	Ezra	Lam.	Lamentations	Song	Song of Songs
Gal.	Galatians	Lev.	Leviticus	1 Thess.	1 Thessalonians
Gen.	Genesis	Luke	Luke	2 Thess.	2 Thessalonians
Hab.	Habakkuk	Mal.	Malachi	1 Tim.	1 Timothy
Hag.	Haggai	Mark	Mark	2 Tim.	2 Timothy
Heb.	Hebrews	Matt.	Matthew	Titus	Titus
Hos.	Hosea	Mic.	Micah	Zech.	Zechariah
Isa.	Isaiah	Nah.	Nahum	Zeph.	Zephaniah

INTRODUCTION

My daughter began a devotional discipline when she was twelve—reading a chapter of the Bible every night, starting with Genesis. She had reached 1 Kings before I learned what she was up to. By the time my son decided to follow his older sister's suit, however, I was more on target; and I tried to make sure that I asked him about what he was reading as he went along. "I'm starting Leviticus," he told me one day. He was eleven at the time. I found myself saying to him, without even thinking, "You might want to skim the thing—you know, just a little here and there, and then move on to the next book." My instinct was to protect him from the *longeurs* of Leviticus. I didn't want him discouraged so early on in his discipline, which after all, is meant to edify, not drag down into boredom. His response, however, was quick and decisive: "I must read every word," he said nobly. "It's the Bible!"

Both reactions—my instinct to free him from the burden of the book, and his to press on through it in every detail—are bound to the character of Leviticus. Origen sums up this inner dynamic: "If you read people passages from the divine books that are good and clear, they will hear them with great joy. . . . But provide someone a reading from Leviticus, and at once the listener will gag and push it away as if it were some bizarre food. He came, after all, to learn how to honor God, to take in the teachings that concern justice and piety. But instead he is now hearing about the ritual of burnt sacrifices!" Origen himself realizes the problem: without the church taking the time deliberately to explain the dull details of the Jews' sacrificial rites, Sabbaths, and the like, they become but "deadly things." "It's the Jews' business; let them deal with it!" people will say in disgust. So he answers: "But begin from the principle that 'the law is spiritual' if we are to understand and explain all the lessons that are read." It is the church's responsibility to show the people that the dull details are filled with promise. "For my part, and because I believe what my Lord Jesus Christ has said, I think that there is not a 'jot or tittle' in the Law and the Prophets (Matt. 5:18) that does not contain a mystery."[1] Yes, Christians are put off by Leviticus; but still, there is something divine to be received within its words.

Despite Origen's hopes, however, Leviticus is today probably among the least read books of Scripture, by Christians anyway. It is rarely quoted in the New Testament itself, there being, on one count, only nine direct citations. But one verse—loving one's neighbor as oneself (Lev. 19:18)—stands as a centerpiece within Jesus's teaching about the law (Mark 12:31) and has thereby proved enormously influential within discussions of Christian moral teaching. Furthermore, the sacrificial cult described in Leviticus provides the major framework for at least one New Testament writing—the letter to the Hebrews. In the contemporary ecclesial culture wars, Leviticus has taken on a special, almost emblematic, prominence, standing as a kind of dark bogeyman, throwing up poorly understood but looming injunctions against certain forms of sexual behavior. These prohibitions, in turn, are tarred by association with a host of other Levitical attitudes we have otherwise long left behind. This detail of historical experience has itself given rise to a specific kind of defense for ethical development, dubbed the "shellfish argument" ("we eat shellfish, don't we? So why can't we also do x or y that is prohibited by Leviticus?"). Thus, despite its alien and unwelcoming character, Leviticus is a book that is hard to escape, even though we feel it would be easier, for a lot of reasons, if we could. Our ambivalence, furthermore, probably ends up informing our attitudes toward certain more central facets of the Christian faith. That Leviticus hovers, unavoidably, over the whole discussion of the cross of Christ, the sacrifice of our Lord, and the ritual of our eucharistic remembrances, not to mention over the forms of our common life and relations, means also that these central elements of our faith are themselves tinged with the very tension and confusion that we feel about Leviticus itself.

Critically, the historical line of commentary on Leviticus has followed a process wherein this ambivalence has harvested an alien fruit. Between Origen (the church's earliest and surely still greatest interpreter of the book) and Jacob Milgrom (the Jewish author of the present era's most expansive critical study of the book) the evolution of interpretation has moved in a distinctive direction: bit by bit the Christian sacrificial focus upon the book has narrowed through ever elaborated historical interest in the sociological details of ritual, to the point that the text's even potential Christian character has disappeared almost wholly. In its place, a vast and towering historical reconstruction of Israelite and Near Eastern social cultus has emerged as the book's residual substance, like a voracious jungle that has overgrown a long-lost human dump and through which readers must move either as painstaking botanists or cruel clearers of the forest, simply to reach the grim detritus of the text itself. Squeezed out completely in this history has been the divinely created and desired breadth of the world itself that the text was designed to comprehend and lay out to view within the context of redemption.

---

1. Origen, *Homilies on Numbers* 27.1; 7.1; *Homilies on Exodus* 1.4 (in Origen 1981: 1.14, 36).

This trajectory of Christian commentary is little more than the outworking of the problem Origen had already noted with respect to the place of Leviticus in popular perception, even in the early church. While the efforts of Christian theologians of his era and after to respond to the range of Manichean-like rejections of the Old Testament were largely successful, at least theoretically, Leviticus itself always proved an intransigently difficult case in the concrete. Origen's pioneering exegesis, both as a whole and with respect to Leviticus in particular, was a deliberate response to the widespread sense in the church that the book was both too hard to parse and finally irrelevant (possibly even hostile) to Christian concerns. And his methods in this regard sought to open the details—the jots and tittles—of the book to the broad range of divine action and purpose in the world of creation and history as a whole. He did this through the use of what he called "spiritual" reading. The complexity of the text's details, from this perspective, corresponded to the almost profligate character of God's all-encompassing work in creation and redemption, and the Christian reader's vocation and privilege was to uncover and engage these details. In this, Origen's approach was in tune with developing rabbinic methods of interpretation, themselves mostly marginalized in today's reading of Leviticus among most Jews, although in each case—Christian spiritual exegesis and rabbinic commentary like the *Rabboth*—there has been recently a minor renewal of interest among historical scholars.[2]

That the only substantial presence of Leviticus in the New Testament—but what a presence!—is given in the letter to the Hebrews, of course, meant that, for Origen and all subsequent serious Christian interpreters of the book, the spiritual reference of Leviticus would be primarily bound to the body and acts of Jesus as the Son of God. More than any other Old Testament writing, Leviticus demanded of the Christian exegete a figural reading, the theologically comprehensive character of which laid the foundations for the whole theory of scriptural figuration itself from a Christian viewpoint. The reality of the law as a shadow (Heb. 10:1) and of particular sacrifices as images of some heavenly pattern (9:23), that is, given its substantive appearance in the fleshly person and sacrificial history of Jesus (10:20), located the entire Old Testament in a relation of meaning and purpose that was novel and peculiar, certainly in reference to Jewish exegetical precedents for spiritual reading like Philo's. It is one thing to say that the letter of the text indicated some higher spiritual truth; it is quite another to identify that truth as Jesus the Christ. Furthermore, by wrapping Leviticus up, as it were, in Jesus— "sacrifices and offerings thou hast not desired, but a body hast thou prepared me"

---

2. See the overview by Wilken 1997. Neusner 1986: 119–25 argues that *Vayikra* or *Leviticus Rabbah*, to which I shall refer frequently, marks a dramatic reorientation of rabbinic reflection on Scripture, taking Scripture more seriously as a self-determining authority, as opposed to using it as a store of proof-texts for mishnaic legal commentary. This evaluation certainly places the *Rabbah* (dating perhaps two hundred to four hundred years after Origen, though based on much earlier material) in analogy with Origen's own dramatic reappropriation of Scripture.

(Heb. 10:5, quoting Ps. 40:6)—Jesus himself was interpretively given over to all the details of that book's (and the Old Testament's) wide reach.

This last is a crucial point: Jesus is rightly interpreted by Leviticus, so that the actual meaning of what he does, what he teaches, and who he is is informed even by the details of, for example, the laws on bodily fluids, sexual relations, genealogy, and planting. This converse effect of the early church's figural connection between Jesus and the Old Testament text is even less appreciated today than is the first. If it is difficult to find the meaning and purpose of Leviticus lodged in the body of Christ, it is even more difficult to find the meaning and purpose—the form—of Jesus expanded and explicated by the rich details of Leviticus. Indeed, the loss of the figural connection at its base has resulted in the squeezing out of the world from Jesus himself. Jesus is a "thinner" figure in contemporary understanding than is the dense personal reality he represented for Origen, in part because a book like Leviticus in particular no longer traces the outlines of his being.

Perhaps the last modern interpreter to engage this density most fully (though only as a hope left unrealized by his death) was Blaise Pascal. For Pascal, the problem with the Old Testament and especially with a book like Leviticus was not its seeming irrelevance to Christians. The book might well be construed in a (subjectively) relevant fashion, but what did that matter if the scope of relevance itself was spiritually deformed? The problem with Leviticus and the whole "law and the sacrifices" was that its details, if taken or dismissed in their simple literal character, mirrored a kind of person whose carnal nature was more interested in a superficial life than in being subjected to the hard realities of selfless love for God. Scripture is *difficult*, Pascal insisted, and no more so than when we attempt to decipher the true meaning of the law and the sacrifices. If that difficulty is avoided—by simplifying literalisms that, through their embrace or rejection, dispense us from grappling with the Scripture's obscurity—then the full depth of God's character, work, and vocation in Christ will be pushed aside as well (1966: frag. 287). "Objections by atheists: 'But we have no light'" (frag. 244); that is, "none of this makes any sense, so why bother?" Scripture's own discussion of the sacrificial ceremonial, for instance, is filled with contradictions, Pascal notes in a lengthy fragment from his unfinished defense of Christianity: in some places (like Leviticus), Scripture says the sacrifices are pleasing to God; in others they are said to be displeasing to God (as in some of the Psalms and Prophets). Yet both cases, because they are Scripture speaking, are the truth itself. Only a figurative reading of the sacrifices, Pascal argues, can reconcile such a contradiction, not in a wooden sense, but by attaching each reality—the positive and negative character of the sacrificial ritual in the eyes of God—to the full historical ministry of Jesus whose own life in the Father's purposes is marked by a deep obscurity that expresses the profound reality of created human nature and redemption (frags. 257–60).

How does this happen? Because Scripture is the living word of God, our engagement with its reading represents God working with us. And the very details of Scripture, as they exercise our understanding and care, are therefore instruments of the primary mission of God in our souls. Leviticus—even before it is examined—must be assumed to be a means by which the truth of God is exposed to us for our eternal destiny. The whole of reality comprises two foundational truths according to Pascal: the redemptive love of God, and the corruption of human life and nature. If, that is, Leviticus stands upon a contradiction regarding the character of its referents and their enduring effect—for example, opposing views of sacrifice—it can only be because these referents themselves must be examined as caught up within and as markers of the contradiction itself. That is, what Leviticus says about the sacrifices must somehow mean something that also comprehends what the Prophets themselves say about sacrifice. The two are not simply alternative readings of sacrifice, to be laid before the reader or church and chosen as discerned for this or that moment of history. Each part of Scripture must also represent and express the reality of the world's actual shape as a whole, as Pascal explains it. It is the holding together and exposing of these two truths of redemption and corruption simultaneously that the Christian faith represents and that Jesus himself embodies in the flesh of space and time and that Scripture's writing and reading enacts.

But in this, the entire world and the world's history is implicated: what it means to traverse the centuries, to encounter creation, to navigate the challenges of heart and being, to be confronted by God and to be taken up by God, is here included. "He is a God who makes [men] inwardly aware of their wretchedness and his infinite mercy: who unites himself with them in the depths of their soul: who fills it with humility, joy, confidence and love: who makes them incapable of having any other end but him" (Pascal 1966: frag. 449). And scriptural figuration itself somehow enacts the sweep of this historical and metaphysical reality in its very challenge.

The obscurity of the Levitical ceremonial, for example, works both a cosmic light and darkness upon the reader that finds its full substance (and actual origin) in the "humiliated" Christ who expresses the divine love that is Scripture's only purpose to articulate: "If there were no obscurity man would not feel his corruption: if there were no light man could not hope for a cure. Thus it is not only right but useful for us that God should be partly concealed and partly revealed, since it is equally dangerous for man to know God without knowing his own wretchedness as to know his wretchedness without knowing God" (Pascal 1966: frag. 446; see also 220, 268).

The whole Scriptures thus work as a concurrent "blinding" and "enlightening," according to Jesus's own explanation of his parabolic teaching on the basis of prophetic speech in general (Pascal 1966: frags. 332–36). "The disciples came and said to him, 'Why do you speak to them in parables?' . . . 'Because seeing they do not see, and hearing they do not hear, nor do they understand. With them indeed is fulfilled the prophecy of Isaiah'" (Matt. 13:10, 13, quoting Isa. 6:9; cf. Mark 4:12). The centrality of this form of speech within the ministry of the Son as whole marks figuration as a supreme instrument of divine love, by which (as Augustine insisted) all readings of Scripture are to be judged: "Look at all the prescribed ceremonies and all the commandments not [explicitly] directed toward charity, and it will be seen that they are figurative. . . . Everything which does not lead to charity is figurative. The sole object of Scripture is charity" (1966: frags. 267, 270). And this charity, encompassed by the exfoliating figurative expositions of the scriptural text, takes in the world: "God diversified this single precept of charity," Pascal concludes (frag. 270), so that whole of creation and our "curious" minds could be comprehended into its referential reach. And this is only because the precept and its scriptural multiplication derives from "the world exist[ing] only through Christ" and "Jesus Christ [being] the object of all things, the centre toward which all things tend. Whoever knows him knows the reason for everything" (frag. 449). Although the forms for reading Leviticus are not given in advance, we therefore know that *any* proper Christian reading of the text will *somehow* detail the redemptive work of the humiliated Christ upon the broken hearts of human beings and of the whole created order. "Figural" reading is the name we give to the outworking of this "somehow."

Pascal's peculiar Augustinian anthropology notwithstanding, the foundation for his approach to Leviticus was both traditional and traditionally expansive, in the line of Origen's early direction:

> The letter is seen just like the flesh [of the incarnate word], but hidden inside of it is the spiritual sense that is grasped like [his] divinity. This is what we shall find as we peruse the book of Leviticus, with all of its descriptions of sacrificial rites, its diverse offerings, and the ministries of its priests. These are all things that, according to their letter—which is like the flesh of the word of God and the clothing of his divinity—both the worthy and the unworthy can apprehend and understand. But "happy are the eyes" [Luke 10:23] that see the divine Spirit hidden within, beneath the veil of the letter; and happy are those who apply to this hearing the pure ears of the inner man. If not, they shall clearly perceive in these words "the letter that kills" [2 Cor. 3:6]. (*Homilies on Leviticus* 1.1)

For Origen, as for Pascal, the incarnational image here is more than a metaphor: the figural meaning of the text represents and encloses the whole history of God's work with the world, the movement of the Logos in creation, judgment, and redemption, and the movement of the human soul within this larger current of divine work. As students of Origen have pointed out, his method of spiritual exegesis—whether considered in its twofold scheme of letter and spirit or in its more elaborate threefold scheme of "history, morality, and mystery"—is less the pursuit of a formal exercise than it is an engagement with a word that is understood to be intrinsically reflective of the full historical work of the Spirit that animates it. We are called to read the Scripture as participants in a divine economy through which the meanings of material realities—worldly and written—are given in these realities' disclosure of divine life.[3] The full range, therefore, of Levitical referents

3. See Marcel Borret's careful introduction in Origen 1981: 1.22–34.

reflects the creative breadth of the Logos himself, in his Spirit-led mission from the foundation of the world and into the church's life as bound to the incarnate one's body. The degree to which and the manner in which figural exegesis is bound up with the development and maintenance of a Nicene trinitarian theology is unclear. Certainly, there is no logical determinism involved. But there is no doubt that the formative, embracing, and creative character of Scripture's written word, in Origen's view, as it comprehends the very shape of history, sustains the rapprochement and finally the identity of Logos and divinity, in a way that some developments of Antiochene exegesis could not.[4] The christological implications of Origen's scriptural figuralism in this sense surmounted those of his asceticism, the latter of which could easily lead in subordinationist and even Arian directions (see Kannengiesser 1991). Jewish figuralism, with the same sense of the word's (and its words') creative initiative, interestingly also founds the development of Judaism's most richly differentiated divine metaphysic, such as that in the Kabbalah.

Origen was not the only reader of Leviticus in the early church, but he was by far the most powerful. Even while other theologians, from Tertullian through Augustine, might approach the book most frequently in terms of its place within the *history* of God's pedagogy of Israel, when it came to the actual meaning of specific texts, Origen's spiritual exegesis dominated. And medieval exegesis tended to follow, rather than build upon this tradition. Origen's influence proved decisive through the sixteenth century, either directly or through intermediaries like Hesychius of Jerusalem and then later compilations like the *Glossa ordinaria*. There are in fact more extant manuscripts of Origen's *Homilies on Leviticus*, in Rufinus's Latin translation and paraphrase, than of his other commentaries on the Hexateuch, for the book itself provided the clearest application of the exegetical method based on multiple senses that was central to medieval reading. Furthermore, the elaborated evolution of the Western church's sacramental culture proved a fertile parallel, figurally and in its own significating right, to the cult of ancient Israel, and the book of Leviticus proved a sturdy imagistic bulwark in this regard to liturgical life. To a real extent, this actually tended toward the desiccation of the exegesis of Leviticus, as the book's objects and referents were increasingly given rote explications that simply followed the fittings of current ecclesial practice.

This observation is important. Even Origen's homilies, especially if read in sequence as a whole, can become wearisome in their unrelenting insistence upon the spiritual referents of the text. But it is crucial to note the character of this insistence, for its limitations lie less in the motive than in the pinched unidirectional dynamic of his interpretations, which jump almost immediately, over and over again, to the New Testament texts dealing with levels of virtue and vice and the ascetic soteriology with which he tended to work, however richly. By the Middle

---

4. Maegher (1978: chap. 1) employs the useful distinction between "disclosive" and "creative" aspects of the scriptural word, which, while they could oppose one another, could also in some theologians (like Origen and Augustine) complement each other.

Ages, this habit had made Leviticus, in many instances, no more than a handbook of Christian tropes that did little, in fact, to open the scriptural text to the fullness of the incarnational implications that Origen himself held as foundational. Curiously, a better place to see this scriptural opening and even incarnational implication is in Jewish exegesis, as it developed its midrashic methods and traditions, which are still employed especially in the orthodox hassidic interpretive communities and founded on the reality that the temple's disappearance redirected the localized cultic laws toward other referents.[5]

The *Leviticus Rabbah* represents a critical, indeed essential, fertile, and in many ways easily adapted exegetical orientation for Christian reading of Leviticus in particular. While the *Rabbah* assumes wider referents—spiritual in a broad sense—for the objects of the text, these are never reduced to what become the free-floating emblematic catalogues of the Christian Middle Ages. Rather, these referents are always discerned through the traversing of the history of Israel and its scriptural persons, from Adam and Cain to Abraham and into the times of the kingdoms and beyond. If, for instance, a purificatory rite is being examined, its meaning is derived only through a dynamic sifting of the lives and intratextual discussions, as it were, of Abraham and David, of Israel and Persia, of Isaiah and Moses, as their own lives engage the realities of sin and forgiveness. Each speaks to the other, with Leviticus as a kind of narrative forum. Obviously, the chronological character of narrative here is drastically loosened, but the narrative and temporal moorings of Leviticus are heightened, not lessened, through its words being suffused by the history of Israel and its people. And this, frankly, is a greater witness to word made flesh—because the landscape of Scripture is always inhabited by a people with whom God is engaged—than are the almost abstracted symbolizations that end up dominating Christian exegesis of Leviticus and that, for all the Reformers' rejection of their fabricated particularity, still inform the Protestant reduction of the Old Testament's cultic and even legal material to contemporized moral allegory. Under the best of circumstances, "the letters of the Jews are black and clean / And lie in chain-line over Christian pages," "hedg[ing]" the flesh of man" (Shapiro 2003: 109, in a poem entitled "The Alphabet"). When the "barbed wire" of Israel's scriptured history is removed, the flesh, as it were, threatens to dash away across the pages and purposes of the Bible like a convict on the run.

Yet even despite the drift into leaden symbolism, the medieval tradition nonetheless managed to keep the "letter" of Leviticus from turning into a mere husk, for concurrent with the formalizing of typological and allegorical readings of the book, Christian exegetes maintained a strong and continued conviction that the interplay between literal object and spiritual meaning within the text was a crucial

5. Babylonian Talmud, tractate *Megillah* 31b says: "Abraham said, '. . . but when [the temple] does not [exist], what will become of [the sacrifices] then?' God said, 'I have appointed for them the chapters about the sacrifices: whenever they read them, I will reckon it to them as they had brought the offerings before me, and I will forgive them their sins.'" Prayer and suffering became posttemple atoning substitutes for sacrifice.

sign of the outworking of *God's* acts of judgment and mercy in the history of the world and of the human soul. The *Glossa ordinaria*, citing Hesychius, introduces Leviticus as the place where God exposes humankind to the "good law" of life and the "bad law" of death, spoken of in Ezek. 20:11, 20 and here given in the single words of the text to the Spirit-led or Spirit-abandoned individual and people (Patrologia latina 113.297). The whole drama of salvation is played out in the text and the text's actual reception, as the figural interpretive enterprise engages the hearts and hopes of the book's readers. This was exactly the view Pascal embraced with a passion: "Each man finds in these promises [of the law and sacrifices] what lies in the depths of his own heart; either temporal or spiritual blessings, God or creatures; . . . [and] those who are looking for God find him, without any contradictions, and find that they are bidden to love God alone and that a Messiah did come at the time foretold to bring them the blessings for which they ask" (1966: frag. 503). And finding God, they find, turning back to the letter of the text, all the creatures of God as they are properly to be loved.

That Leviticus contained the world was a Jewish conviction and, retrospectively rightly ordered in Christ, was a Christian assumption derived from Origen's incarnational reading of the text. And still in the Middle Ages the assumption was elaborated so as to induce sometimes an almost joyful appropriation of the book's referents toward a celebration of creative blessing. Bede had early used Ps. 19's praise of the law to explicate the order of the Pentateuch, with each book somehow illustrating a kind of historical progression from natural law through to the written law and finally to the new law of the gospel. Within this schema, Bede suggested that Leviticus represented a kind of "clarifying" word on the distinctions of these contrasts, with God speaking to the movement from nature to Christ. The call by God to Moses for ordering the offerings of the people that opens the book becomes, in this reading, the figure for the whole world's gathering in faith, and the animals and objects are each laid out in the text as embodied images of the evangelical work of drawing in the nations through time (Patrologia latina 91.331–34). The reader of Leviticus, then, is asked to engage a kind of map that traces the work of God in history and whose apprehension provides a living structure to the actual life of the world in which the reader lives. Although attempts were made to render this kind of exegesis methodical in its ascetic exercise, with one sense of the text purportedly built upon another (literal first, then allegorical, then moral)[6] and following the progress of the soul's ascent to God, the actual practice of figural reading in its details strikes us as conspicuously unordered. Indeed, medieval commentary on a book like Leviticus appears like a random pile of symbols. But the coherence and relationship of the details is given, not so much in a methodological outline of reference, as in the underlying assumption that the book as a whole depicts the work of God in Christ on a cosmic scale, comprehensive enough to demand the wealth of detail figured in the book's verses. In this sense, the associative method

6. See Borret's introduction in Origen 1981: 1.25–34; also Davis 2005: 76–77.

of medieval exegesis, whereby images from the primary text are brought into relation with other parts of the Bible not out of a systematic logic but merely through linguistic concordance, is deliberately arbitrary, from a human perspective, for it submits, first of all, the ordering of the figures to the initiative of the divine letter, given as an array of scriptural articulation that is granted a kind of inherent verbal networking. And, second, it assumes that the economy of Christ has preestablished these connections through the simple reality of his "subjecting all things to himself" (1 Cor. 15:27–28). A power of divine gravity directs the ordering of figuration as a kind of magnetism of form.

The letter to the Hebrews, in fact, locates the work of God depicted in Leviticus in the actual *body* of Christ. This underlying reality, grasped by Origen and made central in all subsequent Christian commentary, includes not only the more obvious sacrificial details of the book, but also the communal laws of Israel's familial and civic relationships, whose referents must ultimately extend to the church as members of Christ. More broadly, the body of Christ in its personal and ecclesial aspects is seen to be the vehicle by which all of creation is brought into the reconciling purpose of God (Col. 1:15–20). Thus, it persists as the referent even of the disparate details of animal and plant existence that populate the text within its legal demarcations. The world-historical character of the exposition in Hebrews of the fate of Christ's body demanded such a sweep (Heb. 1:1–3), and, at least through the seventeenth century, it still informed the reading of Leviticus in a crucial way, as Andrew Willet's elaborate 1631 commentary shows.[7] Just as the Son and the Father are one (John 10:30), and whoever sees the Son has seen the Father (12:45), so the divine will behind the law of Leviticus finds its formal exposition within the body of the Son himself as it reorders the whole of creation.

While some modern commentaries, particularly of a traditional Protestant orientation, maintain a strict figural reading of the sacrificial images of Leviticus, applying them to aspects of a carefully articulated atonement theology, even these have long been cramped by a single doctrinal focus that reproduces, in its own way, the disembodied emblematic universe of medieval exegetes. Calvin's example, though more supple than his followers' approach, nonetheless shied away from all but the most prominent sacrificial metaphors for Christ, leaving most of the book useful only in terms of its depiction of and exhortation to self-disciplined obedience and the virtues attendant upon it.[8] Leviticus fell prey to the general

7. Willet's commentary (part of a series he completed on several books of Scripture) is an extremely useful and detailed compilation of exegetical arguments from both antiquity and his own era, including many Roman Catholic and Reformed commentators. He refers regularly to Rashi as well and despite his own Puritan Anglican convictions treats most of his sources fairly if unimaginatively.

8. Since all the ceremonial law is fulfilled in Christ, their only value now is to show us how, in moral terms, to live now with Christ. Calvin comments on Lev. 3:1: the Israelites' obedience to the details of sacrifice teach us moral subjection to the rule of Christ in terms of different virtues, like scrupulosity of devotion, thanksgiving, attentiveness, and so on (1996: 2.333–35).

skepticism about figural readings that crept over the churches after the Reformation divisions, and its content quickly proved uninteresting to the growing doctrinal-historical approach to the Scriptures that took its place. At best, the book provided sensationalist fodder to skeptical opponents of scriptural authority as a whole, as is still the case. By and large the book has fallen readily into the most marginalizing exercises of historical-critical inquiry. To be sure, by the end of the nineteenth century, the consignment of Leviticus to the dustbin of "Judaic superstition" at the hands of deist and rationalist polemics was alleviated slightly by the rise of anthropological inquiry and the developing interest in comparative religion as a discipline. New insight into the character of sacrifice and holiness as more general elements of *human* religiosity provided Leviticus with a reburnished profile as a major literary example within the collection of data being assembled by scholars to plumb the depths of the religious psyche of humanity. At the same time, the book's place within the evolving theoretical frameworks of documentary criticism of the Bible was always important. But none of this did much to encourage the actual *reading* of Leviticus as a living word from God within the Christian church, and the book continues to languish in the backwaters of last-ditch Bible studies and in the initial rush of introductory Scripture courses.

This commentary takes its place within the course of the traditional reading of Leviticus that came to its end, at least as a living thing, in the early modern period. It is not a history of interpretation, but a theological reflection; and so it uses only a small number of prior readers, Christian and Jewish, more as types of understanding, prying open a hearing in the heart (see list at end of this chapter). My use of Jewish commentary, for instance, will be highly anachronistic and acultural, engaging interpretations of the Torah outside the context, usually, of the Talmud and the talmudic tradition. My goal is not to understand that tradition in itself, with respect to Leviticus, so much as to open lines of interpretation to Christian readers that might otherwise be clouded due to our own historic hermeneutic prejudices and presuppositions. And the approach of this commentary *is* that of a Christian reading, bound to the life of church and its reality as the body of Christ, but deeply informed by the Jewish discipline of treating the Scriptures as a still-inhabited universe. But because of this, it is a difficult reading, attempting to outline the obscurities, not the simplicities, that determine our calling as followers of one of whom "the world was not worthy" (Heb. 11:38), though by whom the world was loved in the Son's own death (John 3:16). The reading of Leviticus, in this sense, is a hard and narrow way (Matt. 7:14); it is a kind of discipleship whereby our own hearts are exposed to the world's edges even as they are challenged and transformed by the world's redeemer. This is a reading filled with images of becoming, as the encounter of the text with Christ's world transforms all that is in it, text and world together. Things and objects become new; they do not only stand for one another. Well might we yearn for protection from such an encounter; but in this we would desire wrongly. If in fact "Jesus also suffered outside the gate" (Heb. 13:12), and in this showed forth the meaning of those beasts burnt outside the camp in Lev.

4:21, so in the very act of apprehending such a truth with joy, we too "go forth to him outside the camp" (Heb. 13:13), we too follow.

If there is a movement that takes place in Leviticus—a movement discovered in its reading—it is not only the movement of the human soul as it is snared by the challenges of a spiritual text and taken to a new place of love, for this could happen only if there were a prior movement of the Spirit, one in which the Son of Man goes forth into the world and through it and with it goes to the Father, and if this prior movement were the foundation of the text and its details. This is the great following we undertake, and through it, the hard reading of this book marks out the good work of his will (Heb. 13:21), in which we listen, with all creation, to the call: "Arise! Let us be going to our Father" (cf. Mark 14:42; Luke 15:18).

Frequently Cited Commentaries

Origen	*Homélies sur le lévitique: texte latin, introduction, traduction et notes.* Edited by Marcel Borret. 2 vols. Sources chrétiennes 286–87. Paris: Cerf, 1981.
Bede	*Explanatio in tertium librum mosis.* Patrologia latina 91.331–58.
Rabanus Maurus	*Expositiones in leviticam.* Patrologia latina 108.247–586.
Rupert of Deutz	*De trinitate et operibum ijus: in leviticum.* Patrologia latina 167.743–836.
Glossa ordinaria	*Liber leviticus.* Patrologia latina 113.295–380.
Bruno of Segni	*Expositio in leviticum.* Patrologia latina 164.377–464.
Calvin	John Calvin, *Commentaries on the Four Last Books of Moses Arranged in the Form of a Harmony.* Translated by Charles W. Bingham. 4 vols. Reprinted Grand Rapids: Baker, 1996 (orig. 1852).
Willet	Andrew Willet, *Hexapla in leviticum; that is, A Six-fold Commentarie upon the Third Booke of Moses.* London: Printed by Aug. Matthewes, for Robert Milbourne, at the signe of the Greyhound in Pauls Church-yard, 1631.
Sifra	Jacob Neusner, *Sifra: An Analytical Translation.* 3 vols. to date. Atlanta: Scholars Press, 1988–.
Rabbah	Jacob Neusner, *Judaism and Scripture: The Evidence of Leviticus Rabbah.* Chicago: University of Chicago Press, 1986.
Rashi	Morris Rosenbaum and Abraham Maurice Silbermann (eds./trans.), *Pentateuch with Targum Onkelos, Haphtaroth, and Rashi's Commentary*, vol. 3: *Leviticus.* London: Routledge & Kegan Paul, 1932.
Nahmanides	Ramban (Nahmanides), *Commentary on the Torah*, vol. 3: *Leviticus.* Translated by Charles B. Chavel. New York: Shilo, 1974.
Me'am Lo'ez	*The Torah Anthology, MeAm Lo'ez*, vols. 11–12: *Leviticus.* Translated by Aryeh Kaplan. New York: Maznaim, 1982.
Hirsch	Samson Raphael Hirsch, *The Pentateuch: Translated and Explained*, vol. 3. Translated by Isaac Levy. Gateshead: Judaica, 1973.

PROLOGUE

Leviticus stands as the third book of the Pentateuch, the Five Books of Moses or the Torah ("teaching, law") of Judaism. The book is known as *Vayikra* in the Hebrew canon, a title taken from the opening verse of the first chapter, meaning "and he called" (i.e., "The LORD called Moses"). The name "Leviticus," on the other hand, derives from the third-century BC Greek translation of the Hebrew Bible, known as the Septuagint, and refers to the members of the tribe of Levi, from which the priests of Israel were taken. The rabbis sometimes refer to this book as "the instruction of (or to) the priests," and the implication is that the book is primarily a manual for priestly functions. While there are obvious reasons for reading Leviticus as a priestly manual—a fact that has dominated and constrained critical studies of the text in the past 150 years—nonetheless much of the book is in fact addressed to "the people of Israel," via Moses, and the content of the instructions, although focused often on ritual realities, is in fact comprehensive of an entire way of life for all people and, as we shall see, for the world and creation as a whole. Although the name "Leviticus" (which was taken over by the Latin church) stands throughout this commentary, on a theological basis the Hebrew title *Vayikra* is a far more accurate way of naming the purpose of the book.

The narrative placement of Leviticus within the order of the Pentateuch is clear. At the beginning of the second year after their departure from Egypt, and following the initial setup of the tabernacle at the foot of Sinai, built according to the specifications given to Moses by God (Exod. 40:16–38), "the glory of the LORD filled the tabernacle." Exodus ends by explaining how the continuing journey of the Israelites through the wilderness was always directed by the Lord's "cloud" lifting from the tabernacle and leading them forward. Leviticus itself takes up this situation and provides a long series of instructions, given by God to Moses and the people of Israel from the now-erected tabernacle.

The tabernacle itself has a form that follows the divine instructions given in the latter chapters of Exodus (Exod. 25–31; 36–39). It provides a spatial orientation for a number of the laws of Leviticus and is worth understanding briefly. Following, as one tradition has it, the ordered levels of approach to Mount Sinai commanded by God in Exod. 19 and Exod. 24, the tabernacle was constructed to enforce a graduated and protected approach into the divine presence. Evidently built as a portable shrine, it was designed to be carried with the Israelites during their journey through the wilderness. Its form later becomes the model of the temple(s) built in Jerusalem. According to the specifications given in Exodus, the tabernacle proper was centrally located in the western half of a large court measuring 100 cubits x 50 cubits. This court was surrounded by a wall of linen hangings or curtains on a wood frame. The tabernacle itself was built as a tent measuring 20 cubits x 10 cubits, oriented to the west, and covered by two layers of skin roofing. Its walls (and an initial covering) were of linen draped over a framework of boards, very much like a large and sturdy tent. The entrance to both the outer court and the tabernacle was from the east. The western third of the tabernacle was separated off by a curtain or veil, and within this section, known as the holy of holies, was placed the ark of the covenant, containing the two tablets of the law. The larger section of the tabernacle contained an altar for incense (before the curtain), a table for the bread, and a golden lampstand. In the outer court, directly in front of its eastern entrance, was found the altar upon which burnt sacrifices were offered and near it the large laver for washing. All these elements come up or are presupposed in the course of the commands of Leviticus.

There has been much debate over the historical and concrete relationship between the divinely described tabernacle and the tent of meeting mentioned in Exod. 33:7–11; Num. 11:1–12:8; and Deut. 31:14–15. Are they one and the same, sequentially confused in the narrative? Does the tent of meeting reflect the original tabernacle, whose elaborate details are really later images from the postexilic era, retrojecting (for ideological purposes?) the temple's shape into a Mosaic period? Is there some other historical confusion at work? Does a previous tent of meeting become incorporated, as it were, both linguistically and practically, into the tabernacle's function once it has been erected (Exod. 40:2)? This last suggestion seems reasonable, but there are still seeming inconsistencies: Exod. 33:7 and Num. 11:16–30 picture the tent of meeting as being pitched "outside the camp," while the tabernacle, once erected, sometimes seems to lie in the center of the camp, surrounded by the people (Num. 2; Lev. 24:10–23). The locales appear confused, and this has given rise to theories positing differing traditions regarding the tent and tabernacle, deriving from differing times and contexts, that have been interwoven in the Pentateuchal material only at a later date.[1]

We are not told where and when exactly the instructions that make up the bulk of Leviticus are given. But when the book of Numbers picks up its narrative, it appears that one month has passed from the erection of the tabernacle (Exod.

---

1. One of the best and most textually detailed summaries of these matters is still Davies 1962.

40:17) and the opening events of Numbers (Num. 1:1). The instructions and events of Leviticus, therefore, seem to fall within this single month.

The events in question may appear limited. By and large, the bulk of Leviticus is devoted to the instructions given by God that regulate sacrifice, worship, and the behavior divinely demanded by Israel's calling. However, several narrative episodes in the book lodge these instructions within the temporal unfolding of history. First, Moses follows God's command by consecrating Aaron and his sons and by performing the associated sacrifices (Lev. 8–9). This takes a week. In Lev. 10, two of Aaron's sons are killed by God, following their offering of "unholy fire" apart from God's direction. But because no time of mourning is allowed, we can assume that these events take place on a single day. After the sacrifices that follow Nadab's and Abihu's deaths, most of the rest of the book resumes its series of divine instructions. These are, however, briefly interrupted by a third event, the blasphemy and stoning of Shelomith's son, in 24:10–23. The instructions of Leviticus, therefore, are either given without interruption (apart from the events just mentioned) or are given sequentially over the course of the remaining month.

There is some ambiguity over the location of this revelation, however, that may inform the question of its timing. Leviticus opens with God calling Moses to the tent of meeting. Leviticus 25, however, opens with the phrase "the LORD said to Moses on Mount Sinai" (see also 7:38). Are we to understand that a part of the revelations was given at the tabernacle and another part directly to Moses on Sinai itself? The book as a whole, however, ends with the summary that "these are the commandments which the LORD commanded Moses for the people of Israel on Mount Sinai" (27:34; cf. 26:46), as if all that is contained in Leviticus was given to Moses on Sinai. The traditional Jewish way of answering this confusion is to distinguish between the general shape of the laws, given directly on the summit of the mountain, and the explanation of the law's details, given later at the tent of meeting or at least explained by Moses to the people in this location. On this reading, Leviticus represents something of a temporally blurred revelation, some of it referring back to the original general revelation, much of it offering the later details of those general laws. Calvin's treatment of the laws in Leviticus as subsets of the Ten Commandments represents a theological version of this solution (1996: 1.416).

However, it seems more straightforward to read "on Sinai" as a general location, referring to the Israelites' encampment around the foot of the mountain (as in Num. 10:11–12), where the tabernacle was located. This has been a traditional Christian reading of the text, at least since the seventeenth century. Indeed, the narrative flow, despite its limited touchstones within the book, depends upon this sequentially continuous reading, which locates the laws themselves within the ongoing struggles of Israel's human life, as the two stories of Aaron's sons and Shelomith's son embody. The character of historical time, along with the agonies of generational loss, is in fact one of the central themes of Leviticus, and it would be strange if the book itself articulated its contents only from within a deep temporal murkiness.

These kinds of questions, however, motivated the critical analysis of Leviticus according to its history of composition, a practice that generally assumed its non-Mosaic authorship. In the late nineteenth century, Julius Wellhausen, applying insights gathered from previous scholars, first formalized this notion that Leviticus derives from a separate documentary source from within the Pentateuch. He called this the Priestly (P) collection of materials and associated it with a late postexilic community of scribes tied to the Second Temple.[2] The theory of multiple sources, both for the Pentateuch as a whole and within Leviticus itself, has since been elaborated and emended many times, in attempts to take account of various linguistic, ritual, and theological divergences identified within the text. These attempts, furthermore, involve the speculative positing of various historical settings from which the particular portions of the text, small and great, might arise—settings and origins that some scholars date back to the preexilic period (either in the northern kingdom or in Judah or even before David).[3] There is great diversity among historical critics over this question of setting and dating. Critics of the documentary method have also emerged, some using critical approaches to argue for an ancient uniform origin to the text's major substance, others to undercut the critical effort altogether.

Many of the conclusions of these historical-critical efforts surrounding the text of Leviticus possess real plausibility, and the questions they address cannot simply be ignored. But their usefulness in understanding the book as Scripture is limited. Whether one adopts a canonical attitude or simply a methodological historical skepticism—where plausibility, in such cases, can never logically rise to the level of probability—a religious approach to the text will require the supposition of a divinely providential coherence to its utilized form. And it is that providential coherence that will demand scrutiny with respect to the text's meaning and application. Theologically, one might say that the name "Moses" and the explicated narrative framework of the book represent just that providential coherence in its historical imposition upon the church and its times. And this is so not only in a symbolically cognitive way—what one might call a heuristic fashion, whereby the names and characters of the text stand in the reader's mind as the indicators of that coherence, but do so more as signs than as historically constituted figures. Rather, the theologically robust claim of providential coherence for the text tells us that Moses and Israel represent that coherence really and historically: God presents and thereby fashions time, through Leviticus, in the form of Moses and Israel as they are depicted in the

2. Wellhausen 1885 remains the critical wellspring for approaching Leviticus from a multi-documentary perspective. A sophisticated modern example is Elliger 1966. The most exhaustive modern commentator on Leviticus, Milgrom 1991–2000, uses a variety of historical-critical tools, but tends to approach the text in terms of a greater (albeit temporally limited and nonecclesial) coherence.

3. Levine 1989 provides a religious (Jewish) commentary that is well integrated with an attempt at detailing critical historical locale.

sacred text.[4] This *is* history, though a history accessible only through God's revelatory display of its force.

The narrative history given in Leviticus is thus central. It is central, though, not because of its temporally limited character and meaning—which, as we saw above, do in fact present inconsistencies—but because the times that it represents are, in God's providence, times that form all times and expose the meaning of all time. And in this perspective, the inconsistencies themselves have a meaning to be pursued. In Leviticus in particular, the narrative depiction of God's call to Moses, the explanation of the laws of sacrifice and other matters, the events of Nadab, Abihu, Aaron, and Shelomith's son—all of this represents the way that God is fashioning time. And this time is, from a Christian perspective, something that exists according the reality of the creating word, made flesh in history. If we look at the outline of the book, we see a range of references that, under the formative sway of Christ Jesus (the Christian definition of providence), gather up the history of creation and the realm of creatures who come from the hand of God and mark out their movement toward God in the grasp of Jesus the Christ.

Leviticus is thus a kind of universal history. Its placement in the midst of the more dramatically oriented books of Exodus and Numbers forms the theological core of these books and offers, not so much a legal insert into their histories, disrupting and confusing their details, but rather an explanation of how the histories of Exodus and Numbers move and what they mean. Within the Pentateuch as a whole, Leviticus similarly orients the varied material of the other volumes. It is for this reason that, within Judaism, Leviticus was often the first book of the Torah taught to children.[5]

The present commentary seeks to display that formative gathering by which history is shaped. Its chapters are divided mainly according to the divisions founded by the speech of God to Moses, Aaron, and the people: "and the LORD said to Moses," "the LORD said to Moses and Aaron," "the LORD said to Moses on Mount Sinai," and so on. These divisions do not always correspond to standard chapters, but often do. In addition, some of these locutionary sections have been merged in the commentary, more for practical reasons of space. In general, the divisions follow the call of God to Moses and Israel and do so according to the explicit account of God's speech articulated at the tent of meeting in the days following revelation on Sinai, the sin of Aaron and the people, and the erection of the tabernacle. The instructions given in Leviticus precede the long journey of thirty-eight years that still awaits Israel and mark in advance the details of their passage through the wilderness that is our world.

---

4. This is true, *mutatis mutandis*, for all the books of the Bible and their characters and for the Bible as a whole. For the general approach adopted here, see Radner 2002: esp. chap. 9; and idem, 2004: intro., chaps. 4–5.

5. In Midrash Tanhuma, tractate *Parshat Tzav* 14, the reason given is that the greater purity of children adapts them best to the performance of the sacrifices and laws of cleanliness and behavior.

LEVITICUS 1:1–2A

The book of Leviticus is, almost wholly, the record of the speech of God, uttered to Israel through Moses from the tabernacle. The Hebrew name for the book, *Vayikra*, is taken from the opening phrase: "And he called." It is the same call as from the burning bush (Exod. 3:4) and from Mount Sinai (24:16). The name of God is not in fact mentioned here, but "he called" to Moses, as the very God who reveals himself from the depths of his own being, into the limited light of human recognition. This is the God, as the rabbis noted, who calls our creation, even the stars (Ps. 147:4); the God who calls and speaks to Adam (Gen. 3:9) and Noah and Abraham (*Rabbah* 1.9); the God whose word spoken into the world creates history and sets it on its path from origin to consummation (Heb. 1:1–4). The words of Leviticus—a title that, in a sense, does disservice to the substance of the book by tying it to a limited category of regulative lore—are rather the words of God's calling into human life itself.

If the words here are the words of God who reveals his very self, then we are called through the words themselves into an encounter with God. The book of Exodus has ended, before Leviticus begins, with a description of the tabernacle "covered" by the "cloud" and "filled" with the "glory of the LORD" (Exod. 40:34). This tangible covering over and filling up of the tabernacle by the presence of God actually prevents Moses from entering (40:35). Yet, we are told, when the cloud lifts it leads the people forward through their "journeys" (40:36–37). From *this* tabernacle, "he called Moses," from the heart of his presence as he leads Israel in the desert. From the midst of this revelation of his purposes in time come forth the words of the book of sacrifices and holiness.

That we are to take Leviticus as a distinctly vocational exhortation is foundational to the book's existence. It is a calling into a purpose that underlies the shape of time. And the purpose is God's. But if this is so, the purpose reaches to the length of God's will—and not only partially. The calling given in Leviticus must include the brute details of its exhortation, which *persist* somehow in time all the way through, to, and in the Christ and his own "pioneering" path (to use the term in Hebrews). These details cannot be segregated, in their specific meaning, simply to a culturally limited era from the past, whose time has come and gone, however meaningful the details themselves may have been in that now-lost context.

This point cannot be overemphasized, since it indicates a direction of interpretation quite different from still-standard historicist approaches to the text, even when they have been attempted in service of the Christian gospel (perhaps especially in such cases). The method, for instance, of reading the historical meaning of Leviticus in terms of its place within the "evolution of a people," the "pedagogy of Israel," and even of the human race, has a long history in the church: at *this* stage in the history Israel, so the theory goes, God sought to mold an incoherent populace into a single *ethnos* devoted to a single God, capable of being the vehicle for the instruction of the nations yet to come. Hence, the rules of Leviticus come down to an elaborate training exercise that, imposed over centuries, hones a people's focus, in form and experience, on the one God of the world. But at a certain moment—to carry on with the theory—the childhood exercises of Israel would be set aside, for the sake of the substantive life of "true worship" and obedience, given in the gospel. This theory was provided by, among others, Tertullian, in his arguments against the Marcionites.[1] It was adopted by many of the Reformers. It became, furthermore, the staple of the more religiously tolerant Enlightenment philosophers, like Lessing. His classic *Education of the Human Race* (1778) explained the Old Testament law in terms of a "primer" by which God would "guide his chosen people through all the degrees of a childlike education," at some point to move on to a new degree, for "every primer is only for a certain age" (1910: 20, 51). In Lessing's case, the final goal was the "gospel of reason," not of Christ; the reach of God's will, shadowed in the primer of Leviticus, stretches elsewhere, leaving the sacrifices and orderings of the past as discarded and crude tools strewn across the past.

Even more orthodox modern scriptural interpreters, like the great Anglican New Testament scholar William Sanday, made the evolutionary model of Tertullian a key element in his "gradualist inductive method" of interpretation, which was meant to integrate ancient and historical-critical approaches to the Bible. But the details of the Old Testament were still hard to hold onto as truly authoritative aspects of divine revelation, apart from a vague platonic search for their spiritual lesson (1903: esp. the concluding chapter). This, of course, has become a common end point for much traditional Christian interpretation that, nonetheless, has had

---

1. Tertullian erects an explanation of sacrifice based on God's intention to wean Israel from pagan idolatry. By presenting the Israelites with an intricate web of self-committing practices that bind them to him, God would make them his own. The more elaborate the ritual and the demands, the more separated the people would become from the snares of relation to other gods (*Against Marcion* 2.18–19). Tertullian calls this divine approach a "rational institution" (2.22), in that its purpose made educative sense, even if the sacrifices themselves were without intrinsic religious meaning.

the effect of eviscerating the enduring power of the text, as the lessons themselves become timeworn and limited. Origen and the rabbis at least maintained the details of the text as concrete indicators of specific religious disciplines. Now it is the disciplines themselves that lie in ruins.

The pedagogical theory, in any case, tends to something other than the Christ. This is why, however useful and perhaps necessary it is to take the historical details of Leviticus seriously enough as to found their experienced meaning in the practices of a time whose suffering might in fact have molded Israelite devotion to a certain developing end—the law is a "schoolmaster" of sorts (Gal. 3:24)—we cannot simply gauge the meaning of the text in terms of its speculated function in weaning a people away from idolatry by stages. Indeed, it is not clear that modern educational theory would sustain such a method as useful in any case. "And the LORD called Moses, and spoke to him from the tent of meeting" tells us, rather, that the words spoken reveal the Lord himself, not only the history of religious formation. The church rightly sees the words spoken as therefore necessarily referring to God, whose purposes call the whole world to its end in him. Such is the reach of his will.

Paul knows well the form of the words that Moses is given as he "enters the cloud" out of which God calls him on the mountain of Sinai, appearing as "a devouring fire" in his glory (Exod. 24:15–18). These words are the words of the law. They are the same words, in the character of their form, as those that God "spoke to him" out of the tent of meeting (Lev. 1:1). Yet they are words heard either "under a veil" or with "unveiled face." When veiled, the words inevitably "fade in splendor" and their meaning drifts into the mists of a past context without purchase on our souls. They die. Yet when heard with "unveiled face," unobstructed through a "turning to the Lord," the words of the law reveal the full purposes of God given in Christ through the Spirit: that we are "being changed . . . from one degree of glory to another" into the very "likeness" of Christ as we "behold the glory of the Lord" (2 Cor. 3:7–18). When he called to Moses from the tent of meeting and spoke to him, then, we are asked to "turn to the Lord" that we might see Jesus.

This is the reach of the purposes of God here revealed. And thus, they are given not only to Israel, but to the church, and indeed to the church that is formed of Jew and Greek together, the church of the "one new man" that stands as the redemption of the nations (Eph. 2:15). Moses is called and told to "speak to the people of Israel, and say to them, When any man of you. . . ." "Any man"? Although the "people of Israel" (or "children of Israel") points to a particular group, the chosen portion of Jacob (Deut. 32:9), God addresses "any man" among them, the man who has been drawn into this great purpose, which is encompassed by the "new man," the man who is both Adam and Israel together. Origen points out that Leviticus is clear enough when it comes to specific sorts of conditions that demand this or that sacrifice or behavior—a priest or chief priest or community as a whole or even a sinful person—but here it is "any man," it is "the human being" as a whole, *adam* (*Homilies on Leviticus* 1.2). This view is shared by the rabbis and medieval commentators, "any man" becoming equivalent in the Vulgate of the *anima* (Lev. 2:1) of human life (the *nephesh* of 4:2) (*Rabbah* 2.7). God speaks through Moses to "any man" (*homo*) who is drawn to God, as the "first man" was first drawn to his maker (Gen. 3:9), given all things and holding all things from God, and bound by God's providence to the gathering up of all things that once were given over to him, in the Second Adam to whom and in whom are all things subjected to God himself, even death, the deaths of man and beast (1 Cor. 15:27–28, 45; Ps. 36:6).

"When any man of you brings an offering to the LORD," then, speaks of the offering that comes from the beginning of time and moves to the end of time. "In the course of time Cain brought to the LORD an offering of the fruit of the ground, and Abel brought of the firstlings of his flock and of their fat portions" (Gen. 4:3–4). What did they bring? They brought what God had given them: "Fill the earth and subdue it; and have dominion over the fish of the sea and over the birds of the air and over every living thing that moves upon the earth" (1:28; cf. 9:1–3). They had brought the objects of God's abundance, yet also of God's mercy (3:21), plant and animal together. When did they bring it? They brought it "in the course of time," as do all people. Yet what is the nature of this time? It was a time bound to the sin and violence of all time, wherein "Cain was very angry" and where "sin is crouching at the door" (4:5–7), whose desire fulfills itself in murder (4:8). "When any man of you brings an offering to the LORD" you bring the first gift and the first rebellion and the time that carries forward gift and rejection. "When any man of you brings an offering to the LORD," it is tinged with the history of "any man" and of "every man."

Yet, if "any man" shall do this, "one man" shall bring "the course of time" to its end, even in the midst of time, by doing what "any man" shall do bound to the taints of time. "When Christ came into the world, he said, 'Sacrifices and offerings thou hast not desired, but a body hast thou prepared for me.' . . . Then I said, 'Lo, I have come to do thy will, O God,' as it is written of me in the roll of the book" (Heb. 10:5–7, quoting Ps. 40:6–9 Septuagint). Christ, the Second Adam, the one new man, brings an offering to God: "Lo, I have come." And in him, the "children of Israel" gather, "sanctified" in his offering (Heb. 10:10) and making their own offerings. "When any man shall bring an offering to the LORD," it shall then be an offering "in him" of "praise" and a "shar[ing of] what you have" (13:15–16), for this shall please the Lord. In the one new man, "any man" shall bring offerings, even the Midianites and the peoples from Ephah and Sheba (Isa. 60:6), for "in every place" a "pure offering" will be made to the Lord (Mal. 1:11).

God calls to Moses, with a call to every person to enter the movement of offering by which the world's life from its poisoned beginnings should be taken to its comprehensive and reconciled ending. There is, of course, a development in this. The words spoken to Moses are bound to particularities of Israel's cultic life, here laid out. But they are so bound because of God's love to move from Adam to Adam: Israel shall carry Adam's line to God in the New Adam, and so the nation is precious and worthy to be addressed and formed and taken by the hand with each word and object that shall reveal God's glory to the unveiled face. "Is Ephraim precious to me?" (cf. Jer. 31:20), the rabbis ask when speaking to these first two verses of Leviticus (*Rabbah* 2.2–3). Yes, it is beloved, for so God speaks to it. Is Moses not precious to God? He is so, writes Nahmanides (1974: 7), for in calling him, God shows his "affection and encouragement." But what is God's love, what is the affection by which he encourages? Is it not the sending and coming, the very offering of his Son, by which the world itself is made the object of divine mercy (1 John 4:14; John 3:16)? And so Ephraim is precious because it is the embodied instrument of such a love for all the world. To the children of Israel "belong the sonship, the glory, the covenants, the giving of the law, the worship, and the promises; to them belong the patriarchs, and of their race, according to the flesh is the Christ. God who is over all be blessed for ever. Amen" (Rom. 9:4–5). Amen, because through its life and time, through the worship and the flesh by which the Son of God is offered, even the failures of disobedience "mean the reconciliation of the world," and its "acceptance [will] mean . . . life from the dead" (11:15). Israel's preciousness, and the care that is given to all the commands of the Lord through Moses, is wrapped up in its own offering by God "as a light to the nations" and as the means by which his "salvation may reach to the end of the earth" (Isa. 49:6). In Zion they were born (Ps. 87:4–6).

God calls Moses to speak to the children of Israel because it is to be the vessel by which "any man," by which Adam, is carried to God in the new Adam. Adam dwells within the people ("any man *among you*"), and the offering of "any man" to God is thus given not alone, but within this movement, through Israel, of Adam to Adam. The very body of Christ, "the Israel of God" (Gal. 6:16) who carries, like the ark, the renewing seed of "eight persons," the whole human race's future through the waters of time (1 Pet. 3:20–21), presents itself "as a living sacrifice" (Rom. 12:1) in the course of history. And in the details of all the offerings spoken by God to the people, we find the promise given to all the world in the flesh of Jesus Christ. This is why and what he calls.

Leviticus is the book of God's call. It is the call to all of creation; the call to Adam and to Moses; it is the call to the prophets and their own calling to the people (Jer. 2:2); it is the calling of judgment and of hope (Isa. 40:2–3; Mark 1:3); it is the calling of Jesus: "If any one thirst, let him come to me and drink!" (John 7:37); it is the calling of the Holy Spirit in our hearts, "Abba! Father!" (Gal. 4:6). "And he called." So that, through Moses, we hear the same voice as that which now "has spoken to us by a Son, whom he appointed the heir of all things, through whom also he created the world" (Heb. 1:2), and therefore all things, even the things of Leviticus, are spoken through him. "If you believed Moses, you would believe me, for he wrote of me" (John 5:46; cf. Luke 24:27, 44). He wrote of Jesus, because he was first called by God "from the tent of meeting," and this tent, the glory of the Father, is given presence in the very body of Christ who becomes the offering of God and humans together. "We have beheld his glory," through the flesh of the word who "set its tent among us" (John 1:14). "Any man among you" is *this* man, whose body is the very tabernacle of the Lord (2:19, 21–22), the very heart of God (Heb. 9:11–14). God calls and gives the answer, and the world is encompassed with his work: "Deep calls to deep . . . ; all thy waves . . . have gone over me" (Ps. 42:7).

These first two verses of Leviticus set in motion the calling of God by which the world should be brought into the full ambit of his love, in the body of Jesus Christ. In this book, we see the passage of this body through the world, as it were, of humans and beast, community and nations, as each is drawn into him and given over to the Father. Jesus the *viator*, called forth and calling forth. "When the days drew near for him to be received up, he set his face to go to Jerusalem. . . . He went on his way through towns and villages, teaching, and journeying toward Jerusalem" (Luke 9:51; 13:22). "When any man of you brings an offering to the LORD," you will go with him, you will go this way, as he draws the world into himself in this one great offering. "Immediately he called them: . . . Follow me!" (Mark 1:20, 17). Leviticus is the image of this "mystery of his will, according to his purpose which he set forth in Christ as a plan for the fulness of time, to gather all things in him, things in heaven and things on earth" (Eph. 1:9–10).

LEVITICUS 1:2B–3:17

God calls the world to himself, and Christ answers, "Lo, I have come!" (Heb. 10:7). The answer to the call of God is not an offering or a sacrifice in purely Levitical terms; for these are things "in which you take no pleasure." Rather, the answer is a "body prepared" (10:5). Nonetheless, the body is continuous with the offerings; it springs from their line and takes their place, so that they thereby are displayed as the figures of that body. "When any man of you brings an offering," that offering (*qorban*) points to all offerings, as they point beyond themselves. The general root word here, almost unique to Leviticus and Numbers, refers to a "bringing near or carrying forward." Hence, it is a movement close to God, and this movement is taken up by the one who says, "Lo, I have come!" Every offering bespeaks the one offering of the body, the movement from the other side, the "coming into the world" of the light (John 1:9).

The movement of *qorban* is measured by the one who comes. In this light, it is a movement easily stymied, a movement whose fulfillment demands the whole of one's integrity as a person. Jesus explicitly upbraids those who claim to be bringing *qorban* when in fact they are seeking a way to hold back, for example, support for their parents. Such offering is a subterfuge for "void[ing] the word of God" in its command to honor mother and father (Mark 7:9–12). If anyone brings an offering, if anyone would come forward to God bearing a gift, then this gift must somehow genuinely carry the whole of one's self, as the story of Ananias and Sapphira demonstrates negatively (Acts 5:1–6). This is perhaps why the opening call to offering in Leviticus is immediately qualified as an offering of a live beast—often translated "cattle," but referring in general to land animals, which can be distinguished here only by their presumed cleanliness as coming from a domesticated herd (Rashi, in Rosenbaum and Silbermann 1932: 2b). A true offering to God implies flesh with its blood (Lev. 17:14), something that is subject to human will and dominion, a "creature" to humans as humans are to

God (cf. the "living creatures" of Rev. 4): "You shall bring your offering of cattle from the herd or from the flock"; you shall bring me the life that is yours.

More broadly, the general discussion here of offerings is therefore a description of the movement of coming, of the "body prepared" or, better, the preparation of the body itself—in relation to the body of Jesus. It is a dying, a waiting, a desire to adorn with spices and ointment (Luke 23:54–56; cf. Mark 14:8), the cherishing of something yet ungrasped, that can only be received. The offerings of Leviticus are a "bringing before" of the body, in a physical hope, a humiliated love; and the true body, in some sense, is given over to the offerers. So the world is brought to God, and God gives the world his Son. The strange paradox of the Eucharist's "offering," in "praise and thanksgiving," by which a body is received and we are "brought near" to God, is contained in this opening statement of summary.

In the three chapters that follow, the shape of this sacrificial preparation is outlined, as a kind of template for all offering. No explanation is given; no theological rationale or theory of sacrifice is articulated as an underlying justification for the shapes described. The form of these opening sacrifices has generally been placed within the category of freewill offering, that is, something offered without reference to a prescribed law or its infraction (versus, e.g., sin offering). Much argument has been given, especially among the rabbis, as to the situations in which such offerings are appropriate—although at a certain point of authoritative definition, of course, they are no longer really free. Furthermore, a more technically identified kind of freewill offering is also explicitly mentioned in Lev. 22:18–25; but this explicitness is missing in these opening chapters. Christian exegesis has, in any case, had less interest in the kinds of distinctions made in the Jewish tradition and has instead taken the literal abstraction of the opening sacrifices as an invitation into a kind of wide and introductory survey of sacrifice as a whole. And in this light, the lack of defined rationale has indicated one of the great challenges of the entire law and of these aspects of the law in Leviticus in particular: they are commanded without persuasion. And therefore their relevance to a nonsacrificing church and culture must seem particularly uncertain.

Calvin's remarks on the opening of the book, in this regard, express a distressing candor: "In these [first] chapters Moses will treat generally of the sacrifices. But since we read of many things here, the use of which has passed away, and others, the grounds of which I do not understand, I intend to content myself with a brief summary," thereby salvaging something "profitable, provided we are not too curious" (1996: 2.323). But the "groundless" presentation of the injunctions indicates, not their opacity as divine commands, as if, in the pedagogical theory of both Jews (like Maimonides) and Christians (including Calvin),[1] obedience is learned only in the exercise of ignorant subjection. Though the Kabbalah, for

---

1. Calvin 1996: 2.328 describes the Israelites addressed by Moses as a "rude people" who needed the training provided by otherwise pointless rules from God so as to avoid self-rule according to "their own foolish inventions." Exact rules about trifles prove to be useful as types of things to come; but more practically, they act as constraints on the people's imaginations and reason (2.333–34).

instance, raised this subjection to a glorifying of God's name in and of itself, the almost irrational character of such devotion remained the motive of its focus. Yet Leviticus is not a part of the Christian Scripture because of its divine *senselessness*. Rather, the persuasive force of these commands comes from their location within the figural image of the body of Christ, which is offered by God. Their meaning is discovered within the life of the figure as it shapes us. Their very apprehension in this placement is itself a kind of preparation for the heart, an opening to the grace of God in Christ. The movement from object to varied referent goes back and forth, and in this stretching and leavening of the text and its hearing, the Spirit enters with its expanding force.

Three kinds of sacrifice are laid out, in their bare form. First is the burnt offering of flesh (1:3–17), the *olah* or holocaust. This is tied to blood (1:5) and to atonement for sin (1:4). Second is the offering (*minkhah*) associated with grain (Lev. 2). No purpose is given for this class of offering, though it is used, like other forms, in covenant ceremonies and was associated, when burned, with "the bread of your God" (e.g., 21:6, 21–22). Certainly, from a human side, the grain offering touches upon the most staple aspect of nourishment, both given and received. And like the burnt offering of flesh, it was "a pleasing odor to the LORD" (2:2). Finally, the peace offering (Lev. 3) is a burnt offering of flesh, primarily of the internal organs and the fat associated with them. Like the burnt offering of Lev. 1, the blood is sprinkled about the altar. And it too offers a pleasing odor to the Lord as it is burned (3:5). The difference between the peace offering and the burnt offering seems to lie in the character of the sacrifice, whose name denotes an offering associated with a condition of well-being (cf. Calvin's "prosperity" [1996: 2.333] or the New Revised Standard Version's "well-being"). Sin and life (blood), nourishment and survival, peace and well-being—all these are covered somehow in these three categories of offerings. They are brought before God and map out the boundaries of human existence as it is lived before God, as it contains the world in which God has placed human life, and as it receives the offering of God.

Burnt Offering

Standing at the head of the outline, the burnt offering becomes the epitome of sacrifice in its atoning character, tied to the laying-on of hands. This is an offering *for* something, for the *homo*, the man, "any man," who would come before the Lord. The rabbis saw the expansive referent here as continuing to work out of the *adam* of the opening call by God, not distinguishing between one sin or another or between one role or office of life and another, but touching all human beings, from Adam across the face of the earth (*Rabbah* 5.1–3; likewise Origen, *Homilies on Leviticus* 1.2, and the medieval commentators).

That this original sacrifice is associated with the atonement for sin (1:4) has puzzled commentators, because it is articulated in such an unspecified manner, and the laws regarding sin and its punishment or atonement are otherwise so carefully detailed. Are willful sins or only sins of ignorance touched here? If so, which? Or are these only sins of the heart, the "secret thoughts" of a person, known only to God and hence without prescribed response except through the freewill exercise of offering such as seems to be at issue here? The rabbinic discussion was elaborate and often polemical on these points.

But the call is to "any man" at any time. And the sacrifice is thus inclusive of such universality. If it is universal, it drives us to the common history of human life. Historical critics sense the need, for instance, to dredge the meaning of sacrifice as a general category from the examples of Genesis; and the intuition is not mistaken, at least in its textual focus. Even narratively, the notion of a universal offering is deliberately embodied primordially in Abel's gift (Gen. 4:4), where the beasts of his flock and their "fat portions" are offered up to God and God "regards" them. The distinction between the sacrifices of Abel and Cain was fodder for Jewish and Christian exegesis together. At least from Philo on, the brothers' sacrifices were read as symbols of divergent sets to the human heart before God, not only in terms of virtue and vice, but even of ingrained sinfulness and grace. Augustine provided a determining historical reading for the church when he used the two as figures of the "two cities" of God and of the world and flesh respectively, which ended up being applied according to schemes of election and heresy as various contexts seemed to justify. Rabbinic exegesis, by contrast, buttressed by a range of diverse legends surrounding the two brothers, never settled on a purely, let alone single, historical or genealogical reading of the contrast and thereby maintained both Abel and Cain as progenitors for Jew and Gentile alike as moral exhortation demanded (Ginzberg 1911: 1.61–68). If, as the outline of the sacrificial typology of Leviticus implies, Abel and Cain stand at the primordial root of its distinctions, then we ought appropriately to engage the historical and genealogical figures they represent, but within the logic of the sacrificial grammar itself, not extraneously.

Therefore it is right to ask, what is this primordial offering of Abel that God regards? Does the offering stand at the acceptable base of human history (cf. Noah's sacrifice after the flood in Gen. 8:20), that is, God regards it, and it shows what it is to come before him? Yet, bound to the fate of Abel (and Noah even), this offering stands as something contradicted by human sin. Cain's anger turns Abel's sacrifice into "blood . . . crying . . . from the ground" (4:10). This crying out is bound to the "cut[ting] . . . into pieces" of the flesh (Lev. 1:6). It is an act that alerts the world to the reality of sin and danger, that releases the demand for redress (cf. the Levite's hewn concubine in Judg. 19–20 and Saul's call to the people to gather against their enemies in 1 Sam. 11). So God regards, and his regard apprehends yet another voice. The sacrifice of the burnt flesh initiates, yet further becomes the maintained line of Abel's martyrdom (Matt. 23:35), which will lead through Jerusalem and comprehend the one who comes to it. Still "Abel speaks" (Heb. 11:4) in all burnt offerings, the voice of despised faith over despair (versus Cain in Gen. 4:6), the voice of confession and desire. This voice now "confesses" the Lord of all offering, the offering itself, in Christ (Phil. 2:8, 11), whose humiliation responds to the crying out of blood before God. In this sense, the burnt offering's sin-taintedness—bound to Abel's death at the hands of his brother—prepares the body, who is the brother who finally responds to spilt blood's supplication.

Read in the context of Ps. 50, the burnt offering that anyone might bring before the Lord is given a lived reality that reflects this faith of Abel: "Your burnt offerings are continually before me," yet "I will accept no bull from your house, nor he-goat from your folds." Rather, "offer to God a sacrifice of thanksgiving" and "call upon me in the day of trouble" (Ps. 50:8–9, 14–15). Abel's faith is this, and his offering is this kind of offering. Yet, from the ground of his murder, his offering draws Cain and his progeny into the current of his heart: dead for sin, faithful for life. From now on, the burnt offering marks the search for righteousness that can die for the sake of life. "The sacrifice acceptable to God is a broken spirit; a broken and contrite heart, O God, thou wilt not despise" (51:17).

Hence, Paul will write that "if I deliver my body to be burned, but have not love, I gain nothing" (1 Cor. 13:3). In this way he describes the passage from Abel to Cain and back again in a renewed and redeemed guise: nothing can be truly given away, even "all I have" (13:3), unless given for the sake of another and for its life. Love determines the nature of burning. So the sweet aroma of the burnt offering (Lev. 1:9, 13, 17)—of all offering—is made in the giving of self in love, first in Christ and then in the church through those who live in this offering of the Son: "Walk in love, as Christ loved us and gave himself up for us, a fragrant offering and a sacrifice to God" (Eph. 5:2), a "fragrance from life to life" (2 Cor. 2:16).

This offering of the whole self in love runs through the burnt offering and all else, coursing from the beginning of human life, taken up in Christ Jesus, the Son given in love for the sinful world. The details of the slaughtered body and its parts draw together the whole of anyone as their sin cries out, and they pull it into the fire of redemption. Nahmanides noted, paraphrasing Ibn Ezra, that the image of the sacrifice encompasses *adam*:

> G-d commanded that when man sins and brings an offering, he should lay his hands upon it in contrast to the [evil] deed [committed]. He should confess his sin verbally in contrast to his [evil] speech, and he should burn the inwards and the kidneys [of the offering] in the fire because they are the instruments of thought and desire in the human being. He should burn the legs [of the offering] since they correspond to the hands and feet of a person, which do all his work. He should sprinkle the blood upon the altar, which is analogous to the blood in his body. All these acts are performed in order that when they are done, a person should realize that he has sinned against his G-d with his body and his soul, and that "his" blood should really be spilled and "his" body burned, were it not for the loving-kindness of the Creator. (Nahmanides 1974: 21)

Thus when Origen enumerates the diverse sacrifices of Leviticus, he invariably returns to Christ as somehow (if not exclusively) being figured by each—whether it be bull or sheep, goat or bird, grain or other offering.[2] Christ is he whose body finally encompasses the bodies of all people, and thus the bodies of all sacrificial beasts who correspond to them. The "male without blemish" from the herd (Lev. 1:3) is associated with the fatted calf slaughtered in celebration of the return of the prodigal son (Luke 15:23), the embodied form of God's converting joy through which the "lost is found" (*Homilies on Leviticus* 1.2). In some sense, however, the details of the specific sacrifice become pointers to the breadth of the forms through which the love of God given over for the reconciliation of a sinful world—the legacy of Abel—in the incarnation and death of Christ is exposed, over and over again in multifarious color. In this primary giving of God's self in love, the array of the world is caught up, and its character as a vast created network of life and signs bound to its creator is made manifest.

The sacrificial animals, then, are not distinguished because of their specific efficacy within the sacrificial system; they stand for distinction itself, the diversity of the creature whom a human being, "any man," might offer and in this offering entail the history of Abel's seeking and whose offering must be taken up by Christ. Distinctions can be made speculatively, of course: "from the flock" distinguishes sacrificial beasts from animals that are hunted and so perhaps represent what is more intimate to a human life; turtledoves, besides being cheap enough for the poor, are distinguished by their mating fidelities and so perhaps point to the desired devotion of Israel to God (while the pigeons are to be "young," before they mate at all and are thereby tempted into infidelity); cocks, in any case, are "lewd" and thus inappropriate (Nahmanides 1974: 25–26).[3] But these distinctions are worth making only to the degree that they cover a range, that they in fact include typically, rather than exclude inherently. (Why not, after all, the cock, whose lewdness also mirrors human souls well enough in its own way? Bede will say that the goat mirrors human sin [Patrologia latina 91.333–34]. But that is the point: it is the human sin, not the nature of the goat that is at issue.) The designation of animals in Leviticus, in this sense, is more a bestiary than it is an exposition of the intrinsic qualities of oblationary force linked to individual creatures. The bestiary, as in the *Physiologus* and its medieval progeny, enumerates the world of God's purposes as and within a display of creatures, each of which contain the truth of the world allegorically through the image of their form. Likewise, Isaiah's bestiary of redemption in Isa. 11:6–9 or 43:20 draws together those creatures that have been opposed through the force of sin; but it does so typically, not specifically.

2. See also Origen, *Homilies on Leviticus* 3.5: Christ is the figure in *all* sacrifices. Calvin likewise declares that all the sacrifices were sacramental in that they were really about Christ's sacrifice ("testimonies of the grace" of Christ) and in this way were analogous to baptism today (1996: 2.324).

3. The notion of Maimonides (*Guide to the Perplexed* 3.32) that the choice of sacrificial animal was tied to God's attempt to wean Israel away from the nations' *worship* of these particular creatures is roundly rejected as historically fallacious and theologically shallow.

And Jesus too articulates a bestiary, of sheep and oxen, sparrow and ravens, even dogs and pigs. Bull, sheep, goat, turtledove, pigeon—these belong to humans: they carry the hopes and failures of human beings in their limbs, they are given over to the Lord as the extension of the world that human beings inhabit, have made, and have dismantled in blood.

Grain Offering

Abel's offering is transformed by sin and becomes the form, or at least a kind of historical motive, for all offering. What shall we say of Cain's? It was he, the unwitting shaper of his brother's sacrifice, who in fact gave the first bloodless offering of his crops (Gen. 4:3). Some explain the seeming rejection of Cain's offering by God on the basis of its supposed laxity. But the text says nothing of this, and God addresses Cain's lack of patience, trust, and self-discipline, not his slipshod offerings (4:6–7). And in his own way, his brother Abel turns Cain's failures in this regard into thanks. The body that is consumed upon the cross, Abel's voice crying for a judgment that masks mercy, returns itself as "grain" fallen on the ground and sprung up to new life, ground and baked and shared (John 12:24; Mark 14:22). This is a strange passage, by which two separated brothers are finally reconciled, at least within the body that God offers back to the world of their children.

The grain offering begins this passage, but does so in great fragility. Banished and wandering (Gen. 4:14), toiling and wasting (3:17–19), Cain's continued line furthers the murder of others (4:23–24) and remains under the curse of his father, joined to the resentment of labor's deadening force. He is the link that passes down Adam's punishment, and he does so as a harassed worker of the soil. Yet even in this, God's mercy is still embodied (4:15). The offering of grain, beleaguered and exhausted in Cain's fate, is yet the hope of sustenance that will finally blossom. "He that goes forth weeping, bearing the seed for sowing, shall come home with shouts of joy, bringing his sheaves with him" (Ps. 126:6). Hence, the grain offering is the peculiar shadow of grace, cast by the sinner who carries it forward to God. It is normal life, replete with the abnormalities of the creator's love.

As normal, it is also humiliated and humbled. The rabbis associated the grain offering, in its initial description as a "handful of . . . flour" (Lev. 2:2), with Eccl. 4:6: "Better is a handful of quietness than two hands full of toil and a striving after wind." The imagistic association here was hardly random: the "toil" of this life in sowing, harvesting, milling, and cooking is offset, is refashioned in the grace it represents even, indeed especially, for the fallen. "Quietness" becomes the gift discovered in the midst of normal life. And it is given over to the tired and the beaten, to the poor and the downtrodden (*Rabbah* 3). The "soul" (*nephesh*) of Lev. 2:1—"when any one brings a cereal offering"—refers to the nakedness of the sinner who does not even see clearly to the hope of Abel, yet for all that becomes its heir, its purpose, the brother "kept."

Not for nothing did the medieval commentators then see the church in particular as the agent of this offering, the soul that is the Holy Spirit animating the body of Christ. The church is the flour, leavened by this gift, gathered as many grains into one loaf. Yet it is also brought forward to God as anyone, the normal, the people of God who have nothing to bring but their own neediness as shaped by the quotidian demands of temporal existence: "My grace is sufficient for you" (2 Cor. 12:9), the Lord speaks to the weakened toiler. The church can offer only prayers, supplications like incense, the cry of the empty-handed (Bede [Patrologia latina 91.333–35] and the *Glossa ordinaria* [Patrologia latina 113.301–4]). Even such offerings as these are distanced, as it were, from the altar of the Almighty. If unleavened, they can be burned (Lev. 2:2), but if leavened, if bound to the more routinized character of the day, they cannot (2:11), but can be offered only through a kind of memorial proxy (2:16). The grain—parched, cooked, and ground— awaits its blood, its life. It feeds humans—the priests—but it is not the food of a god. There is something intrinsically human, and therefore limited and mortal, about this offering.

Nonetheless, even this offering can be sanctified, made "most holy" (2:3), made edible even at the altar. Thus, Abraham feeds the Lord at Mamre (Gen. 18:6), turning the grain into cakes of hospitality whose offering unveils a blessing for the nations. Israel's eating of the unleavened bread in haste marks the deliverance of God in the midst of oppression and death (Exod. 12:8, 18–20). The flour, through Elijah, becomes the miraculous instrument of feeding for the poor and the helplessly faithful (1 Kgs. 17:8–16). Just like the bloodied bodies of Lev. 1, brought to God, so the grain and flour carried to the altar are transformed into an offering given back by God: the holy bread is given to the tired men of David's band (1 Sam. 21:1–6), to the hungering crowds (Mark 6:30–44), to the traveling disciples (Matt. 12:1–8), to the church (Mark 14:22), to the world: "The bread which I shall give for the life of the world is my flesh" (John 6:51). Cain's offering is restored, is newly regarded, in the flesh of God. And the sin that crouched at the door of Cain's heart is resisted in the one who not only proclaims, but fulfills in his body, that "man shall not live by bread alone" but by the word of God who comes into the world (Matt. 4:4). Much of the *Rabbah's* emphasis, in this chapter, upon the teaching of the priest—otherwise seemingly out of place—derives from this sense that Aaron's sons partake of a transformative blessing through their receipt of a part of this offering: "true instruction" proceeds from their mouths, because the word of God is given back as a gift within the prayers of the people, showering them with grace, that is, "made holy" (3.6).

This is where the figure of the church as especially present in the grain offering is given weight. The church serves "any man," not simply as a vessel for human brokenness, but as the vessel that would transform, through the offering of that brokenness, the stale lot of life into the recipient of grace. The church prays for the world, goes out into the world, serves the world, finally dies within and for the world in Christ (Col. 1:24). Hence, the wandering of Cain is appropriated into the pilgrimage of the church, precisely through the church's offering of the world's labors in its intercession and devoted service. These are the oil, the frankincense, and the salt that are added to the various offerings (Lev. 2:1, 2, 4, 5, 13) and that provide the "pleasing odor" (2:2, 9, 12) that draws these sacrifices into the ambit of the fat of the beasts. The church's humble service, anointed and baptized by the "oil" of the Holy Spirit, lifted by the "incense" of its prayers (Ps. 141:2), enlivened by the "salt" of its faithfulness and teaching (Matt. 5:13), embeds itself within the life of the world. It is the breadth of this worldly normalcy, now gathered for God, that is transfiguring. Rashi (Rosenbaum and Silbermann 1932: 8) refers to an apparently medieval midrash regarding the "salt of the covenant" (Lev. 2:13; cf. 2 Chr. 13:5) and relates it to the ocean's willingness at creation itself to be bound by God in return for its taste to be offered daily at the altar. The savor here is one of cosmic rootedness, drawn out of chaos, whose direction in offering is meant to touch, from God's side, the whole of that to which God grants being. In the church's prayers, as well as in its witness and suffering ("for every one will be salted with fire"; Mark 9:49), "earth is joined to heaven." "Have salt in yourselves, and be at peace with one another" (9:50).[4]

From this vantage, the church's offering of daily bread reflects the incarnation of God in Christ, who takes his place within the wanderings of Cain's children: the growing child, the carpenter, the itinerant and pilgrim, the one who takes to himself as his own death the very mark of the defeated offering of toil. Rabanus Maurus thus sees this entire chapter, at least in its hovering imagery of the oven and of baking, cooking, and burning (Lev. 2:4, 5, 7), as an echoing declamation of the gestating redemption of the Son, emerging from the depths of the Trinity, from the womb of Mary "in the fulness of time" (Gal. 4:4), and hidden in the midst of human time, as its "bread of life" (Patrologia latina 108.259).

The poverty of Cain's fate; the thorns and thistles of his destiny (Gen. 3:18); the promise of thin soil, the stony ground, and the withered heart (Mark 4:3–7) that cannot listen to the promise simply of "doing well" and the "well-being" that comes from such a faith (Gen. 4:6–7)—all this is gathered up and cracked open in the offering of grain and in its place is returned abundance (John 10:10). The portion of the "daily bread" that is handed over to the priests, to Aaron and his sons (Lev. 2.2), stands as a surplus—what is left over—and it is made visible as a

4. The early church—a practice continued until Vatican II—used salt (placed on the tongue or mixed with water) as part of the rite of baptism. It was generally associated with exorcism, driving out the powers of decay and corruption, the "attack of the unclean spirit" and "the terror of the poisonous serpent." Later, the salt was associated with a range of other figures, especially the gift of wisdom, but including the promise of suffering for the faith in the course of witnessing to the world (John Chrysostom, *Homily* 15.6–7; Confraternity of Christian Doctrine 1954: 129–34). In July 2002 John Paul II compared salt to holiness, as it figures the saints who have giving their lives to God: "Let us remember only a few of them: Agnes of Rome, Andrew of Phú Yên, Pedro Calungsod, Josephine Bakhita, Thérèse of Lisieux, Pier Giorgio Frassati, Marcel Callo, Francisco Castelló Aleu or again Kateri Tekakwitha, the young Iroquois called 'the Lily of the Mohawks'" ("Message to the Youth of the World," on Matt. 5:13–14).

glistening overflow, the light of an oil running down the beard. Again, the church's location within Cain's trajectory, yet embracing its forms for the sake and in the power of its redemption, draws together "brethren in unity" (Ps. 133:1) and brings forth fruit in abundance. Grace overflows (Luke 6:38).

The rabbis too sensed this promised reversal of the natural order of things that is embodied in the grain offering, quoting a psalm of deprecation for the purpose of blessing:

> R[abbi] Hananiah bar R[abbi] Aha went to a certain place and found the following verse at the head of the order: "And what is left of the cereal offering shall be for Aaron and his sons" (Lev. 2:3). With what verse did he commence the discourse in that regard? "From men beneath your hand, O Lord, from men whose portion [in life is of the world, may their belly be filled with what you have stored up for them; may their children have more than enough; and may they leave something over to their babes]" (Ps. 17:14). (*Rabbah* 3.6)

God's blessing on the community provides more than enough for the landless tribe of Levi. And the oil of this abundance is the reconciliation sown within the people and given by the law of God from the lips of their leaders: "The Holy spirit answered [Moses], 'Behold, how good and pleasant it is when brothers dwell in unity. [It is like the precious oil upon the head, running down upon the beard, upon the beard of Aaron, running down on the collar of his robes]' (Ps. 133:1ff.)" (*Rabbah* 3.6). Daily bread, prayed for by Jesus himself (Matt. 6:11) and in a sense prayed for too in the offering of the grain, becomes the "bread from heaven" (John 6:32–33) that never passes away (6:27, 51), the "one loaf" made of "many" members (1 Cor. 10:17–18). The prayer offered by Jesus turns the church into the fullness of its own sacrifice, "receiving who you are, becoming what you receive," to paraphrase Augustine on the Eucharist (Sermon 272).

This moves naturally to the question of the firstfruits in Lev. 2:14–16. Christ, we know, is "the first fruits of those who have fallen asleep" (1 Cor. 15:20, 23)—Paul using the image of the grain that is "crushed" and dies to be given a more glorious body (15:37–39). But so too is church itself among the firstfruits of those in the world whom Christ's rising touches (Jas. 1:18), both of whom are anointed with the Spirit's initial outpouring (Rom. 8:23). In this, the whole character of Israel's purpose is given as the template for the world's redemption: Israel, the firstfruits of the Lord's harvest (Jer. 2:3), whose history as such, driven by Cain yet restored as Abel, will carry the world's resurrection into new life: "For if their [the Jews'] rejection means the reconciliation of the world, what will their acceptance mean but life from the dead? If the dough offered as the first fruits is holy [cf. Num. 15:19–20, esp. in the Septuagint], so is the whole lump; and if the root is holy, so are the branches" (Rom. 11:15–16). Paul here speaks to the nations, who are both pressed and pulled by Israel into this life, their existence leavened by Jewish Israel and thus transformed. There is always one who comes before us. The life of each person, called and protected by God, leads forward into a larger realm, drawing others along, from Cain to Abraham to Jacob to Christ, from the remnant Israel to the world of Jew and Gentile, from Adam to Adam. Time is the marking of redemption as a sequence of an accumulating offering.

Peace Offering

"He is our peace, who has made us both one" (Eph. 2:14). But who are the "two" here? Paul speaks of Jew and Gentile. But in the sacrifices, these first chapters of Leviticus speak of the origin of Jew and Greek, of the chosen, the "regarded," on the one hand, and of all the rest, of the wandering and waiting, on the other. So Abel and Cain are reconciled, and "he is our peace." Rashi speaks of the peace offering as being "so called because [it] bring[s] peace into the world" (Rosenbaum and Silbermann 1932: 9). Nahmanides speaks of the peace offering's "male or female" victims (Lev. 3:1)—not exclusively one or the other, as in the burnt offering and sin offering—as bringing together the range of God's attributes, harmonizing the breadth of God's purpose (1974: 37). "He is our peace," for he, Christ Jesus, comes into the world and gathers into one. "And I have other sheep, that are not of this fold; I must bring them also, and they will heed my voice. So there shall be one flock, one shepherd" (John 10:16); "that they may be one even as we [the Father and Son] are one" (17:22). And so the peace offering is listed after the burnt offering and grain offering, because it marks the resolution of the two.

The peace offering, for Origen and the Christian tradition, represented a kind of perfection. Peace in this sense meant "salvation" itself, as the term was sometimes translated in Latin (and even in the New Revised Standard Version it is called a sacrifice of "well-being"). And this third form of offering was thereby seen to be the perfecting of the others, in an almost historical sense: the image of peace, in this case, was strongly eschatological, the place where history has come to its consummation, for the individual as well as for the world. The "whole" person, in the fullness of his or her virtues (hence the male and female victims, encompassing both the higher and lower virtues of the soul, as Rabanus Maurus insists [Patrologia latina 108.262–64]), are brought before the Lord. But this is only because God has first given all, has poured out his grace and showered his goodness. The ceremonies of the covenant in Exod. 24:5; Num. 6–7; and Deut. 27:7 are all accompanied by peace offerings and rejoicing. Both the law and the promise are received and sealed here, and thereby the end of Israel's purpose is given, and, even if not made explicit, the world's end is also implied.

We understand this ending and perfection as the sign of God's redemption. Although the peace offering has often been associated with a communal feast (Exod. 24:11)—only the designated fat portions of the inner organs being burned, the rest supposedly being shared in a common meal—nothing is said of such a meal in Lev. 3. Still, the peace offering is elsewhere associated with a shared banquet (e.g., Solomon's feast for his servants in 1 Kgs. 3:15). And the concern with the offering of fat to God is at the center of peace offering, a traditional association with pleasure and satisfaction and hence with a kind of overflowing of abundance that can touch all. Fat is good in that it derives from a condition of well-being. (The lack of opprobrium for stoutness within the rabbinic tradition, in this regard, is well noted.)[5] The offering to God of fat has often been seen as a demonstrated sign that we must locate the core of our well-being with God (Babylonian Talmud, tractate *Gittin* 56b).[6] It is all his, as is all grace (Lev. 3:17).

So the peace offering is rightly bound to the same joy as is marriage and feasting. It is the mountain of the Lord, and "a feast of fat things" (Isa. 25:6—though the word for "fat" here is not the same as in Leviticus). It is Jesus eating and drinking (Luke 5:33–35; Matt. 11:19) and the peoples coming from east and west into the kingdom of God to "sit at table" (Luke 13:29). But also, it is still an *offering*, a coming before the Lord. Perfection is reached by and in this offering, so that salvation itself is shown to *be* an offering. When Paul speaks of the reconciliation wrought by God in Christ, he speaks of the offering of church to the Lord, "without spot or wrinkle" (Eph. 5:27). This is a reality not only accomplished by but given in the offering of Christ "in love" in his own body, which sweeps up the church itself into his self-giving (Col. 1:22). Although it is correct to speak, as has become common, of "the biblical concept of peace [*shalom*]" as the experience of a kind of integral social prosperity and justice, the sacrificial character of its "coming before" God is given a special emphasis through Leviticus. The offering *is* peace itself; and peace is given in the offering. The body and its fate define what a just society must look like, not the other way around: "He is our peace."

This identity of offering and salvation is what opens the text up to the broad moral range of interpretation given by the church to this section—exegesis *moraliter*, as the commentators put it. Israel comes before God in a movement into and through holiness, as the whole of Leviticus makes clear. But this is done, in this context, through sacrifice. The victim "without blemish" (Lev. 3:1) is given in perfect love, like the husband for the wife (Eph. 5:25–33), but, so too, like the bride presented to her husband (2 Cor. 11:2). This peace is one of communion, of the "one flesh," of "abiding in," and of the participation of character; but because of that, it bespeaks the "being perfect" (Matt. 5:48) and "being holy" like the Father (Lev. 19:2) and the life of mission like the Son. The peace offering implies, then,

---

5. See Babylonian Talmud, tractate *Bava Metzia* 84a, and Tosafot commentary on Rabbi Yishmael son of Rabbi Yosi and Rabbi Elazar son of Rabbi Shimon, whose respective girths were so great that an ox-drawn cart could pass between them even as their stomachs touched.

6. Calvin, rejecting all objective allegorical referents for fat, preferred to see it as a moral symbol: God should always get the best of what we have to offer, and we should have our gluttonous appetites reined in by giving up fat (1996: 2.335). See also Schneersohn's discussion (1997: 155) of this in terms of self-transcendence. The discussion regarding the exact anatomical identity of this fat, denoted by a different Hebrew word from the fat of Lev. 1:8, has been intense, given the practical consequences for butchery and cuisine (see, e.g., Nahmanides 1974: 39–44).

the life of holiness and the mission of the church as an aspect of self-giving that is identified with salvation: "Peace be with you. As the Father has sent me, even so I send you" (John 20:21). "Greater love has no man than this, that a man lay down his life for his friends" (15:13). "Whoever keeps his word, in him truly love for God is perfected. By this we may be sure that we are in him: he who says he abides in him ought to walk in the same way in which he walked" (1 John 2:5–6).

Much of the medieval commentary on this chapter, therefore, has to do with the nature of this walking, and the details of the offerings—entrails, fat, kidneys, liver, the "appendage" or "tail" of the liver—are related to elements of human nature that are offered to God (generally through the Mass) in subjection to his will: heart, passions, desires, concupiscence, virtues. Each part of the body images an aspect of the human character, which "God tests" (in the Vulgate, in terms of kidneys and heart or liver—Ps. 26:2; Jer. 11:20). All are to be given over to God for his use and transformation in a spirit of love (*Glossa ordinaria* [Patrologia latina 113.304–5]). From this perspective, the peace offering represents a change in the human person that has been effected through the act of divine self-giving into which the church, its members, and finally the world itself are caught up.

It is important to note at this point in the book these aspects of both transformation and participation, for they bear upon the moral character of holiness as it is increasingly asserted within Leviticus as a whole. The offerings found the ethical codes that will follow, not the other way around. And while this seems to reverse the rational order by which modern sensibilities approach religious life—whereby today we prefer to construct and evaluate worship, for instance, on the basis of informing ethical principles—it orients the scriptural revelation qua revelation in its fullness: "*This* is love, not that we loved God but that he loved us and sent his Son to be the expiation for our sins. . . . We loved, because he first loved us" (1 John 4:10, 19). That he *is* our peace means that he does not bring to us a peace that exists apart from and not intrinsically within him. Indeed, when peace is understood as such an external object, defined outside of Christ and his form, he brings not peace at all, but a sword (Matt. 10:34). Since he brings himself as an offering, such an offering is received only with a sword, only violently and by murder, by those who are not redefined by the offering itself (26:55). The peace he is, such as it is, exposes us and in so doing either transforms us or reveals our violence.

He is our peace, because coming as he does he actually reconciles Cain and Abel. It is not as if the two now become pacified, a smoldering anger quenched, like Jacob and Esau (Gen. 33). Such pacification is but the shadow of true reconciliation, though it passes for such in a world where difference is seen as radically ingrained in creation. But Christ is our peace because the two become one, the "one new man in place of the two, so making peace" (Eph. 2:15). And Christ Jesus does this as a "creation in himself," as something making new, as one who oversteps all the wreckage of time by his own self-offering. The peace offering maintains its continuity with the burnt offering and grain offering by creating them anew as "one," yet "in him" they are not destroyed so much as fulfilled, "made perfect," as the "perfect man" (4:13 Authorized Version) is grown up in Christ within the church. The act of laying on of hands (Lev. 3:2, in continuity with 1:4) displays this growth and this oneness. Often seen simply as the symbol of the victim's "bearing of sins" (the sins of Israel and of humanity, according to Rabanus Maurus [Patrologia latina 108.265–67]), the image extends further, for the "head" of the victim in this case is "the head of the body, the church . . . the first-born [and firstfruits] from the dead" (Col. 1:18)—both burnt offering and grain offering find themselves in this head—and he shares the "fullness of God" with the members who are joined to him in this self-offering.

The laying on of hands is a joining of sorts, an effective act of solidarity and participation, as when the people lay hands on the Levites for their consecration, and the Levites in turn lay hands upon the victims for sacrifice, and so all are joined in the power of the one act (Num. 8:10–13). But God too "lays his hand" on persons and nations (Exod. 7:4; Ezek. 39:21; Ezra 8:22), for good and ill, for the sake of furthering the purposes of his providence. Jesus lays his hands upon the sick for healing (Mark 6:5; 8:23), and the Holy Spirit is given through such touch (Deut. 34:9; Acts 8:17–19). When, therefore, it says that "if a man's offering is a . . . peace offering . . . he shall lay his hand upon the head of his offering" (Lev. 3:1–2), we must ask: who, then, is this man, and whose head is touched? And the answer is given in the initial character of the burnt offering and grain offering: the offerings of Abel and of Cain are here being given over to the offering of Christ, who, in his re-creation of the human person, allows the two brothers to make their offering perfectly. Their hands become his hands, for the head of the church also works through the hands of the church; "any man" is taken into the one man; all are joined, so that perfection is given in the offering of love for hand and head and foot together (1 Cor. 12:12–26).

If the "sons of Aaron" (Lev. 3:2, 8, 13) are often identified, prophetically, with Annas and Caiaphas (John 18:13–14) (Rabanus Maurus [Patrologia latina 108.265–67]), and thus if the victims here, as always, are linked with Jesus himself, it is important to see this connection as more than simply the figuration of a future event, that is, of the passion. Rather, the figures of the peoples themselves are brought into view here, the history of the children of Abraham in their extent, of Israel and the nations together. "[Caiaphas] did not say this of his own accord, but being high priest that year he prophesied that Jesus should die for the nation, and not for the nation only, but to gather into one the children of God who are scattered abroad" (11:51–52). So the "gathering into one" is the peace offering. And the offering is the work of God for the redemption of the world and the bringing to fulfillment of creation's purpose. This is why the "sons of Aaron" are also the leaders of the church of Christ and not simply signs of the agents of the Savior's death; they are the apostles and their heirs. And this is why too the peace offering is the image of the church's mission and not only of its end. As one whose head has had hands laid upon it, as one who is thus joined to the one offering of reconciliation, the church's life becomes this offering, and the "gathering into one of the scattered children of God" becomes its work accomplished through this offering. Pope Paul VI writes that evangelization is this offering of the church's self-giving peace (*Evangelii nuntiandi* 12, 16).

The peace offering is thus the foundation of the ecclesiology of Leviticus—the historical joining of Abel and Cain through holiness and mission, through blood, fat, and fire. Through *blood*, so that Abel's own, in its cries to heaven, is taken up by heaven and returned in love (Lev. 3:2); so that the provoking of its cries by Cain is taken in and carried through by such a love; and so that such a blood that cries is now made the lifeblood of the church itself and given over for the world (Col. 1:24). Through *fat*, for the fat of Abel's offering (Gen. 4:4), which became a burning anger for his brother, is turned to laughter, into the rejoicing over the lost who are found and over the dead who are given life (Luke 15:23–24); for one lamb has died so that the flock can be made whole (John 1:29; Luke 15:3–7); for the whole body's offering of member to member now provides a pleasing fragrance lifted high into the heavenly realms, not with cries but with praise (Phil. 4:18). Through *fire*, because fire has burned from Eden to Jerusalem and to the ends of the world (Rev. 8:8), beginning in God's heart (Exod. 3:2; 19:18; Ezek. 1:4, 13) and reaching out beyond the impermeability of human rebellion (Gen. 3:24); because it surpasses the curse of love's end that saps all families' hope (22:3, 8, 13) and promises the end of lovelessness by a miraculous cleansing of the Spirit (Matt. 3:11; Acts 2:3); because such cleansing in the Spirit comes *as* a body consumed (Luke 12:49), and our own bodies are joined and changed by such consumption (1 Cor. 3:15); because the offering of our bodies in Christ (Rom. 12:1), Cain's lost love returned on earth (1 John 3:11–12), *is* the actual worship of the consuming fire who is God (Heb. 12:29).

This historical joining of Abel and Cain, through the breadth of offering, represents the history of humanity. This history is, in its forms of burnt offering and grain offering as a coming near to God, a preparation of the body of Christ. Abel's and Cain's lives and deaths, stretched out over the centuries, gathered into the actions of Israel, are drawn by the Father to the Son (John 6:44). This drawing "prepare[s] the way of the LORD" (Isa. 40:3–5), a preparation that is described in terms of the friction of hard hedges, of landscapes smoothed, for the sake of the Lord's revelation, the glory that is the Son's exposition of his body (John 12:23–24). The rendering in Leviticus of *qorban* in terms of Abel's and Cain's forms of offering makes this history of preparation a universal history and thus lays the ground for any theology of cultures and religions, outside of Israel, as bound to the theology of this preparation. But declaring a *praeparatio evangelica* in this case is not a matter of finding presentiments of Christian themes within past or foreign cultures, certainly not of Israel, as if it were the type of what is foreign to the truth! It is rather the assertion of the actual working out within all peoples of the movement of offering given in the forms described by Leviticus for Israel, in preparation for the revelation of a redeemed body. This is the "yearning" of all creation over all the years (Rom. 8:19, 23). "Any man" who makes an offering during this time—this time of "any man" and therefore a long time and thus of all human life as it is drawn to God—is molded by his or her offerings into the form that can be joined to the perfect offering, the image of the invisible God (Col. 1:15), who fills the church with his fullness (Eph. 1:23) in the "fulness of time" (Gal. 4:4).

LEVITICUS 4:1–5:13

The sacrifices of Lev. 1–3 are given generally. They lay out the form of human history that is gathered up in and by Christ, but they do so with a sweep that universalizes the character of that history of redemption. As the next chapters unfold, we are taken to a more concrete plane, one in which the forms of history are particularized in the actions and consequences of individuals or groups in time. The sacrifices enjoined in this section will take the form of those outlined already—for example, the sin offering of Lev. 4 explicitly partakes of the forms of both the peace offering (4:10) and the burnt offering (4:4, 12). They are sacrifices, then, that specify, that elaborate, that engage in the particular stories of the larger history. But they do not alter it or provide alternatives.

The Christian tradition has therefore tended to read these details almost, in musical terms, as improvisations upon the central themes of the types of Christ's death that were seen as originally laid out in the first chapters. As already noted, Origen was explicit in this claim, and when he comes to these chapters he uses it to bolster his summarizing exposition: "Almost every victim that is offered partakes of some aspect of the image of Christ, for in him every sacrifice is 'recapitulated'" (*Homilies on Leviticus* 3.5). This is temporally proved, he says, by the historical fact that, once Jesus died upon the cross, all these particular sacrifices "ceased" (at least for the church).

Origen is well aware of the redundancy this may create in Christian interpretation of a book like Leviticus: everything will inevitably sound the same theme, over and over again. In response, the Christian reader of the book's details will engage in a kind of *jouissance*, to use Roland Barthes's description, of interpretive experiment, so long as it remains tethered within the central christic figuration that the text exposes. The sacrifices are, in each case, the same offering of *himself*, but seen from the perspectives of redeemed and fallen flesh respectively. (And this accounts, therefore, for the different treatment of and emphasis upon the fleshly details of skin and excrement in Lev. 4 in contrast to Lev. 1 and Lev. 3.)

Similarly, and on a more specific basis, Origen will take up the differing aspects of a particular sacrifice, as in 4:1–12, and relate each to elements of Christ's own self and mission: the kidneys that are burnt refer to Christ's freedom from carnal perturbation; the seven sprinklings of the blood by the priest represent the seven gifts of the Spirit; the four horns of the altar that are touched in blood are tied to the four-gospel renditions of the passion; the lobe of the liver stands for human rage, consumed at the altar; and the blood that is poured at the base of the altar points to the final grace of Israel's conversion, which will take place after all the nations are brought in by the church (*Homilies on Leviticus* 3.5).

In all this, a history is explicated and fills out the core meaning of the sacrifice as being Christ's. Still, we might wonder if this history has already been somehow circumscribed by the tight typological fit given it, and in the unidirectional fashion with which it is applied, so that Leviticus itself ceases to elucidate in its own right even the figure of Christ, by the time of the Reformation (e.g., Calvin 1996: 2.345).

By the time we reach Calvin, we see something of this pinched character emerge more clearly. If the sacrifices of Leviticus exist for the *purpose* of indicating Jesus, on what basis do they offer any divine sustenance today for those who know Christ clearly and therefore need no further signs drawn from the obscure reaches of the past? The pedagogical theory—the law as training wheels for the infantile Jews—is dusted off, and the clear sacraments of Christ are retrojected into the Israelites' life as a kind of image staring out from the murky depths of time, but the details of the text—the kinds of animals, the actions taken, the parts of the bodies cut—are important only because they demand care in worship, and of course all people must be careful in their devotion to God. It is a good lesson to bear in mind.

There is an incipient, and understandable, hermeneutic at work in Calvin, comparable to the contemporary practice of engaging foreign cultures on the basis of some purported and radically shared existential experience. The Israelites did things so strange to us that we are left trying to find some basic, if only general, bridge by which to make any sense of it (e.g., just like us in our best moments, they tried to be scrupulous in their devotion, they were held to an external account for their behavior, they recognized a God beyond their own manipulation, and so on). The irony is that this kind of fallback on a putative species of common human religiosity derives from a tenacious Christocentricity. The problem, however, is not with the typological framework itself that Calvin uses, which is both inevitable and necessary, but with the historical meaning of its linkages. Not only should the character of the sacrifices be elucidated by the figure of Christ; but, if the subjecting and formative power of the word at work and visible in the Scriptures is to be honored, the figure of Christ ought to be, in a sense, explicated by the sacrifices.

In this case, the movement into the sin offering, and its peculiar character in Lev. 4, represents not simply a restatement of the central dogma of atonement, but rather a detailing of sin's shape as it is engaged by Jesus. And thus, the contours of the Christ are here clarified in a way that would be impossible apart from the fullness of the Scriptures given in this book in particular. Christ's ingathering journey goes through this landscape not only contingently, but essentially.

One of the key elements in this landscape of human offering, of coming before God, is the form of sin as it shapes human life. In Lev. 4, the sacrifices discussed are those offered in response to the "unwitting" sin (4:2) or sin of "ignorance" or, perhaps more literally, sin done "in error." It has been a presupposition of both Jewish and Christian exegesis that atonement for sin, in Leviticus, is given only for sins of ignorance and that all willful sinning is due a punishment of some kind, including in certain cases death and excision from the people. The distinction between the atonement made in Lev. 4's sacrifices and those in Lev. 1's burnt offering (1:4) has therefore caused some difficulty: what kind of sin is implied by these earlier sacrifices, if they are not simply included in Lev. 4 and subsequent texts? A major Jewish tradition (e.g., see Nahmanides' discussion [1974: 11–12] of Rashi) has therefore viewed the freewill offerings of Lev. 1 as valid only and necessarily for (even willful) sins *unspecified* in the law as to their punishment (of which there are a few, such as violating the commandment to dwell in a booth on Sukkoth). Leviticus 1's sacrifices of atonement, the argument goes, deal with all sins for which punishment is *not* otherwise specified by Scripture. It is a kind of catchall. The particular force of the sin of ignorance in Christianity, however, has been less clearly defined, precisely because the sacrificial antitype of Christ has been so inclusive. While enumerations of sins and the shape of their penitential responses have an elaborate history within the tradition of the Christian confessional, the formative hold that these details have on the understanding of Christ's sacrifice has been loose: if all sacrifices are types of Christ's atoning death on the cross, and that death is for "the sins of the world," what more needs to be said? Indeed, Christian commentary on this section regarding sins of ignorance has tended to elide ignorance into the previous willful faults by which habitual sin has taken root in the soul (Rabanus Maurus [Patrologia latina 108.270–79]).[1]

But just this character of ignorance or error is at issue in this chapter. Leviticus approaches it as a category whose particularity is given within the human locales of the sin's commission, the persons or groups affected: priest (4:3), community (4:13), political authority (4:22), and common person (4:27), each of whom is an example of the designation "any soul [*nephesh*]" (using the literal Hebrew): "If any soul sins unwittingly" (*Rabbah* 4.1). Although a sacrifice of atonement is mentioned in Lev. 1, the sacrifice specified for *sin* is first laid out specifically in *these*

---

1. The Catholic distinction between mortal and venial sin—biblically based especially on 1 John 5:16–17—is obviously critical. Venial sins are precisely those that are committed in some fashion either without our consent or in a condition of ignorance as to their sinfulness (Thomas Aquinas, *Summa theologiae* 1a2ae Q. 88). The medieval reading of Lev. 4, however, tends to overlook this difference, despite its often elaborate articulation elsewhere during this period, in large measure because the unwitting sin here requires blood sacrifice all the same.

terms, the terms of human action and location. That is to say, the sins for which these sacrifices are given are the sins of Aaron and Abiathar, Eli and Jeremiah; they are the sins of Benjamin, Ephraim, Judah, Samaria, and Jerusalem; they are sins of Saul, David, Ahab, and Manasseh; they are the sins of Uzzah, Naboth, Ruth, Job, and Amos. This breadth and particularity together somehow define the error of the sin involved. And this breadth and particularity is somehow atoned for through the sacrifice and through the antitype to which it points.

Further, this breadth and particularity inform the character of an unwitting sin and unveil its power. *Rabbah* 4.1 is wonderfully intent on dealing with this reality of *extent*. It does so by immediately linking the sin of ignorance with Eccl. 3:16: "Moreover I saw under the sun that in the place of justice, even there was wickedness, and in the place of righteousness, even there was wickedness." Why this fundamental linkage? Because what is called ignorance is in fact a function of sin's extent, of what, in Christian terms, is called corruption. Ecclesiastes 3:16 is applied to all creation, for all was made good, yet in its midst what does one find? Wickedness. Where the law is given, where worship is made, where mercy is offered, where liberation is granted—that is, in the midst of every narrative of the Scripture through which the life of humanity, even in its elected focus within Israel, is explicated—just *there* and always there, one finds wickedness. Thus, *this* sin, which is called unwitting, is the sin of "any soul," of any life, that is, of exactly that which God has made good at the beginning in the very center of a human being.

The *Rabbah* will not let go of this line of thought, for it goes to the heart of all things: "There are three who are ingrates: earth, woman, and the soul" (4.2). That is, we must follow here the order of creation and fall itself, as described in Genesis. The human soul, given all things, squanders its gifts in abject ingratitude: "Whatever I have created on the six days of creation I made only in your favor, and yet you go and sin, steal, and grab." The soul, highest of all things, is given a mind and body: yet it refuses to gain knowledge, and shies from subduing its passions. Thus the claim to sin unwittingly, the claim to ignorance as some kind of justification, is both an evasion and a blasphemy against the created power, goodness, and gift of God. Though the words used are different in the two cases, the dynamic is common: the sin called error and ignorance turns into the wandering and vagabondage of Cain (Gen. 4:12). No one, as Jesus demonstrates with the woman caught in adultery, can claim to be "without sin," however one wishes to construe it (John 8:7). Negligence, as Rabanus Maurus remarks (Patrologia latina 108.276–78), is engrained in the soul by sin itself.

And so the *Rabbah* uses the reality of the unwitting sin to trace a range of irresponsibilities that end up covering the human being as a whole: the mind is called to inform itself and to gain knowledge (this is its engraced vocation); the soul is called to control the body and all its fleshly temptations and drives; the community is called to hold its religious and political leaders accountable to justice and truth and vice versa. In every locale, among every person, within every relationship, the demands and opportunities for righteousness are lodged and so too in fact is the subversion of righteousness. "I forgot," "I did not know," "no one told me," "I am weak," "we all make mistakes," "they are too strong." True enough: and that is why, and only why, "in the place of justice, even there was wickedness, and in the place of righteousness, even there was wickedness." That is why "there is no longer any that is godly" and "the faithful have vanished from among the sons of men" and "every one utters lies to his neighbors" (Ps. 12:1–2). That is why "they are corrupt, they do abominable deeds, there is none that does good" (14:1). That is why both rich and poor alike are not to be trusted (62:10), and that God "put[s] down the mighty from their thrones, and exalted those of low degree" (Luke 1:52; cf. Ps. 146) demonstrates utter and undemanded grace. This is Paul's certain and stark conclusion, as he describes it in Rom. 1–2, to the cascade of sin as it seeps into the corners and cracks of human existence, and lurks unwittingly: "Therefore you have no excuse, O man, whoever you are" (2:1); for "any soul," any and every life sins.

The locale of sin, then, in its unwitting or *ingrained* reality, becomes the reflection of the particular character of grace as God creates and re-creates. The Gospels lay out the range of lives and (ir)responsibilities marked out by Lev. 4 as brought into the orbit of Jesus's life—priests and rulers, peoples and commoners: Zechariah and Caiaphas; Herod and Pilate; Nazareth, Siloam, Chorazin, Bethsaida, and Capernaum (Luke 10:13–15); Jerusalem and Rome; Peter, Canaanites and Samaritans, centurions and Pharisees, Mary and Joanna, children and beggars. The Christian tradition that would find in Christ the condition of every human being finds it first within the locale of "any man" whose unwitting life surrounds the Lord and presses against him. The medieval commentators, thus, will find the specificity of, for example, the priest of Lev. 4:3–12 in a figure like Caiaphas, unwittingly facilitating the world's offering (John 11:49–52), but also in the fallen yet providential vessel of the whole catholic church, a "kingdom of priests," and finally, in the figure of the first man, Adam, primordial priest of Eden's holy sanctuary (Bruno of Segni [Patrologia latina 164.389–94] and Rupert of Deutz [Patrologia latina 167.774–75]). "Any man" is also "each man"; "any priest" is also "each priest"; "any priest" is also "every man."

From this arena, we understand that Jesus enters into sin itself, only to the degree that "any man's" sin becomes the place where the life of Christ dwells. And the Son of God enters into human life, setting up his tent and tabernacle within human flesh (John 1:14), because here he finds the unwitting sin of "any man." The particularity of the locales of sin mentioned in Lev. 4 drives paradoxically toward the tearing down of all distinctions before God. "You have no excuse, O man, whoever you are." Ecclesiastes speaks again to this character of the unwitting sin of error: "There is an evil which I have seen under the sun, as it were an *error* proceeding from the ruler: folly is set in many high places, and the rich sit in a low place. I have seen slaves on horses, and princes walking on foot like slaves" (10:5–7). And Paul wrote of a god who took the form of a slave, and a slave who was exalted into the heaven and heavens (Phil. 2:5–11). If "all have sinned" (Rom. 3:23)—something we know in part from the *diversity* of sin's manifestation that touches all particular social locations—then God's mercy (if God *is* merciful) will come and touch all places and people. There is an opening up of the world to God precisely in the bringing of the sin offering. There is a taking up of the world by God precisely in the breadth of human offering comprehended by the coming of the Son of God.

The reality of extent as undergirding the character of the sin of ignorance informs the two contexts that are explicated immediately following the outline of locales: the touching of an unclean thing (Lev. 5:2–3) or the failure to uphold an oath (5:4), through a public call to witness (5:1) or through a vow made privately (5:4). The matter of contamination looms large, especially later in the book of Leviticus, and will be treated more fully in subsequent chapters. But here we have opened to us a window upon the inescapable network of sin that besets a human life (and so shapes the vocation of the Son of Man)—what or who one touches, or what or who touches us, what surfaces and edges we move along and brush beside. When Jesus passes through the crowd, and the woman with a flow of blood comes up behind him and reaches out to his robes for some momentary contact, he turns and asks, "'Who touched my garments?' And his disciples said to him, 'You see the crowd pressing around you, and yet you say, "Who touched me?"'" (Mark 5:30–31). Is not the press of human flesh too confused even to note? Yet Jesus knew the touch of the world, of this or that person, of this one woman in particular. His power (5:30) had met the unwitting power of the world's sin and scraped against it.

Origen and the Christian tradition will spiritualize the nature of contamination in an attempt to move away from the seemingly superstitious claim to infection through physical contact: to touch something unclean, in this reading, is a way to indicate the fact of following sin; any purely physical interpretation, like the Jews' interpretation, is simply "vain" (*inutiliter*). In this vein, the human cadavers of the text figuratively refer to Christians who have lapsed in their faith; animal cadavers refer to uninformed Christians, whose purity or impurity is determined by their ways of life in following Christ (*Homilies on Leviticus* 3.3). The spiritualizing of contamination and impurity is not wrong—nor is it exegetically without Jewish roots itself. But the warning of the resurrected Jesus to Mary, "do not touch me" (John 20:17), is coherent precisely because *bodies* must be changed before they can apprehend the Lord's glory fully (1 Cor. 15:42–50). And in Lev. 4–5 the power of touching displays the supple and secret integration of sin within the world's interstices, its wandering and taking up residence in the physical realities of human life. Dead bodies lie like Abel's on the ground, and their blood, filled with the life and soul of God's creative grace, is squandered on the ground, for life and soul is the blood of any creature (17:14)—any life and any soul. To live, to wander and walk the earth, is to touch and be touched by this reality through which sin and mortality are joined.

So the unwitting sin is a description of the world's sin—invasive, infecting, growing with almost organic inevitability. To describe the unwitting nature of sin is a way of speaking about life within the world. The *Rabbah's* clear move in blurring the line between witting and unwitting sin is motivated by this sense of the sin offering's unveiling of something far more entrenched than occasional negligence in keeping the law (5.8); and, by contrast, this unveiling goes deeper yet and divulges the consequent miracle of divine mercy itself. If God can forgive what lies about us like the earth itself, what some might think is simply the inevitable fate of human life, then how should we wonder at his remittance of the most blatant and heinous of willful violations? Which is easier? Which goes to the heart of a human? The offerings for unwitting sin say less about a human being and the subtleties of human rebellion; rather they say, finally—and contra attempts to put a wedge between the kinds of sin that stalk us—everything about God.

And what do they say? They describe, not some lesser and more primitive form of sin,[2] but rather the very act of God's own offering of himself: "Father, forgive them; *for they know not what they do*" (Luke 23:34). Indeed, the most deliberated assault upon God's own being—"you . . . killed the Author of life" (Acts 3:15)—is called unwitting, a sin of ignorance (3:17). How strange that the cross has turned the enormity of horror into the path of thoughtlessness! Or is it not that thoughtlessness has raised itself into the towering form of horror? The parsing of evil, in this case, is shown to be a false pursuit; and casuistry, while serving gentle purposes, dissolves before the offering of Christ. The words of every martyr echo from this moment, as Stephen follows out his Lord's assertion: "Lord, do not hold this sin against them" (7:60). Why? Because "they know not what they do"? Because knowing, their deed is less than that of killing the Lord of life? Jesus himself, at one point, seems to make a distinction between knowledge and ignorance in the face of God's wrath: "That servant who knew his master's will, but did not make ready or act according to his will, shall receive a severe beating. But he who did not know, and did what deserved a beating, shall receive a light beating." Yet he explains this in terms of the gift: "Every one to whom much is given, of him will much be required" (Luke 12:47–48). And what has he been given? "I gave you everything" (Gen. 9:3; cf. Luke 15:31). If sin would distinguish, "God shows no partiality" (Acts 10:34). The witting and the unwitting are swept up together.

In this perspective, the perspective of the one who comes with the offering of himself, blindness—and thus unwittingness—is a sin in its own right and is healed in its own locale. The people are blind though they have eyes (Isa. 43:8; Jer. 5:21; Ezek. 12:2), through their own fault, yet also as a consequence of God's holiness (Isa. 44:18; John 12:40) and of "the god of this world," whose work has ensnared them (2 Cor. 4:4). The unwitting are so because of a long history that

---

2. Calvin 1996: 2.345–46 would have us think that propitiation for such minor habits of sinfulness was a kind of encouragement given by God to the Israelites in order to keep them on their moral toes, so as not to slip into the horror of "deliberate impieties."

itself has carried darkness with it. The offering of the Son of God itself exposes this blindness and thoughtlessness (Matt. 13:13–17; John 9:39), yet also brings light into the midst of ignorance's darkness (John 1:5; 9:5; 12:46; 1 Cor. 4:5). As he stands there (Mark 9:2), even as he hangs there (John 12:16, 28), the glory of God shines out, and the unwitting are filled with knowledge: "Truly this man was the Son of God!" (Mark 15:39).

There is, then, a deep moral uncertainty attached to the condition of ignorance in the face of God's coming: unwittingness masks a wide deception and is itself unmasked. Hence, the response in the midst of its awareness leads to confession as the main pronouncement of the sacrifice for sin: "When the sin . . . becomes known" (Lev. 4:14); "when a man is guilty in any of these, he shall confess the sin he has committed, and he shall bring his guilt offering to the LORD" (5:5–6). He shall confess it, because light has shown in the darkness, and the offering is sign of such a light. He shall confess it, because the nature of the offering of the one who comes is light itself, is truth telling before unwitting and sinful rulers (1 Tim. 6:13) and before all the world (John 18:20; 1 Cor. 4:9; 1 Tim. 6:12). Just as the reference to uncleanness and the touch of death in Lev. 5 speaks to the nature of unwitting sin, so the concomitant concern with witnessing and swearing (5:1, 4) that is mixed up in the same chapter speaks to the nature of sin's exposure in the light of God's self-offering as a sturdy truth telling. The good confession of Jesus exposes the failure to confess and the false oaths of Peter and of all his followers, the range of human life gathered around the one who speaks the truth. "He began to invoke a curse on himself and to swear, 'I do not know this man of whom you speak'" (Mark 14:71). And "many bore false witness against him, and their witness did not agree" (14:56). The offering for sin seeps out from the ignorance of these failures and these oaths. The hidden (Lev. 5:4) is made plain: "Nothing is hid that shall not be made manifest, nor anything secret that shall not be known and come to light" (Luke 8:17). "When the sin . . . becomes known," he shall confess the sin: "Peter remembered how Jesus had said to him, 'Before the cock crows twice, you will deny me three times.' And he broke down and wept" (Mark 14:72).

Plain speaking, which says yes and no, which leaves oaths to another era, is commanded by Jesus because "any one sins unwittingly." Human words are a tangled covering upon the land, and we can never know their beginnings and endings, and we are lost in them. "A fool's voice [comes] with many words" (Eccl. 5:3), writes Solomon, in the same place where he speaks of oaths. Because "any one sins unwittingly," there is only one confession and one oath that can be trusted, only one truth that can be uttered. "For all the promises of God find their Yes in [Christ Jesus]. That is why we utter the Amen through him, to the glory of God" (2 Cor. 1:20). "Lo, I have come" (Heb. 10:7) is a word the Father can believe; it is the only word that is faithful (2 Tim. 2:13), the only son or slave who does what he says (Matt. 21:28–32). So all commentators on Lev. 5 have seen the command to a sin offering for rash oaths and unfulfilled trusts as a light upon the word of God in all its immovability: "The LORD has sworn and will not change his mind,

'You are a priest for ever after the order of Melchizedek'" (Ps. 110:4; Heb. 5:6; 7:21), the medieval exegetes discover in this text. "He took an oath to them, and they took an oath to him" (cf. Deut. 29:12–15), announce the rabbis as they consider those who keep their word and the Lord who makes covenant (cf. Luke 1:73; Heb. 6:13–20). "See now that I, even I, am he . . . ; I kill and I make alive; I wound and I heal" (Deut. 32:39), recalls Origen on this verse, as the Lord speaks to Israel and shows that the commitment to follow Christ in the spirit is a gift of the one faithful God, and of no other, not even of the selfsame spirit (*Homilies on Leviticus* 3.4). God's word alone is true from beginning to end (Ps. 119:160). And so the offering of the word is truth and grace together (John 1:17).

When Paul therefore speaks of his status as a sinner, he does so by holding together both his misdeeds as one ignorant in his actions and his condition in these actions as a blasphemer and insulter of Jesus Christ himself (1 Tim. 1:12–17). He is, even in his ignorance, "the foremost of sinners" (1:15). In what way is it blasphemy if done in ignorance? Because, in doing as he did, Paul denied the very oath of God made in Christ. And yet this oath, this "sure and acceptable saying," is the word of the Son who says, "Lo, I have come" and brings his body, and so "comes into the world to save sinners," even the foremost of them, even the ignorant blasphemers. The unwitting sinner is a sinner in the light of his sin's forgiveness. He offers because there is a God who offers first (2 Tim. 4:6). This God's oath stands before and over all human speech; it is a witness given by Father, Son, and Holy Spirit together. Yet the oath is certified, as it were, within the coming of this witness into the history of the world, whose form draws out God's testimony as it speaks within the realm of human sin and is heard as water, blood, and the confession of the saints (John 8:18; 1 John 5:6–9).

The first sin discussed in Leviticus is the unwitting sin, because this sin shapes the world for God's mercy, for the revelation of the light and truth of God in the one who comes into it and brushes against it and leaves himself within it in order to "draw all men to [him]self" (John 12:32). The Hebrew word translated by English "atonement" (*kipper*) has been traced by some (e.g., Milgrom 1991–2000: 1079–84) to the meaning "rub" or "wipe" (Jer. 18:23). Entangled, enmeshed, and ingrained in the world, a place where high and low make their way, sin's extended grasp and roots become the place of God's self-offering. The nature of the repeated sacrifices for sin is not so much an indication of their weakness and inefficacy, as Hebrews is usually taken to mean (9:11–14, 25) and as the Christian tradition has generally insisted. Rather, it is a figure of the ongoing grace of God as it engages the realities of time—and who but the Lord of time enters time?—which Leviticus underlines through the miracle of a forgiveness that extends into the hidden crevices of time and heart, through the laying out of men and women, of all times and places, before the Lord's light as it comes into their midst and gathers. Jesus rubs against their repetitions, that is, against their time. In doing so, he shows the world for what it is.

LEVITICUS 5:14–19

The previous instructions have dealt with unwitting sins as the ground out of which sins of all kinds emerge. As we turn to this section, a specific form of the unwitting sin is now discussed, which engages the reality of guilt and restitution for the first time, stated in terms of some transgression with respect to "the holy things of the LORD" (Lev. 5:15). A particular vocabulary is used here, whose definition has been a matter of much dispute. Calvin's impatience with the distinctions that may or may not apply to various ways of describing sin, in this and other cases in Leviticus, is mirrored even by some of the rabbis. Coordinating the various words and situations used and addressed throughout the book becomes both complex and, as many note, perhaps misguided. But even without attempting at this point to wade into these distinctions, we can see from the start that this "sin" (*maal*), a word sometimes translated "breach of faith" (Revised Standard Version) and hence "betrayal," is bound up with the breaking of trust. The topic here is sandwiched between the unwitting violation of certain oaths (5:1–13) and the failure to make good on certain promises to one's neighbor (6:1–7). Rashi points out that early authorities like Akiba always saw God as the defrauded party in any broken oath made even to a human being, because God is always the divine witness to this promise (Rosenbaum and Silbermann 1932: 19). Hence, at its most general, the section has to do with the defrauding of God.

It is a concern, as we have seen, lodged in the very character of offering itself, of coming before the Lord. Jesus discusses the manipulation of *qorban* (Mark 7:11–13), and the incident of Ananias and Sapphira (Acts 5:1–6) demonstrates the seriousness of its deformation. Holding back, diverting, and using the claim of God for the sake of personal indulgence, and doing so under the cover of some word made to God—all of this represents a terrible cheating of God out of what is rightly his. What, then, specifically are "the holy things of LORD"? Since the discussion extends itself to unwitting violations of God's commands in general (Lev. 5:17–19), and the context itself locates these holy things as part of a wide practice of defrauding God, we may well consider the focus here to move beyond the particular altogether. The guilt associated with the sinner in these texts (5:15 and 5:17 especially) was in any case seen by the rabbis as describing the effective outcome fundamental to all sin, even and especially the unwitting sin, for it describes the action as, before all else, a pernicious *disregard* for God. But what is the nature of this disregard?

The matter of holy things has already appeared in Lev. 2:3, 10 in relation to the portion of the grain offering given over to the priests. The context there spoke to the transformation of the offering into something of God, the figure of his word, filled with grace. But the question of what exactly constitutes the holiness of this portion, and in a way that connects it with other realities deemed holy, was not discussed (see the commentary on 19:1–2). Here, we are instructed as to an unwitting defrauding of God with respect to "the holy things of the LORD." The Vulgate explains this with the explicit word "ceremony" and so locates the sin involved here with elements of the sacrificial cult in particular, a specification that allowed most commentators to focus, in a Christian context, on aspects of liturgical negligence (e.g., not listening to the words of the Mass, not praying). But the text does not in fact specify what these holy elements are, a matter that exercised the rabbis, even as a certain common sense of the cult's implication here was accepted. Still, the lack of precision, especially as it is lifted up in this first specific sacrificial action devoted to something holy, allowed for a wider reflection on the nature of holiness itself.

If defrauding God is at issue, then we are speaking of things that somehow belong to God. This has, in fact, been an aspect of the root word's meaning that philologists have underlined: if—as is most commonly done—the base for the Hebrew family of words designating "holy" (*qad*) is linked with some basic sense of "separateness," then one crucial element of being "set apart" in this context is the goal: set apart "for God," becoming, as it were, the "possession" of God. The "holy ground" upon which Moses is called to step before the Lord's self-revelation (Exod. 3:5) demands the removal of his shoes and hence the customary recognition of the Lord's ownership of that space. And the call to Israel to be a "holy nation" is bound to the claim that God has made upon it, among all other nations, to be his "own possession" (19:5–6). Holy things, then, are those that are the Lord's own. Yet is this not too large a claim? Jesus's injunction that we are to "render . . . to God the things that are God's," despite its potential limitation by the assertion that there may be things that also belong to Caesar (Mark 12:17), has always raised the possibility that an offering that properly fulfilled this demand would engulf the whole self. Within this section of Leviticus especially, where money is required to be given over to priests, the offering of which Jesus speaks opens a larger vista, for, as he points out with regard to the widow, it is the offering of "her whole life," measured not by the strict rule of the sanctuary's shekel (Lev. 5:15) but by the relative extent of her self-giving, that garners the Lord's attention (Mark 12:44). Are not *all* things in their most fundamental the actual possession of the Lord?

"Behold, to the LORD your God belong heaven and the heaven of heavens, the earth with all that is in it" (Deut. 10:14); "the earth is the LORD's and the fulness thereof, the world and those who dwell therein" (Ps. 24:1).

What has God given, or loaned, that any soul might defraud him of it? We return to the reality of creation's extent, mentioned above: God has given over all things to Adam (Gen. 1:28). Yet that is only because all things are God's. It is significant to note that the first mention of holiness in Scripture comes as a summary to the divine work of creation itself: "So God blessed the seventh day and hallowed it [made it holy], because on it God rested from all his work which he had done in creation" (Gen. 2:3). So-called documentary analyses of the scriptural text here, by identifying this phrase with the Priestly editor, have tended to dismiss the canonical force of its summarizing scope: the holiness of the Sabbath is embedded in the nature of time and of creation as its very *sign*. The act of creation is designated by the reality of holiness, and that reality emerges to view because God is the creator of all things. Thus, God will later speak of Israel's call to holiness in terms of the very separation it embodies from the other peoples, that founds the division of elements into the forms of being and matter and, furthermore, distinguishes the clean from the unclean: "I am the LORD your God, who have *separated* [*badal*] you from the peoples. You shall therefore make a *distinction* between the clean beast and the unclean.... You shall be holy to me; for I the LORD am holy, and have *separated* you from the peoples, that you should be mine" (Lev. 20:24–26). "And God said, 'Let there be light'; and there was light. And God saw that the light was good; and God *separated* the light from the darkness.... And God said, 'Let there be a firmament in the midst of the waters, and let it *separate* the waters from the waters.'... And God said, 'Let there be lights in the firmament of the heavens to *separate* the day from the night'" (Gen. 1:3–14). The Havdalah ("differentiation") prayer that ends the Sabbath reads: "Blessed art Thou, O lord our God, King of the universe, who distinguishes between sacred and profane, between light and darkness, between Israel and the other nations, between the seventh day and the six days of labor. Blessed art Thou, O Lord, who distinguishes between sacred and profane!" (see the commentary on Lev. 11).

If, in fact, the sins in question in Lev. 5:14–19 refer to transgressions with respect to tithes (Exod. 30:13) and firstfruits, this is only because the holy things draw into their reach the whole of God's creation, itself the sign of God's nature, for which these offerings are tokens of recognition: "For what can be known about God is plain to [all people], because God has shown it to them. Ever since the creation of the world his invisible nature, namely, his eternal power and deity, has been clearly perceived in the things that have been made" (Rom. 1:19–20). Paul goes on to add: "So they are without excuse"—that is, they are guilty before God for lives that lack this recognition. The guilt that Lev. 5:15 associates with the transgressions of holy things—the offering required is a guilt offering in distinction from the sin offerings of Lev. 4 (though guilt is also present in 4:3)—is then a reflection of the violation of the gift given over by God to Adam in Adam's creation as the steward of all the earth.

These sins are a violation of the stewardship of creation. Thus the term for the offering, *asham*, is linked with a sense of "liability," as in the case of a trust, deposit, or debt, whose demands extend, in case of default, to some kind of punishment and restitution. But guilt is bound to the gift, embedded in God's act as creator. "Every one to whom much is given, of him will much be required" (Luke 12:48). How much? "Your soul is required!" (12:20). This is why liability or guilt is semantically linked with desolation, that is, the wasting away and death of created being. "Samaria shall become desolate" (Hos. 13:16), as the Authorized Version translates what in the Revised Standard Version becomes "Samaria shall bear her guilt." But this desolation is precisely how some rabbinic commentary, like Nahmanides (1974: 56–57), understands the force of the judgment etymologically: given much, holding on to much, losing all. "He has made my flesh and my skin waste away" (Lam. 3:4; cf. Ps. 31:10 for the more exact verbal analogy). And so guilt becomes a despoiling, a withering, even a death. "When thou dost chasten man with rebukes for sin, thou dost consume like a moth what is dear to him; surely every man is a mere breath!" (Ps. 39:11). When any soul sins, it is this very created fragility that is at stake.

Yet guilt is removed through giving! The guilt offering here represents a giving away, a giving back that surpasses the debt itself, or rather, whose doubled character—a ram and its value added—points to a condition that goes beyond the bare quantity of the amount owed. What could possibly equal the character of God's creative power and gift ignored? "Truly no man can ransom himself, or give to God the price of his life, for the ransom of his life is costly, and can never suffice" (Ps. 49:7–8). "For what can a man give in return for his life?" (Mark 8:37). Yet, through some form of giving, all is forgiven. Unless this movement is clearly seen—from God's creation, to its rejection and the rejection of its character, to the desolation that attends such guilt, to the restitution that such a desolating and self-expending offering embraces—then the figure of Christ that is necessarily lodged in the midst of this passage cannot be discerned. Yet to the degree that guilt is forgiven at all, it is done only through the offering of a gift that surpasses even created life itself. To throw away one's created existence, bound as it is to the substance of the earth and the gift of God and destroyed through the avoidance of its nature as such, is to embrace annihilation. Or what? Or to call forth a new creation itself, an offering that itself brings new life. If Anselm's description of the atonement in terms of an infinite offering to an infinitely aggrieved divine honor is articulated in categories that derive from a culture of esteem no longer in place (see Pelikan 1978: 143–44), nonetheless he rightly captured the sense of guilt as an overturning of created reality that lies outside our power to restore except by the incursion and engagement of creative life itself.

The key proclamation of the gospel as the reality of divine forgiveness is rightly, then, expressed in terms of a new creation: "Therefore, if any one is in Christ, he is a new creation; the old has passed away, behold, the new has come. All this is from God, who through Christ reconciled us to himself . . . not counting their trespasses against them" (2 Cor. 5:17–19). But Jesus himself understands this as the remission of a debt, the resolution of the demand that a defrauded God would place before those who had ignored their responsibilities. "Forgive us our debts," he teaches us to pray (Matt. 6:12), binding our petitions to a merciful master (18:23–35). The remission is itself the new creation, not an adjunct to existing life in fusing it with added force. It is a wasting life's replacement, the presence of the creator himself in his work, inserted into the midst of death, so that holiness is once more made apparent. We have a hint here that what religion has known as vicarious sacrifice is not, within the gospel, a matter only of "standing in the place of" another. It is rather the imposition of the life of God into the center and darkness of desolation, and thereby a new separating out of being and light. And conversely, the forgiveness enjoined by Jesus upon his followers—"forgive us our debts, as we also have forgiven our debtors" (Matt. 6:12) and "forgive, and you will be forgiven" (Luke 6:37)—is not a matter only of imitating another's action of remittance. It is rather the joining of oneself, the coming close, to God's own re-creative act in the midst of death.

"For what can a man give in return for his life?" (Mark 8:37). He can give nothing that could suffice. Only God gives life (Isa. 42:5). When Jesus says from the cross, therefore, "Father, forgive them," he speaks as one giving new life, creating it anew, in the face of the debtor's guilt. But he creates as one who offers in the midst of those who cannot offer enough. Isaiah 53 speaks of this in the same context of divine creation and likewise describes this forgiveness as the bearing of sin itself, the carrying of transgression. The restitution of the debt to which Lev. 5:16 refers, is a forgiveness because it is new life. But it is new life only to the degree that God has placed his work and self into the midst of life's demise. The reading of this passage as a figure of Christ's life and death together—of the order of restitution and sacrifice in a temporal sequence—has had a long history (e.g., Kellogg 1988). It is important to see here, however, that such a divine re-creation made in terms of an offering is the offering of life itself; it is an entry, an engagement. Jesus's incarnate life renews a wasting and guilty creation by replacing it with his own life, and each of his actions thereby "fulfil[s] all righteousness" (Matt. 3:15) by restoring to fullness what human beings have ignored as God's own gift.

This is the implication of restitution in any case: making whole and right, in the manner of the peace offering, what has withered and decreased. The offering of the ram and its monetary value, along with the superadded value of a fifth as a portion for the priest, has given rise to a variety of interpretations, although the central feature of the victim's character as tied to Christ is universal within the church's exegesis.[1] Given the centrality of guilt and restitution in this passage,

1. The variety of referents discovered here is unusual. Origen's interest in linking both the extra shekel (the plural of Lev. 5:15 was frequently understood in terms of the number two) and the

however, it seems best to see the details precisely in terms of this restorative divine act—that is, it is possible to retell it in narrative terms—by which desolation is replaced with new abundance, rather than in terms of the numerological figure of the added fifth in the narrative of Joseph and the offering to Pharaoh of a fifth of the rich harvest for the sake of surviving famine (Gen. 41:34; 47:24, 26). Jesus is a Josephan figure, going "into Egypt," into the world itself with all of its alternating wealth and oppression, and turning need into abundance for the sake of Gentile and Jew, through the exercise of a strange wisdom. As the entire Christian tradition of reading the Joseph narrative in this way is extravagantly loose, yet personally vivid in this regard, so too are the sacrificial details of the Levitical text related to this figurative narrative in a broad way.[2] Jesus goes to the "far country," in Barth's rereading of the prodigal son (*Church Dogmatics* 4.1.59.1), yet there transforms hunger into life through the giving of his own body.

This form of restitution, then, marks the giving of the one life that suffices, through its sharing of the life that cannot suffice. We must refine our discussion of forgiveness in this light. Re-creation is not the same as *creatio ex nihilo*. It is instead *creatio ex morte*, creation from death, a new thing taken from a preexisting lapse of being. And *this*, then, marks the peculiar way in which guilt is healed through a divine participation. God *enters* the dying world, he does not simply replace it; he is "baptized" within it and drags it with him into his own creative life. Again, the follower of Christ follows into this way, not to mimic it, but to be swept up into its direction and embodied dynamism (Mark 10:38–45; Rom. 6:1–4).

If we are, then, to maintain the Christian, and especially Western, reading of "holy things" as in some sense "ceremonies," we must do so only in the most extended way. I shall speak of the later distinction of ceremonial and moral law in the commentary on Lev. 18, but here I can note that, at its best, it is a difficult distinction always to maintain. Even if, and just because, the ceremonies described in 5:14 refer, from a Christian plain-sense perspective, to the Eucharist, as many commentators insisted ("holy things for holy people," in the early and still-used invitation to Communion), one is thrust through this reference into a reality that comprehends the deepest moral content. As we know, eucharistic piety and its theological underpinnings are existentially expansive in the Christian tradition. And the Eucharist here, as it is indicated in this Christian reading of Leviticus, is understood in its broadest reach as the body, the body of Christ given over, the

---

superadded fifth (the sense beyond the five senses of the body) to the true faith needed to receive the grace of Christ did not become standard (*Homilies on Leviticus* 3.8). Later commentators saw in the two shekels the two Testaments (Bruno of Segni), the two precepts of charity for God and neighbor (Rupert of Deutz [Patrologia latina 167.770]), the number five as pointing to Pentecost and the gift of the Holy Spirit by which grace is offered (the *Glossa ordinaria* [Patrologia latina 113.310–11]), etc.

2. The reading of Joseph in typologically christic terms begins as early as Justin Martyr and reaches fullness in, e.g., Ambrose's *De Joseph patriarchia*, which sets out what become standard patterns of correspondence.

body received and created within the church, the body given for and upholding the weak, the body as that through which and for which "Christ died" (Rom. 14:15). It is not inattentiveness to the prayers, lack of focus, and laziness in worship to which Leviticus could primarily speak here in this context. Rather it coheres with Paul's own exhortation that what is at stake is "discerning the body" itself in the life of the world (1 Cor. 11:29), that is, the act of God by which his life enters the world and into which, in all of its forgiving, we are drawn. To forget, let alone turn from, this is raw faithlessness.

That "the holy things of the LORD" are bound to the Lord who creates and thus to the Lord who redeems—that is, who restores by restitution, who pays the debt that is his own, who forgives—was one of the assertions of the great French spiritual writer Pierre de Bérulle. It was an assertion, curiously, with some parallels to the Kabbalah's mystical doctrine of creation. Bérulle suggests that at the very center of God's being there is a willingness to separate his own self from its true nature, to let go of himself so fully that the infinite could become mortal and limited. "[God] left [his Son] for a while in infancy and powerlessness, in swaddling clothes and the crèche, in persecution and flight, in a life both known and unknown, on the cross, in death and in the tomb. Oh, what a strange division and wondrous separation, even between what is the Divinity and the glory of the Divinity!" (*Discourse on the State and Grandeurs of Jesus* 8, quoted in Thompson 1989: 144).

But why this separation? What good might it do? How is it holy in and of itself? Why would God, perfect in all goodness, somehow (and we cannot ever know just how) be literally ripped from the condition of divinity? Only for love. For Bérulle, this separation is the very essence of love itself, this willingness to be separated from one's own self. Love is holiness; love creates, even as it gives itself over:

> O Jesus, love draws you out of the bosom of the Father and leads you outside, as you yourself state, to live in a foreign nature and land. . . . Love [then] separates your human nature from the human person to offer it up again to another Person [God the Father]. . . .
>
> O love that divides and no longer unites! . . .
>
> O Jesus, may this love that is in you, be in us! May this love that acts in you, act in us. May this love that triumphs over you, triumph over us. May this love that creates separation and division in you, divide and separate in us. May it separate us from sin, the earth and ourselves so that we may live for you. May this love absorb us in you, draw us to you and fill us with you. (*Discourse on the State and Grandeurs of Jesus* 12, quoted in Thompson 1989: 155–56)

LEVITICUS 6:1–7

Some Christian commentators saw, in the two shekels associated with Lev. 5:15, a reference to the "two precepts of charity" given in Jesus's summary of the law: "You shall love the Lord your God with all your heart, and with all your soul, and with all your mind. This is the great and first commandment. And a second is like it, You shall love your neighbor as yourself. On these two commandments depend all the law and the prophets" (Matt. 22:37–40; cf. Rom. 13:9–10). The connection was hardly arbitrary if taken in the context of the juxtaposition of Lev. 5:15–19 and 6:1–7 (numbered 5:20–26 in the Hebrew Bible and Septuagint), for the one deals with defrauding the Lord and the other with defrauding one's neighbor, though in the explicit shadow of sinning against God: "If any one sins and commits a breach of faith against the LORD by deceiving his neighbor" (6:2). The relation between the two was viewed by both Jews and Christians as one of coherent subordination: to cheat a neighbor *was* in a sense to cheat God, especially if an oath (using the Lord's name) was involved (so Rashi [Rosenbaum and Silbermann 1932: 19], following Rabbi Akiba, Rabanus Maurus [Patrologia latina 108.290], and Calvin 1996: 2.358–59). The link with the two precepts of charity, however, goes further, at least in Christian terms, than asserting a moral continuity, for it raises the christological import of the "neighbor" with a special urgency, and with this question, Leviticus points forward to the vocation of the church's history among the nations.

In Mark's version of the summary (12:28–34), Jesus is commended by the inquiring scribe for his answer, and he in turn extols the scribe. But in Luke 10:25–29, the lawyer who speaks to Jesus "desir[es] to justify himself" and so says to Jesus: "And who is my neighbor?" This question is not asked by most commentators of Lev. 6:1–7, but it cannot be avoided once the historical context of

---

the sacrifices is grasped, the context that engages Israel and the peoples together in their common origin and fate.[1]

In Luke 10 Jesus replies with the parable of the good Samaritan. The priest and the Levite, bound to Jerusalem and its sacrifices, ignore the wounded man and pass by on the other side of the road. But the heretical Samaritan stops, tends the man, and gives of his money for his care at the inn. Jesus asks the lawyer: "'Which of these three . . . proved neighbor to the man who fell among the robbers?' He said, 'The one who showed mercy on him.' And Jesus said to him, 'Go and do likewise'" (10:36–37). Augustine most famously (with Origen leading the way) had identified the Samaritan with Christ himself and the wounded man with Adam (*Quaestiones evangeliorum* 2.19). This framework, with a sometimes florid variation, became standard through the Middle Ages and continues to be used pedagogically (and negatively) as a paradigm of the allegorical method. It is the identification itself, the Samaritan as Christ, that is the most daring and finally pertinent in this trajectory, for "being a neighbor" as an answer to the question "who is my neighbor?" engages the word of God to Moses that "any one . . . [who] deceiv[es] his neighbor" in a particular way within the context of Leviticus. The neighbor—a single English (and in the Septuagint a single Greek) word used for two Hebrew synonyms—makes his appearance in Leviticus only here, before taking a more central role in Lev. 19 (e.g., 19:18). In large measure, modern readers have seen the neighbor in Israel as standing in some contrast with the sojourner or stranger, at least as legal matters go. But, as scholars more recently argue, there is in Leviticus a very clear move whereby, just in those sections where the neighbor becomes a prominent explicator of the law's concerns, the stranger also makes an appearance as a positive participant in the injunctions (Seitz 2005). The neighbor is not only an object of justice (19:33–34), but also one to whom the law applies as an agent (18:26). Indeed, this inclusion of the sojourner within the practice of the law extends even to the sacrificial injunctions (or at least some of them), a fact that in this case dissolves somewhat the distinction between moral and ceremonial that some might see at work in these passages (17:8–13).

Who is my neighbor? There is a real way in which Leviticus moves toward the blurring of the lines between neighbor and stranger, but drawing both into the clear demands and effects of the law. Leviticus 19:33–34, furthermore, locates the press toward this blurring in the common historical experience of sojourning, shared by Israel and those foreigners who live within its midst. Not only does Moses name Israel according to this reality (Deut. 26:5/Gen. 12:10), but it

---

1. The rich man asks the same question in both in Mark 10:17 and Luke 10:25: "What must I do to inherit eternal life?" And Jesus offers to the rich man the commandments of the Decalogue. Calvin 1996: 2.358–60 notes that the sin addressed in Lev. 6:1–7 is, on a particular basis, prohibited by the eighth command and to that degree can be read through a plain-sense and very concrete lens. Yet in Luke 10 Jesus answers the question with the summary itself and so embraces something larger than the one commandment, indeed something that comprehends (or "fulfills," in Paul's language) all the commandments. The figure by which this is personified is that of the neighbor.

becomes paradigmatic of what it means for Israel and the Israelite to exist at all, the most human of the human creature: "Hear my prayer, O LORD, and give ear to my cry; hold not thy peace at my tears! For I am thy passing guest, a sojourner, like all my fathers" (Ps. 39:12). From Cain, driven out and wandering, to Abram, setting out from Aram and moving into Egypt, the movement is consistent, such that it is taken up by Hebrews as the culmination of its paean to history's temporal meaning: "By faith Abraham obeyed when he was called to go out to a place which he was to receive as an inheritance; and he went out, not knowing where he was to go. By faith he sojourned in the land of promise, as in a foreign land, living in tents. . . . And what more shall I say? For time would fail me to tell of. . . . They went about in skins of sheep and goats, destitute, afflicted, ill treated—of whom the world was not worthy—wandering over deserts and mountains, and in dens and caves of the earth" (Heb. 11:8–9, 32, 37–38).

The matter here of blurring the line between neighbor and sojourner is not one of subverting Israel's false separateness, as the anti-Judaic tendency of modern universalism has always insisted. Rather, it is a matter, within the sacrificial locus of offering, of indicating Israel as the place of refuge for the world, as the living sign of that land of promise, the "city which has foundations, whose builder and maker is God" (Heb. 11:10). "Behold, Philistia and Tyre, with Ethiopia—'This one was born there,' they say. And of Zion it shall be said, 'This one and that one were born in her'" (Ps. 87:4–5). Born in Zion, because of the one who is the neighbor there.

Who is my neighbor? "Out of Egypt have I called my son" (Matt. 2:15, quoting Hos. 11:1; cf. Exod. 4:22). So Jesus takes his place within this sacrificial interchange, the neighbor from afar who stands beside. He will rightly say, with Moses and Israel's prophets: "You know the commandments: 'Do not kill, Do not commit adultery, Do not steal, Do not bear false witness, Do not defraud, Honor your father and mother'" (Mark 10:19). How then would you treat Jesus? The matter of sin against God as that very sin of defrauding neighbor finds its glaring sign in him and its explicator in the cross. Around Jesus gather lies and betrayals, false witnesses, bribery, stolen clothing, broken oaths. "Help, LORD; for there is no longer any that is godly; for the faithful have vanished from among the sons of men. Every one utters lies to his neighbor" (Ps. 12:1–2).

"If any one sins and commits a breach of faith against the LORD by deceiving his neighbor," then what? Then "every eye will see him, every one who pierced him; and all tribes of the earth will wail on account of him. Even so. Amen" (Rev. 1:7). All the tribes will wail with Israel and within it. The discovery of the passion, the neighbor's home within Jerusalem, here in Lev. 6 is hardly an importation of concern. "I was a stranger and you did not welcome me" (Matt. 25:43). Yet Jesus was a neighbor too. And if Jesus is both stranger and neighbor, he draws all people into the midst of his own life, even those who defraud and reject. One of the central claims of Leviticus, that God comes close to sinning Israel and the world and bears the burden of such proximity, is here broached.

Jesus is neighbor and friend: "I have called you friends" (John 15:15). "Behold
...a friend of tax collectors and sinners!" (Matt. 11:19). Though "my friends and
companions stand aloof" from me (Ps. 38:11) and "my equal [a man like me,
anthrōpos/homo, any man], my companion, my familiar friend" (55:13) "taunts
me" (55:12), yet "greater love has no man that this, that a man lay down his life for
his friends. You are my friends if you do what I command you" (John 15:13–14),
if you "love one another as I have loved you" (15:12). Who is my neighbor?
Jesus's answer, "go and do likewise" (Luke 10:37), is the same call as that to the
commandment-keeping rich man, "come, follow me" (Mark 10:21), the neighbor
sinned against, the neighbor who offers himself.

Far from leaving behind the concrete elements alluded to in the text of Leviticus—deposits, securities, robberies, oppression, lying—the reality of the neighbor
who is Jesus gives these injunctions roots within the life of human flesh. All Christian commentators from Origen on have dwelt upon the practical character here
of the concern for responsible and honest dealings with money and with people,
with the poor, with word and sacrament. "The faithful and wise steward" (Luke
12:42) is the one who cares for all that God gives to him or her, with the same
care as God himself. "It is required of stewards that they be found trustworthy"
(1 Cor. 4:2), even of the full "mysteries of God" (4:1), which embrace the fullness
of our vocation in word and deed toward others.

On the one hand, Origen finds the greatest trust to be the image and likeness
to God that each of us were created as bearing (Gen. 1:26) (*Homilies on Leviticus*
4.3). Hence, to tend to this image's redemption and health in ourselves and to
honor it in others—this likeness is in fact what makes us neighbors and what draws
strangers into this similitude—impels our self-discipline and self-giving, the very
work of sharing the gospel's wide-netted truth. And this likeness is expressed in
reflecting God's own nature, his mercy and care for the good and the evil. "You
have heard that it was said, 'You shall love your neighbor and hate your enemy.' But
I say to you, Love your enemies and pray for those who persecute you, so that you
may be sons of your Father who is in heaven; for he makes his sun rise on the evil
and on the good, and sends rain on the just and on the unjust.... You, therefore,
must be perfect, as your heavenly Father is perfect" (Matt. 5:43–48).

On the other hand, Origen sees especially in the character of the "security"
(Lev. 6:2) an image of something greater than the individual's single worth—the
church itself and its communion with the triune God (*Homilies on Leviticus* 4.4).
The Hebrew for this term indicates perhaps the "hand of fellowship," an unusual
phrase whose translation opened up a wider perspective. Thus, the Septuagint
(*koinōnia*) and Rufinus's Old Latin version (*societas*) focused upon the social
(rather than the material) aspect of this particular sin, and later exegetes used it
as the basis for reflection on the stewardship of the body of Christ in particular
as the image of God's own life (using texts like 1 Thess. 4:6; Phil. 2:11; 1 John
1:3; 2 Pet. 1:4). To sin against the body, then, in the manner discussed by Paul in
1 Cor. 11–12 or by Jesus in Matt. 18:5–22 becomes the framework in which the

neighbor's character is especially torn asunder and the reality of God most horrendously blasphemed. The profound moral and spiritual implications of ecclesial integrity and virtue are thereby sketched—and with them an ecclesiology of unity and humility as bound to the neighbor who *is* Jesus giving and receiving—that speaks directly to the struggles of the modern church.

Certainly, the image and reality of the body of Christ is given to the church as a trust to steward. This trust also reflects a larger promise granted the church for the sake of the world of civic neighbor: it must draw all those around it to itself, just as Israel draws the stranger into its midst. Paul will address the Gentiles as once being "alienated from the commonwealth of Israel, and strangers to the covenants of promise," even as "having no hope and without God in the world" (Eph. 2:12). The "one new man" that Christ creates of Jew and Gentile, is however, granted "in himself" (2:15), the neighbor defrauded and healing, which is the church, the new *societas* of his passion (Phil. 3:10). While the relationship of neighbor and stranger is more deeply engaged in later chapters of Leviticus, here, in this closing of the first section on sacrifice and its human offerers, it is tied back to the primordial history of Abel and Cain and bound up with its resolution in Christ. And just in the center of this stands Israel as the sign of its origin and goal.

It is worth noting the way in which the figural bearing of Leviticus is unpacked. The ethical details regarding honest dealings with one's neighbor are firmly established and mark out the character of a host of particular sins and virtues: "The wicked borrows, and cannot pay back; but the righteous is generous and gives" (Ps. 37:21). This literal sense, as the tradition would have it, forms the basis of the textual dynamic set in motion and informs the divine framework of that motion's scope. Yet Leviticus itself will raise questions about the lines that are to distinguish neighbor and stranger especially with respect to the demands of the law. Israel, as it were, draws into its law the "scattered" "children of God" (John 11:52) by outlining the shape of the divine neighbor who makes the exile his friend. It is here that the body of Christ emerges, as both neighbor and stranger, law-abiding and sinned against, Israelite and outcast, ground of sacrifice and victim. Yet how could it be otherwise? He is the "first-born of all creation" and "in him all things were created, in heaven and on earth, visible and invisible ... all things were created through him and for him" (Col. 1:15–16). Jesus, as creation's center, articulates the movement already instigated within Leviticus and mirrors it back into the text of Leviticus itself. In this way, the world is seen as Israel itself, yet through Christ. The figures of Leviticus can thus be defined as follows: they are the revealed particulars of Israel offered to the world that, through Christ, conform the world to their expanded contours.

This reading depends upon the confidence that the details of the text can and must be explicated by the acts of God in Christ. "In many and various ways God spoke of old to our fathers by the prophets; but in these last days he has spoken to us by a Son" (Heb. 1:1). And we are invited by this voice into a refashioned Israel: "No longer strangers and sojourners, but you are fellow citizens with the saints and members of the household of God, built upon the foundation of the apostles and prophets, Christ Jesus himself being the cornerstone, in whom the whole structure is joined together and grows into a holy temple in the Lord; in whom you also are built into it for a dwelling place of God in the Spirit" (Eph. 2:19–22).

LEVITICUS 6:8–7:38

In Leviticus 6:8–7:38 (6:8–30 is numbered 6:1–23 in the Hebrew Bible and Septuagint) a shift takes place now in the perspective of God's instructions. Until now, God has called Moses to tell the people how to offer their sacrifices. Now he tells Moses to "command Aaron and his sons" (6:9). Command them about what? About the same sacrifices already described, but now approached from the side of the priests. In addition, a new sacrifice is mentioned (6:19–23) to be offered on the day of the priest's anointing, and new details about some of the other offerings (e.g., the peace offering) are given. But the shift of perspective raises questions: why go over the same material again? Why do the priests receive their own instructions, now buttressed as "command," unlike the words given to the people? And finally, what are we to make of the ordering of this section, which provides instructions for matters that are perhaps already performed (e.g., in Exod. 40)?

Let us begin with the question of chronology. On this there has been disagreement among interpreters, though in general Christian commentators have not been exercised over the matter. But the rabbis wondered whether Exod. 40:16–33 appears to say that many of the sacrifices, including the consecration of the priests, had already taken place before the words spoken by God in Leviticus. The easiest way of dealing with this was to see the entirety of Leviticus as a kind of explanatory subsection to be fitted into or upon the last chapters of Exodus, and the dating of Exod. 40:17 and Lev. 9:1 are coordinated in a seamless temporal scheme. This was Nahmanides' solution (1974: 3–4), who argued for a strict chronological sequence of the two books.[1] But Rashi recognized, in a sense, the challenge posed by this attempted chronological systematization—that is, plain sense was somewhat stretched. From his point of view, one must simply admit, even affirm, that

---

1. One of the (minor) motivations for Calvin's use of a harmony to deal with the last four books of the Pentateuch was to pursue this chronological sorting out, although the principle of theological organization of these books' content was far stronger in his case.

"there is no 'earlier' or 'later' . . . in the Torah" (Rosenbaum and Silbermann 1932: 30). This, of course, is more than a documentary description, for it undergirds an entire method of reading the Scriptures that became intrinsic to rabbinic exegesis: the dissolution of the temporal uniqueness (and therefore sequence) of scriptural referents and their apprehension as determinants of everyday realities, not so much repeated as variously embodied as the means by which God absorbs the world into his (scripturally articulated) plan (Neusner 1986: 75, 91). That there is neither earlier nor later in the Torah means, in the case of the sacrifices and their participants—people and priests—that we are to understand them as descriptions of our own lives and temporal existences.

This seems right. And from a Christian point of view, it directs our answers to the next two questions regarding the change of perspective in this section on the sacrifices. First, the distinction between people and priest marks our relationships with God even now. And second, these relationships in distinction are moored in the commanding of God: "Command Aaron and his sons."

Why does God tell Moses to issue a command? There is here a new urgency, some inescapable demand, and it is received primarily through the priests, through their work and obedience. The explanation given by Leviticus itself comes at the end of this section, in 7:35–38. The blurring of chronological lines is important here, for we are to read the apparent reference to Exod. 29 and Exod. 40 in these concluding verses as temporally applicable, whatever we make of the historical sequence at issue: the priests have been commanded and the people together commanded from the Sinai itself "on the day" that God spoke to Moses. And that is the day when—through the obedience to these commands—the Lord "will dwell among the people of Israel, and will be their God. And they shall know that I am the LORD their God, who brought them forth out of the land of Egypt that I might dwell among them; I am the LORD their God" (Exod. 29:45–46; cf. Lev. 26:12). A command is given for the sake of God's dwelling. And the movement from people to priest in this section of Leviticus represents a movement, speaking in terms of theology, from anthropology—"what is man that thou art mindful of him?" (Ps. 8:4/Heb. 2:5)—to its basis, to God the abider, through him "who for a little while was made lower than the angels" (2:9). This is what the priestly perspective unveils.

The priestly presence stands as the cipher for the object of God's abiding, the community as a whole. This stands behind the notion of shared priestly guilt in Lev. 4:3: "If it is the anointed priest who sins, thus bringing guilt on the people. . . ." But the direction of relationship is important: the priest is people insofar as God abides and insofar as the people receive the vessel for this abiding, the commandments. Where "priest" is written, we read Israel as a whole and as the tabernacle of God. Christian commentators, like Rupert of Deutz (Patrologia latina 167.774–75), will thus see these chapters as particularly pertinent, not to the individual Christian, but as explanatory of the shape of the Christian community, the church as a whole, the "nation of priests," following 1 Pet. 2:5, 9 (and Exod. 19:6). These chapters of Leviticus therefore now review the earlier ones from the perspective of God's relationship with the community as a whole, in terms of his indwelling. Aaron's sacerdotal blessing, after all, is the sign of Israel's unity with God (Ps. 133). Yet Aaron is also the quintessential communal sinner, the perpetrator of the golden calf (Exod. 32), which becomes the quintessential sin of Israel as a people.[2] In the first chapters, the priests function as ancillaries to the figural narrative of primordial human life caught up in Israel's mission. If there is converse at work, then, it is that Israel itself is now addressed through the commandments that God will use for the world's redemption.

What then are the contours of God's abiding? They are given sacrificially, through the offering presented by "any man." But what offering will this be? Now the offering is commanded from Israel as a people, for the sake of God's saving of all people. "If a man loves me, he will keep my word, and my Father will love him, and we will come to him and make our home with him" (John 14:23). "This is my commandment, that you love one another as I have loved you" (15:12)—"a *new* commandment" (13:34; cf. 1 John 3:23). The relationship between commanding and abiding is given in offering: "Greater love has no man than this, that a man lay down his life for his friends" (John 15:13; cf. Rom. 5:7–8). The commandments given on Sinai from the fire become the commandments given on the mountain in Galilee, from the light of Tabor: "Go therefore and make disciples of all nations, baptizing them in the name of the Father and of the Son and of the Holy Spirit, teaching them to observe all that I have commanded you; and lo, I am with you always, to the close of the age" (Matt. 28:18–20).

We should follow Origen here, who gives a surprising amount of attention to these verses in Leviticus (*Homilies on Leviticus* 4.6–10). Although we might, from one perspective, focus on the various particular elements of the priestly duties and portions associated with the sacrifices, we need to return always to an undergirding reality—that of the word's depth, difficulty, and promise. This is symbolized in the primary sacrifice of the holocaust, the whole burnt offering that points to the word in its fullness, without revision or compromise. The details therefore can do no less than beckon the spirit into an overwhelming land. Yet this very promise ends up being the topic of the text itself: each detail—grill, fire, priestly clothing, portions of the grain, the consumed fat—points again and again to the reality of something deeper that the Christian is called to enter, the fullness of faith and the miracle of life in the Spirit granted by Christ, who has come to dwell in the human flesh that carries the word within the world. "Command Aaron and his sons" becomes the call of Jesus to the disciples to the assumption of all their being—to love, to deny, to give themselves to unity within the church and to obedience to God. Rupert of Deutz (Patrologia latina 167.772–80) also senses something similar. Over and over, with an insistence and continuity rare

---

2. So *Rabbah* 7.1 will insist as it treats the later chapters of Leviticus and discusses the whole significance of sacrificing a bull, even including the initial and paradigmatic sacrifice of Lev. 1:3.

in the skip-and-scatter method of medieval commentary, his reflections on these passages return to the fire of the priestly ritual and point to the Spirit of charity, which is to light and consume all aspects of the church's life, all details of its faithfulness, so that it becomes transformed into the shape of its promise, which is God's indwelling in its body.

"But will God indeed dwell on the earth?" (1 Kgs. 8:27). He will dwell with a people who keep his commandments. Solomon renews the commands of Moses regarding the cult, in answer to his own question. And the gospel continues, by declaring that "behold, something greater than Solomon is here" (Matt. 12:42). In all cases, however, we are to see the range of sacrifices revisited in Lev. 6:8–7:38 in terms of the care for God's life within the community that obedience provides. The portions—and the object of the portions, altar, ashes, and so on—become the signs of the intersecting of love and abiding that mark out God's tabernacling presence upon earth (John 1:14). Although Calvin overly restricted the purpose of the commands here simply to obedience in its own right, he was correct to see—as did many Jewish commentators—that obedience in and of itself, without reference to rationality, was a source of tremendous blessing: although "God prefers obedience to all sacrifices, he was unwilling that anything should remain doubtful as to the external rites, which were not otherwise of great importance; that [the people] might learn to observe precisely, and with the most exact care, whatever the Law commanded, and that they should not obtrude anything of themselves, inasmuch as the purity of the holy things was corrupted by the very smallest invention" (1996: 2.363).

Within this context, the resummarizing of the main categories of sacrifice from the perspective of the priestly community becomes a set of images of various forms of self-dedication in faith, ecclesial practices as it were. The burnt offering marks the reception of the whole of God's self-offering in Christ, the fullness of the word as we have said with Origen. Its touch, like the sin offering's, sanctifies, like the woman with a flow of blood, and so calls the church to a constant and deep immersion in the word's teaching and to total faith that does not shy away from going ever further along the pathway of learning. The offerings are burnt during the night both to symbolize the quotidian character of their demand during this mortal life and to recognize the fundamental humility and hiddenness with which the church is called to pursue faithfulness. The grain offering, on the other hand, is presented in the light of day, the "good works" by which the Father is glorified (Matt. 5:16) in the eyes of the world, rid of the leaven of vanity and conceit. The particular grain offering associated with the priesthood in particular is given over wholly to the Lord and represents the way in which the church's service qua liturgy is without self-regard.

The anthropological scope of the original description of the sacrifices in the opening chapters of Leviticus, which drew all within the ambit of the primordial human life and its redemption, is left aside now, as the aspect of ecclesial obedience to God simply gathers together the range of devotional conduct.

And so the priestly redescription of the sacrifices now brings in the sin offering and guilt offering (a distinction that many commentators, like Calvin 1996: 2.369–72, are hard-pressed to explain). Each calls forth from the church an interior self-giving through which repentance becomes the continuous current of approach to God. The peace offering comes last, and now it is sketched according to several motivations—thanksgiving, votive, freewill—along with a new gesture in their performance, the "waving" of the portions of the breast and thigh given over to the priests. Both the motives and the gestures point to the set of the church's heart in an encompassing array of situations, now oriented toward God and lifted up in a communally enacted statement of praise and thanksgiving. This core element of the peace offering, the thankful worship of God with heart and soul, represents the highest and in some sense most essential aspect of all sacrifice for *Rabbah* 9.4–9, and so it is discussed last of all, as the epitome of offering itself.

It is important to see that there is nothing extraneous to the text in the explication of this sacrificial summary in terms of communal character oriented toward God. These are the forms of life by which God will dwell with his people. And thus, each form, commanded for the sake of such abiding, grows out of a desire for God and out of the contexts in which such desire is formed, from self-denial to Eucharist. And each of these contexts, elicited by the divine command, now demands attention and awareness on the part of the people. "Will God indeed dwell on the earth?" they ask; and they answer only as they thirst after the living God. "Thou hast said, 'Seek ye my face'"—that is, "Command Aaron and his sons"—"My heart says to thee, 'Thy face, Lord, do I seek'" (Ps. 27:8), that is, "Lord, to whom shall we go? You have the words of eternal life" (John 6:68). Thus all is done in order, for deep in the heart of the church it cries out: "Hide not thy face from me" (Ps. 27:9).

All that the church does, it does out of its desire for God's dwelling. And it will do all things: "I will lay down my life for you" (John 13:37). We will follow Jesus anywhere. All things we give to him. One of Origen's most famous passages is written about the sin offering. We are each, he says, a kind of microcosm of the world from which the sacrificial victims are gathered:

> Look for them [the victims] within yourself, and you will find them at the center of your soul. Do you see? You have inside of yourself herds of cattle, blessed in Abraham. Do you see? You have herds of sheep and goats, by whom the patriarchs were blessed and multiplied. Do you see? You even have within you the birds of the sky. And do not be surprised when I tell you that all of this is within you. Don't you see? There is within you another world in miniature—a sun, a moon, and all the stars. Why else would the Lord have said to Abraham, "Lift up your eyes to the skies, and gaze upon the stars. Can you count their multitude? These will be your descendents." (*Homilies on Leviticus* 5.2)

And all these we give to God.

The encompassing desire for God is described in the details of the priestly sacrifices, and they must be read, variously but assiduously, in connection with the Scriptures of Christian service, for in this case there is no sequence, but all is taken up by God in the moment and place of his coming as Christ. There are, indeed, a host of such connections. There is an altar placed within its center—the worship of the Lamb, placed in the midst of the martyrs (Rev. 5:6–14). Even the church's life is given over here. Upon the altar burns a fire, miraculously sustained (as both Jewish and Christian commentators have recognized) by God's grace through night and day, for all time, from Alpha to Omega. It is the fire of God's love, his Spirit cast by Jesus to enflame a world offered up to the Father, consuming sin and purifying the hearts of men and women by the great holocaust of his own body (Isa. 31:9; Luke 12:49). And what shall be left? Only the dregs of a defeated death, the ashes of mortality (Gen. 3:19) from which God will bring new life. "O death, where is thy victory? O death, where is thy sting?" (1 Cor. 15:55, quoting Hos. 13:14). Their empty shells will be banished from the place that God has chosen, that is, "outside the camp." "Behold, the dwelling of God is with men. He will dwell with them, and they shall be his people, and God himself will be with them; he will wipe away every tear from their eyes, and death shall be no more" (Rev. 21:3–4).

And who shall dwell within this people? Neither the "the dogs and sorcerers and fornicators and murderers and idolaters, and every one who loves and practices falsehood" (22:15). Instead, the gates of the city are protected by a court of holiness, a place where all that is not of God is left behind, where repentance—the killing of the beasts of sin—is made the hall of sustenance and reformation the table of the feast. The people clothe themselves with garments of purity, no longer wandering about as fugitives in the skins of animals (Gen. 3:21), but garbed in a linen woven from the gifts of a newly benevolent earth. Here is labor of love in service of the Lord, anointing with oil, washing feet (Luke 7:36–38), serving meals (Mark 1:31). Oven, pan, and griddle are tools by which God's people press their hospitality upon a God who sits with them, as they listen to his every word (Luke 10:38–42).

This story of the church's desire and service for its Lord is meant to take in the breadth of its effort and its breath—each portion of the peace offering, each corporeal aspect of the ritual as some reflection of this ecclesial service. The hands that carry the victim and wave its sections "before the LORD" point to the exercise of the Spirit's gifts; the fat is the heart purified for God's love; the tail of the liver is a soul stripped of distorting passions; the shoulder of the beast is a faith strengthened by devotion and learning and separated from evil living. This, and much more, can be said (as Origen and others have said), not as a single reference, but as a part of an inexhaustible whole.[3]

---

3. Even from a social-scientific viewpoint, such ramified meanings across the scriptural text make perfect sense. In most cultures, the practical deployment of food and sacrifice is purposefully

The reader of Leviticus is called to discern precisely these formal projections of Israel's and the church's own communal vocation in the pursuit of and welcoming of God's own life in its midst. The seemingly strange explanatory silence within Scripture regarding the purpose and meaning of sacrificial ritual is, in itself, a divine demand for responsibility, for identifying and engaging the full network of scriptural forms by which God would order our lives according to his plan. "Command Aaron and his sons" is quite literally the call to Israel to live in a manner (and to struggle for such a life) that coheres with the formal promises provided, for instance, in the eschatological vision of Isaiah:

> On this mountain [i.e., the mountain from which God commands] the LORD of hosts will make for all peoples a feast of fat things, a feast of wine on the lees, of fat things full of marrow, of wine on the lees well refined. And he will destroy on this mountain the covering that is cast over all peoples, the veil that is spread over all nations. He will swallow up death for ever, and the Lord GOD will wipe away tears from all faces, and the reproach of his people he will take away from all the earth; for the LORD has spoken. (Isa. 25:6–8)

There is a direct line between the commands to Aaron and his sons and the ethical challenges even of modern liberation theologians just because of this literal call to the discernment of sacrificial food in the hands of priests: we are called to eat together the satisfying food of God's provision, for God has laid this out for us. How shall this take place? What therefore shall we do? The abiding presence of God among his people, explicated specifically by the Christian tradition following Origen here in terms of Father, Son, and Holy Spirit calling, forming, and empowering the church, demands that the people be shaped according to the fullness of the scriptural world of its words and not simply by the limited referents of a past culture. "Lo, this is our God; we have waited for him, that he might save us. This is the LORD; we have waited for him; let us be glad and rejoice in his salvation" (Isa. 25:9). The exclamation "this!" is Rashi's discernment of the always and interchangeably chronological present of the Torah (Rosenbaum and Silbermann 1932: 30).

It would be wrong, however, if we were to see the priestly sacrifices only in terms of demand, the demand pressed by God's abiding, the issuing of command, for what is at stake, even on the terms of the sacrifices themselves, cannot only be the church's faithfulness. It is also and primarily a matter of God's grace. As the

---

aimed at exposing the widest and most entwined meanings of religious existence, and this has given rise, beginning in the nineteenth century, to the burgeoning speculation on sacrificial theory, such as William Robertson Smith's theory of sacrifice as a communal meal with a god (1886, 1888). Smith's ideas became standard fare in popular scriptural commentary (e.g., Cook 1953: 112, 118). For recent discussions of symbolic anthropology (and not only in religious contexts) as related to the study of food, see Sahlins 1990; Fieldhouse 1995; Douglas 1972; and Counihan 1999. This approach, even in its decided secularity, is useful to the religious reader of Leviticus, precisely because it trains us to take seriously the meaning of carnal (literally) detail.

rabbis cited in *Rabbah* 9.1–3 emphasize, there is a reason why, just as the peace offering is listed last in the opening chapters of Leviticus, here too in its priestly explication it is presented last and explicitly in terms of thanksgiving, for is not thanksgiving the highest form of sacrifice, because it expresses the deepest reality of the people's relationship with God and with the promise (and demand) of his abiding? That is, God *chooses* Israel, God has come to it of his own desire, he offers it the means to desire him. "For you are a people holy to the LORD your God; the LORD your God has chosen you to be a people for his own possession, out of all the peoples that are on the face of the earth. It was not because you were more in number than any other people that the LORD set his love upon you and chose you, for you were the fewest of all peoples; but it is because the LORD loves you" (Deut. 7:6–8). And even *this* choosing, this separating and distinguishing, is but the form of all God's choosing, that is, of all God's love. Hence, we can only thank God, before all else; and such thanks can come only in the forms of separated and distinguished, of particular beasts and foods. *Rabbah* 9.4 goes on to say here that the priority of God's grace and love is, as it were, so metaphysically foundational that there is a real sense in which we must say that God "himself offers the thank offering," not Israel at all. But this is only to say that "he is our peace," the Lord himself, that God who first abides among us (John 1:14).

The marvelous grace of God's self-giving to the world, which calls forth praise, is thus at the center of this priestly explication; and the reader is called to an enumeration simply of the ways this must be so, a catalogue of praise, as in Ps. 147. We will see later (i.e., on Lev. 11) how this hymnic embrace of creation itself, in the form of the animals, stands behind the distinctions that are made among them. But even here we can note how the reality of the sacrificial acts related to God's presence among his people affirm—contra any ancient or modern gnostic denigration of created matter—the goodness of the whole of what God has made. It is only on the basis of this value, given in its loving distinction from God, that the sacrificial exchange of love, so emphasized by Rupert of Deutz in this context (Patrologia latina 167.772–75), makes sense, and must make sense: what God has given—himself in the fire of the Holy Spirit—dwells within his people, as a formative love that offers itself in return. Thereby is the world's goodness, as wrought by God, unveiled.

LEVITICUS 8–9

There is no doubt that many readers experience the first sections of Leviticus on sacrifices as tedious. This may especially be so with respect to Lev. 8–9, which appear to press repetition to an extreme. Did we not hear about much of this material regarding the forms of the priests' consecration and about their clothing in Exod. 28–29 in the shape of a commandment given to Moses? Were these not revisited, as being actually fabricated, in the last chapters of Exodus? And in Exod. 40, did we not read that "Moses finished the work" and that "then the cloud covered the tent of meeting, and the glory of the LORD filled the tabernacle" (40:33–34)? Did we not hear, in Lev. 6, something of the sacrifices to be offered on the day of the priests' consecration? And, in any case, were not these sacrifices in their general order already set forth in earlier chapters? For Calvin, the discussion in Lev. 8–9 is by and large "wearisome" and as usual filled with things that "we do not understand," nor should we worry about our ignorance (1996: 3.422–23).

Origen goes only a bit further (*Homilies on Leviticus* 6.2). These particular chapters represent a "recapitulation" (*anakephalaiōsis* [Eph. 1:10]) of material already discussed. The repetition, in this case, is meant to do more than drive information home. Rather, it is designed to restate something first presented as "carnal" and "historical," so that we might be prodded to go further and see its spiritual import. Something is clearly being pressed, he recognizes. But, as Calvin himself noted (1996: 3.421), it is precisely the *historical* and not the spiritual that unfolds in these chapters: "The LORD said to Moses, 'Take Aaron and his sons with him . . . and assemble all the congregation at the door of the tent of meeting.' And Moses did as the LORD commanded him" (Lev. 8:1–4). The remainder of the two chapters lays out the *actions* performed within time ("on the eighth day Moses called Aaron"; 9:1) and in fact are carried through, in Lev. 10, with a shocking human dénouement to this sequence of sacral events.

So what is the action that is being done? In a sense these two chapters provide the account of a palpable fulfillment of the previous instructions and constructions

of Exodus, as well as the initiation, in practice, of the sacrificial outline given in
the opening chapters of the book, which themselves explicate the summary given
at the end of Exodus. To that degree, they stand as an impression *in* history of
the commands of God to Israel: that which God has spoken has taken place. The
consecration of the priesthood and their first sacrifices within the erected tabernacle is now a fact in time. And this fact has thereby established a process that
will be continued in time. The uniqueness of this moment is marked by certain
divergences from the general instructions for, for example, cereal and wave offerings in Lev. 7, the strange transition from Moses as provisional priest to Aaron and
his sons as perpetual priests. Indeed, sacrificial time is now inaugurated by God
himself, who sends down his fire and consumes the final burnt offering laid out on
the altar (9:24). We are given a moment in time that affects all time, wherein the
movement of God's glory takes hold of a space and a relationship with a people,
for whom God is present today in his fullness (9:4, 23).

It is this sense of a newly inaugurated form of temporal existence that draws
these chapters into relation with the great inauguration of the cross: "After this
Jesus, knowing that all was now finished, said (to fulfil the scripture), I 'thirst.' . . .
When Jesus had received the vinegar, he said, 'It is finished'" (John 19:28, 30). It
is in this reality of accomplishment and finishing, tied to the work of perfection
and filling up, that the law is fulfilled and the times fulfilled and the word of God
fulfilled (Rom. 10:4; Jas. 2:8; Rev. 17:17; 20:3). "It is finished" is the declaration
that presses upon world and human lives what God has declared, not raising the
word into a heavenly realm, but asserting its reality in time. Thus Lev. 8–9 gathers
up the components of previous divine explications and places them within a narrative that takes up the world within it, rather than leaving it behind. The word
of God is fulfilled by taking upon it the flesh of the world. And trust in the word
becomes a matter of beholding the word's presence in the world, as moving and
visible in the flesh and blood, in this case, of Israel, as active. The nature of prophecy
is thereby revealed as a faith in the divine dynamics of incarnation itself.

It is in chapters like these that the limitations and exegetical dangers of Origenistic and medieval interpretation become apparent. The tendency to treat all of
the law in emblematic terms transforms the referents of Leviticus into free-floating
significators. While Origen notes the historical turn of these chapters, it is for this
reason that he feels compelled to search for something beyond their carnal reference, and temporality itself is ripped from the text (*Homilies on Leviticus* 6.1–6).
Origen himself will usually engage the literal details of the passage upon which
he speaks in a preliminary way. But even his own exegesis, and most especially the
medieval tradition that grew out from it, presents a Leviticus devoid of people, a
landscape almost akin to the metaphysical art of de Chirico, populated by forlorn
statues and images. Not surprisingly, then, the discussion of the consecration of
Aaron and his sons becomes, in the hands of Christian commentators, an enumeration of symbolic articles that bespeak the virtues of the ordained priesthood, the
character of the hierarchy, the nature of true doctrine and preaching (e.g., the Urim

and Thummim), and, embedded in the carnal-spiritual distinction, the claim to the church's supplanting of the sinful Jewish nation's crude commitments. Indeed, the anti-Semitic tendencies of this dynamic are intrinsic to the method, for the atemporal referents of the ceremonial law, stripped from their human agents, are often deployed as weapons against temporality itself, that is, against a world in which nations and peoples live and struggle and grow and die. "Take Aaron . . . and on the eighth day . . . Aaron and his sons."

To be sure, the determined rejection of the figural character of these texts by Calvin can have an almost similar endpoint, as the alien actions of the text so distance the narrative's actors from the present as to render them uninteresting and at best taxidermic specimens of a stunted past that can only offer moral warnings for the still unwary. Turning to the *Rabbah's* sequence of discussion is helpfully instructive (10–11) and provides a necessary corrective to traditional Christian exegesis. Certainly, rabbinic exegesis will lift up the symbolic character of much that one finds in these chapters, just as do the Christian commentators (e.g., priestly vestments). But it does so in a very particular way, by gathering up human history, experientially, into *Aaron's* life, as a person with a divine vocation that indeed touches all people, yet only through his temporal existence. Thus, the *Rabbah* begins its reflection with an extended (if characteristically elliptical) discussion of Aaron's righteousness as a kind of prophet, called in the line of Abraham, and continuous with the prophets of Israel into the future. Did not Aaron's sin at the time of the golden calf preclude his choice as an instrument of God's word fulfilled? Yet the reflection—which takes up, for instance, the call of Prov. 24:11 to "rescue those who are being taken away to death"—moves to a complex meditation on repentance and forgiveness, which, after all, lie at the heart of atonement itself, the atonement provided through the vessel of the sacrificial cult that is Aaron's to inaugurate. We are led to see Aaron as standing in the midst of a history of sin that stretches, as the *Rabbah* explicitly states, from Cain through Sodom to the treachery of Joseph's brothers and only then to the golden calf and from there most certainly to a future of sinfulness that the sacrificial cult addresses, challenges, and redemptively embraces. Hovering over this is the reality of sin and loss, as well as forgiveness and mercy, that Lev. 10's story of filial tragedy will bring upon Aaron's spirit. Both the *Rabbah* and *Sifra* 98.1 before it, thereby turn to Aaron, in the particularity of his actions and hard challenges, as the one who unveils, now in the particularity of his calling and duty, the movement of God's life within the history of humankind. "Take Aaron and his sons" becomes a command to memory and promise together, given in a moment of time, through which God acts to touch all time.

This sense of temporal gathering, which stretches across history, is indicated in the command of 8:3 that Moses is to "assemble all the congregation at the door of the tent of meeting," a command immediately fulfilled in fact (8:4). How could this be? Should the hundreds of thousands (Num. 26:51) all gather in one small area before the tabernacle? Yet this was always considered a miracle of notable proportions (even by Rashi [Rosenbaum and Silbermann 1932: 30]), which *Rabbah* 10.9 and many other interpreters understood as pointing to the great miracle of redeemed creation's own gathering before God, the heavens themselves and the hosts of the resurrected in the last time, "all men from Adam," the cosmos itself drawn into Zion (Ginzberg 1911: 3.180 and n373). "Let the waters under the heavens be gathered together into one place" (Gen. 1:9). Gathered in Aaron, Aaron is "any man" transfigured. But transfigured how? By righteousness and love, by grief and joy together. Aaron, in the tradition, is a sinner redeemed, who is able to share (thereby bear) the redemption of sinners. Though liable at the scene of Israel's apostasy with the golden calf, yet he is seen as one who also worked hard to stall their descent into idolatry while hoping for Moses's return. He is a pursuer of peace, tirelessly reconciling husband and wife. And he is famously lifted up by Hillel as the exemplar of a "lover of all creatures." At the same time, he is the father who takes joy in his children and, as the Jewish commentators struggle to indicate in these chapters of solemn festivity and grace, one for whom the grief over their children's death is haunting fate (*Rabbah* 10.3; *Pirqe de Rabbi Nathan* 25.25b; Mishnah, tractate *Avot* 1.12).

The tabernacle has therefore become the focal point for this gathering, now concentrated through the lens of Aaron and the people of Israel. As the central locality around and within which the chapters on the Levitical cult unfold, the significance of this spatial complex is ever more deeply indicated: the glory of God that descends at the end of Lev. 9, described as the "orb of the Eye of the world" (*Rabbah* 11.7), will, in the course of elaborated Jewish exegesis, become almost synonymous with the tabernacle itself (and then the temple) as the very living center from which creation itself is sustained. The idea that at the base of the temple lies the foundation stone from which the whole world was formed derives from this conviction (Babylonian Talmud, tractate *Bava Batra* 4a; Midrash Tanhuma, tractate *Qedoshim* 10). In the sequence of praise that begins *Rabbah* 11, this centering is used to explain the continuity of the world's history, which is the product of God's wisdom (based on Prov. 9:1–6, wherein wisdom is joined with a cosmic sacrifice [upheld by Ezek. 39:17–20]): from creation to the temple to the giving of the Torah to final eschatological feast—all is undergirded by the consecrated reality that attends Aaron's initiation into the priesthood, whereby the glory of God is joined to the earth in the form of Israel and extended in all directions temporally by the sacrifices themselves. Later explanations of an earthly and heavenly sanctuary mirroring each other and opening up the world of angels to the human world maintain this sense (*Numbers Rabbah* 12.12; see also Ginzberg 1911: 3.185). The point here is simply, yet massively, that Aaron's time provides a vision of the whole creation's time as given by God.

The basic claim of Christian figuralism asserts that "these are only a shadow of what is to come; but the substance belongs to Christ" (Col. 2:17). But what is the substance (literally "body," *sōma*) itself that Christ constitutes, as well as the means of apprehension through which the type is understood? Both Catholics and Protestants took the figural practice seriously, even and especially around matters discussed in Lev. 8–9, but there was wild divergence as to the particularities of application involved, in large part because of the temporally free-floating symbolism that the text was seen to be exclusively capable of providing. Had they taken Christ's body to mean all the types more seriously, they would have taken more seriously, as *Rabbah* 11 rightly does, the world into which Christ came, for as the image of God (Col. 1:15) he both bears upon him the impress of the creator (Heb. 1:3) and also passes this image on in various ways to and through the range of created forms (Col. 1:16–17; Rom. 5:14; 1 Cor. 10:2, 6, 11). These imprints of the antitype upon creation, as Franciscan tradition well understood, are not things that are thrown away in the course of history so much as they become temporal passages through which the fullness of their referent is revealed. Unfortunately, as the question of the ceremonial law came to be defined and then explicated in later Christian tradition, there was always the temptation to equate temporality purely with provisionality, when in fact the Aaronic narrative of the cultic institution of the sacrificial cult speaks of temporality as revelatory at its base. The world gathers around the tent of meeting so that, as God is present, so too are all things seen in their truth and blessing.

In terms of the particularities of figuralist readings of the text, it is therefore better not to dwell upon the images of, for example, the priestly vestments as symbols of abstracted virtues. This was Origen's major focus, as the virtues he discerned (e.g., through the tunics and thigh bandages) were read, given his scriptural concerns, mainly in terms of spiritual powers of listening and teaching. By the time twelfth-century Norbertine Adam Scot wrote his treatise entitled "On the Three-part Tabernacle," a lengthy treatment of a genre that had been popular since Bede, the Jews, Jesus, and the Christian soul had each become long and involved doctrinal and ascetic referents for every item of the sacred complex described in Exodus and Leviticus (*De tripartito tabernaculo* [Patrologia latina 198.633–792]). It was, however, now done in a way that overwhelmed Aaron and the created order that his life was designed to bring close to God in the course of human history.

If Christian figuration was to be properly applied, it required a broader reading that was able to open the text up to the movement of time that the hieratic tableaux of Leviticus were meant to solemnize, not smother. As an example, Ambrose takes up the priestly ephod and undergarments in a discussion of the nature of the Son of God, whose twelve names (source, radiance, image, bounty, wisdom, power, etc.) are represented by the twelve stones in Aaron's robe and inscribed with the names of the twelve tribes of Israel (*De fide christiana* 2.4–15). Hebrews speaks not only of Jesus as the antitype to Aaron (Heb. 4:15; 5:1–5; 7:28; 8:7); more importantly, it speaks of the *fullness* of divine reality represented in these types, one that is not merely semiotic, but that overflows into the very character of creation. Thus, Ambrose dwells upon the colors of the fibers, cloths, and stones, because they signify in various ways the actual elements of the created order (air, water, fire, and earth) "from which the human body itself is formed." This is, in fact, a traditional piece of Jewish exegesis regarding the priestly robes, and Ambrose's design is to show how the reality of the Son of God is precisely that which draws together the realms of natural and historical being that are bodily brought near to God through the acts of Israel at worship. The exact referents are actually less important here than that the reader should allow the fullness of the world to be gleaned in the performance of the new sacrificial order. Why should this not include the colors even of the world's surfaces and surroundings, the gleaming of its blues, purples, and scarlets, the sounds of its bells heard by the angels and the thrill of its lush pomegranates containing the seeds of all the earth and church (as Exod. 28 describes it)? Jewish and Christian exegesis come together here.[1] Indeed, the reading of the Levitical text itself provides a "bringing near" of the world in variously construed and apprehended configurations, and the reader offers not so much a standard of figures as a constantly reapprehended portion of the world's actually incomprehensible variety, in a reiterated fashion. And in this sense, Leviticus is to be read as Victorinus encouraged us to read the book of Revelation: as an encircling (not sequentially chronological) embrace of history's forms into the ordering power of God, recounting the same story over and over again from different perspectives, until all becomes, through this prayerful exposition, that which is all God's (1 Cor. 15:28).

What then of the story itself? Do not Moses, Aaron, sons, and Israel stand for some cosmic action? Rather, it is they who become and lay out the actual form of cosmic life in which we participate. Moses therefore has gathered through the law, through receiving and sharing it: "Take Aaron and his sons"—take them through the command and the commandments that the Lord gives. All is taken up in the word of God, actually embraced and carried. Carried where? Carried to the tent of meeting, to the place where God's glory shall come and shall abide. Moses himself will clothe and anoint and provide the first offerings. He is, in this regard, also a priest—indeed, the tradition struggled to both affirm his priesthood ("Moses and Aaron were among his priests"; Ps. 99:6) and distinguish his priesthood as assisting and provisional, rather than perpetual. And this was not without reason, for Moses himself was a sinner and had withdrawn too genuinely from the calling of God to be given the most blessed of gifts, to dwell in the house of the Lord. It was Aaron who "long[ed], yea, who faint[ed] for the courts of the LORD" (84:2). And the yearning gave rise to a fullness of indwelling (Lev. 8:33–36), seven days and nights of prayer and life and rest. The service of consecration—washing,

1. Jerome is one with Ambrose, who in some respects works within the tradition of Philo, whose elaborate exegesis of the tabernacle vestments and furnishings he summarizes by saying that the "arrangement of the sacred dress of the high priest [is] a representation of the universe, a marvelous work to be beheld or to be contemplated"; *De specialibus legibus* 1.17 (trans. Yonge). His readings, in turn, whether directly or otherwise, are part of the long rabbinic tradition, elaborated endlessly, and have crossed over to medieval Christian readers (e.g., Bede, *De tabernaculo* [Patrologia latina 91.485–87]) as well.

clothing, anointing objects and priests with oil, anointing blood (8:23–30) on the symbolic parts of the whole person, the sacrifices themselves (sin offering, burnt offering, peace offering)—all of this is described as a great assembling of commands, desires, labors, and hopes. And they are physically, even in the bodies of Aaron and his sons, brought near to the Lord.

The narrative character of this ingathering is, as noted earlier, deliberately suffused with the humanity of Aaron and of his fate—the righteous man, the patient man, the yearning and praying man, the loving and peaceable man, whose very distinction from his brother Moses forces us to discern the particularities of his going near to the Lord. *This* man is consecrated with his sons, two of whom, Nadab and Abihu, will, in a short while, be struck down by God even in the course of their offering. This we know, for the story is told and time has passed. Therefore, the going in and the dwelling in God's courts, the self-giving and therefore cleansing and offering that is embodied in the elaborate ritual of sign and sacrifice—this is snared in some larger scheme of giving and losing, yearning and lamenting, which, in its sacrificial scaffolding upholds, as Moses says, the reality of atonement (8:34). So the tradition has looked back on the seven days and nights that Aaron spent in the tabernacle and has seen a time of mourning before the fact—or perhaps a carrying into the tabernacle of a mourning already swept across the earth, a mourning by God over the creatures struck down by the flood, over sin and violence, over Cain and his burning anger and wandering search. Outside is death (8:35); inside are the tears that wash clean the surface of the world (Jerusalem Talmud, tractate *Moed Qatan* 3.82c; cf. Ginzberg 1911: 3.181, esp. n375 for references).

The bond between creation and mourning is one that is intrinsic to this story. Newer English translations of Lev. 9:1 ignore the full verbal form of the temporal explication of this verse, simply locating the narrative "on the eighth day." Yet the Hebrew says, quite explicitly, that "*it came to pass* on the eighth day" (so the Authorized Version), and this "coming to pass," this phrase of happening *into* time and *through* time and pointing *beyond* this one time, becomes the source of much reflection in rabbinic interpretation. The *Rabbah* points out (11.7) at great length that "it came to pass" becomes the basis for an exegetical principle, such that "any passage in which the words, 'And it came to pass,' appear is a passage that relates to misfortune." Many examples are cited: Abraham (Gen. 14:1), Ahaz and Isaiah (Isa. 7:1), Jehoiakim (Jer. 1:3), Esther (Esth. 1:1), and Ruth (Ruth 1:1). The history of Israel retold as the course of time in God's hand is filled with misfortune. Yet what of creation itself? "And God said, 'Let there be light'; and [it came to pass that] there was light" (Gen. 1:3). Rabbi Ishmael responded by noting that "this too does not represent good fortune, for in the end the world did not have the merit of actually making use of that light." And so, "it came to pass on the eighth day that Moses called Aaron and his sons and the elders of Israel" into a time in which the grace of the world's being as made by God will give rise to sorrow. *Sifra* 99.1 itself observed that this "eighth day," which marked the coming of God's glory, is the first day of creation (i.e., Sunday), the day of the great separation of matter that God provided out of love itself for the sake of all things' being. The first priestly work and first sacrifices and first benedictions and so on (the "ten crowns" of the day, as they became known) are all liturgical acts that are bound to this "first day" of all days (the first crown itself). Yet, as Rabbi Ishmael recognized, even though a crown of glory, it is one that reflects the nature of history itself, of Adam's life and thus Israel's, in all its calling and yearning and failing and restoration. This is Aaron, the high priest, whose temporal body in *this* sense, this sense given on the first and the eighth day, of glory tinged with mourning, passing through the same ambivalence of David's agonized blessing, is taken up by Jesus on the "first day of the week," always the "Lord's Day."

"And so, when Aaron died, it says that *all* the congregation mourned for him [Num. 20:29]. But when Moses died, it says that those who wept were the children of Israel, not *all* the children of Israel [Deut. 34:8]" (*Avot de Rabbi Nathan* 25.25b). This is because Aaron carried the mourning of Israel himself, in his own body, into the holy of holies before the presence of God. It is because Aaron was like "any man," but a man whose desire for God drew him near. Not only do the sacrifices of the consecration ceremony fulfill a command, then, an event that is particular to the events at hand, but they are representative in this particular way, as allowing the man Aaron himself to represent others, clothing with the joy of God's promised presence the temporally networked admixture of sinfulness and loss that "any man" would bring before God as "it came to pass" that they should live and seek God's face. When, in Lev. 9:6, Moses says, in the singular, "This is the thing which the LORD commanded you to do," this "one thing" implies *all* things that Aaron would do, all in the sense of unity of Israel's life brought before God (Hirsch 1989: 1.244), joined one with another in the temporal realities of struggle, sin, and self-offering. And all this, in the end, is blessed (9:22–24), this one day and one thing that points to all things "that come to pass" and that are taken up on the eighth day by a Lord who makes that one day of all days his own. As Aaron enters the tabernacle and the sacrifices begin, time becomes God's in a new way, a way that seeks its own fulfillment in God's final entering of its corridors. *Then* "it shall come to pass" that all things—now marked within the consecrated tabernacle's utensil-stocked premises—shall be inscribed "Holy to the LORD" (Zech. 14:20), for if "it came to pass" represents misfortune, surely when it says "it *shall* come to pass" (as Rabbi Ishmael also taught [in *Rabbah* 11.7–8]), it must "signify good fortune."

Aaron and his sons come into the tent; God comes into the world. This reciprocal dynamic is heightened and resolved in the cry of Jesus, as he "came into the world, [and] said: 'Sacrifices and offerings thou hast not desired, but a body hast thou prepared for me'" (Heb. 10:5). Not, in the time to come, "all these sacrifices," but this "one sacrifice"; not "any man" coming, but "one man" with his one body, "in [whom] the whole fulness of deity dwells bodily" (Col. 2:9), "the tabernacle of God . . . with men" (Rev. 21:3 Authorized Version), "the word become flesh and [tabernacled] among us" (John 1:14). But it is one, not because it has cast aside the others, and his is all that remains. It is one because it has gathered them up, in all their colors, in all their yearning, in all their wandering, in all their loss, in all their rejoicing. This high priest (Heb. 8:1) is not unclothed and naked, but like Aaron even in his tabernacle of groaning (2 Cor. 5:1–5) is dressed in the fullness of creation's light and form and sound, bearing the robes to which are attuned the eyes and ears of the angels.

What distinguishes Origen's figural explication of these chapters from that of later Christian writers is his profound sense, for all his unmoored emblematicism, that the fabric of that reality to which these texts point can be got at only in wrapping oneself as fully as possible with its words, which themselves hold all the words of law and gospel together (*Homilies on Leviticus* 6.2). Aaron in the tabernacle is first and foremost he who has gone into the word to meditate upon it "day and night." He entered the flesh of Jesus, that great temple by which the lowly is raised up (John 2:19–22; Luke 1:52), and there found the vision of light through which all things can be seen in their truth and order. For Origen this unveils a kind of life shaped by the virtues of listening, humility, openness, and thirsting for God—Aaronic in its center. For later Christians, it became clear that this tabernacle, and this Aaron who carries in his flesh our own cries to be given over to the cry of Christ, is entered in the Eucharist itself, for which time has indeed become sacrificial time, the time of God's offering through which heaven and earth are joined as a landscape inhabited by God's creatures.[2]

2. This way of framing the eucharistic character of the text in more cosmic terms distances these chapters from the particular liturgical-doctrinal elements upon which subsequent Christians fixated. It proved a focus that robbed the texts of their suffusion in human historical experience by cutting them off from a broader figuration of creation. The Reformation debates deployed many aspects of these chapters, for instance, in the service of Protestant-Catholic polemics over the nature of the Eucharist, from the metaphysical definition of the sacrificial substance to matters of "reservation," vestments, and so on. See Willet 1631: 144–48 at length on this matter, with many citations.

LEVITICUS 10

God's glory is shared, we see in Lev. 9:24, and this sharing stands behind the reality of God's own gift of himself to Israel and the law and the tabernacle together. Yet at the same time, the gift of God's own self uncovers a yawning chasm of difference between creature and creator, and finally of death. The people are unworthy. Into this chasm the story of Lev. 10 unfolds.

And a true story it is. Leviticus 10 is one of the few truly narrative sections in the entire book, extraordinarily brief though this passage may be. There are, of course, other moments in the book where agents actually perform actions in time—such as the two previous chapters. But in Lev. 8–9 the actions themselves—setting up the tabernacle, consecrating the priests, and so on—are all bound to normative rituals whose repetition in time has always rendered their meaning, for readers, as indicative of some larger metahistorical reality. Thus, their important referents have generally been interpreted in symbolic ways. But with Lev. 10, something happens in a most unrepeatable way, to two named persons, Nadab and Abihu, sons of Aaron. And what happens is shocking, and the consequence of this happening rumbles through the rest of the chapter and the relationships of Moses and his family to such a degree that the episode is remembered in passing three other times in the Pentateuch as a warning and a sad memory (Lev. 16:1–2; Num. 3:4; 26:61).

The story is clear enough. But given its stark brevity, it is worth noting the details again. Nadab and Abihu held a special place among Aaron's sons and were called up to accompany Moses, Aaron, and the seventy elders as they beheld God and worshiped him at the time of the law's initial receipt (Exod. 24:1, 9–11). Here, in Lev. 10, after the glory of God has appeared to the people at the tabernacle and the divine fire has consumed the initial offerings of the priests, the two sons each take a censer and offer to God an "alien" or "unholy fire," such as the Lord "had not commanded." Immediately a "fire . . . from the presence of the LORD," parallel to that at the end of the preceding chapter, comes out and "devour[s] them" and they die. Moses tells Aaron a word from God he has received, wherein God declares he will show himself holy to those who are near him and will glorify himself to the people, presumably a comment on what has just happened. The rest of the chapter details how the bodies of the two men are to be disposed and who shall do it within the family, how mourning is to be or not to be expressed, what offerings should and are given by Aaron's remaining sons in the midst of this surprising and tragic set of events; and in the course of this, God speaks directly to Aaron regarding the duty of distinguishing holy and unholy and teaching the people. What comes out clearly in this long aftermath to the sons' death is a struggle, a struggle over grief as it is rightly held and expressed within the parameters of God's presence. And this grief itself becomes a context that bears the weight and confusion of the law in its demands and offerings, a context that draws in a breadth of family relationships among Moses, his brother, and his nephews and cousins and suffuses them with the hints of conflict and misunderstanding, as well as of difficult resolution.

Indeed, it is the injection of human emotion into this most unemotional book of the Bible that is so remarkable and disturbing. God's glory, as we have seen, has come among the people in a visible way, and the events that follow show us that this divine approach ought also to be read in as historical a way as possible, for it is this living being, bound up with a fire that can touch human life, who immediately overturns the joyous moment among the people by rushing out upon Aaron's two sons and killing them in an instant. God's glory appears within the community, but in its very presence it sets up a terrible tension, humanly speaking, with human grief, shock, and bewilderment. Moses proclaims the Lord's will with respect to this divine killing; yet Aaron falls silent—perhaps grimly, surely dazed and sorrowful. This tension, embedded in the actual lives of these individuals, sets in motion a new theological dynamic, in which all the normative rules of the revealed law come explicitly up against the contingent realm of human experience. And in this confrontation, the sacrificial system discloses God's being as explicated through individual relationships, in this case of loss and regret.

This story is deeply disturbing in its violence and in the stark demands of response to human suffering that are depicted, demands that raise real questions about the character of God. Before suggesting a way to answer these questions from within Leviticus, I will briefly survey some of the standard interpretations of the story, for these—both Christian and Jewish—bespeak a certain fear and evasion of the story's reality and significance. In the process, however, they actually illuminate by contrast the thrust of the text's real purpose.

The most common approach to this chapter has been to read it as the exposition of human sin—Nadab's and Abihu's—and its deadly consequences. The chapter, thus, functions as a warning, and an especially pointed one, set as it is in the middle of the Levitical revelation, designed both to underscore the critical nature of obedience to these laws in particular and to divine command in general. On the one hand, this has led to a comprehensive application of the text to moral allegory with a limited theme as well as, in Jewish contexts, to the explication of a detailed calculus of sacrifice itself, such as might be capable of unraveling the specific duties that might explain the sin of Aaron's sons and the confusion surrounding proper conduct in the wake of their death as well as the means of avoiding such missteps in the future. Curiously, this press toward defining a sacrificial calculus has coincided, in the last 150 years, with historical-critical interest in outlining as carefully as possible the practices and beliefs behind the story. This juxtaposition of interests in the calculus of sacrifice itself has fueled the general and unconscious anti-Judaism within the academic guild, as historical-critical description has voided the relevance of doctrinal claims within the text and left traditional Jewish exegesis seemingly a grab bag of fanatic superstition. The old deist and anti-Semitic argument of all scriptural literalism (even Christian) as "rabbinic" lurks in the background.

I bring up this last point because it speaks to an important aspect of Christian interpretation of this chapter (and many other portions of Leviticus). Christian interpretations of Nadab's and Abihu's deaths are generalized and diverse, to be sure. But most traditional ones have moved in a single direction, reading the story in terms of the exclusiveness of the community, where the tabernacle and its severely demanding rituals, associated with the proper demarcation of space, refers to the church and to the salvation granted exclusively within its precincts. So, for many Nadab and Abihu represent "heretics" and "Arians" (the *Glossa ordinaria* [Patrologia latina 113.326–27] and Bruno of Segni [Patrologia latina 164.412–14]), whose attempt to innovate religiously according to their own whim was greeted with a divine destruction. But the spatial-membership logic of this use of the story was inevitably caught up in the current of the more basic church-synagogue distinction that informed so much Christian exegesis from the time of the fathers. In this light, the heretics themselves represent most fundamentally the Jews, and the story of Nadab and Abihu became, in Christian hands, a quintessential figure—ironic, to be sure, given its Levitical location— of Jewish ill will toward God's true desires, by which the entire sacrificial system was judged and condemned. Rupert of Deutz (Patrologia latina 167.792–94), among others, sets a standard for this anti-Semitic reading, making the two sons of Aaron stand for the entire Jewish nation, mired in a willful insistence (using an etymology for Nadab's name) on the value of the carnal rites of sacrifice. Rupert (like the *Epistle of Barnabas* long before) goes so far as to say, referring to Isa. 1 and Ps. 50, that the entire sacrificial system is here condemned as being the invention of Jewish self-regard and that the fire that killed Aaron's sons is a figure of God's judgment (Deut. 32:22) upon the Jews and their temple as a whole, fulfilled in the Roman destruction of Jerusalem following the foundation of the Christian church at Pentecost. The rest of the chapter is insistently interpreted according to this scheme of carnal superstition overcome by the church. Of course, the further inclusion of this kind of judgment upon the forms of *Christian* life also has been the indiscriminate leveling achievement of the modern critical sensibility.

It is true that Rupert of Deutz can note the force of grief in the story and link it to Jesus's mourning over Jerusalem and Paul's anguish over the Jews' fate in Rom. 9. But it was important not to let such lamentation shape one's sense of God's purposes, which were squarely geared toward the destruction of a sinful nation. Aaron's silence here becomes virtuously paradigmatic. Indeed, Christian understandings of the emotional tension within the story itself have usually tended in the direction of vilifying the tension altogether: Aaron's grief was itself dangerously close to contravening God's will and here represented a temptation to temper the force and justice of God's wrath. The moral allegory of the human aspect of the narrative, according to this view, is precisely that this human aspect should be resisted in the face of God: emotion is at best distracting from the truth.

Jewish interpretations of the chapter—except for the particular tradition I will discuss below—are more cohesively ordered toward the moral of obedience: God's commands cannot be even minutely compromised, on pain of death, both physical and spiritual. Shorn of most of the figural details of his predecessors, Calvin's reading of the text (as of most of the sacrificial and ritual content of Leviticus) comes down to the same lesson, clearly and repeatedly articulated (1986: 3.430–37). By the nineteenth century, this basic focus had not shifted, although with Hirsch (1989: 1.251–58) it was now able to address cultural developments in attitude and ideas, so that the chapter becomes, in his hands, a treatise against romantic individualism, embodied by the yearning and enthusiastic spirits of the two sons, whose inability to control their own personal religious stirrings contradicted the quintessentially Jewish insight that places every individual in the service of the corporate self and its common obedience to God's will.

Among Protestant Christians especially, however, just this turn to the individual in the nineteenth century meant that Aaron's grief could not quite be left behind. A Victorian struggle with family affection and the wounding of death pressed interpreters (e.g., Gray and Adams 1903: 296) to linger on the feelings of Aaron, to wonder at the silence of his response to Moses's declaration of God's word to him (Lev. 10:3), and to speculate on the depth of pain (not virtuous self-control) that holds his tongue even from complaint. These kinds of wonderings cast a question mark over the moral certainties about the exemplar given by the story that had commonly reigned. Yet at the same time, Protestants continued to admit to the typical character of this episode, as pointing to the atoning sacrifice of Christ (the aspect of atonement being mentioned in 10:17). These two elements were never integrated, however, as deliberate vigor was exercised (Willet 1631: 198–99) to deny any link between this type with the character of suffering borne in love, as given in the human emotional dynamic implicit in this story. Christ hovers on the horizon, but no more, and we are left with an unresolved tension between human grief and divine atonement.

I survey, however summarily, this history of interpretation only because its consistent clarity stands in a sharp contrast, an ultimately uneasy and fragile one, with a more supple and morally disjointed tradition of reading the story that prevailed among certain sectors of Jewish reading. The contrast is almost unconsciously deliberate and self-protective, certainly on the Christian side, for, in fact, from the earliest times there was an increasing ambivalence about and searching exploration of the narrative of Nadab and Abihu that ended up circulating as a kind of undercurrent in Jewish exegesis until the present. Its outline is provided in *Rabbah* 12's comparatively vast reflection on the story. Although the *Rabbah* contains a careful consideration of the sins of Aaron's sons, the word "contain" is appropriate, because the consideration is carried within a larger set of concerns: the reality of grief, not as blasphemy but as an illumination of human life and God's own heart, the fate of the righteous, and finally an almost experimental discernment of glory in the two young men's own destiny. God himself mourned the deaths of Nadab and Abihu "twice as much" even as Aaron, the *Rabbah* insists. What kind of God is this, what kind of world is it in which such a God is sovereign, and how could such a world exist in a time over which God reigns?

Rabbah 20.1–12 begins its discussion of the story (actually based on Lev. 16:1–2) with a meditation on Eccl. 9:2, that "one fate comes to all, to the righteous and the wicked" together. Nadab and Abihu, therefore, are placed from the start with the righteous, and the strange ways of God are laid out to ponder in the face of the sweeping victory of death. This leads to a commentary on the transitory character of joy, particularly the joy of parents over their children (like the mother of Aaron's sons), which takes us back to the Preacher's comment that "I said of laughter, 'It is mad'" (2:2). And God? God stands in the midst of the unsteady and vulnerable world as one whose own presence brings death! Job is quoted, transferring the destiny of the eagle to God's own work in the world: "He spies out [his] prey . . . his young ones suck up blood; and where the slain are, there is he" (Job 39:29–30). After raising severe questions about the meaning of human life and affection, of divine compassion, and of theodicy itself, the *Rabbah* then moves to an extended discussion of the various sins of Nadab and Abihu that brought punishment upon them. These include the deduced and the speculated as well as the highly imaginative: arrogance of taking initiative and teaching in the presence of their master Moses, drawing near to the holy place, making an offering that God had not commanded, bringing in a fire from their kitchens, failing to take counsel with each other, drunkenness, wearing the wrong clothing, failing to wash their hands and feet, having no children of their own, never marrying, being snooty over the low quality of Israelite brides, secretly wishing to take over Moses's and Aaron's places when the latter died, indulging their spiritual appetites by "feasting their eyes upon the presence of God." Yet having presented this cascade of possible sins, the *Rabbah* closes with a completely new thought: why are the two sons and their death mentioned again at the opening of Lev. 16, which describes the Day of Atonement? Is it not because their death as righteous persons (so, the opening of the discussion) itself achieves atonement? As with Miriam in Num. 19–20? Or Aaron even?

This conglomeration of thoughts is significant, for it contains a remarkable, and hardly resolved, range of concerns, worries, and hopes. One is left with the sense that something deeply powerful, if mysterious, is being disclosed in this story: that sin and its destruction are bound up with goodness and its self-giving; that love and pain are intertwined; that power and justice do not simply reorder life, but burrow into the recesses of the human heart and turn things inside out. Many of the details found in the *Rabbah* reappear in more developed forms and stories in later Jewish legend (Ginzberg 1911: 3.381–87). They were ensconced in Talmud and elsewhere. In all, this far-flung tradition indicated a web of complex conflict within family and motive. But also prominent was the notion of Nadab's and Abihu's righteousness before God and therefore a sense that the episode recounted the outworking of a special relationship with the Lord (*Numbers Rabbah* 2.23). Certainly, a growing sense of paradox can be seen within the tradition, which finally was given voice in the judgment that the death of Nadab and Abihu was the expression of God's actual *love* for them, and in this respect the two priests were too good for the world! So the *Zohar* eventually raised the two to the level of saints, standing in the place of sinning Israel and demonstrating the value of righteous suffering on behalf of others.[1] Commenting on Lev. 10:1–6, *Sefer Emet* (by nineteenth-century Rabbi Yehuda Aryeh Leib Alter) explained:

> "But your kinsmen, all the house of Israel, shall bewail the burning." It is apparent that it is incumbent upon every Jew to weep for them, as we learn in the *Zohar* (*Aharei Mot*). And the reason can be said as the following: They were completely righteous. And our sages have said, "in the place where the repentant stand, the truly righteous cannot stand." Therefore, they were punished on our behalf, this is why we must weep for them. And it is better not to go on at length about this point. (trans. Arian)

Philo (*Allegorical Interpretation* 2.57) had already raised the possibility of the two sons' justice and the probability of their living with God, and even Rashi (Rosenbaum and Silbermann 1932: 39) had wondered whether the bodies of Nadab and Abihu had not been consumed, like a burnt offering (a question that puzzled some Christian readers too). He repeated the explanation that the fire had killed them from the *inside*, as it were, passing through their nostrils and indicating their interior desire for God. And in a sense, he argued, they were being used by God's presence (Lev. 10:3) precisely because of their righteousness.[2]

1. The *Zohar* (2.26b; 3.57b, 217a) also uses Nadab and Abihu as a examples of its controverted teaching regarding the transmigration of souls—these two righteous persons inhabiting the souls of other righteous individuals and strengthening them (e.g., Phineas) and also thereby fulfilling their duties to bear children (having died childless on earth).
2. *Sifra* 99.3 had already emphasized the righteousness of Aaron's sons and therefore indicated that their death was a demonstration of God's positive use of good people. Rashi (Rosenbaum and Silbermann 1932: 39) notes this reading, without however, drawing any conclusions about God's purposes and the history of God's chosen. Still, the tradition of Aaron's sons' *positive* character

The major point struggled with in all of this tradition is the seeming reality that God takes the *righteous* to himself. "I will show myself holy among those who are near me" (10:3). And how shall God do this? By joining them, somehow, even to the destructive aspect of his self-sharing, his glory before which no one can live (Exod. 33:18–23; 40:35). Death comes to the righteous *because* they are close to God, a closeness that devours them. However one may wish to detail the particular sin(s) of Nadab and Abihu, few interpreters have claimed that they were *more* sinful than others among their people. Not only their office, but the character of their lives within this office brought them into contact with God's own self, and to that degree it was their righteousness that killed them.

The paradox, precisely in the context of the figures of fire, has been felt by Christians too. On the one hand, there is the rejection by Jesus of just the kind of destructive flame from heaven that seems to have overcome Aaron's sons: met by inhospitable Samaritans as Jesus's party begin their journey to Jerusalem, the disciples ask Jesus, "Lord, do you want us to bid fire come down from heaven and consume them?" His response (especially in the fuller version of the text) seems to repudiate the Levitical story altogether: "But he turned and rebuked them, and he said, 'You do not know what manner of spirit you are of; for the Son of man came not to destroy men's lives but to save them'" (Luke 9:51–56 Revised Standard Version margin). Yet at the same time, the favorite Levitical antitype on the topic of sacrifice is provided by Luke 12:49: "I came to cast fire upon the earth; and would that it were already kindled!"—a vocation whose concrete character of destruction is explained in terms of "not peace, but division," within the most sacred intimacies of families, just as in Aaron's case, and with all the implications of horror and grief that Jesus's lengthy description of households torn asunder would have evoked (12:51–53). Yet the implication is that such horrible grief is something that might itself save. Thus, Rupert of Deutz's notation (Patrologia latina 167.793–94) of Jesus's lament over Jerusalem and Paul's over his people in the context of Aaron's mourning ought not to be dismissed. Gethsemane proves a place of agony and sorrow (22:44–45), as if a fire had been turned upon him, the very "cup" of fire, brimstone, and scorching wind (Ps. 11:6), Paul's own "curse" of love (Rom. 9:3). The image in Hebrews of Jesus dying on the cross "through the eternal Spirit" (9:14), that is, the Spirit of Pentecostal fire itself, embodies and extends this paradox so completely as to astonish.

Certainly, the thrust of this story cuts against the entire modern sense of what is the nature of mercy and love, which we rightly associate with God, but here is shown to be a compassion that burns to dust. And surely this is one reason why Leviticus is so offensive, and has been for so long, for it is, not least, a reminder of

---

was well established. And whatever Hirsch's later strictures (1989: 1.251–53) against romantic religious subjectivity, it is clear therefore that when he argued against Nadab and Abihu's individual religious enthusiasm, he was not arguing simply against a nineteenth-century shift in religious outlook about the story, but rather against a deep stream of Jewish rumination, then upheld by the backward-seeming Hassidim.

God who is encountered in Jesus Christ, whose glory "we have beheld" (John 1:14) and whose glorification we have gazed upon (12:23; 13:31; 17:1; Mark 15:39). The medieval depictions of this apprehended visage—*Ecce homo!*—an image that is the face of God, still encourage us, now more than ever, to turn our eyes. And in turning, we become complicit in the very crimes that so discomfort us.

The reality of atonement, as apprehended by the trajectory of Jewish interpretation of this chapter, is indeed founded upon the prior reality of this antitype, through which God's own fire of glory is allowed to consume his own self for the sake of those who have come near or even, in their nearness, have exposed their more primordial distance. That Moses is an atoning figure became assumed in Judaism, basing itself upon passages like Exod. 32:11–14 and Num. 14:10–19 and then elaborating the matter through a variety of narratives and speculative assertions (*Numbers Rabbah* 2.14; 18.5; *Deuteronomy Rabbah* 1.2; the *Yalkut* compilation of Haggadoth, *Ki Tissa* 388). But, as mentioned above, this paradigm was extended to include an array of scriptural characters—Miriam and Aaron himself—and finally explain a basic aspect of Jewish and even human life in its ethical destiny. Here we have further members of Moses's own family brought into this circle, in this case, dying "on behalf" of the people and even on behalf of their own father (as some traditions had it) whose sin with the golden calf had not yet been dealt with. And all the characteristics associated with Nadab and Abihu are swept into the dynamic of this coming near to God that takes them up into the force of God's own love for his people: the young die for the old, the zealous and desirous for the indifferent, the light for the fading. We have here, and traditionally (as *Rabbah* 12 and 20 explored) with all the same resonances, a foreshadowing of the disturbing yet also sanctifying revelation given through the Holy Innocents—the "first martyrs" before the fact, as Augustine himself observed (*Sermon* 373.3 [Patrologia latina 39.1664–65]).

As with the reality of Christ's own crucifixion, the presence of God near at hand before the people and most intimately with Aaron's two sons sets in motion and is fulfilled by the act of self-giving. A coming near—that is, an offering—becomes the vessel though which holiness appears. It is because glory appears—that is, God himself in his substance—as an offering that it brings with it a strange conjunction of death and grief. The question here has concerned Christian exegetes, who have (oddly enough, given their own christological focus) generally understood Lev. 10:3 as indicating exclusively the punishing aspect of God's self-disclosure, the explanatory text being Ezek. 28:22–23: "Behold, I am against you, O Sidon, and I will manifest my glory in the midst of you. And they shall know that I am the LORD when I execute judgments in her, and manifest my holiness in her; for I will send pestilence into her, and blood into her streets." Augustine writes: "God is sanctified also in punishing" (*Questiones in heptateuchum* [Patrologia latina 34.689])—"also" in the sense of "in addition to his mercy." But "also" must surely be "as": the judgment *is* merciful and especially its brilliance is made manifest when given in the form of self-offering.

This manifestation, it seems, is what lies behind the conflicted reactions of onlookers like Aaron. The early modern return of stoic endurance—both Catholic and Reformed—seems to have dictated the general sense that Aaron's silence (Lev. 10:3) was a virtuous expression of his blunt acceptance of God's will in this affair (Cajetan's 1639 *Quinquelibris Moysis* [cited in Willet 1631: 185] and Calvin 1996: 3.433). What was there to say? Aaron becomes a kind of enforced Job, quietly articulating, through holding his peace, that "the LORD gave, and the LORD has taken away; blessed be the name of the LORD" (Job 1:21). How then should we mourn? We interpret the character of Aaron's subsequent sacrifice simply as a resigned and humbled carrying on, even while the corpses of his progeny are being borne outside the camp. Yet Jewish reading here, as we have seen, discerns a struggle within Aaron's own heart, a cry and an unrequited sorrow. He carries on with the ritual grain offering and peace offering (Lev. 10:15), both under duress, but also pushed on by some interior desire to engage the very power that has taken his children from him. Expectant and hopeful, despite his pain? This is basis for the glimpse of atonement. "He did not revile in return . . . he did not threaten" (1 Pet. 2:23).

Aaron moves forward and proceeds with a new coming near, entering the very precinct of offering by which glory slays (Lev. 10:3). And so the subsequent refusal to eat of the final sin offering (10:16–19), which so upsets Moses. Normally due—and even bound to this provision of grace and communal solidarity—a portion to be eaten (6:24–30), Aaron allows the sin offering to be wholly burnt (6:8–13). In this, he binds himself rather to the very death of his sons, affirming the tragedy even as he sacrifices wholly to the God whose presence lies behind his loss. His response to Moses (10:19) is by no means obvious, but at the least his goal is to be acceptable in the Lord's sight *just because* of the nature of his sons' death in the course of offering their own offerings, sin and burnt offering together. Should we suppose our own offerings to be different or more pleasing to God than theirs? He bows, as it were, to the sharing of, if not their fate (though that was possible, he seems to imply), at least the status of their gifts. Hirsch's definition (1989: 1.10) of the burnt offering in terms of an ascension (via the rising smoke), as the epitome of all sacrifice in its embodiment of going near to God, comes to mind. Moses's own reaction of fear and anger to this obscure wrestling within Aaron's motives simply underscores the fundamental reality that coming near to God is too difficult and confusing if taken only on the terms of a calculus of survival.

The strange story of Nadab and Abihu points to something deep at the center of God's coming, recounted in 9:23, which goes beyond a simple revelation or a simple gift. Rather, we are directed toward a kind of overturning and transformation in which some of the deepest pain in the world, and in its Christian apprehension *all* of the world's pain, is concentrated. This touches on the reality of holiness, at least as it is disclosed here. The surprising word of God spoken directly to Aaron (rather than through Moses) after his sons' death seems at first, as many have taken it, simply to prohibit a behavior that may have led Nadab and

Abihu astray, namely, drunkenness. Or, as is more likely (Nahmanides 1974: 121) the wine impaired their judgment about other matters, that is, the distinguishing "between the holy and the common, and between the unclean and the clean" (10:10). Somehow, it is this distinguishing that the priests' death brings into view. Is the alien fire that they brought the occasion of this word from God that will now set out a task for Aaron and the people? Or does the display of God's glory, devouring in its proximity, also uncover the basis for such distinctions in the world? Whatever the case, we have seen, as have Aaron and all the people, that such distinctions have about them a kind of woundedness, and in the context of this episode, stretching out toward the glory of the humiliated Jesus, the holiness of the holy one has about it a kind of wounding of the self.

We are therefore granted a clue about something that will unfold further in the next chapter. Is it all—the laws, the demands, the distinctions—a matter of subjecting oneself to the Lord's will, however that will is framed (and Leviticus will frame it in as unyieldingly unself-evident a way as possible)? Is this what it comes down to, and here are two priests who go their own way, and such a way must lead to death? While Hirsch (1989: 1.252), for instance, does indeed wish to see these matters under the heading of "simple obedience," nonetheless his insight that "a Jewish priest is entirely at one with, and part and parcel of, the nation," and thus defined by an "objectively corporate" reality, gets at the nature of this obedience and its connection with holiness: holiness is for others, inasmuch as it is for God; holiness is "for the sake of." This, somewhat, bridges the gap between the subjective and objective aspects. But a gap there is: holiness, as (etymologically) separateness, uncovers this gap between persons, even as it leaps into it. A man cannot see God and live (Exod. 33:20), unless he be holy (Heb. 12:14). But what holiness can this be, that cannot die? "We have beheld his glory" (John 1:14), we have even "touched [it] with our hands" (1 John 1:1), for it "came among us." Yet in doing so, this weight of glory, which we saw and touched, in which we saw and touched it, hurtles into a chasm.

LEVITICUS 11

Readers of Lev. 11 have often seen its placement after the account of Nadab's and Abihu's deaths as way of distinguishing its teaching in the context of a warning. God directly addresses Aaron after his sons' demise and only now instructs him to teach the people about the distinction "between the holy and the common, and between the unclean and the clean" (10:10)—only now, that is, after a demonstration of what is at stake in failing to follow the detailed commandments of the Lord. Whether this verse refers to 11:47 and so has in mind the actual distinctions between the clean and unclean creatures, or whether it points simply to the root violation of Nadab and Abihu in their particular missteps, their story acts as a general admonition to take seriously the commands of God. But we have also seen that an ambivalence has been at work in how one understands the deaths of Aaron's sons, to the point that some have even considered their destruction as an act of grace and reward, even an act of vicarious atonement (e.g., *Sefer Emet*) that, in Christian eyes, would clearly prefigure the form of Christ. As with Abel, death is turned into something that carries with it life.

If the fire that consumes Aaron's sons is a warning, it is also a revelation of sorts. What might it disclose? Nothing less than God's own character and power, which founds and precedes the mission he gives to his servants. The burning bush marks the giving of God's name and the call of Moses (Exod. 3:2–6); the smoking mountain upon which "the LORD descended . . . in fire" (19:18) marks the giving of the law tables and the call of Israel to the law; the consuming fire establishes the divine purpose of the temple cult (2 Chr. 7:1) and later sets in motion Elijah's prophetic judgment upon Israel (1 Kgs. 18:38). If a revelation of God's power precedes the revelation of his mission, the mission itself is given in the form of fire in particular, for although even these marks are temporary, the final gift of God's being, the "kingdom that cannot be shaken" is given in the God who *is* "a consuming fire" (Heb. 12:28–29) and whose fire constitutes his kingdom: the one who proclaims that "the kingdom of God is in the midst of you" (Luke 17:21) is also he who tells all that "I came to cast fire upon the earth" (12:49). Rupert of Deutz (Patrologia latina 167.796–801), among others, is therefore right to draw this fire as a referent into the realm of the very Spirit of God: "He will baptize you with the Holy Spirit and with fire" (Matt. 3:11). And as the portent and energy of God's vocation, it is given most clearly in the gift of Pentecost through the Spirit's "tongues . . . of fire" (Acts 2:3).

What does this mean in terms of the teaching of distinction that Aaron is called to give to the people? For Rupert of Deutz (Patrologia latina 167.796–801), the pentecostal focus in Lev. 10 explicates the framework of Lev. 11 in terms of the mission to the Gentiles entrusted the church by God. That is, the outline of distinction that Aaron (and Moses) provide the people—in terms of animal life, food, and even the touching of carcasses—properly embraces the distinctions of the peoples and their place within the providential calling of God. From the perspective of the New Testament, this coordination of elements is almost natural. It is, after all, Peter himself, in the course of his calling by God to turn to the Gentiles with the church's first deliberate Christian evangelistic effort in their direction, who is presented with a threefold divine vision treating specifically the question of clean and unclean foods (Acts 10:9–16). Peter, in the midst of prayer, is suddenly beset by a feeling of hunger, but falling "into a trance, [he] saw the heaven opened, and something descending, like a great sheet, let down by four corners upon the earth. In it were all kinds of animals and reptiles and birds of the air. And there came a voice to him, 'Rise, Peter; kill and eat.'" When Peter objects that he has "never eaten anything that is common or unclean," the heavenly voice declares that "what God has cleansed, you must not call common." Rather than seeing Peter's vision as a simple nullification of the Levitical laws of distinction, Rupert of Deutz understands these laws as the reflection of this single providential goal, by which the whole of the world will be brought into right relationship with God, gathered together in the heavenly sheet. The vision sets in motion Peter's visit to the Gentile centurion Cornelius in Caesarea, who is baptized despite his fundamental nonadherence to the breadth of the Levitical laws. Hence the Levitical laws pertain to—they advance toward and present—this goal of Gentile baptism, both in terms of reference and object; they do not contradict it.

But how can this be? To draw Aaron's distinctions into some providential correlation with Peter's Gentile mission is seemingly to suggest fulfillment through subversion. The connection is obvious on some level, however. Peter's vision explicitly contains three orders of animal life not only dealt with in Lev. 11, but more importantly, categorically laid out on the fifth and sixth days of creation (Gen. 1:20–25) and reiterated as being saved from the flood (7:8) and delivered into human hands after the flood (9:2): animals, creeping things, and birds.[1] In

---

1. The seeming absence of the aquatic animals in Peter's vision is debated. They are perhaps included in the term *thēria* used by Peter in Acts 11:6. But while this inclusion would allow for the convenient covering of the animal spectrum, the usage seems doubtful. There were no fish, obviously, in the ark, and Jewish tradition has it that this is because the fish themselves had not sinned.

some basic way, the elements within the sheet let down from heaven are tied to the creative ordering of God, both in their visionary origin and in their connection with the earth's first and restored inhabitants. The enumeration of the beasts in Lev. 11 is evidently tied to this creative ordering. Furthermore, that the distinction between clean and unclean beasts is established even before the flood (Gen. 7:2)—however Noah himself is able to understand it before being taught—emphasizes its status as an element intrinsic to the world's form. If God speaks to Peter about the distinctions between beasts and food, even in terms of that distinction's disappearance, it is because God addresses a matter that links the divine purposes for life across epochs and conversely defines epochs according the purposes for life that belong eternally to God. The inclusion of the Gentiles marks the breadth of that purpose and therefore is tied to the ordered reach of created life upon which that purpose is founded.

If we turn to the story of Noah, we see that the distinction between clean and unclean beasts, as it preexists the delineation of Leviticus, is also ordered toward a sacrifice that preexists the sacrificial laws of the tabernacle. How is it that God can command Noah to distinguish the beasts and later sacrifice them accordingly before the giving of the law itself? The question is asked here not with respect to the means of Noah's knowledge, which could have been gleaned in many possible ways. Rather, the question is about purpose: in an era before the law is given to Israel—given, as most Jewish and Christian commentators assert, for the main purpose of distinguishing it from the nations—what was the meaning of the distinction during the time of the flood and demise of almost all peoples? We must admit that the only revealed purpose lies in the link between the distinction and sacrifice itself (Gen. 8:20). Only the clean animals are offered at Noah's altar after the flood. And only the clean animals are given by God's command to be saved in a sevenfold magnitude more numerous than the unclean (7:2). On the basis of this linkage and this measurement, we must conclude that the clean beasts, in their greater number, are saved for the purpose of dying as ritual victims and in so doing providing a "pleasing odor" to the Lord (8:21), while the unclean beasts, in their lesser number, are saved for some other purpose altogether. That is, the clean animals exist for the sake of all the others, sacrificing themselves, as it were, in the world newly restored and in the place of the unclean (including the unprotected fish, which fill the oceans covering the world). The "distinction [made] between the unclean and the clean" (Lev. 11:47) is therefore a distinction made for *offering*, that is, for love, as it touches the whole world's realm.

I have already noted the way in which separation is an active aspect of love itself, in that it both stands as the basis of creation—the invention of the other who is loved—and also thereby orders the giving of love as the costly embrace of separation's chasm of being and identity. The boundaries frequently referred to

---

In this case, the absence of marine animals in Peter's vision is somehow linked in its significance to the renewed primordialism of Noah's covenant.

in Job (14:5; 26:10; 38:11; cf. Ps. 104:9; Jer. 5:22; Acts 17:26) represent the very character of what it means for God to bring something into being.[2] To distinguish is (from a human perspective) to learn to love, by analogy with the creating act of God; to love in this way, distinctively, is to learn to reconcile. The Greek word translated "reconciliation" (*katallassō* and its cognates) had an original economic implication of adjusted levels of "exchange"—labor, money, salaries. As the term was later applied, in a standard fashion, to the reconciliation of estranged parties, the notion of adjustment remained fundamental and pointed to the capacity for distinct agents to order themselves toward one another away from hostility and in favor of peaceful engagement. Certainly reconciliation presupposes difference, but it also maintains it in a transfigured fashion. There is no love without otherness, nor can reconciliation count as anything without offering.[3] Hirsch's great comments (1989: 1.304–20) on the meaning of uncleanness in the Levitical text provide a clear example of his "etymological exegesis" on just this matter: *tame* (unclean) is related, he argues, to a root that paradoxically indicates wholeness. But in this case, wholeness does not constitute perfection, but implies an illegitimate admixture, a merging of what is distinct by nature into a destructive absorption.[4] If the value of creation as an object and embodiment of God's love—that is, as

2. See Beauchamp 1969 for an exegetical discussion of this in terms of the creation narratives of Genesis. For a less scriptural rumination on difference and creation, taking in the mysterious distinctions between animals and humans and the dangers and losses of obscuring such fundamental distinctions, see the social philosopher Baudrillard 1998: 129–41. If "love separates," in Bérulle's stark formulation (in Thompson 1989: 155), this is because creation itself is an act of love, and love, in its perfect form, creates. The Arian worry over an impassible God, a God whose love cannot admit of the separative cataclysm that creation implies, demanded their rejection, it seems, of an incarnation and cross-bound death as the temporal embodiment of God's love. See the remark of Demophilus, Arian Archbishop of Constantinople, that God "would have been under the necessity of either making everything gods to be worthy of him, or else everything would have disintegrated by contact with him" (quoted in Hanson 1988: 101). The Kabbalah saw a similar problem as the Arians, and both sought a solution in the speculative positing of some kind of intermediary between God and creature.

3. The debate surrounding Jewish philosopher Levinas's religious treatment of otherness—is it actually congruent with Jewish or with Christian religious presuppositions in its implication of self-offering for the sake of relationship?—is pertinent to a discussion of distinction and sacrifice. On his general ethical theory, see Levinas 1991. On this rather crucial argument as to religious congruence, see Sibony 2000.

4. In Lev. 19:19 the question of mixing is made explicit. In this latter case, however, as a statute designated *khoq* (as opposed to *mishpat*), the reason for the injunction against certain kinds of mixing is, according to Jewish tradition, deliberately veiled in God's hidden will. There is a relation of purpose between Hirsch's etymological speculation (1989: 1.304–20) and the popular theory of anthropologist Mary Douglas, who argues that the laws of clean and unclean in Leviticus, especially as applied to animals, were designed to outline the necessary distinctions by which the creative ordering of the world by God is exhibited. According to this theory, what is unclean is precisely that which somehow "crosses the line" of difference and blurs the character of order (e.g., animals that live both on land and in the sea, rather than exclusively within one respective sphere of existence). See Douglas 1970: chap. 3.

true creatures, in the plural—is to be upheld, then, in a world where created life (distinctions) comes under threat, only self-offering can sustain reality.

Thus, the clean die for the unclean, and in this is the very act of the creator's love exposed, and what is other is lifted up. There is some connection here with the very tragedy of Cain and Abel, now transformed. The two brothers have difference turned to enmity, by the very distinction of God's regard, and thereby the ordering of love turns into murder. Yet Abel's death, as the tradition understood his own prefiguring, also indicated the way forward, by which sacrifice through the giving over of a self to distinction's anger would in fact prove its reconciliation. The very forms of Levitical sacrifice announce this. In difference made and difference given over, there is new life, the life bound to the very creative act of God who first made "man and beast" and who is most certainly the one who saves both "man and beast" (Ps. 36:6). How shall God save them? By submitting their distinctions to the cost of love, by subjecting self to another, one difference to another, a subjection that finally must be infinite (1 Cor. 15:28; Mark 10:45; Eph. 5:21).

The allegorical reading—both Jewish and Christian—by which the sacrificial animals of Leviticus refer to those beastly, irrational, or wild (Maximus the Confessor [in Palmer, Sherrard, and Ware 1979–95: 2.273]) aspects of the self that require subjugation is in fact congruent with and perhaps even founded upon the presuppositions of this reality of distinction and offering. Allegorists like Hirsch or Origen can identify the animals as symbols of personal sin, even as they also and at the same time construe the animal referents as positive aspects of the soul itself. How do they maintain this referential contradiction? The common issue has to do with subjection, in this case subjection of the self for the sake of knowing that which is other than oneself, creation, and, in an infinite way, God: proper control of the self transfigures the soul into something beautiful and becomes, in itself, a worthy offering. In the posttemple reality of Judaism, the laws of sacrifice are transferred to the acts of prayer, and in this the self is ordered and distinguished in its complex identities for the sake of world and maker.[5] This is the way life is and must be, this ordering and offering of distinctions within and as creation, if there is to be such a thing as love enacted. The Lord is one who saves both "man and beast," but does so, not globally or categorically, but specifically in the demands of justice and obedience as related to every aspect of a world whose diversity constitutes the otherness invented by creating love. The heart mirrors the world in this respect.

But what does this love look like in point of fact? And how does it relate to the enunciation of the clean and unclean animals of Lev. 11, where nothing is actually said to indicate such a spiritual logic? Returning to Peter's vision and its

---

5. The notion that prayer can stand in the place of sacrifice is apparent already in, e.g., 2 Chr. 30:18–19. Later posttemple Judaism made this a (temporary) dispensational standard (Babylonian Talmud, tractate *Megillah* 31b). There is "nothing left but prayer" (*Midrash Psalms* 5:4).

narrative context, we can observe the specifics of Peter's sermon to Cornelius and those with him (Acts 10:34–33): Jesus, according to Peter, is sent to embody a "word ... to Israel," a word of peace. This word is one anointed by the Holy Spirit and power; it leads Jesus to the broken and the demon-possessed, healing them; it leads him throughout Israel and finally to his self-offering by hanging on a tree; it raises Jesus from the dead and places him at table to eat and drink with his companions. Finally, this word, incarnate in the dead and risen Jesus, sends the disciples out on their own mission of witness that brings Jew and Gentile together and represents God's own act of cleansing the "common or unclean" (10:28–29, 45) through the gift of the Holy Spirit to the Gentiles, the fire of God's own self. This entire story of Jesus's mission, as recounted and enacted by Peter, is one that both explicates and embraces the distinctions of the world, among the animals as among the peoples, and subjects them to the self-subjection of the word of God upon the cross, by which they are all brought together in the comprehensive love of God. God cleanses all things, in the sense of reconciling them: "For in [the Son, Jesus Christ,] all the fulness of God was pleased to dwell, and through him to reconcile to himself all things, whether on earth or in heaven, making peace by the blood of his cross" (Col. 1:19–20). It is not as if the distinctions disappear; rather they are taken up by God, literally in his own flesh.

This vision, in its ultimate resolution, stands in sharp contrast to the *Rabbah's* enumeration of the distinctions of uncleanness solely in terms of the nations' wickedness and opposition to Israel; what is unclean ever remains disgustingly so, according to the *Rabbah*. And perhaps the *Rabbah's* sense in all this—the camel, badger, and the hare's uncleanness referring to Babylonia, Media, and Greece; the pig to Rome; and all the unclean beasts to the blasphemy of the Gentiles—that "Moses foresaw what the evil kingdoms would do [to Israel]" (13.5), is right, historically right and inescapable, and finally horrific and demanding of a final and annihilating judgment. There are only Jews and Gentiles in the world, as even Vico (*New Science* 1.105) insisted; and Abel and Cain inhabit their spirits. But so too do Abel and Cain together inhabit the spirits of Jew and Gentile with each individual separately and within their respective families. And though "in Christ" there is "neither Jew nor Greek" (Gal. 3:28; Col. 3:11), yet the distinction itself is not effaced as a historical fact (as Paul's frequent references to just such distinctions in the church make clear).

Even the animals, therefore, cry out to God on behalf of Israel, as crying out for the whole world, before God's altar, just as all "creation waits with eager longing for the revealing of the sons of God" and in that waiting "groan[s] in travail" (Rom. 8:19, 22). Yet even here, Peter's vision does not contradict the reality of this opposition and longing and groaning as a historical fact, as if the distinctions themselves had all been a misperception. Rather, the vision places that fact within the self-offering (i.e., the subjection to its force) of God himself, hanging on a tree, for in this offering, which stands at the basis of all things, a distinction submitted to that cries out the lament of all distinctions, of distinction left to its own dangling isolation, "my God, my God, why hast thou forsaken me?" (Mark 15:34), there is yet a re-creation, a saving of man and beast.

The world of distinctions in Lev. 11 is thus the phenomenal image of the creating and *reconciling* love of God in Jesus Christ, one that takes in the breadth of the world (2 Cor. 5:19). And this claim founds the rationale for reading, marking, and digesting Leviticus in its details as markers of reality. To see how this is so, from a particularly Christian perspective, we need only trace the Jewish interpretive parallel to its incarnational conclusion. Hirsch's commentary (1989: 1.304–6), for instance, looks at the distinctions of clean and unclean as a matter of ideas—ideas that in fact order life in its entirety: the subjection, as I noted, of the whole of human existence to God. The comprehensive character of the laws of clean and unclean is essential to grasping their purpose. Although the animals, in this case, and the prohibitions attached to them are symbols of these ideas of human subjection, they are themselves objects that are part of the practice of a God-subjected existence, according to Hirsch. Thus, they are a particular kind of symbol; they are each a synecdoche in their referential meaning (an actual part standing for the whole), not an abstracted representation. The objects and laws do not simply stand for the reality of human subjection to God; they in fact form a part of that subjection, dragging us into its fullness through their limited practice, dragging us, indeed, into the whole world's subjected destiny. Hence, the objects involved—food, clothing, and so on—must be phenomenally real and must engage a historical obedience; and the law, for Hirsch, is immovable in its particular demands, not translatable into new or more modern forms, despite its symbolic character.[6]

The difference between the Christian and Jewish application of this conviction lies, not in phenomenality, but in the matter of legal demand. For Origen, the world and its objects are spiritually meaningful, but not legally so (*Homilies on Leviticus* 7.4–7). The animals and beasts truly speak their messages of their own (in the Spirit)—the scaly and nonscaly fish telling human beings about the distinctions between higher and lower forms of understanding—but they do so without the mediation of legal requirements in order to be heard. Why? Because the same comprehensiveness of direction demanded by Hirsch (1989: 1.304–6,

6. It is common to understand Christian symbolism, particularly as applied to the spiritual reading of the Old Testament, in a very different way, that is, as a detachment of phenomenal realities described in the Scriptures from their referential meaning. But when Origen, for example, explains animal distinctions in Lev. 11 as referring to levels of spiritual discernment (e.g., scaly fish supposedly dwelling in the surface or higher and warmer waters of the Spirit, and nonscaly fish dwelling in the nether depths of carnality), he is in fact maintaining a phenomenal rooting for his referents (*Homilies on Leviticus* 7.7). The specific words (and their objective referents) in Leviticus are spiritual, not because they are linguistic metaphors enabling a cognitive apprehension of a deeper truth. Rather, they are spiritual in a robust pneumatic sense: they *are* the Holy Spirit at work in us, or the very instruments of this work in us, who read them and perceive them. And the objects represented by the text are effective in that they seek out their spiritual purpose within the actual phenomenal world. And this is a conviction that Origen shares with Jewish exegetes.

310–20) is carried to its legal fulfillment in Christ's own body. The practical law of Leviticus focuses on the breadth of bodily existence in the world, and Jesus *is* that body wholly and fully existing in the law; he is its end in the sense of its perfect embodiment (Rom. 10:4). The Scripture's referents and objects, however, remain the same.

They remain the same, but they are gathered in the word made flesh, who speaks them and contains them. The forms of Scripture—the clean and unclean, the animals, the sacrifices—are the same for the church as for Israel, although their legal embodiment is now located in the existence of the one man. Jesus assumes the whole of the world, including its sin and its curse (2 Cor. 5:21; Gal. 3:13) and including therefore and precisely the distinctions among the beasts as they are made in time and space. In a way that comprehends the matter that sustains the distinctions of love and sin, Jesus chews the dust of death and life together, eats and ingests it into himself, allows the cells of the earth's very being to become his own. "Christ the Incarnate One assumed flesh—organic, human flesh; he was nurtured by air and water, vegetables and meat, like the rest of us. He took matter into himself, so matter is not alien to him now. His body is a *material* body—transformed, of course, but transformed *matter*. Thus he shares his being with the whole created order: animals and birds, snakes and worms, flowers and seeds. All parts of creation are now reconciled to Christ" (Gregorios 1987: 89). If "God looked into the Torah and created the world" according even to its letters (*Zohar* 2.161b), he did so on the basis of a word whose body comprehends, in its tendons and limbs, the very reaches of created reality (*Zohar*, tractate *Terumah* 165b; *Shaar HaGilgulim*, tractate *Hakdamah* 11). Such is the separating and separated love of God. "*This* is love . . . that [God] loved us and sent his Son to be the expiation for our sins" (1 John 4:10). Love founds, comprehends, and gives itself over completely to the reality of created distinction.[7] The black letters of the Scripture that hedge in the world, as Karl Shapiro writes (2003: 109), are also the "black letters written in the sky" by the bees in Francis Jammes's poem "The Church Clothed in Leaves" (1976: 58). And both are writ into the flesh of Christ.

To say that the comprehensive scheme of Leviticus is fulfilled in the body of Christ is also to say that the body of Christ is defined by the realm of distinguished creation and of the death and life tasted by Jesus. Hence, in this case, the animals

---

7. From the viewpoint of metaphysical categories, nothing could be more fundamental to assert, for this reality is often misconstrued. Feuerbach, for instance, summed up what has become a platitude of modernism in claiming that love "universalizes" and "identifies," while faith "distinguishes" and "separates." Hence, in Feuerbach's view, traditional Christianity has foundered on a contradiction between a love that would make God and humans one thing, and all human beings one common people, and a faith that would separate creation from God and persons from other persons, bringing about intolerance, violence, and death. Get rid of faith in a distinct and separate God and in a consequently distinct and separated creation, and the world would be a better place (1841: chap. 26 and app. 19). Yet Leviticus, rightly, insists that nothing is more deadly than the demand to erase distinction; and nothing is more loving than the suffering embrace of distinction itself. Faith is simply the knowledge that love is possible at all and real in fact. That is, faith is only in God.

remain in their clarity of identity, yet they emerge in the posture or reconciliation as much as do Jew and Gentile in Peter's vision: "The wolf shall dwell with the lamb, and the leopard shall lie down with the kid, and the calf and the lion and the fatling together, and a little child shall lead them. The cow and the bear shall feed; their young shall lie down together; and the lion shall eat straw like the ox. The sucking child shall play over the hole of the asp, and the weaned child shall put his hand on the adder's den" (Isa. 11:6–8). The animals are still named, they are still given over to the world by God, but clean and unclean stand together, at peace, no longer in a relationship of destruction. That this is the shape and histori-cal reach of Christ's body is what differentiates such a vision from Hirsch's. But the end is the same: "For the earth shall be full of the knowledge of the LORD as the waters cover the sea" (11:9), that is, that God should be "all in all" (1 Cor. 15:28).[8]

The relationship, however, between the referents of Leviticus and their gathering in Christ is not given in a single movement. The law is subordinated to its own fulfillment, yet that fulfillment is repeatedly reordered by the contents of the law. If Origen's tradition can be faulted, it is in its reluctance to return to the text and its objects as referents of the world's actual landscape. Moral allegory, relentlessly pursued, tends to squeeze out the phenomenal world as a whole. The animals are about humans, Origen (*Homilies on Leviticus* 7.6) and the entire medieval tradi-tion insisted. Each beast individually and as a class refers to some moral condition that a human being might instance. While Hirsch (1989: 1.301–8) would, in a sense, agree with this, he is unable to leave behind the individuals and classes precisely because they are bound to human beings through their legal engagement, even when allegorized after the temple's destruction in terms of forms of prayer and service, and in this they act as concretized and consistent reminders of their meaning. Yet so too with Christ: the discrete character of the literal referents in the text of Leviticus is in fact given in Christ as their creator and also as their reconciler. From this fact the referents can indeed apply to human life and moral order, but only as tied to the animals.

What, then, shall we say of the animals? We should first reject the notion—for example, in Maimonides (*Moreh Nebukim* 3.48) or Nahmanides (1974: 130–43)—that their status as clean or unclean depends upon some intrinsic moral character they embody or to which they refer—whether it be the irrational or evil instincts of certain creatures or the physically unhealthy and poisonous elements of their makeup. Augustine makes this clear—they are distinguished not because

---

8. Whether the animals themselves are fallen along with all of creation is a murky matter in its specifics. Doubtless they are in some general way—evidenced by a world of reconciled beasts like lion and lamb—but this is never discussed in Scripture in any clear fashion, except insofar as all of creation is reconciled by Christ. Seventeenth-century theologian Thomas Burnet, who argued eloquently in his *Sacred Theory of the Earth* (1684) for the corruption of the whole natural universe through the fall, found many smaller indicators of the fallenness of individual animals. How else account for the existence of mosquitoes?

of some "fault of nature," but to indicate symbolically human characteristics that are the virtues or "sins of choice" (*Reply to Faustus the Manichaean* 6.7).[9] Calvin points out (1996: 2.63) that there can be no question of the animals' intrinsic character in the distinction between clean and unclean if in fact Jesus could declare "all foods clean" (Mark 7:19) and if the world could in fact ingest them without harm (unless, of course, that pronouncement actually altered the nature of the animals in question). Rather, their differences entail the distinctions of creation that are ordered by and toward divine love. Each is constituted by a particular act of God's will and is ordered in a particular way within God's purposes. The particularity or distinction is phenomenally evident, even if the divine desire for each, in its true meaning, remains mysterious to humans.

Among the unclean animals, for instance, we find many whose character is one of integrity before God, praised by the very words of the Scripture.[10] The lion, of course, is a symbol of Israel (Num. 23:24) and even of God (Hos. 5:14). Camels and horses are prized and denote wealth (1 Chr. 27:30; 1 Kgs. 4:26). The soaring of the hawk and the "spread[ing of] his wings toward the south" is an emblem of God's wisdom (Job 39:26). Likewise, the flight of the eagle into the air is a sign of God's renewing mercy (Exod. 19:4). Ravens are the servants of God's generosity and actually feed Elijah in the desert (1 Kgs. 17:4–7). The bee gives its name to one of Israel's great judges, Deborah. David takes the worm as his own image (Ps. 22:6), as does Christ in quoting the psalm. Behemoth in Job 40 (whether it be a hippopotamus or an elephant) and Leviathan in Job 41 (who is clearly the crocodile) are both unclean, yet here mark the awesome limit of God's unfathomable wisdom and power. Even the snake is endowed with beauty and grace (Prov. 30:19).

Clean and unclean do not refer to some moral status, therefore, but to the reality of distinction itself that lies at the heart of God's creative love. In this they point to the offering that love itself embodies. And so all creation, all the animals exist to praise their Lord equally, and their being is given over to such praise. The *Perek Shira*, of the first centuries AD, puts these songs, whose words

9. Augustine follows, therefore, a standard figurative reading, based on the symbolic character of the ceremonial law (see the commentary on Lev. 18).

10. At the same time, the very forms of God's creation, including the scriptural images of animals and humans together, are sometimes assumed by demons who insert themselves into our imaginings, "sleeping or waking," and distract our souls from our purpose—so St. Gregory of Sinai in a long and vivid discussion of contemplation entitled "On Commandments and Doctrines": "The demons of desire turn themselves sometimes into pigs, sometimes into donkeys, sometimes into fiery stallions avid for copulation, and sometimes—particularly the demons of licentiousness—into Israelites. The demons of wrath turn themselves sometimes into gentiles and sometimes into lions. . . . The demons of greed appear sometimes as wolves and sometimes as leopards, those of malice assume the form sometimes of snakes, sometimes of vipers, and sometimes of foxes, those of shamelessness the form of dogs and those of listlessness the form of cats. Finally there are the demons of lechery, that turn themselves sometimes into snakes and sometimes into crows and jackdaws" (quoted from Palmer, Sherrard, and Ware 1979–95: 4.224–25).

are taken directly from the Holy Scriptures, into the mouth of every beast, clean and unclean (translation from Isaacs 2000: 165–74):

> The vulture says: "I will whistle to them and gather them, for I will redeem them; they shall increase and continue increasing." (Zech. 10:8) . . .

> The fly, when Israel is not engaged with Torah, says: "A voice rings out: 'Proclaim.' Another asks: 'What shall I proclaim?' All flesh is grass . . ." (Isa. 40:6) . . . "I will create a new expression of the lips; peace, peace for the far and near says God, and I will heal them." (Isa. 57:19) . . .

> Leviathan says: "Praise God, for He is good, His steadfast love is eternal." (Ps. 136:1) . . .

> The insects say: "Let Israel rejoice in its Maker, let the children of Zion exult in their King." (Ps. 149:2)

> The serpent says: "The Lord supports all who stumble, and makes all who are bent down stand straight." (Ps. 145:14)

> The scorpion says: "The Lord is good to all, and His mercy is upon all His works." (Ps. 145:9)

This unveiling of the creature's hidden purpose and nature is given impetus in the Christian encyclopedic naturalist tradition from the Middle Ages onward—including the bestiary, the Renaissance descriptive collections of Conrad Genz, and the seventeenth-century botanical and zoological investigations of John Ray—and reaches an apogee in the handbooks of scriptural geography and natural history of the mid- to late-nineteenth century, by such popular writers as H. B. Tristram. And obviously it takes a special devotional and even metaphysical root in the platonic outlook of the Franciscan tradition, shared also with certain earlier Eastern Orthodox ascetic disciplines (e.g., St. Peter of Damascus's Sixth Stage of Contemplation).

But even the *Perek Shira* demonstrates, in its placement of Scripture on the tongues of the beast, how this particular catalogue of creaturely praise is tied to the nature of Israel's vocation in particular, something each animal addresses in some fashion. Israel is called to distinguish the clean from the unclean and in so doing uncover the nature of the world as God's gift or offering to be offered back. The earth speaks of sacrifice. The demanded differences that are embodied in the legal prescriptions drive Israel, as Hirsch (1989: 1.310–20) argues, into an intense examination of life before God in all of its particulars. And within this context, the allegorical associations of the beasts that both Jewish and Christian commentators proposed gain legitimate force, even and especially in their profuse variety: do birds of prey bespeak the ravenous passion, or does reptilian dragging upon the earth point to the dust of death, or cloven feet to the two Testaments, or chewing cud to the rumination upon the word or law, or flies and all swarming things to the filth of corruption and mortality? In a world where distinctions are the essence of purpose and where every purpose is bound to God, such careful examination and parsing, however shifting and varied, becomes itself the apprehension of the truth, what Eastern Orthodox contemplatives called discrimination. The reinjection of all things into the forms of the Scriptures orders all things toward God.

In this process, the traditional association of the unclean with the realm of death and sin, however secondary and, metaphysically speaking, inapt, becomes permissible (Rev. 21:27). And the placement of the carcass at the center of this ordering of the unclean (Lev. 11:24, 31–39) grounds this interpretive move, for the nature of death is constituted by its contrast to the grace of God's creative gift of life. Because of this, it is exactly what is common to all creatures—humans and beast, "any man" and any beast, must perish: "For the fate of the sons of men and the fate of beasts is the same; as one dies, so dies the other. They all have the same breath, and man has no advantage over the beasts; for all is vanity" (Eccl. 3:19). This is made yet more precise in 9:2: "One fate comes to all, to the righteous and the wicked, to the good and the evil, to the clean and unclean, to him who sacrifices and to him who does not sacrifice." In this light, death lies as the negative base of creation and the separated otherness of love, for what is common is precisely what cannot be, and what is living is constituted by its distinction. Death dissolves; love—as life itself in God's act—reconciles. As the unclean animal stands as a constant reminder of this reality, surrounding Israel with the echo of love's ultimate contingency, God's profile emerges from the shadows of human self-regard. The swarming beasts are teeming with life, as Mary Douglas points out. They are not in themselves dirty; they are directly God's, because he is life-giver, and outside the realm of Israel's domain (1999: 157–66). But because they are God's, like Israel is also God's, they are gifts, fragile, gossamerlike in their sparkle and vulnerability.

Origen's assertion that "the animals refer to men" (*Homilies on Leviticus* 7.6) then becomes, in its diverse and particular deployment, a constant prod away from self toward the power and person that gives life. The dirtiness of the chameleon and the gecko, slithering across the floor and up the wall late at night or especially in the middle of the bright and sullen day, brings within the realm of daily existence the glimmer of sinful fragility and merciful grace, the very touch of creative distinction. And is not the human made last of all, after even the gnats, as the rabbis pointed out? Israel is a "worm" (Isa. 41:14), after all, and all human beings die just like the "flies" (51:6). Yet even this points out God's miraculous love.

This is the movement by which creation itself takes rise from God's hand. God makes the distinctions between himself and all else, between light and dark, creature and creature; but in this, he would have all creatures refer to him, offer to him what is first offered, and death is therein given over to life. Jesus "eats" the world of matter, as Gregorios writes; he eats the very dust and finally the death of the world. Yet this turn away from himself, living even "with the wild beasts" (Mark 1:13), gives life to all things. So God himself cleanses the world of its commonness, its own singular fall into death, as Peter's heavenly vision reveals (Acts 10:15).

And so too, as Peter testifies to Cornelius, Jesus "is the one ordained by God to be judge of the living and the dead" (Acts 10:42), that is, distinguisher of creatures, of light and dark, of the thoughts of men and women (1 Cor. 4:4–5), of love and nothingness. He "tabernacles" among us (John 1:14), and to his temple are brought all creatures for their offering (Rev. 21:22–27), that is, to be made new (21:5). The great distinction of clean and unclean on the part of Aaron and Moses takes place on the eighth day (Lev. 9:1), and this day, as some Jewish tradition has it, is the extraordinary day: "Seven is the number of the days of the week, the measure of earthly time, a symbol of the human dimension. Eight signifies the more-than-human; it is the symbol of holiness."[11] God cleanses what is common because God himself eats it, becomes common himself, becomes like the beasts and the Gentiles, and so turns the common into life again on the eighth day, the Lord's Day, the day of resurrection, where "death is swallowed up" in the purifying meal of God (1 Cor. 15:54).

And this is divine holiness, the holiness that Israel is called to embody in common now with God as the summation of these instructions (Lev. 11:44), this distinguishing by which love is given, and death is taken into the self, and life is thereby granted. In my commentary on Lev. 19, I shall say more about what holiness is and how God is holy. But here I can say at least that once every part of life is thus distinguished, discerned, and devoted, it becomes "holy to the LORD," even "every pot in Jerusalem" (Zech. 14:21). As St. Neilos the Ascetic wrote in "Ascetic Discourse," the animals *know* their boundaries and live within their order. Hence, the saints of the desert fled the dens of human wickedness in the cities and instead chose to live with the beasts, "trust[ing] the animals as their friends; for animals do not teach us to sin, but revere and respect holiness" (quoted in Palmer, Sherrard, and Ware 1979–95: 1.246, 241). In this he was reiterating the prophetic comparison of the animal as the embracer of distinction, over and against human iniquity: "Even the stork in the heavens knows her times; and the turtledove, swallow, and crane keep the time of their coming; but my people know not the ordinance of the LORD" (Jer. 8:7). And the work of such distinction and discernment and devotion, taken to its furthest limit, the limit of its very existence and of the brink of death and creation, is the work of "the Holy One" himself (Mark 1:24; Acts 3:14). To reconcile is not to erase these distinctions, but to fulfill the mission of offering on behalf of others, that is, to "love . . . to the end" (John 13:1).

When the church reads Leviticus here, it sees the body of Christ laid out upon the earth and all the creatures of the earth swarming upon its rest, gathering, each

---

11. Schneersohn 1986: 172 refers to the classic Pentateuch commentary (the *Kli Yakar*) of sixteenth-century Rabbi Shlomo Ephraim of Lunshitz.

of them one by one, each in its intricate particularity—the osprey, the stork and the heron, the winged insects, the weasel and the mouse, the lizard and crocodile, the pigs and the whales—each in its "ending," the place where its very form arises out of nothing and sinks into nothing. And it learns and follows to the same place, the same brink and chasm (Rom. 12:1; Luke 16:26; 1 Pet. 3:19), as seen in Richard Grossman's poem "Home" (1990: 494):

> The animals all yearned now
> for home:
>
> to be isolated and reduced
> to where they had been.
>
> For a time we functioned
> in this interstice, they said.
>
> Learning and enjoying.
> Sharing our deadness
>
> and our lives that fuel deadness.
> And the spark, entire, separate
>
> and clear. The spark guarded
> from the rest of the universe.
>
> We made our small candles
> burn bright in the black endlessness:
>
> a galaxy
> where the stars whispered.

LEVITICUS 12

Jesus comes as a body into the world of distinctions. He comes as a body (Luke 17:37) and ends as a corpse (Matt. 24:28)[1] that is raised from the dead as a spiritual body (1 Cor. 15:44), though a body nonetheless (15:38). Around him gather the beasts of land and birds of air. His flesh is eaten and his blood is shed and drunk. The very being of things, the very act of creation, the center of love, the entering of the chasm that is the separation of God, he enters and takes to himself, not to destroy the distinction of bodies, but to reconcile them with God.

Childbirth is, in history, the distinction into which Jesus comes, the place where this chasm is beheld and touched, not only as the passage of our own being, but now by God who touches creation itself, becoming that which he does, subjecting himself to the clean and the unclean, the holy and the common. Riven by impurity and pain, yet the very means of existence and thereby belovedness, childbirth stands as the meeting place of the creation of and assumption of time by God. Given its central role in Leviticus, childbirth also displays how time itself is an instrument of distinguishing within the realm of creation; temporality undercuts any notion of common or universal being among creatures. And finally, Lev. 12, as being a key moment of the Christian gospel's appearance and recounting, becomes central also to Leviticus itself as Scripture.

In some ways, in fact, of all of Leviticus, this chapter is the most closely bound with the New Testament, other than, perhaps, the various sacrificial elements found in Hebrews and, after all, only inexactly drawn from Leviticus itself. Origen first saw this clearly, grasping that Lev. 12 must, in a primary way, be drawn into relationship with Luke 2:21–24, wherein Jesus's circumcision and Mary's purification after childbirth are described in a manner that follows the Levitical prescriptions fairly accurately (*Homilies on Leviticus* 8.4). But what exactly is the relationship that is

---

1. Compare "wherever the [dead] body [*ptōma*] is, there the eagles will be gathered together" (Matt. 24:28) with *sōma* ("body") in the same phrase in Luke 17:37.

to be necessarily drawn? A major issue is whether the prescriptions surrounding childbirth stand here in some kind of shadowed contrast with Jesus's birth, as the incomplete reality that remains to be fulfilled by Jesus. In such a case, Mary's situation—and Jesus's too—is thereby seen as different on some basic level from what is talked about in Lev. 12. But this historically contrastive approach has, I believe, led to a number of confusions, not least of which are christological.

Origen, for instance, would free Mary from actual need of purification (*Homilies on Leviticus* 8.2). Noting that 12:2 applies to a "woman who conceives [i.e., receives seed] and bears a male child," he insists that Mary, as a "virgin" touched rather by the Holy Spirit, did not receive any semen and therefore is not impure. The issue, of course, is the virgin conception and birth of Christ. "Let regular women bear the burden of the law, but let virgins be exempt," he writes. Having distinguished Mary in this way—and by implication the child that she bears— Origen (*Homilies on Leviticus* 3.3) then lays aside the evangelical meaning of the text and seeks to explain Leviticus on its own terms. Why the impurity of childbirth for all other women? Here, he sets out a remarkably insistent list of proofs for the inherence of sin in conception and birth itself, enumerating the many Old Testament verses that refer to birthdays as "curse days": Job 3:3; 14:4–5; Ps. 51:5; Jer. 1:5; 20:14–18; and so on. Only self-inflated sinners like Pharaoh and Herod celebrate their anniversaries. Although Origen does not address the question of original sin in these terms, he affirms its reality and points to infant baptism as a proof of remitting the sin of simply being human that afflicts all people. Later Christian interpreters like Rupert of Deutz (Patrologia latina 167.801–3), following Augustine, made much of this, attaching the transmission of sin to the sexual act itself, which, as the *Glossa ordinaria* (Patrologia latina 113.331) explains, first took place only outside of Eden.

The Catholic tradition as a whole, thereafter, made much of the distinction between Lev. 12's referents and the actual birth of Jesus, thus differentiating Jesus from other men, but also, more and more, separating Mary from other women. Assertions that, for instance, Mary's womb miraculously closed again following Jesus's birth and that no blood or placenta emerged soon became standard claims, thereby placing the matter of childbirth described in Leviticus within an ancient realm of covenantal (and still-fallen human) anachronism.[2] Rupert of Deutz (Patrologia latina 167.801–3) points out—in a manner that would certainly provoke

2. A long-standing Christian feast day (February 2) devoted to the "Purification of the Virgin" may therefore seem incongruous. But the day itself was used to underline Mary's difference from other women, indeed her paradoxical need *not* to be purified. The Franciscan St. Anthony of Padua (thirteenth century), for instance, explained it thus in a sermon for the celebration: "The Lord spoke to Moses, in Lev. 12, saying: If a woman having received seed shall bear a man child, she shall be unclean seven days [12:1–2]. This is in distinction to her who gave birth as a virgin. Neither the child nor the mother needed to be purified by sacrifices; it was to free us from the fear of the law, that is, from keeping a law which is observed in fear" (forthcoming). Anthony goes on to use Mary, not as a person in her own right—she does not herself "fit," after all—but as a figure for the Christian soul, which, of course, *does* require various kinds of purification and is therefore

modern sensibilities—that the ritual distinction between male and female births (the latter requiring double the period of purification) was but a sign of the first sin's narrative, Eve first succumbing to the serpent's temptation and proving herself the instrument of Adam's fall (1 Tim. 2:14). But, he goes on to say, this narrative itself is removed from symbolic expression by Christ, in whom "there is neither male nor female" (Gal. 3:28). The same sacrificial victim, after all, is required for both male and female births (Lev. 12:6)—a lamb, that is Christ Jesus!

Later Protestant exegesis was concerned that this differentiation had gone too far in subsuming Mary into its net. Sensibly observing that Mary herself in fact performs the purificatory ritual demanded of a new mother, they countered their Roman Catholic adversaries by insisting that Mary too was stained by original sin—no immaculate conception here—just like all the rest of us. Jesus, however and of course, was not. Interpreting circumcision (12:3) as an atoning rite for the male, Christian interpreters tended to explain its application in Jesus's case as a kind of "fulfillment of righteousness" on his part, much like his baptism (Matt. 3:15), a demonstration to others of his willingness to obey, even if, for his own person, unnecessary in itself. Hence, especially in Protestant hands, the Levitical rites described in Luke 2 are seen as pedagogical signs, but in themselves as ineffective ones.

The problem with this entire Christian tradition is not only its slightly jumbled application that ends by evacuating the very figural symbols that are deployed in the reading of Lev. 12. Even more so, the tradition fails to comprehend the actual richness of the text, whose christological application would otherwise be granted a far greater depth. The matter at hand in the Lord's address to Moses (12:1) is, after all, the great distinction between clean and unclean among the creatures upon the face of the earth (11:46–47). As Jewish tradition has commonly noted, not only the order of creation in Genesis, but the order of the discussion of sacrifice and distinction in Leviticus places the animals before humans, largely to inculcate humility on the part of Adam (and Israel): human beings are but one part of a chain of createdness, in which "the gnats precede them." This created similarity between beasts and humans is initially described, in the Levitical narrative, through the experience of familial tragedy (in connection with Nadab and Abihu at 10:10), as it applies specifically to parents and children. When the question of childbirth is thus explained by God also in terms of cleanness and uncleanness, its meaning finds its shape within the context of this particular reality of distinguishing what drives the destiny of creation: clean and unclean, life and death, male and female.

Leviticus 12 is therefore a matter of how things are, how they exist, and their relation to God in a primary fashion. It is only this given of the order of the world, once established, that is taken up by Jesus, not left behind. In this sense the chapter

called to the humility of submission. The feast day is, understandably, given the confusions, now known as the Presentation.

cannot serve, in any basic way, as the means of a contrast between the Testaments. Rather, it functions as an explication of who Jesus is and the nature of his body as one who is in the world: Jesus assumes distinction, he does not abolish it. And to this extent, furthermore, the meaning of the chapter also stands in enormous conflict with the kinds of claims to universalized being and existence that modern theology and politics have been pressing for so long. Given the importance of this topic, which merits its own separate treatment, what follows can be only a summary of some of the many elements that are comprehended by this assumption of a body by Jesus that Lev. 12 in fact elucidates.

First of all, how shall we understand the descriptive phrase of 12:2, which deals with the woman's seed? All interpreters have observed the redundancy, or perhaps backward logic, of the expression: women usually simply conceive, by receiving the seed of the husband. In this case, however, the Hebrew verb, *zara*, indicates a sowing or scattering of the seed, a function one would normally associate with the male. Yet the Lord says, literally, "if a woman sows her seed." Origen's response, as we remarked, is to see the identification of seed here, which he associates exclusively with the husband, as a prophetic contrast with Jesus's later virgin birth, where no husband is involved. But Jewish exegetes have instead noted how the emphasis here is placed on creative physicality. Hirsch (1989: 1.321) explains that the expression dealing with seed using the verb *zara* appears elsewhere in Gen. 1:11 in reference to the plants when first created by God. In this light, we are to relate human conception and birth to the same process—God's creation from lifeless matter—that upholds the existence of trees and plants. *Rabbah* 14.2, from a different angle, dwells upon the miracle of the woman's receipt of the man's semen—but a "drop"—through which God allows the fetus to come into being and to form. It is a process, however, that is no different than that given to the animals. And just as the creation of human beings in Eden only follows the order of the other animals, so too does the human fetus in the mother's womb grow into a distinct being by passing through the forms of other animals, beginning with the appearance even of the locust! The sowing of the seed in this verse, then, is meant to make a generalized statement about what it means to be a creature, not to explicate (at this point) some aspect of the sexual act. Rather, it emphasizes the humiliating factor by which we are to understand the common character of human creation—common, that is, to all things that come from the sovereign and gracious hand of God.

But this commonality of origin does not entail some uniform substratum of character. As scholars have noticed, there is a tendency in rabbinic interpretation of Lev. 12 to drift into an encyclopedic enumeration of physiological theories regarding conception and gestation. But the focus in these seeming naturalistic (if often fantastical) digressions is more fundamentally about the character of differentiation itself that defines human existence as a divine creation, and the questions it poses are therefore a *necessary* aspect to the reading of the text. When and how does the seed become a human being rather than the strange being that looks, as a fetus, so much like other beasts? When does sexual differentiation take place? The *Rabbah* considers the starting point of conception—indeed of the human race itself in Eden—as a kind of amorphous mass: "When the Holy One, blessed be he, created the first human being, he made him an unformed mass, and he spread it from one end of the world to the other" (14.1). Why the vast extent of this mass? To demonstrate that the human creature is nothing until it is *formed* into particularity. It is only this that it has in common with the beasts, that it is *distinct* as created by the will and hand of God. Likewise, as Lev. 12 underlines with its particular rituals of purification, sexual differentiation itself arises from this creative distinction. There was, for instance, wide-ranging exegetical speculation regarding the interaction of the mother's blood and the father's semen as the causative factor in sexual difference (Nahmanides 1974: 157). But these attempts to uncover the mechanisms of human sexual differentiation were driven, not simply by an uninformed human curiosity so much as by the conviction that such sexual difference represented the obvious creative source upholding human reality at its base.

This becomes the central theological claim of Lev. 12, in its interpretive weight: the key to gestation and distinction is God's act. Nahmanides (1974: 157) will speak of the "three partners" to human conception—the blood (from the woman) provides skin, flesh, blood, hair, and eyes to the fetus; the semen (from the man) provides sinews, bones, and whites of the eye; and God himself gives mind, soul, and spirit. But this last miracle is primary, from which the other partners gain any force of their own in any case. This miraculous act is judged to be an expression of God's righteousness in its most substantive sense (Job 36:3), and the *Rabbah* describes its demonstration in many forms, from the "little white drop [of semen] in private" that the Lord turns into "whole and beautiful souls in public," to the hiddenness of the fetus gifted with light, to its "upside down" survival in the womb, to the wonderful providence of the noble breasts that give milk for sustenance, gloriously transforming the woman's blood into a source of food. "Is this not an example of 'life and steadfast love' [Job 10:12]?" (14.3). God's righteousness is demonstrated in the creation precisely *through* the distinctions of male and female, which constitute for human beings the distinctions of a new creature.

In rabbinic exegesis of Lev. 12 (and in talmudic discussions of conception) one of the central interpretive texts applied to the task of explication is Ps. 139. This is not surprising in that the psalm speaks intently of the "wonder" of human gestation (139:13–16). In contemporary discussions, these verses are often deployed in arguments over abortion, particularly to point out the divine hand in the actual formation of the fetus from its "unformed substance." Curiously, however, the traditional applications of the psalm to Lev. 12 avoid this ethical question and are usually aimed at the broader issue of created distinction itself: how long from conception, for instance, does it take for a fetus to become a human? Forty days, according to the tradition (Hirsch 1989: 1.322), because it is only then that it is possible to discern distinct features that differentiate a human from either another beast or the unformed substance with which God begins his work. (The features in question include the forehead, eyebrows, eyes, cheeks, and chin, according to the Babylonian Talmud, tractate *Niddah* 23b.) This applies even to a fetus that is otherwise malformed or miscarried. Yet the basis for this judgment is not some abstract definition of the human as a quality or ideal; rather it is the visible and distinguishing marks of matter molded in a certain way by God that make something a human being.

God's righteous distinguishing and creating, just because it is located here in Lev. 12 with respect to the reality of conception and childbirth, is thereby located within a history of divine relationships in time. As with so much of the fundamental orientation of Leviticus, this turns us back to Cain, the first man who is conceived and born through a mother's womb (Gen. 4:1). This first mother, Eve, is already told in Gen. 3:16 that her "pain in childbearing" will be multiplied. Now comes the fulfillment of this word of God that marks the end of Eden's home. Yet the first child's name, Cain, indicates, not a curse, but the way in which conception and birth are a gift received from God. And the story of Cain that unfolds from this primordial human birth moves, as it were, from blood to blood: from the word in Gen. 3, fraught with the reality of childbirth's wounding, to Abel's murder and the blood that cries to God "from the ground" (4:10). Blood is traditionally tied to woman, as we saw above, and thus to the consequence of exile from paradise. But blood is also tied to life within the history of God's gracious dealing with humanity as a race that exists through the gift of procreation. And therefore blood is tied to the reality of a people who exist in time and whose relationship with God exists in time; that is, blood is tied to a vocation. Blood, in a sense, *is* history—blood given for the continuance of life, blood shed for its ending, blood shared (as becomes clear in Christ especially) for life's reconciling fulfillment (see the commentary on Lev. 17). Any discussion of the meaning of blood in Leviticus and in its cultic apparatus—both so central, but also so masked in obscurity—must reflect upon this fundamental revelation of blood given in the extraparadisiacal birth of Cain and in his fratricide, for blood reflects the divine grace of temporality that is also formed by the reality of human choice and life with God. And from the perspective of Gen. 3:14–19, the distinction of human sexuality is given in terms of life extended (woman and childbirth) and life endured (man and toil). If we were to extract, at this point of the discussion, a provisional conclusion, it would be that sexual distinction is bound to the historical vocation of the human race in God's eyes and hands.

But why the impurity associated with childbirth? As it is, the exact nature of the uncleanness associated with childbirth is not explained either in Leviticus or elsewhere in the Scriptures. But it is clearly tied to the blood that the woman both utilizes but more importantly expels in the course of giving birth. And it will require, furthermore, not only purification but an atonement (12:7) that completes this making clean. It is the ambivalence of the blood's historical character and signaling capacity that seems to be at work here, as explained above. Blood is both set *within* the distinctions of the world—woman as different from man, blood as different from semen, childbirth as different from toil—and is itself one of the distinguishers of the world, being an instrument of fetal differentiation, of nurturance, and of death. The blood marks, through this historical coming-to-be and carrying-on, existence itself with God through his creative grace. And thus the blood contains in its passage into and through the world the whole history of freedom, choice, sin, oppression, forgiveness, suffering of sin's outcome, and some kind of redemption through all this. The woman's childbirth *is* all of this at once and hence gives rise to and embodies the fullness of this history. It is not so much that history needs to be cleansed. Rather, history is itself the work of cleansing what is unclean, even as what is clean is being made impure. If history is changed in Christ, somehow, it is *this* character of history that is transformed. But whatever transformation there may be, it will be one that brings into light, not some new direction of divine will, but the nature of that will itself, which is one of exercising love in the face of the creature's distanced helplessness.

But this history is therefore rightly understood as bound up to the very nature of sexual differentiation, not as a gnostic element of the fall, but as the stuff with which God works in time. I have mentioned already how Ps. 139 proved a key explanatory text, in Jewish interpretation, for Lev. 12. More important even than its discussion of God's mysterious fashioning of the human creature within the womb, however, is the psalm's claim in 139:5 that God ("thou") "dost beset me behind and before." This is an odd focus, taken up in *Rabbah* 14.1 and in the Babylonian Talmud (tractate *Berakhot* 61a), among other places. Of interest here to the commentators is the sense of there being two faces, turning to the front and turning backward toward God. What are these faces? Are they not a reference to the male and female realities that constitute the human race? Some rabbis entertained the possibility that the human creature was originally an androgyne, both male and female together, and that this original androgynous Adam was separated into distinct sexual beings only at a secondary stage of divine creation. In general, however, this mythological view was rejected, and instead "before" and "behind" were understood, not Janus-like of a single creature, but chronologically, male first, female after, both of which encompass the fullness of human history, literally understood in terms of creation and consummation (*Rabbah* 14.1). Differentiation is at the root of temporality and hence also of relationships of sequence and spatial divide.

Philosopher Emmanuel Levinas provides an extended talmudic exposition on just this topic and rightly reflects on the way in which the "before" and "behind" of sexual difference represents the most profound element of human history as an encounter with otherness and difference, an encounter that *constitutes* createdness under God (1990: 160–77). This is more than the deployment of postmodern categories (that he himself helped to invent) to biblical texts, for Levinas draws the conclusion, utterly antithetical to postmodern sexual ethics, that human createdness, precisely because it is a particular expression of the distinction that underlies all creation as created, must therefore have lodged within its sexual differentiations the historical reality of inequality. Inequality here designates a difference in time and time's experience and embodiments—the facing of the chasm between beings that is confronted only bit by bit—not a difference in value (something that rabbinic teaching generally rejected).[3] The challenge to our self-understandings is great on this score. Certainly, there is nothing about love, the love between a woman and man, let alone the love between any creature or the love between a creature and God—there is nothing in this love that implies equality as some intrinsic evaluation of the actors themselves. Just the opposite. While the chasm of created otherness may well relativize the final judgment upon differences, it cannot do anything but leave these differences standing in their temporal givenness and incommensurability. It is the nature of love that it be exposed to and embrace this incommensurability of creatures.

Thus Eph. 5:21 speaks of a call to "subject[ion] to one another," not as an expression of creaturely equivalence, but as a form of embraced and spiraling inequalities, wherein what we are is constantly given up in the face of what we are not. Furthermore, this call to mutual subjection is made "out of reverence for Christ," that is, in subjection to the one who initiates most sweepingly the embrace of inequality itself as a divine action: "Christ Jesus, who, though he was in the form of God, did not count equality with God a thing to be grasped, but emptied himself, taking the form of a slave, being born in the likeness of men" (Phil. 2:5–7 Revised Standard Version margin). Being born in the world is an aspect of sexual difference, and this difference binds us to a realm of experienced inequalities.

In Jesus's case, his maleness "turns about face" and thereby shows the face of God as coming "from behind" in a new way. And Mary's choice of sacrificial victim, the two turtledoves or young pigeons (Lev. 12:8; Luke 2:24), bespeaks the engagement of a concrete inequality of indigence that is bound to this network of differences. As Origen, Augustine, and the entire Catholic tradition understood, this offering of the poor by Mary established Jesus himself as a creature taking his place among creatures, one whose commonness lay in the difference, in this case of material poverty, that he assumed. It is *not* the case that Jesus "is like all other men" from a historical perspective. His life is marked by difference and inequality. So too, when the church has read the offered turtledoves as the "cries" and "lamentations" of the church on earth (Rupert of Deutz [Patrologia latina 167.802–3]) we are to see this as the expression of the creaturely limits and differences within ecclesial existence

3. The equal standing of women and men before God was a commonplace in rabbinic teaching, one that often explicitly denounced the unjust ways in which human beings oppressed others, including men oppressing women. *Sifre Numbers* 133.49b revealingly speaks of equality in terms of divine compassion, not social function: "The compassion of God is not as the compassion of men. The compassion of men extends to men more than to women, but not thus is the compassion of God; His compassion extends equally to men and women and to all, even as it is said, 'The Lord is good to all, and His mercies are over all his works' (Ps. cxlv,9)" (quoted in Montefiore and Loewe 1960: 510).

itself—the cries are what alone can cross the chasm of creation that exists in time. This is made explicit in Paul's discussion of mutual subjection in Eph. 5 when he provides as the epitome of such existence the relationship between husband and wife, given in a mortal self-offering on behalf of the other, one that itself is embodied in Christ's love for the church and his giving "himself up for her" (5:25). The church is not the place of equals, of sameness, but of the relentless giving over of the self to that difference that draws life out of death.

Elizabeth Barrett Browning, in her *Sonnets from the Portuguese* no. 3, detailed the history of her love for her husband:

> Unlike are we, unlike, O princely Heart!
> Unlike our uses and our destinies.
> Our ministering two angels look surprise
> On one another, as they strike athwart
> Their wings in passing. . . .
> And Death must dig the level where these agree.

Here we begin to see why discussions of sexuality—including homosexuality—that rely on an abstracted understanding of otherness and on generalized virtues of other-relatedness cannot make sense in the Levitical context of the Christian faith, for it is the *particularized*—and hence *unequal*—distinctions of historical existence that determine createdness. And for human beings, these are enmeshed in the outplaying of sexual differentiation and its historical struggles, most profoundly given in the agonies of childbirth, childrearing, and growth and the concomitant realities of disappointment, self-expenditure, loss, and death. These are not matters that can be historically extricated one from another, but rather are the fibers of human history itself. The incarnation cannot, by definition, possibly transcend this reality in any essential fashion.

The conviction that sin is a part of childbirth seems to arise, therefore, because childbirth is the vessel of human temporality and history. Both Jewish (*Sifra* 122 as well as *Rabbah* 14.5 and beyond) and Christian interpreters (Origen, *Homilies on Leviticus* 8.3; *Glossa ordinaria* [Patrologia latina 113.331–32]; and subsequent Catholic and Protestant exegetes) insisted on this root connection between coming into the world, living in it, dying, and intrinsic sin, pointing to, for example, Ps. 51 and Job 14, with their insistence on the uncleanness of transitory life. At the same time, especially Jewish readers understood that redemption is also bound up in the whole unfolding of childbirth as it is extended in time—and in this sense, the atonement sacrifice for the newly delivered mother is not so much a correction of some corrupted natural process as it is an occasion for establishing, in the heart of the mother herself and her community, a more accurate assessment of that process's character.

Nahmanides (1974: 163–64), for instance, suggests that the mother must atone for the cursing that she does at the time of her travail, when she demands in the midst of her pain that God grant her an end to more sex and more children. By her offering of atonement, she is then reopened to the grace that is also essential to childbirth. And the whole of the natural process is a kind of dragging of history—of Eve's curse and God's mercy—into the present, conjoining in an apprehended fashion the consequences of human sin with the righteousness of God's gracious miracle of created life. It is crucial to see that Jesus is born into *this*, completely and not partially. He too comes into the world through blood and weeping and leaves it, for a time at least though quite fully, as a cadaver. But now, because it is God's own bearing of creation's chasm, with a completeness that comprehends all things, blood and weeping reach out, even in time, toward resolution.

Travail—the pains of childbirth—thereby becomes the great sign of God's redemption. Beginning as a curse, to be sure, from the time of Eve (Gen. 3:16), travail continued to be seen in this negative light, though increasingly (as with Jeremiah) as the figure of existence's burden in the face of human sin and divine judgment (Jer. 4:31; 13:21; 22:23; 30:6; 49:24; 50:43; but also Isa. 13:8; 21:3; 26:17–18; 42:14). But precisely because the judgment here is God's and not that of some blind fate, the character of this painful act is bound to the original creative blessing from whose deformation it proceeds. Jesus points to this when he appropriates the image of travail at childbirth as a figure of his own mission and ministry as it is finally shared with the disciples. In doing so, he underlines the final joy of creation that emerges from the agony of the birth as the mother takes delight in what God has given her (this is one of the "miracles of God's righteousness," mentioned by *Rabbah* 14.4—that a "nauseating" mess such as childbirth should be transformed into an immediate object of tender affection): "When a woman is in travail she has sorrow, because her hour has come; but when she is delivered of the child, she no longer remembers the anguish, for joy that a child is born into the world" (John 16:21). The hour of travail here is, of course, the hour of Jesus own sacrifice upon the cross (12:23, 27; 17:1). The mother's travail *is* in fact the figure of salvation, as Jesus's flesh assumes it in Mary as the actual hinge of human history, the "fulness of time" (Gal. 4:4 Authorized Version): this is the "great portent" itself that "appear[s] in heaven, a woman clothed with the sun, with the moon under her feet, and on her head a crown of twelve stars; she was with child and she cried out in her pangs of birth, in anguish for delivery," and the church carries this portent as its own figure upon earth (Rev. 12:1–2). First Tim. 2:15 points to the broader reality of Jesus and the curse itself, as the cross is revealed truly to be that which gathers to it the death that lurks in life and fulfills the life that is planted in death.

Mary is not immune to this history, as she fulfills the prescribed Levitical offerings at Jesus's birth. Rather, she is immersed in it, and Anna's prophecy in Luke 2:35—"a sword will pierce through your own soul also"—is less a prediction aimed specifically at the cross than it is an acknowledgement of the history of all mothers that, in fact, the cross will take into its arms. The Catholic subtraction of Mary from blood—wrongly, despite her virginity—has tended to obscure this reality and has thereby opened the door to sentimental versions of motherhood and childhood that ill serve a proper understanding of human existence. Mary, instead, properly[4] forms the closing figural end piece to Aaron's beginning, wherein both lose their children as each states, through their extended travail demonstrated in the sacrificial rite, the character of historical existence—the drifting away of love in time, whose only receipt might be God's. Aaron and Mary, in this way, also mark the historical life of the church itself, who is "in travail until Christ is formed" within its own children (Gal. 4:19).

The concern with sexual distinction lodged within human history that marks Lev. 12 is revelatory of the character of human life at its root. But just how? We know that Jesus will contrast the sexually differentiated form of human life in this world, at least as it founds the reality of marriage, with the world after the resurrection, when human beings "neither marry nor are given in marriage, but are like angels in heaven" (Mark 12:25). Is this not linked to Paul's assertion that "in Christ Jesus" "there is neither male nor female" (Gal. 3:28)? Is not the redeemed nature of the human person somehow beyond sexual difference and all that it implies? And so the salvation given in the cross, in the assumption of travail by God for the sake of a fulfilled love, must do away, not only with the impurities of blood, but with the differences of male and female histories of purification (as they are outlined in Lev. 12).

Yet we remember how, by and large, the notion of the original androgyne as the first Adam was rejected by the tradition in favor of an original distinction. In this light, if there is a complementarity of the sexes, it is not akin to the Platonic image from the *Symposium* of a quest for some primordial sexual oneness that then drives the temporal search for love. The angels, to whom Jesus compares risen human beings, are after all themselves distinct—they have individual names and are distinguished morally by their actions, proclivities, and functions. It cannot be distinction itself that is removed in human redemption; rather such distinction is part of what is redeemed. How so? Freed from temporal conditions, in this crucial case, distinction is no longer bound to blood: there is no blood in the garden, nor is there any blood within the kingdom of God, except the blood of Christ who still stands enthroned as a Lamb, "standing, as though it had been slain" (Rev. 5:6). The "blood of Christ" brings Jew and Gentile together, breaking down the "dividing wall" (Eph. 2:13–14). This is a way of expressing that history, including male and female in their distinction, becomes entirely the possession

4. The otherwise sober-visioned von Balthasar uncharacteristically scolds the seventeenth-century French school for its "harsh, almost somber, picture of the nature of childhood," in favor of the pacific Thérèse of Lisieux. But this is because there is no wonder experienced at the "nauseating" character of childbirth itself—in, e.g., rabbinic terms—in its wider reality, having been immaculately banished from Christ's coming by the prior fencing in of his mother's physicality. On the other hand, von Balthasar is readily willing to transfer some of the suffered reality of motherhood—now seen in terms of widowhood—onto the church as Mary's figure, enveloped by the pains of childbirth (1968: 249–58, 310).

of Jesus. Yet male and female—as do all distinct peoples and nations—maintain their particularity even as his possession. And as temporal sexual beings, that particularity is given in blood, the blood that gives birth within travail, that extends life, and that bears the agony of assaulted love.

All else, as the rabbis noted, would be but an amorphous mass. The indivisibility of the human person is one that is forged from the alien seed that has joined itself to an ovum, a father and mother—neither two fathers nor two mothers. Sexual particularity within history, then, remains tied to marriage and procreation from which the individual arises and not to some abstract set of virtues such as mutuality or even fidelity in which individuals participate.[5] Love in time is always bloody. Moses is a "bloody husband" (via circumcision), as his wife designates him in Exod. 4:24–26, a strange story in which bloody love is bound up with perseverance in a divine vocation. The Christian ascetic vision that has sought to live "like the angels" even now—that has, in a sense, sought to escape history—has paradoxically contributed to the modern desexualization of life. Within this desexualized realm, sexual passion has reasserted itself, unmoored in the blood that marks our sexual beings; it has reverted to a kind of precreative amorphous polyvalence of free-floating sexual indulgence. This observation bears upon the later discussions in Leviticus of sexuality and sexual behavior (e.g., in Lev. 18).

Jesus is born into this. It is not clear that he needed to be male rather than female according to some discernable logic of incarnation. But he must be one or

5. Defining sexual differentiation in terms of complementarity is an assertion with a long history from Plato on and is often reiterated today in Roman Catholic documents, most famously by John Paul II in his "Catechesis on the Book of Genesis: Original Unity of Man and Women" (1997: 43–57). Clearly the account of the creation of the woman in Gen. 2 indicates something of this. But can this story be definitive of human sexuality, for one of the key texts on the nuptial difference in sexual identity, Eph. 5:21–33, has nothing to do with male and female complementarity? Rather, the distinction is based, by analogy, on the distinction between Christ and his church and, in this sense, between God and his creature. This has nothing to do with two partial natures that, once joined together, make up something fuller, perhaps even more whole. The entire passage, which speaks piercingly about true love, is about the suffering of and through difference, and the suitability of the two parties' natures is in fact contradictory to the meaning of Paul's teaching. The difference between Christ and the church, the husband and the wife, is intractable; and that is why the love that joins one body to the other in procreative power is the cross. (It is also why homoerotic partnerships are simply not comprehended within this vision.) To be sure, Christ loves the church as "his own body," a body that, in his incarnation, he has taken to himself. Yet this taking of a body by God is precisely what is at stake in the Levitical claim to the sacrifice of differentiation: Jesus does not find his "missing self" in being born in human flesh. Rather, as God, he dies for the ungodly (Rom. 5:6). And the difference between a man and a woman does not lie in a range of feelings or attitudes that, if collected, would somehow gather the whole of human emotional life. Indeed, the difference is unfathomable, it is a *differentia ignota*, as unknown one to the other (by analogy) as is God by the creature. Men and women are made one by sheer grace, though it be a grace lodged within the nature of human purpose. This is why the differentiation itself is given, not in the articulation of diverse sexual essences, but simply by the acts that each performs one to the other, epitomized in the procreative context. Hence, the proper Levitical method of speaking about sexuality is the law, not a treatise on the nature of subjective impulse and satisfaction.

the other. He cannot be both, and he can relate to the other only in terms of who he is and was formed as being. The male-female distinction, as we have seen, is a *created* distinction and does not represent as symbol some further set of eternal essences. Born a male, this is who Jesus is, no more and no less. And this is how he loves, bound by the shapes of his body and the character of his distinction. As the progeny of Mary's travail, his distinction as a male, differentiated from his mother's blood, provides an indicative breadth to the character of human history that God takes as his own. Hence, his birth as Messiah is one accompanied by birth pangs and maternal tribulations; and his reign as king is one in which such suffering is joined (Col. 1:24–26). To his maleness attaches the circumcision (Lev. 12:3) that, along with childbirth, provides the distinction that fuels human creation and its history in the world. Circumcision is the occasion for the shedding of male blood, not in the extension of life according to God, as with woman, but in the subjection of a rebellious life to God, a sign of Adam's endurance in toil under God's direction. Hirsch (1989: 1.325–27) speaks of this male subjection, along with its shorter period of purification for the mother and in contrast to the longer and extended bloodletting and purification associated with the female child, as simply two sexually distinct ways of formation, religious at root, that are pursued in time. Whether one wishes to follow this out in a speculative psychology is doubtful. Nonetheless, we must emphasize that circumcision itself is about distinction: male from female, Israel from nations, law from nature.

The chasm of creation denotes these distinctions, and the fleshly circumcision represents the place of human life, as creature, within this realm. The figural extension of this distinction into the realm of redemption, of the creation gathered up fully in God, is something both Jews and Christians together perceived, although with varying understandings of how this impinged upon physical existence. "Circumcision" of the heart or of the lips or of the ears, in any case, became a standard image (Exod. 6:12; Deut. 10:16; 30:6; Jer. 4:4; 6:10; 9:26; 32:39; Ezek. 11:19; 36:26) and was included as a traditional Christian trope (Rom. 2:29; Col. 2:11). Here the reality of creaturely distinction by subjection to God is made prominent for both male and female together. But for the Christian church, this distinction was now drawn in an exclusive fashion as being bound to the person of Jesus himself. The "circumcision of Christ"—"made without hands" (Col. 2:11)—becomes definitive. Is this "circumcision of Christ" located somehow in Lev. 12 and its Lukan fulfillment?

The key to answering this question lies in the connection between circumcision and blood that is so central to Lev. 12 as a whole. The definition of maleness in Judaism came to rest in the possibility of deriving several drops of blood from the assumed sexual organ of the infant through the ritual itself.[6] If this was not possible, then the child could not be considered a male. This standard was ap-

6. *Sifra* 123.1 on Lev. 12:3 speaks of a single drop of blood as defining the act of circumcision in doubtful cases.

plied very practically in cases of hermaphroditism (as opposed to those without sexual organs at all, the *tumtum*), proselytes, and, by conjunction, to questions of fetal viability (Babylonian Talmud, tractate *Shabbat* 134b–35a). The issue here has to do with the distinctions necessary to a creaturely body, which were tied to an identifiable sexual organ from which blood could be taken through cutting. Jesus is circumcised in this fashion, thereby binding him to human history as a creature, a subjected creature furthermore, who lives with God in a relationship of obedience "in the flesh" (Gen. 17:10, 14; Phil. 2:7–8).

It is from this single subjection of God to the inequality of creaturehood that all creaturely redemption flows. No longer does the sexual organ in and of itself act as the focus of loving distinction, but the flesh as a whole, yet still bloodied as it were: Paul will dispense with circumcision—"for neither circumcision counts for anything, nor uncircumcision, but a new creation" (Gal. 6:15)—but he does not, thereby, reject the bloodiness of love that circumcision embodies. Now— as both male and female—the Christian is gathered into the whole of Christ's circumcised body, which is filled out upon the cross for all human beings and for all creatures: "Henceforth let no man trouble me; for I bear on my body the marks of Jesus" (6:17). What are these marks—literally *stigmata*—except the final and perfected distinction that God bears in the flesh that is his own? This circumcision is the eighth day's (Lev. 12:3) in its issuance in a new creation, a new flesh given in the resurrection (1 Cor. 15:42–50) that proceeds from the love that gives up life (15:36).

It is still flesh, still blood, that Jesus draws Paul into, and with him the whole church. But now this flesh is oriented to the redemption of creation itself. If we are to speak theologically of the kenosis of the Son of God, it is not toward questions of internal consciousness that we must turn, as was the case with English theologians like Charles Gore, who pressed the kenotic theory as a means, in part, of navigating cultural differences especially in the reading of the Bible. Rather, it is to the fullness of blood, of creation's chasm itself, that divine kenosis is bound. Jesus carries humanity into himself: formed first in the sense of being the first patient of distinction (the Adam of 1 Tim 2:14), bound to a woman (Gal. 4), like Cain, as the product of fall and grace, covered in blood at his birth, subjected in blood to God at his circumcision, he dies in the shedding of his blood, taking upon him the endurance of Adam and the travail of Eve both. "My little children," Jesus calls his disciples (Mark 10:24; John 13:33). As a sexualized being, whose very flesh becomes wholly that distinction that sexuality embodies—the "bloody marks"—he becomes father and mother to all, even the "scattered" "children of God" (John 11:52). But there is no gnostic escape in this from sexual distinction. There is, instead, the embrace and offering of such distinctions, for the sake of the world's whole-ness, to God in his own distinct body. The grand affirmation of the sacrificial vision in the letter to the Hebrews is founded on this reality: he is "tempted as we are" in "every way" (Heb. 2:18; 4:15). This was Tertullian's conviction, announced with such clarity against Marcion's distaste over Mary's and her child's filthiness and birth:

> Come now, beginning from the nativity itself, declaim against the uncleanness of the generative elements within the womb, the filthy concretion of fluid and blood, of the growth of the flesh for nine months long out of that very mire. Describe the womb as it enlarges from day to day—heavy, troublesome, restless even in sleep, changeful in its feelings of dislike and desire. Inveigh now likewise against the shame itself of a woman in travail, which, however, ought rather to be honoured in consideration of that peril, or to be held sacred in respect of (the mystery of) nature. Of course you are horrified also at the infant, which is shed into life with the embarrassments which accompany it from the womb; you likewise, of course, loathe it even after it is washed, when it is dressed out in its swaddling-clothes, graced with repeated anointing, smiled on with nurse's fawns. This reverend course of nature, you, O Marcion, (are pleased to) spit upon; and yet, in what way were you born? You detest a human being at his birth; then after what fashion do you love anybody?" ("On the Flesh of Christ" 4 [trans. Holmes])

Tertullian's lens here is love; and it is a love fastened to a more basic divine attitude that has been ever at work in God's turning toward creation's nature as distinct yet powerless, as bloody, yet requiring blood. Ezekiel's description of God's love for Israel, although focused here on the infant rather than the mother, nonetheless matches the substance implied by Tertullian's details: "And as for your birth, on the day you were born your navel string was not cut, nor were you washed with water to cleanse you, nor rubbed with salt, nor swathed with bands. No eye pitied you, to do any of these things to you out of compassion for you; but you were cast out on the open field, for you were abhorred, on the day that you were born. And when I passed by you, and saw you weltering in your blood, I said to you in your blood, 'Live, and grow up like a plant of the field'" (Ezek. 16:4–7). Here, the motherless child is left in her own blood, and God saves her (a girl child, as seen in 16:7), to watch her grow into a young maiden, now menstruating (16:9), whom God marries. The whole range of bloody life, bound to the woman's being, is reached out to and drawn close by God.

The centrality of Lev. 12 to Christian theology in its enunciation of the incarnation is obvious. Further, the force of this Levitically informed Christian message to a modern culture confused by bodily distinctions and creaturely subjections is enormous. In fact, from the perspective of both realities, much of the legal and ethical implications of this book find a crystallizing focus in this discussion of childbirth. It is not, however, exhaustive in its explication of human history's divine purpose. That is why it is located only within a larger discussion of illness, desire, and sacrifice.

LEVITICUS 13–14

Immediately following the discussion of childbirth and human sexual distinction, the focus of Leviticus shifts to disease, and not any disease, but the disease of the flesh and skin. This shift represents a turn from the character of human relations in time to the appearance of such relations' dissolution. Skin disease, more than anything else, displays to the eye the falling away of visible difference and the alienation of touch, and Lev. 13–14 thereby becomes a meditation upon the historical reality of the human creature's demise—sin's work—and upon God's response.

Physical disease is, of course, something that has a direct bearing upon daily life quite apart from its ritual or theological implications. Not surprisingly, then, Jewish exegesis, even after the destruction of the temple made the sacrificial "remedies" for the disease no longer accessible, maintained a strong concern with the descriptive details of the ailments under consideration, especially in Lev. 13. *Sifra* 127–47's long and involved treatment of this text seeks to analyze the quantitative meanings of the size and coloration of the leprous diseases described here. To this degree, exegesis is aimed still and very vividly at actual diagnosis. A question arises, therefore, as to why Christian interpreters paid so little attention to the medical aspects of these chapters. The movement directly to symbolic exegesis occurs, it seems, from the start of Christian reading. Were Christians unconcerned with the medical realities of leprosy? Certainly not, as the robust medieval response to leprosy (generally admitted as such today, along with other possible diseases) well attests.[1] But, given the lack of authoritative priestly structure outlined in the scriptural record, diagnosis among Christians was far more diffused even among

1. For a helpful overview (despite political tendentiousness), including references, see Moore 1987: 45–65. For a historical overview of the disease, including medieval Europe, see the opening sections of Steger and Barrett 1994: 319–54. For leprosy placed in a historical context of diagnosis and treatment, see Cohn 1989.

untutored laity and followed patterns of local direction as much as common tradition. This robbed Lev. 13 of medical leverage in Christian circles and left the identification and treatment of skin disease to other developing strategies.

In some ways, this was understandable, for more than any other text in the Bible, these chapters describe the concrete minutiae of the human body itself and in ways that are almost overwhelming and confusing in their detail. We need, therefore, to begin our discussion of Lev. 13–14 with a survey of how the text has been applied within the exegetical tradition for one main reason: the varying and ultimately restrictive ways in which these chapters have been approached represent the actual topic of their discussion, that is, the turning away from disease and its divine message and the demand to engage disease through the act of divine grace given in the body of Christ. Only by squarely facing this reality can we enter into the disease's precincts in a way that allows our passage through them. There are moments when the history of interpretation is an act that unveils Scripture's authoritative address to us, allowing it to make itself felt, to touch and to speak, and this is one such moment. The "corruption of the flesh," as these chapters describe it, is an encounter in time from which we have been running for centuries, and to permit that encounter anew we must see how the way is blocked. Or, to put it another way, leprosy is a disease with a history in which we are involved and that describes us.

Calvin was among the first to raise questions openly about the particular pathological referents of the text (1996: 2.13–16). His open disdain for specific allegorical and figural exegesis at this juncture, in addition to expressing a general skepticism he had about such methods, derived in this case mainly from his sense that there was great obscurity with respect to the exact nature of the symptoms and diseases that Leviticus might be attempting to describe. On this score, Calvin may well have represented the end to a long Christian development that, frankly, simply found the Levitical texts too murky to offer clear medical direction—a sentiment that had long freed the text for Christian spiritual exegesis with a vengeance.

Calvin, in any case, took the first explicit step in the modernist passage that ended by voiding these chapters of any specific theological substance, largely through the blurring of physical distinction. Having rejected figural exegesis from the start, he advanced a general historical theory about disease that rendered the text experientially inaccessible to contemporary readers: diseases, he noted, change over time and according to place, and the diseases mentioned in Lev. 13–14 are obviously those of another era. After all, what do we today know about houses struck with leprosy (as in 14:33–42)? Calvin is not doubting the reality of such domestic pathogens, only considering them beyond our ken. Willet (1631: 329) follows Calvin on this score, pointing out how each age has its own plague, such as, in his day, "the French disease" (syphilis). And just as Calvin was left to fall back on the broad moral allegories that were alone left him—Israel and the Christian by extension are here taught the value of a pure and chaste life in the service of God—so Willet presses this a little more particularistically: is not disease in general caused, in some quasiscientific mechanism, by evil living? The French disease is, after all, rather pointedly linked to sexual promiscuity ("venery," in Willet's term); but so too is dropsy caused by drunkenness, and so on. The road to the disappearance of Leviticus in the mishmash of pseudoscience and moralism is already well marked.

As it turns out, modern (and often quite pious) medical research agrees with Calvin's historical relativism regarding the disease in question. Based not only on the specific dermatological descriptors of Leviticus, but also on a range of paleopathological research, the current consensus is that what has been commonly translated "leprosy" in the Levitical texts (and perhaps the New Testament as well) is by no means the same as Hansen's disease (after nineteenth-century Norwegian scientist Gerhard Armauer Hansen, who first identified the causative bacillus). Only the latter is properly associated not only with at least some of the leprosy located in the European Middle Ages (subsiding by the early modern period), but with the better known contemporary forms of the disease that were and continue to be found around the world since the nineteenth century. By and large, the most notable feature of modern leprosy is the nerve damage wrought by the disease in the extremities, causing a loss of sensation that usually proves devastating to victims; yet this salient and destructive feature is not mentioned in scriptural discussions of leprosy. Furthermore, the specific symptoms carefully enumerated in Leviticus do not well correspond, in any coherent way, with Hansen's disease and match, more adequately, a range of other ailments with dermatological indications: eczema, psoriasis, ringworm, and syphilis itself (which may not in fact be the New World disease long assumed; see Spinka 1959 and Cochrane 1963).

Dermatological historians, as well as other researchers in the new field of paleopathology, have raised the possibility that descriptions (both written and visual) of disease from many ancient cultures are bound to religious symbolization. This has been studied most carefully with regard to Mesoamerican cultures, from which a large number of surviving ceramic figurines depict, among other anomalies, a spectrum of skin lesions and deformities. What might be called the "stylized representation" of disease, which articulates not so much clear physiological symptoms as their inscribed religious meaning, becomes an open interpretive question even with respect to Leviticus (Servain-Riviale 1999; Vérut 1973; von Winnig 1987). Hirsch (1989: 1.331) himself was adamant that the diseases described in Lev. 13–14 were and are not known human maladies. This is not because, like Calvin, he assumed some historical epidemiological variation across epochs. Rather, Hirsch argued, it is because the leprosy of Leviticus is a peculiar *divine* affliction that has no natural roots. Noting that, for instance, the actual laws relative to seclusion are hardly systematic and that rabbinic legislation in any case made the waiting periods secondary to more primary religious obligations (e.g., marriage rites), Hirsch insisted that there was no real sense in Leviticus that the disease in question was contagious (nor does the Scripture ever say that it is). The symptoms themselves are not linked to any known disease, furthermore, as even Jewish commentators like great sixteenth-century rabbi, exegete, and physician Obadiah Sforno had concluded. For Hirsh, the linguistic key is given in the Hebrew term *tsaraath*, translated "leprosy" (which in turn comes from the Greek word for "scale, scab"). *Tsaraath* refers, most especially as joined in Leviticus, to the accompanying term for "disease" (*nega*), an affliction literally pressed upon a human body by, in Hirsch's view, the "finger of God." This is a divine disease, whose origins lie outside the natural world and whose purpose is given in response to particular human sins, in this case, the sins that break the bonds of Israel's peoplehood and community. The remedies, especially those associated with seclusion and segregation, are therefore embodied responses to the assault *upon* community made by the individual consequently afflicted by the disease: sin is combated with its own weapons, and the sinner "falls into the hole which he has made" for another (Ps. 7:15). At the same time, the sinner is given over completely to the control of the divine community, being left at the mercy of the priest's evaluative powers, scripturally ordered. Only thus, according to Hirsch, is the human-divine relationship of responsibility reestablished.

Hirsch's interpretation represents the end point of a certain mystical literalism: a historically enacted and experienced affliction whose meaning is completely subsumed in religious realities, and to this degree it attempts to resolve the modernist scientific challenge in a daring historical application of traditional claims. The disease is as particularistically embodied, for Hirsch, as in any modern literalistic account; but its substance is outside natural categories of definition. The standard parsing of the text tended, in fact, to focus on the religious dimension of the illness. From Philo on (*That God Is Unchangeable* 122–30), at least, in both Jewish and Christian circles (with Origen's *Homilies on Leviticus* 8.5–11 as the great exemplar), leprosy was seen as primarily an imprint—whether reflected physiologically in a historical sense—of human sin and divine response. The details of the disease point to the details of sin.[2]

For Origen the main issue in all of this is less the specific category of sin that each type of leprosy embodies as it is that of sin's perdurance in the human person over time—its long-lasting marks and influences.[3] The locating of sin and its

2. Origen uses this section of Leviticus—one of his most extended within his extant homilies on the book (*Homilies on Leviticus* 8.5–11)—to outline the fundamental body/soul distinction and relationship that exists as a reflection of the basic scriptural typology of "shadow reality" mentioned in Heb. 10:1. Six types of leprosy are described in Lev. 13, he explains, and each of these is a type for a particular form or effect of sin, to which are attached specific kinds of remedies and purifying acts: ulcers point to inner impure passions that, even when forgiven, return to affect the soul in a hidden manner; sores from burns refer to evil appetites of ambition and anger, whose malevolent fruits linger over time; sores upon the bald head indicate the return of sin to a soul already cleansed; and so on. Protestant exegesis, interestingly, later took up a similar allegorizing of details, using them as a foil to Christ's redeeming sacrifice, which was read as being indicated in the many specifics of the birds, lamb, sheep, etc., in the text.

3. Presumably drawing on the Septuagint's translation of Hebrew *seeth* ("swelling, rising") in 13:2 as "scar" (Greek *oulē* and Latin *cicatrix*, although the word does not appear in the Vulgate),

healing within a long temporal process was noted also by Jewish interpreters as a major element in the Levitical discussion of leprosy (Nahmanides 1974: 198–200). Schneersohn (1986: 184–86) explains that the insistence upon the use of the future tense, beginning in Lev. 13:2 ("he *shall* be brought") and continuing throughout the section, encloses a special meaning: healing is given in a divine promise that works itself out only over time. And, as with Origen, this happens only within the matrix of intricate and developing relationships. Altogether, this focus upon time provided both Origen and later Jewish commentary with a complex, psychological, and especially communal treatment of the text, wherein the symptoms of the disease were approached as lively symbols of a range of human failures and transgressions and where their place within a divine schema of gradual redemption included the breadth of human relationship. Among medieval Christian interpreters, this breadth was given in the bodily referent of the disease, as they saw, as being the church itself.[4]

Taken in themselves, all these interpretive approaches are theological dead ends, straining at maintaining a place for these chapters, but in the end fitting them to prearranged theories of history and typology. By contrast and for all the limitations of his moral-allegory-by-default, Calvin was always intensely aware of the way in which the Old Testament proved a constant judgment upon the church, rather than simply a template by which to identify its enemies. In this case, his sense of leprosy's unspecified referent led him to look for wider meanings. Given his methodological concern with harmonizing Leviticus with the other books of the revealed law, he approached Lev. 13–14 only through, as he put it, the defining moral lens of Deut. 24:8 and Num. 5:2, texts that warned of Israel's own moral defilement. A way was opened here for a more narrative placement of the leprosy texts. By drawing them into engagement with Deuteronomy and Numbers, Calvin sought to hold up Israel—and the church, of course—in a parallelism with the nations whom Israel passes through or defeats: it too will suffer from the plagues visited by God upon the Egyptians and others—and

---

Origen moves from this first dermatological marking to create an elaborate interpretive structure by which each form of leprosy speaks to "remains" of sin's power that demand ongoing spiritual discipline and penitence to overcome (*Homilies on Leviticus* 8.5).

4. Hesychius, with Rabanus Maurus (Patrologia latina 108.371–92) relying on him, develops and passes on a long and influential meditation on the character of the church as a body subject to pathological effects of sin, which in fact envelope the whole of the individual's life in this bodily fashion and point to deep realities of spirit. It is disturbing, however, to see how this description of ecclesial disease applies to the "sins of leprosy" a founding supersessionist paradigm of communal history: the Jews constitute, in a figural way, the "sores" upon the body of the church, transgressing a law they foolishly insisted upon keeping; while the Gentiles represent the purified body made clean through Christ and his gospel. Using Matt. 12:43–45 as a figure of history's course, the "sores" of ecclesial leprosy return again and again (the old "demons" of the Jews having been swept away only to be replaced) in the form of a sequence of heretics and "immoralities." These, like the Jews, require excommunication "outside the camp," just as does the leper of Lev. 13–14. Within this enclosing historical paradigm, the particulars of the text are parceled out to particular doctrinal errors and heretical follies of discipline, all of which are invested with tremendous powers of contagion.

for the same reasons (Deut. 28:27: "The LORD will smite you with the boils of Egypt, and with the ulcers and the scurvy and the itch, of which you cannot be healed"). Leprosy is but the universal image of rebellious humankind, defined here in terms of the church's own gross, yet common, pollution. But humankind, by definition, has a history.

This is, as it turns out, a major concern of rabbinic exegesis as well, beginning with the *Rabbah*, and it is this lead we should now follow, for the disease and its remedy assert themselves despite our attempts at evasion. After all the meanderings into specific symbolizations of symptoms, *Rabbah* 15.9 rightly ends by drawing together the fate of Gentile and Jews alike within the scope of affliction. Having linked, in what was a common trope, each form of leprosy with a different manifestation of Gentile oppression (e.g., Babylon, Media, Persia, Greece), the infected house and its final destruction stone by stone is referred directly to the temple. The scope and progress of the disease leads to the outreaches of exile and abandonment. Paradoxically, while *Sifra* 155.6 (on 14:34) speaks of there being no leprosy within the temple precincts, here the precincts themselves are destroyed, and this proves the very embodiment of the disease's unstoppable voraciousness. Although *Rabbah* 17.7 does not make the explicit connection, its final reckoning of leprosy as Jerusalem's demise recalls the images of Lamentations (e.g., 3:4; 4:8; 5:10), where the "wasting away" of the skin, its "blackening" and shriveling, become the sign of Israel's judgment and repentance both.

But the *Rabbah* has also bound all this, in a more primary way, to the grace of God as the healer and savior of Israel. So it turns to Isa. 57:17–19 in order to explain how leprosy fits into the divine economy: "Because of the iniquity of [Israel's] covetousness I was angry, I smote him, I hid my face and was angry.... I have seen his ways, but I will heal him . . . creating for his mourners the fruit of the lips. Peace, peace, to the far and to the near, says the LORD; and I will heal him" (*Rabbah* 16.9). God alone heals, as Origen (*Homilies on Leviticus* 8.1, 5, 11) and others also insisted in reflecting on the relentlessly religious context of this otherwise thoroughly materialistic and carnal outline. The question then becomes one of finding the promise embedded in the disease, so to speak. That is, how is the telling of a tale that leads ultimately to a whole people's demise, in the grip of an infection over which they have lost control, capable to unveiling God's merciful work? Obviously, the sacrificial and purificatory rituals described in Lev. 14 refer to this divine work, but can they do so in a fashion that goes beyond functional gestures that, in both the posttemple and Christian contexts, are in any case no longer accessible?

In rabbinic interpretation (though not in Christian exegesis), including the *Rabbah*, this grasp of the disease's redemptive figure is achieved mainly through the narrative location of leprosy elsewhere in Scripture, most pertinently, given the dramatic context of Leviticus, within the story of Miriam and Aaron: "Miriam and Aaron spoke against Moses because of the Cushite woman whom he had married; . . . and they said, 'Has the LORD indeed spoken only through Moses? Has he not

spoken through us also?' And the LORD heard it" (Num. 12:1–2). After addressing
the two and asserting his choice to speak indirectly to other prophets but directly
to Moses, the Lord's "anger . . . was kindled against them," and "when the cloud
removed from over the tent, behold, Miriam was leprous, as white as snow. And
Aaron turned towards Miriam, and behold, she was leprous" (12:9–10). Aaron
pleads with his brother, Moses intercedes before God, and Miriam is shut out of
the camp for seven days. After this, she is "brought in again" (12:15), presumably
healed. This story, bound up with the chief players of Leviticus, became the great
exemplar of leprosy's historical meaning (although other scriptural texts were
also cited; see *Sifra* 155.1 on Uzziah in 2 Chr. 26:16–21 and especially *Rabbah*
16.1). And through the lens of Aaron's and Miriam's complaint, as well as through
Moses's prayer, the character of leprosy's divine purpose is explicated.

That character is tied most specifically to human pride as it is expressed in the
spoken word. Aaron and Miriam complain publicly. What do they complain
about? About God's choices and the particularities of his speaking: why to Moses
and not to us? And this complaint is lodged within and against the relationships
that bind together the functioning of the Israelite community in its most basic
way, in this case Moses and his wife, a wife who herself is a racial stranger to the
Hebrew people. Speech, then, becomes the issue of leprosy in the rabbinic tradition, speech that tears apart the social bonds of affection and authority both.
Leprosy is a punishment imposed directly for the sin of gossip, according to *Rabbah* 16.1; and Rashi (Rosenbaum and Silbermann 1932: 57), citing *Sifra* 143 (on
13:46), assumes this as a fundamental given. As Rashi later observes (Rosenbaum
and Silbermann 1932: 60), again referring to *Sifra* 155.8 (on 14:35), the use of
the birds in the remedial sacrifice is a way of linking the sin behind the disease
with the "twittering" of the corresponding victim. Similarly, the use of the hyssop
and cedar points to the power of lowliness (the hyssop) as the remedy for pride
(the cedar), a comparison that became proverbial in later Jewish literature and
that would link leprosy to the salve of humility forever (*Pesiqta Rabbati* 60b in
Montefiore and Loewe 1960: 473).

More deeply, though, the pride lurking behind leprosy is that of rebelling against
divine distinction itself. These chapters, after all, are embedded in the discussion
of distinction that comprehends the character of creation and its purpose. The
other famous scriptural narrative of leprosy, that of Naaman in 2 Kgs. 5, is fiercely
oriented toward these distinctions as they have been divinely ramified in the world
of human and geographical difference: Naaman the Syrian, enemy to Israel, must
go to Israel's prophet for healing, and it is the water of the Jordan alone that proves
the instrument of this healing. Against all this he bristles: "Are not Abana and
Pharpar, the rivers of Damascus, better than all the waters of Israel? Could I not
wash in them, and be clean?" (5:12). The answer is, of course, no, and Naaman
is healed only as he subjects himself to this intractable set of distinctions within
which are lodged God's renewing power. Job's case is more subtle (and his skin
ailments, for all the debates over pathological detail, seem clearly to fall within

the general range of the descriptions of Leviticus), for his own affliction is given him—"satanically" as it were—in order to test the genuineness of the distinctions by which he lives, that is, his righteousness before God. While to some degree his uniqueness as a human creature in comparison with other persons is relativized through his fate, in the end it is the chasm of creation itself that is unveiled in its awesome breadth and that, once acknowledged by Job, finally leads to his healing. Thus, the wisdom of Leviticus resolves itself, in part, at the same place as Solomon's, whose proverbs and songs multiply according to the distinctions of the world: "He spoke of the trees, from the cedar that is in Lebanon to the hyssop that grows out of the wall; he spoke also of beasts and of birds, and of reptiles, and of fish" (1 Kgs. 4:33). The notion that pride would seek to erase these multiple distinctions of creation, laid out specifically in Leviticus itself (the catalogue of Solomon's interests is notable here), coheres with Miriam and Aaron's own verbal assault on Moses's marriage and on the ordering of their service before God in Israel. Their assault is aimed, finally, at the very life of the gathered people of Israel, and, as Hirsch (1989: 1.358) insisted, the consequence of such behavior—the unsociability that is leprosy—is punished by segregation.

But what is the nature of the skin and flesh described in Lev. 13 as truly infected? While rabbinic diagnosticians have sought to quantify the characteristics for the sake of accurate analysis of symptoms, and exegetes have tried to link specific sins with each dermatological aspect of the description, and paleopathologists have attempted to trace these aspects in continuity with known contemporary diseases, Scripture has attached to the leprotic affliction some underlying elements that point in a very different theological direction. In Num. 12:12, Moses pleads with God that he not leave Miriam "as one dead, of whom the flesh is half consumed when he comes out of his mother's womb." It is a strange locution. Again, when Naaman is cured, "his flesh was restored like the flesh of a little child, and he was clean" (2 Kgs. 5:14). The focus here upon an incomplete birth, whose fetal flesh is "half consumed" and stands in contrast to a child's well-ordered flesh, identifies leprosy as a kind of unformed reality, the shadow of an unfinished or even reversed creation.

This sense is reinforced by an examination of diagnostic standard for the different types of leprosy listed in Lev. 13 (and such scrutiny, if often obsessive, is hardly unhelpful): in general, a leprosy is identified when it enters the flesh more deeply than most surface sores and rashes (13:3) and exposes the flesh in its rawness (13:10). This would appear to indicate a kind of running sore or ulcer, in which the flesh can be seen as suffused with blood and other fluids. This understanding of the diagnostic standard is not congruent with the Septuagint, the Vulgate, or even Rashi (Rosenbaum and Silbermann 1932: 51–52) (who, however, apparently here made use of the Old French translations of the Hebrew that were in turn based on the Vulgate), for in these versions, the "raw flesh" of 13:10 is translated "healthy" (hence, in Origen's organizing principle, "healed over," however incompletely; *Homilies on Leviticus* 8.7). Willet (1631: 317) and Reformed exegetes noted the incongruity of this reading, for it would seem to lead to the irrational idea that "healed flesh" is a sign of leprosy. More accurately, "raw flesh," designated by Hebrew *chai*, is living, that is, filled with blood (cf. the "living" beings of Gen. 1:21, 24; 2:7; 9:12, 15, 16; similarly Lev. 11:10, 46; and the sacrificial bird here in 14:6). And the "flesh" (*basar*) in question is the very flesh of Adam (Gen. 2:21), from which, through sexual intercourse of spouses, human life is formed (2:23–24). What is being identified here, therefore, are sores that are, in effect, a "bloody mass" (as *Rabbah* 15.2–3 [cf. 14.8–9] uses the term) that bespeaks the unformed fetus or human discussed in conjunction with Lev. 12 above, immediate to the moment and process of divine creation. In leprosy, the skin is wasted away so as to reveal the matter that stands at the origin of life.

Why is such exposure of the living or raw flesh problematic, so as to render a person unclean? Is it not because it represents a breakdown, somehow, of creative purpose? Leviticus itself does not attach this breakdown to particular sins. Rather, the disease is laid out as a kind of general description of *consequence* that will then be applied elsewhere in the narratives of the Scripture, to Miriam and Aaron paradigmatically, but also in a host of other stories (as listed by *Rabbah* 16.1: Isa. 3:16–17; 1 Kgs. 2:32/2 Sam. 3:29; 2 Kgs. 5; 15:5; Exod. 32:25; Gen. 12:17). In all these cases of sinfulness, what is living loses the direction of its purpose—something that represents, in fact, the nature of sin within time. And to this degree sin marks a turn toward the original chaos now lodged within creation itself, the crumbling of what God's own will has wrought (cf. Jer. 4:23 on the lurch into "formlessness and void" caused by sin versus Gen. 1:2 and Isa. 45:18–19). When Gen. 6 (looking back at Gen. 3) speaks of sin, violence, and social disintegration, the outcome to this steady path of rebellion is self-destruction through the weakening of the flesh: "Then the LORD said, 'My spirit shall not abide in man for ever, for he is flesh'" (6:3). Mortality and death expand their reign within the scope of Adam's skin and bone.

Leprosy marks that "in the midst of life we are in death," as the burial service of the Book of Common Prayer famously expressed it. Its real meaning is, literally, the corruption or decomposition of human life. This is Job's interpretation of his own skin disease, whose sign is "flesh . . . clothed with worms" (Job 7:5), whose presence marks nothing more than the return to the pit of death and nothingness (17:14). When Calvin speaks of the mysterious and unknown illness that destroys even homes and clothing (1996: 2.18), he notes that, although the specifics of "leprosy of the garments" may be obscure, we know well the deep significance of its purpose: for "in fact, [God] has surrounded the human race with rottenness, in order that everywhere our eyes should light on the punishment of sin." "'What shall I cry?' All flesh is grass, and all its beauty is like the flower of the field. The grass withers, the flower fades" (Isa. 40:6). "They will all wear out like a garment" (Ps. 102:26).

Jesus's interaction with lepers was not nearly as frequent (or at least not mentioned) as some imply (Mark 1:40–45 and parallels; Luke 17:11–19). But those few places where mention is made link it with his mission of entering the "strong man's house," as it were, and overcoming the reign of corruption and decomposition. To John the Baptist's question "are you he who is to come?" Jesus answers: "Go and tell John what you hear and see: the blind receive their sight and the lame walk, lepers are cleansed and the deaf hear, and the dead are raised up, and the poor have good news preached to them" (Matt. 11:4). Likewise, the disciples are sent out by Jesus in order to "heal the sick, raise the dead, cleanse lepers, cast out demons" (10:8). It is into this realm of corruption that Jesus walks—"by this time there is an odor, for he has been dead four days" (John 11:39)—takes his stand, and does his work.

The earliest Christian preaching saw this clearly and celebrated it as the great mission of Jesus: he comes to confront the corruption of Job's flesh (Job 17:14) and yet, as God's Holy One, to overcome it. Peter preaches: "For David says concerning him . . . 'For thou wilt not abandon my soul to Hades, nor let thy Holy One see corruption' [Ps. 16:10]. . . . [And thereby] he foresaw and spoke of the resurrection of the Christ, that he was not abandoned to Hades, nor did his flesh see corruption. This Jesus God raised up, and of that we all are witnesses" (Acts 3:25, 27, 31–32). We are witness, Peter attests, to the very hope of Job, that "I know that my Redeemer lives, and at last he will stand upon the earth; and after my skin has been thus destroyed, then from my flesh I shall see God, whom I shall see on my side, and my eyes shall behold, and not another" (Job 19:25–27).

This is the "promise embedded in the disease," that is, that the grace and power of God who has created will also redeem a creation that human beings would destroy and to a real extent have in fact destroyed. Schneersohn (1986: 186) ponders why the Torah reading for Lev. 14 now known as *Metsora* ("the leper") was once called (e.g., by Rashi [Rosenbaum and Silbermann 1932: 60] and others) *Zot Tihyeh* ("this shall be"—from Lev. 14:2: "this shall be the law of the leper"). Is it not because the entire section stands as a *promise*? According to Schneersohn, "only in the time to come will we witness the ultimate transformation of darkness into light," the darkness upon the face of the deep (Gen. 1:2), but "the light of men . . . [that] shines in the darkness, and [that] the darkness has not overcome" (John 1:4–5). We may now, without discomfort, call this section *Metsora* because, according to Schneersohn's messianic alertness, the time to come, the promise, is already upon us and is no longer looked at from a distance: "The light is breaking through the wall that separates us from the 'time to come': the light of the age when 'night will shine as day' [Ps. 139:12]."

But the center of this hope, bound to the healing of God that envelopes this entire passage and that is insisted upon universally by Jew and Christian alike, lies in the paradox of mortality as itself bound up with the grace of creation that comes from the hand of the same God, much as Isaiah proclaimed: because I made you, I will heal you. Mortality and even fleshly corruption, just because it derives its wavering being from the hand of God, is a seed for something else far more glorious (1 Cor. 15:35–41). Within the context and language of Leviticus, cleanness is directive; it moves by and toward this promise and reality of God's creative intentions and nature, while uncleanness (commonness) is a movement away from it, toward disintegration. In Christ, the chasm of creation—the yearning of corrupted and festering mortality swallowed up in childbirth and death (Hos. 13:12–14)—is now shown as altered. Now mortal love, which is a dying, is taken up by God to overcome and swallow the chasm itself (1 Cor. 15:54–55).

Leviticus 12–15 deals with a common theme, therefore, from childbirth to the body's external and internal workings: the precariousness, inherent danger, ultimate finitude, and entrenched temptation to sin that is bound up with being a creature of God. Although some commentators see these chapters as applicable only to Israel, the character of being a creature in this case is suffused within humanity as a whole. *Sifra* 127.2–3 on 13:2–3 tells us that leprosy existed before the Torah and then goes on to ponder how one might make an accurate diagnosis upon the skin of differently pigmented persons like Germans and Ethiopians. Clearly, the flesh of Adam is at issue and not simply of the Jews. And it is this flesh, though aimed at final worm-riddenness, that is taken up by God in Christ—taken up by grace, because given initially, thereby making good the original gift. Leviticus 16 will speak of this "making good" in what will become the paradigmatic sacrifice of the Old Testament. Yet already here, the "taking up" of corrupted flesh is considered through the individual remedies of Lev. 14.

These are given through the richness of God's gifts as a whole within creation, and it is interesting that "the law of the leper" (14:2) contains some of the most diverse and distinct elements of the created order, from water, trees, plants, and birds and other animal victims to the fabricated objects of human culture, like pots, woven cloth, and the communal camp and houses made with human hands. Creation's gift is renewed here, redirected to the distinctions by which their integrity can be gathered in by God. The leper's running sores are sprinkled with the running blood of the live bird, killed over the running water (all of which are qualified by the term for life). Cedar and hyssop, in their strength and lowliness, are brought to bear in this process, as are the potter's and the weaver's wares, all in ways that bring back into an intricate relationship of reordering. In this respect, Origen's complex remedial process of ecclesially centered conversion, engaged in the sacramental elements of the church's life, provides a suitable figure for these directives within the new context of Christianity (*Homilies on Leviticus* 8.10–11). But the basis for this must be understood to lie beyond simply the formal means of repentance and growth in holiness. Rather, they point to the complete reconstruction of created being given in the redeemed flesh of Christ as it is given over to the distinctions of the world for their "gathering in" (Eph. 1:10; Col. 1:19–20).

From a Christian perspective, this is most notably clarified in the final section regarding infected houses (Lev. 14:33–53). As we saw, Calvin was mystified by the disease in question, knowing nothing about a leprosy that could affect buildings, and he therefore theorized the historical evolution of sickness. Others took up the challenge and sought analogous structural infections, like saltpeter (calcium nitrate, in this case, which could disintegrate mortar), mildew, or mold. For Calvin, at any rate, it was a predictive threat to Israel—"when you come into the land of Canaan"—and pointed to Israel's future faithlessness (1996: 2.27–28). For Rashi (Rosenbaum and Silbermann 1932: 64), however (drawing on *Sifra* 155 on 14:34), it was part of a roundabout promise from God, for the people of Canaan, hearing of the Israelites' approach, sought to hide their riches within the walls of their homes. Having been dispossessed, the advent of the "house leprosy" would force a Hebrew family to dismantle parts of the structure, thereby disclosing the treasure lying within. There are, that is, riches to be discovered within the rotting walls. One can see the movement toward paradoxical grace in this midrash, for while *Rabbah* 17.9, as we saw, finally identified the completely infected and dismantled home with the temple, still hoping in the healing of God in the time to come, the Christian gospel straightforwardly resolved the question of "treasure in decay" (2 Cor. 4:7–12) with the coming of the word in human flesh. If leprosy is about mortality and corruption, then so too the "house" that succumbs to this sickness that lays waste. "'Destroy this temple'"—and one thinks of the demand, in cases of recurring leprosy, to "break down the house, its stones and timber and all the plaster of the house, . . . carr[ying] them forth out of the city to an unclean place" (Lev. 14:45)—"'and in three days I will raise it up.' . . . He spoke of the temple of his body" (John 2:19–21), that is, of the triumph of incorruption brought through Jesus's subjection to the forces of corruption. Upon this assumption of decay within the power of incorruption is built the literal practice among later Christians of assuming leprosy through love of the leper, from the medieval custom of considering lepers as *pauperes Christi* (the poor of Christ) deserving of service and even physical touching and kissing of wounds, to the more modern examples of ultimately infected caregivers like the famous Damien in Molokai and, forty years before, the less-well-known Moravians in South Africa.[5] This is the Lazarus of Jesus's parable (Luke 16:19–31), the poor man covered in sores, licked by dogs (i.e., by the nations gathered in the church), carried into the bosom of paradise, thrust to the edge of the precipice that separates heart from heart, and humans from God, mortal life yearning for redeemed life given, standing before the incomprehension of a resurrected flesh.

5. On medieval attitudes, see Moore 1987, including his discussion of those who actually prayed to *become* lepers for the sake of assuming a proleptic purgatory and hence escape from eternal death. On the Moravians in South Africa, see Bonar 1978: 40–41, who quotes, in a now-famous passage, an account given him and Robert McCheyne in 1839. After describing the leper house, he asks, with evangelical pleading: "But you will ask, who cares for the souls of the hapless inmates? Who will venture to enter in at this dreadful gate, never to return again? Who will forsake father and mother, houses and land, to carry the message of a Saviour to these poor lepers? Two Moravian missionaries, impelled by a divine love for souls, have chosen the lazarhouse as their field of labor. They entered it never to come out again; and I am told that as soon as these die, other Moravians are quite ready to fill their place. Ah! my dear friends, may we not blush, and be ashamed before God, that we, redeemed with the same blood, and taught by the same Spirit, should yet be so unlike these men in vehement, heart-consuming love to Jesus and the souls of men?"

And so here, in the touch of lips to sores, in the binding of the sick and the well in one common fate (though a fate first given in the incorruptible one), we are indeed tied to the life of a people and of a race and to that people's own internal orderings as they are knotted into the future's promised course. If the temple is Christ's body, it is therefore also the church's, in all its complex relationships, including stone and beam, wall and roof, in the kind of image given by Eph. 2:17–22. This goes far beyond Hesychius's concern (see Rabanus Maurus [Patrologia latina 108.372–401]) with the contagion of heresy, for here we see the body of the church displayed in its corporeal reality and history, as subject to the effects of self-giving love. The church is leprous, its skin is blackened, and the substance of its flesh is exposed for all to view. But what kind of flesh does it carry? A flesh now taken over by the Lord of life, a love that "descends to the dead" in the flesh, even as it rises in the spirit (1 Pet. 3:18). The lepers of Lev. 13–14 therefore provide a figural hint at an entire history that is to follow. But, as with the whole of Leviticus, this history is contained in the details of bird and beast, sore and stone, as a kind of catalogue of realities gathered up by one man.

LEVITICUS 15

The life and history of corruptibility moving into incorruptibility, the journey of Israel and humankind in the vessel of Jesus, passes through the waters of sexuality as they flow from the body's internal organs. This is not a place where even the most erotically imagined picture of Jesus has found a comfortable passage; most "body-affirming" theologies of today in fact *recoil* from the material in the central chapters of Leviticus. Yet the passage itself is inevitable. The present chapter, which deals with male and female bodily discharges, has been seen in the Jewish tradition as connected with the preceding laws regarding leprosy. *Rabbah* 18.1–5 interprets it in this way, and the weekly Torah readings place the sections together under the title *Metsora* ("the leper"). The connection implies, at the least, a common significance to the subject matter, something perhaps not self-evident to modern sensibilities. Indeed, there is a real contemporary instinct that would deny any relationship between physical disease and bodily fluids associated with the sexual lives of men and women. But, as we saw, the character of leprosy in Lev. 13–14 is determined less by natural physiological symptoms than by the exposure of life to the decay of history—mortality and sin "in the midst of life." Likewise, the meaning of the law regarding discharges as bound to this focus is itself less about disease than it is a further comment on the nature of created existence in time. Certainly, the body's subjection to the reality of time is logically implicated in sexual life, just as is the integrity of human flesh. And, in any case, as ordered by the law given by God to Moses and Aaron, both these elements will rightly find their clarification in the life of Israel itself. Bodily fluids go out into the realm of a partner's procreative purpose, will, and desire; or they go out into the world, shaping history according to a logic of waste and decay whose only redemption is to be taken up by God's own suffering of their corruptive power.

This general perspective, however, has not been shared by Christian exegetes, except perhaps on a marginal naturalistic plane. Medieval commentators, for instance, agreed that intercourse with menstruating women might itself engender babies infected with leprosy, but this was not a matter that attracted their concern to any great degree. Instead, in the Origenistic tradition (although Origen's extant homilies in fact omit comment on Lev. 15) the corporeal character of the laws here was always, from the start, transferred to a symbolic level. Following a note of Gregory the Great, the semen of 15:2 was foundationally identified with the word preached and taught. As some exegetes noted, the Vulgate of Acts 17:18 uses the pejorative term *seminiverbius* in a way that literally links these two realities of seed and word together. To be sure, Jesus's parable of the sower in Mark 4 was, for example, more substantively pertinent to this interpretation. In general, this left the bulk of Lev. 15 dealing with male emissions as a figural description of the evils of false teaching, heresy, and malicious gossip (e.g., Rupert of Deutz [Patrologia latina 167.816–18], much in the vein of the rabbinic interpretation of the sin of leprosy). As the male of the chapter stood for the teaching hierarchy of the church, the woman stood for the church as a whole or for the individual soul in its original corruption, and her menstrual flow was identified as either impure thoughts or idolatry. In the eyes of Hesychius (Rabanus Maurus [Patrologia latina 108.403–13]), the writer who most influenced the Western medieval exegesis of this chapter, these two elements are bound up in a grand history of redemption, symbolized by the seven days of purificatory separation (which could also indicate the seven penitential gifts of the Holy Spirit), wherein the sins of Jewish false teaching and Gentile idolatry are together resolved by the evangelical doctrine rightly preached in the church after the advent of Christ.

These figural assertions are not without value. But they rightly stand only as possible conclusions to a more fundamental interpretive movement that moors the text in the bodily realities that are so vividly discussed in the chapter, realities that Christian exegesis has generally found distasteful in both early ascetic and modern critical perspectives. Given the context of the chapter, these bodily realities are here bound primarily to the act of sexual intercourse as the basis for created sexual distinction. Men have semen, women have blood, and each of these fluids is defined as life-giving when they act together in their particular ways. The frustration of this coordinated action is discussed in this chapter, and this frustration, fastened to the body, ties these laws to those regarding leprosy and childbearing that precede it.

The opening command, "when any man has a discharge from his body, his discharge is unclean" (15:2), orients the rest of the chapter (15:33). But what is this discharge that proceeds from his body? Is it an illness? If so, is it generalized or localized? Is it properly associated, as by many modern interpreters, with either urethritis or gonorrhea (Calvin 1996: 2.31), one of whose symptoms may be the oozing of pus or other fluid from the penis? This might explain, for instance, the possibility of the stoppage alluded to in 15:3, and if it is gonorrhea it is linked not only to impurity but also to sin. Christians, by and large, have had little interest in the physical aspects of this question. The entire reality of discharge or flow (*zub*) has, where its sexual connections have been noted, usually implied fornication or some general sexual misbehavior that has been left unexplored in detail (Willet 1631: 350–52 and references).

But the text itself makes no reference to pain, and the discharge in question is not described in any way as to appear abnormal. Although *Sifra* 160.1 raises many possibilities (including that this may apply also to women and not only men), as Rashi explains it (Rosenbaum and Silbermann 1932: 68), the "body" here is clearly the penis (by parallel with 15:16). The only discharge properly associated with this is semen, although in this case (versus 15:16), the seed is not mentioned. Perhaps there is reference here to the discharges associated with various venereal diseases or preejaculate fluids. And although concern is expressed regarding other bodily fluids (e.g., urine, tears, blood, even sweat; see *Sifra* 160.4) that themselves might be contaminated through contact somehow with the impurities leaving the penis, in the end the main distinction accepted is between a "white flow" for a male and a "bloody flow" for a woman (*Sifra* 161.4). Hence, the text is speaking, from the beginning, about male emissions, abnormal or normal. The difference, in 15:3, between running and stopping discharges, Rashi goes on to say, has to do with the nature of semen itself in each case and probably refers to its coloration (clear or cloudy) and not to symptoms linked to a particular illness (Rosenbaum and Silbermann 1932: 68). Calvin, who agrees with this general point, quickly applies it to a general moral lesson: the sweeping linkage between male emissions and impurity served simply as a constant reminder to Israel of its uncleanness, that is, of its original sin and therefore of the consequent and incessant need for spiritual cleansing (1996: 2.31–32). For the Jewish tradition, however, the opening and seemingly generalized law regarding emissions applies to any case in which a man's discharged semen fails to enter the body of woman—from masturbation to asexual stimulation. The distinction between this case and that discussed in 15:16–18 is that the latter is a particular instance—and a most important one—in which deliberate sexual intercourse results in lost semen.

It seems correct that we see Lev. 15 focusing, with respect to men, primarily on the reality of a *sexual* discharge, rather than on disease, however it might influence such discharge. It furthermore takes seriously the long tradition of meaning associated with semen that has grown up around or alongside the Levitical law itself. The rabbinic tradition saw semen as embodying life and often expressed the ancient idea (shared with, e.g., Galen and, in various guises, still accepted well into the seventeenth century) that semen is itself a developed form of blood, as is breast milk in women.[1] Job 10:10 ("didst thou not pour me out like milk and curdle me like cheese?") was, among Jewish and Christian interpreters alike, un-

1. Semen and milk were thought to be delivered through a vein, like other blood, although, in the course of its long journey through the body, this blood was distilled for the particular life purposes promoted through sexual intercourse and gestation. Among others, Leonardo da Vinci expounded this theory; see the opening lines of Leslie Adrienne Miller's poem "Wandering Uterus": "Leonardo believed that semen came down / from the brain through a channel in the spine. / And that female lactation held its kick off / in the uterus" (*Kenyon Review* 28 [2006]: 1).

derstood in terms of the semen ("milk") "curdling" the woman's blood into the formal shapes of the human fetus.[2] Indeed, semen, like blood, contained the life (Lev. 17:14), and therefore thinkers like Maimonides considered the loss of semen as life-transferring to the point that he warned against too much intercourse as a cause of physical degeneration (e.g., loss of strength, hair and teeth falling out, bad odors) (*Mishneh Torah* 1.4.19 [*Book of Knowledge*]). This identification of semen with the blood of life led to equating masturbation with actual bloodshed or murder, and there are numerous texts in which the sins of violence preceding the flood (Gen. 6:5, 11–12) are actually interpreted in terms of wasted male seed (Rashi, *Shabbos* 41; the *Zohar* on Gen. 39:9; the nineteenth-century legal compendium of Shlomo Ganzfried, *Kitzer Shulchan Aruch* 151).

The uncleanness of emitted semen is explained here in terms of teleology, of the semen's failure to fulfill its purpose; and the material problem is one of non-coordination between the sexual roles of the man and the woman. The issue has profound implications for sexual ethics and identity. Emissions of semen without sexual intercourse with a view or window to procreation stymies the semen's creative purpose. A diseased semen, due to some illness, is a visible sign of this frustrated purpose. Similarly, the flow of a woman's blood outside her body (Lev. 15:19–24) without its procreative joining with semen represents another obstacle to the blood's creative purpose. Finally, sexual intercourse between a man and a menstruating woman (15:24) renders the man unclean for a similar reason: life is somehow frustrated. This last notion was, until the Middle Ages, generally accepted among Christians also—Augustine called the prohibition a moral law and *not* a figural one. And reasons usually given were not only the medical claims that children so conceived were usually diseased, but more importantly that conception itself was usually impossible during a woman's period (*Questions on Leviticus* 18–19).[3]

The issue at root, therefore, is the procreative purpose, inherent in blood and semen in their coordinated admixture, that takes place during sexual intercourse.

2. Thomas Aquinas writes: "Next he treats the making of man with reference to the work of propagation by which man is generated from man. Note here that he attributes every work of nature to God, not so as to exclude the operation of nature, but in the way things done through secondary causes are attributed to the principle agent. Similarly the operation of the saw is attributed to the carpenter. That nature operates comes from God, who instituted it for that purpose. In the generation of man, first comes the release of the seed and to express this he says, 'Did you not pour me out like milk?' For just as semen is the product of nourishment, so too is milk. Second, the physical mass is joined together in the womb of the woman and he expresses this saying, 'and curdle me like cheese?' For the seed of the male is related to the matter which the female furnishes in the generation of man and other animals like the coagulant is related to the generation of cheese" (2002: 270).

3. Augustine notes that, in addition to the Levitical prohibitions (18:19; 20:18), punishable (he believes) by death, Ezek. 18:6 mentions it in the context of very clear violations of the moral order of justice. On the medical dangers of conception at this time, see Jerome's *Commentary on Ezekiel* on Ezek. 18:6 (Patrologia latina 25.173); Rupert of Deutz on Lev. 15 (Patrologia latina 167.816–18); and Thomas Aquinas 2002: 170–71. Likewise, Nahmanides 1974: 207–8, on this text, asserts the same likely harm, on the basis of menstrual blood's inferior "nutritional" value. *Apostolic Constitutions* 28, accepted as part of Eastern Orthodox canon law, maintains the prohibition.

Both Jewish and Christian traditions have, until recently, steadfastly proscribed (although according to various casuistic frameworks) both deliberate contraceptive measures and male sexual emission that is not at least aimed at the possibility of conception (a prohibition that obviously includes masturbation). Thomas Aquinas represents this governing rationale of life purpose when, in his discussion of the sin of fornication, he notes that sexual intercourse must not only be open to the possibility of conception, but must also engage the commitments of the two partners to raise and care for any child so conceived.[4] The idea that discharges render one impure and under some circumstances even guilty (and hence requiring sacrifices of atonement) is therefore founded on the need to keep life within the body itself, where it can fulfill its purpose for either promoting or generating created existence.

The matter of separation because of uncleanness in its own right is directly linked to this founding goal. Leviticus 15 speaks to two forms of impurity, although both fall within this same governing category of meaning. The term *niddah* (after which a talmudic tractate on the subject of female impurity is named) describes impurity given in the course of some natural act, in this case, a woman's monthly menstruation (15:20, 25). Separation and cleansing are required, but no sacrifice. The impurity associated with either a willful or unnatural loss of semen or blood (15:2–12, 25–30) is designated by a different word, *zavut*, which renders a man (*zav*) or a woman (*zavah*) unclean and requires an atoning sacrifice.[5] Even in this case, however, the sacrifice (15:14, 29) is the same as that associated with

4. Thomas Aquinas writes in *Summa contra gentiles* 3.122: "Hence it is clear that every emission of the *semen* is contrary to the good of man, which takes place in a way whereby generation is impossible; and if this is done on purpose, it must be a sin. I mean a way in which generation is impossible *in itself*, as is the case in every emission of the *semen* without the natural union of male and female: wherefore such sins are called 'sins against nature.' But if it is *by accident* that generation cannot follow from the emission of the *semen*, the act is not against nature on that account, nor is it sinful; the case of the woman being barren would be a case in point. Likewise it must be against the good of man for the *semen* to be emitted under conditions which, allowing generation to ensue, nevertheless bar the due education of the offspring [i.e., versus fornication, because childrearing is necessary, not just generation]. . . . The above assertions are confirmed by divine authority. The unlawfulness of any emission of *semen*, upon which offspring cannot be consequent, is evident from such texts as these: *Thou shalt not lie with mankind as with womankind: Thou shalt not lie with any beast* (Levit. xviii,22, 23): *Nor the effeminate, nor sodomites, shall possess the kingdom of God* (1 Cor. vi,10). The unlawfulness of fornication and of all connexion with any other woman than one's own wife is clear from Deut. xxiii,17: *There shall be no whore among the daughters of Israel, nor whoremonger among the sons of Israel: Keep thyself from all fornication, and beyond thine own wife suffer not the charge of knowing another* (Tob iv,13): *Fly fornication* (1 Cor. vi,18). Hereby is refuted the error of those who say that there is no more sin in the emission of the *semen* than in the ejection of other superfluous products from the body" (1905: 283–85, emphasis original). This last thought derives from the notion that emissions of other fluids are to rid the body of impurities, and some thought semen and menstrual blood did the same.

5. Detailed talmudic casuistry determines what constitutes the kind of discharge discussed first in Lev. 15, rendering a man a *zav* (a talmudic tractate named *Zavim* is devoted the subject). At least seven kinds of ejaculation are ruled out as causative factors: overeating, overdrinking, illness, heavy

childbirth itself, which is certainly bound up with the natural in the best sense, so that the reality of sin here is less a matter of deliberated hostility to God than it is an ingrained bond to such hostility—the original element of sinfulness. The impurity in both cases—described generally as *tumah*—derives from some association with death, clearly given in the thwarted lifework of the spilled or unmixed sexual fluids of the man and woman. The spillage may well be natural (in the woman's case, the *niddah* of normal menstruation, or lost semen in the midst of intercourse), but it is still a sign of a kind of frustrated life embedded in the course of fallen time. When the spillage is either voluntary (masturbation, *coitus interruptus*, etc.) or unnatural (uterine bleeding of some sort), this frustrating of life rises to the level of a kind of cry to God, like Abel's blood, a revolt against time itself. In this case, atonement—that is, a reapproach to God with renewed purpose for life—is made.

It is important to note that the character of sin is defined by this relationship with the teleology of life. The separation of the *zav* or *zavah* or of the couple made unclean during intercourse or of the woman in her period was not only a sign of frustrated life-formation but also a time to reorient oneself toward the power of such movement toward life. "Rabbi Meir said, Why did the Torah teach that a woman was in a period of *niddah* (ritual impurity) for seven days. . . . So that she will be beloved by her husband as on the day she entered the marriage canopy" (Babylonian Talmud, tractate *Niddah* 31b). During this time apart, a new force—purity—is given to a refocused procreative goal. This is defined as love itself, even colored by sexual passion. The separation that summarizes these laws (Lev. 15:31)—"thus you shall keep the people of Israel separate [*nazar*, as in 'Nazirite'] from their uncleanness, lest they die in their uncleanness by defiling my tabernacle that is in their midst"—represents an enactment of the history of creative distinction itself: male and female are both described in their particularity, drawn together in their intrinsic purpose, though now displayed as thwarted in their goal. The sexual distinction of the human creature, embodied in the male/female difference, is creatively fulfilled in procreation; it is also underlined, through its undermining, in unproductive sexual discharges. The entire chapter, therefore, speaks to this sign of fallenness, of the chasm of creation, wherein life granted in its specificity of difference does not propagate itself and becomes mired in a separateness that cannot move beyond itself.[6] The character of sexuality as oriented to God is fundamentally given in its procreative purpose. Obviously, this places the sexual ethics of Leviticus at the base of what has become a well-articulated Catholic tradition.[7] It also indicates the wider concerns that direct later teachings on sexual relations in Lev. 18 on.

---

lifting, rigorous exercise, visual stimulations, or thoughts. See *Sifra* 160.4; Hirsch 1989: 1.396–97; and Milgrom 1991–2000: 907.

6. On impurity here as somehow associated with death, see Milgrom 1991–2000: 1000–1004.

7. See *Catechism of the Catholic Church* 1652; and, most famously, the general and particular thrust of John Paul II's encyclical *Evangelium vitae*: as human beings, should we pursue love or

In this perspective, we can understand why *Rabbah* 18.1 founds its discussion of sexual discharges upon the opening verses of Eccl. 12, an otherwise incongruous connection: "Remember also your Creator in the days of your youth, before the evil days come, and the years draw nigh, when you will say, 'I have no pleasure in them.'" Solomon speaks not simply of youth, but of *lost* youth; and he defines that loss in terms of a dripping away of life divorced from its creative nature given by the hands of God. Time is provided for life received from and offered back to God, fruitfully, richly. The spilling of semen and blood each point to the loss of such purpose, seeping away or thrown away through the crevices of bodily existence. The traditional rabbinic notion of the flood's figuration of this profligate loss of cherished and mortal existence through the squandering of seed is relentlessly consistent. "Do not waste life!" is the accusation that emerges from sexual insouciance, whose inbuilt bodily censure within the uncontrolled outflow of male and female fluids may indeed, in Calvin's view, be a constant reminder of our corruption before the creator (1996: 2.31–33).

On this basis, in any case, the Christian medieval understanding of the semen as the word of God sent into the world to bear fruit makes good sense, as long as it is not simply stripped of its corporeal exigencies. Bede (Patrologia latina 91.350) raised the question, in this chapter, of a warning given to those who fail to use their natural gifts and innate goodness for the sake of church and world. And Jesus's parables regarding stewardship in the deepest sense—from that of the talents to those of various servants—are rightly connected to this reality of physical existence as both gift and responsibility, summed up in his judgment that "every one to whom much is given, of him will much be required; and of him to whom men commit much they will demand the more" (Luke 12:48). Bodies are gifts and trusts. But the judgment is given substance most particularly in the call to give over one's own self, to "go, sell what you possess and give to the poor . . . and come, follow me" (Matt. 19:21). It is a call made most particularly to a *young* man (19:22), a man capable of and ready to shed his seed for the sake of life, still vigorous in the "days of [his] youth . . . before the sun and the light and the moon and the stars are darkened and the clouds return after the rain . . . and the strong men are bent, and the grinders cease because they are few, and those that look through the windows are dimmed" (Eccl. 12:1–3). In this call, it is one's own blood that is given over for the life of the world.

From the vantage of Lev. 15, however, this call takes form and is heard within the shape of man and woman, married, sexually active, aiming at new life, driven toward one another even in the midst of their wasted gifts, staked there in the chasm of creation itself. The cross of Jesus marks its place here, amid these spilled

---

procreation? Philosopher Anthony Kenny raises this question with pointedness when he asserts that a Thomistically oriented "virtue-based" life would favor love (2006: 143). But procreation, through the coupling of creaturely difference centered in the demands of family life, *is* love. This is a part of the great message of the gospel of the incarnation, the cross, and the resurrection as it illuminates the revelation of God in creation.

fluids, where the distinction of the creature is given over in love—in marriage and sex and procreation—but is also violated and stumbled over. We know nothing of the discharges that emerged from the body of Christ, the flesh of his own male organ. That his body was formed within the reality of these discharges, however, is affirmed by the tradition.[8] And marriage, we are told, became his own vocation, though oriented widely toward the body of the church (Eph. 5:25, 32), a body for which and into which he shed his very blood, in order to bear fruit and to waste nothing. For Paul, this is more than a symbol; it is rather a mystery that reveals the very workings and shape of created history.[9]

So, Lev. 15, like so much of the book, exposes from one vantage the history of giving life. This becomes Israel's vocation—God's calling from the beginning, calling out to Moses and through him to the people that they are to come near to him with an offering (1:1–2). Here, this offering is described in terms of a life that is formed and defined by this staking out of a common life of sexual union within the chasm of creation itself. But this staking out itself reflects and articulates the larger historical vocation of Israel in time. The *Rabbah's* discussion of Lev. 15 presents the total picture in its sweep. It begins, as I noted, with a reflection on Eccl. 12: physical deterioration creeps up upon one because of old age, and this will involve the demise of sexual activity itself. Discharges and leprosy go together, in terms of meaning, for they are each signs of enmeshment within the wasting reality of time, here attached to the "sins of one's youth" (*Rabbah* 18.1). But the *Rabbah* continues: Israel itself gives rise to a world in which life is broken down and squandered. Evil comes from *within* the body, pressing out into the world of relations (18.2), and these sins began as soon as Israel was given the law, a sign of its intrinsic implication in this evil (18.3).

We recall Jesus's teaching, in Mark 7:21–23, that a defiling evil "comes from within" a person and then "goes out." The issue here is not primarily the contrast between the material (food) and the spiritual (matters of the heart), but the contrast between what is foreign to a person, coming in from the outside, and what is genuine and intrinsic to a person, originating from within and then going out into the world. That fornication is included by Jesus in the list of things that go out from the heart indicates that he is working within an emissive framework that goes beyond simply the immaterial. His judgment is one that is profoundly coherent with Lev. 15, especially with its sense of turning interior realities into waste (Mark 7:19).

The people's complaints and craving came to embody this excretion of rebellious passion, and, for instance, Num. 11:20 is cited, where Israel "vomits out" divine

8. While still controversial in some regards, Leo Steinberg's famous 1996 essay, *The Sexuality of Christ in Renaissance Art*, provides incontrovertible evidence at least of the deliberated representation of Jesus's penis as a true sexual organ (often depicted in erection). The incarnational argument of these paintings seems certain, if less documented in their self-consciousness.

9. This is von Balthasar's argument regarding Jesus's virginity: what he calls the "vertical mystery" by which Jesus's "fruitfulness" is born within the church in a kind of direct participation "downward" of divine life, apart from physically experienced sexual intercourse (1968: 309).

food that has become "loathsome" to them in their greed (the roots of the two words are similar). This action now stands as its own kind of discharge, a kind of "coming out" from the body of something good, but whose expulsion is now its own punishment (*Rabbah* 18.4). Similarly, with respect to the woman's flow, both in her anguish and separation she stands for Israel bereft of God and the law in its sins (cf. 2 Chr. 15:3), embodying in her seeping life fluids the loss of her divine life in the course of her history (Num. 19:4–6). Yet in this rapidly enveloping history of demise, God shows that he is different from all others because he heals with the very affliction he imposes: leprosy and the flow of discharge themselves lead Israel to repentance (18:5; 19:6).

It is worth noting that this historical view of the discharges is variously alluded to throughout the Old Testament. The land itself, and its place within Israel's vocation, is seen in a primary way as a marital partner. There is perhaps some residual Near Eastern symbolism in this. The frequent mention of Canaan's promise as a place "flowing with milk and honey" (Exod. 3:8, 17; Lev. 20:24; Deut. 6:3; Jer. 11:5)—a unique phrase that takes up the language of the discharge exactly—may well conjure up images of fertile interactions, as the flow of these elements has often been linked to male semen given over to the woman.[10] The land of Israel, to be sure, is promised as a bride to the Israelites: "Your land [shall be called] Married" (Isa. 62:4). And there is some purpose to these resonances, although less of a historical-genealogical kind than in the way they point to the figural embodiments of divine history within the experience of physical life in time both for individuals and for the people as a whole. Israel's life is a synecdoche of the life of women, who themselves (along with men) embody the character of Cain and the human race as a whole, where the fluids of life are spilled upon the ground and the creature is left waiting in the uncleanness of its separated incapacity to love. So Scripture traces the image, in Ezekiel, of Israel and Jerusalem as a menstruous woman left alone in her impurity, and her interior discharge not simply as the referent of Levitical prescriptions, but as indicating the actual shedding of blood in the cause of idolatry that has taken place across centuries (Ezek. 36:17–18; cf. Lam. 1:17).[11] And just as Israel within the wilderness disgorges in cravenness the gifts of God, eating to the point of loathsome satiety, so too Leviticus itself says that the land of Canaan will vomit out Israel as a wasted fluid of its own, in this case because of the disorientation of the very fluids of sexual blessing (Lev. 20:22). The complicated elements of impurity's transmission to physical objects (15:4–12, 20–24, 26–27), so consuming of clarification in talmudic reflection (see especially tractate *Niddah*), represent the going out into the physical world of this loss, enveloping the landscape of life.

10. The most famous instance of this is in the Sumerian account of the god Dumuzi and goddess Inanna's wedding nuptials (see Jacobsen 1987: 19–23).

11. In Lev. 23 the life of Israel in the wilderness is compared to the cleansing of a menstruous woman and is represented in the seven weeks between Passover and the Feast of Weeks, the purifying counting of the omer.

The discharges of Lev. 15, then, indicate an entire history. But it is one given not only in that history's articulation of decline, for the very reality of cleansing contained in the Levitical precepts also becomes the figure of Israel's future and of the human race. As we saw with respect to Lev. 12, Ezekiel's prophecy of Israel as the blood-covered infant, abandoned in the field, provides the occasion for God's rescue, adoption, and finally betrothal to the matured maiden she has become. "You became mine," God says. And with this marriage, "I bathed you with water and washed off your blood from you, and anointed you with oil" (16:8–9). This is the figure of Eph. 5:25–33, now conjoined to Moses's own prophecy at the end of his life, the unforgotten song of the nation taken up by Paul in Rom. 9–11, whereby God himself "makes expiation for the land of his people," for blood shed, through the shedding of blood, now clearly somehow his own (Deut. 32:43). The Jerusalem Talmud makes this connection between expiation on the part of God and the *mikvah* ritual bath for the menstruous woman; the two represent the center of the one hope who is God: "R[abbi] Akiba said: Blessed are ye, O Israel. Before whom are ye made clean, and who makes you clean? Your Father in heaven; as it is written, 'And I will sprinkle clean water upon you and ye shall be clean' (Ezek. xxxvi,25). And again it says, 'O Lord the hope [*mikweh*] of Israel' (Jer. xvii,13)—as the *mikweh* cleanses the unclean, so does the Holy One, blessed by He, cleanse Israel" (tractate *Yoma* 8.9, quoted in Montefiore and Loewe 1960: 151–52).

Who is the Lord, the hope of Israel? Unless one is able to discern this historical framework that informs the theology of discharge, one cannot answer this question, for the history leads to its own logical fulfillment in the Lord who discharges himself, for the cleansing of his people and of the world. This is he who, on the last day of the Feast of Booths, the day of the law's joy, stood up and proclaimed of himself that "out of his heart shall flow rivers of living water" (John 7:38)—a flow of life that washes clean the land, the world, and all its people. This is he who was raised up on a cross, pierced in his side with a spear, "and at once there came out blood and water" (19:34; cf. 1 John 5:6)—a flow that marked a mixing of his own life-fluids with the water of the world's bathing, a *mikveh* of hope.

And only from this perspective can we properly understand the significance of the bleeding woman, afflicted with a flow of blood for twelve years, who touches Jesus's robe and is healed (Matt. 9:20–22 and parallels). Too often this is interpreted in terms of Jesus's breaking down of the social barriers caused by her "merely" (and hence small-mindedly) ritual impurity: he "brings her back into the community," from which she had been thrust by Jewish religion. But the epiphany given by this event is related, not to the woman's social location, but to Jesus. She herself remains unknown, despite the many legends subsequently attached to her identity; and she is apparently a stranger, for Jesus does not send her to the priest, as he did with the local lepers whom he healed. It was the touch that somehow healed, the proximity with his flesh, bound up with life and with a near outflowing. This is the flesh that will soon be wounded and into whose rawness Thomas is invited to thrust his hand (John 20:27) and that all the disciples are encouraged to hold and to handle (Luke 24:39), as indeed they did (1 John 1:1). Touching has to do with being joined—as it is negatively shown to be in Lev. 15 with respect to the cascade of tangible contagion through proximate palpable objects like beds and chairs and vessels—and this is the history of the woman with the flow of blood: if her flow of blood has ceased, it was only because of the blood of her Lord discharged. There is no marriage without coitus and its life-giving purpose. The discussion in Eph. 5 regarding marriage into "one flesh" as the "mystery" of Christ's own joining of flesh—and thereby fluids, which is the significance of fleshly unity—with the church comes into focus just here: the impurity of wasted life is not somehow now made pure; rather, love now allows itself to be wasted within the scattered realm of life for the sake of life itself. The woman is healed in the same way that one spouse consecrates the other or that parents consecrate their children (1 Cor. 7:14): Jesus touches her with his own blood shed, his own life laid open in the midst of the separated realities of creator and creature. There is no healing apart from this.

This indicates why simply relegating Lev. 15 to ritual law, now overcome some- how by Jesus, misses the point. The marriage bed remains something kept undefiled in its purpose (Heb. 13:4), and for all the same reasons as given in Leviticus. This was Augustine's point in insisting that this law was moral: while the *body* that is cleansed and does the cleansing has been assumed by God in Christ Jesus—his blood, his fluids, his discharges from a flesh laid bare and poured into the chasm of the world's being—the character of created life remains the same, aimed at life propagated, nurtured, and expended in love. Although there have been shifts in both Christian and Jewish attitudes toward the legitimacy of sexual intimacy apart from conception, the vocation to maintain with integrity the admixture of bodily fluids between male and female as husband and wife has remained steady, in large part because the teleology of life within the embodied existence of the human creature is so fundamentally established.[12] Homosexual sex, masturbation, deliberated and intrusive birth control, and abortion all remain transgressive of the actual being of the creaturely body. They are not unforgivable sins, to be sure,

12. The 1968 encyclical *Humanae vitae* 14, 16 spoke more plainly to sexual intercourse as "an act of mutual love" and as having a purpose in addition to procreation, which may even admit of an intention to avoid having children (within certain parameters). More recently, however, the procreative character of human life has been reasserted in a broad way ("integral procreation") that embraces family and society in a rich outline of sustenance and formation that (without explicit reference to it) remains faithful to the Levitical vision; see Pontifical Council for the Family 2006. Jewish talmudic casuistry has generally forbidden any sexual act not aimed at conception that might involve male ejaculation. However, there are arguments that the "seed going forth" refers only to an emission that lies outside the body of the wife; and therefore oral sex that includes ejaculation is permissible as long as it does no physical harm (as anal sex might do). Sophisticated discussions on this topic can be found on the well-known internet site www.avodah.org. The framework even for these wider interpretations, however, remains that of spousal sexual relations geared, at least in their overall purpose, toward or from procreative potential.

and the shape of their overcoming is now given in the body of Jesus, rather than in the practices of cleansing and animal sacrifice. But that is the nature of figural reality: it is real, not imagined, and its reality is given in a diversity of physical and historical shapes, not mental ones. Birth, illness, wasting, marriage, and its dissolutions are all fleshly and rightly remain so. The resurrection of our own bodies has not yet taken place (2 Tim. 2:18) and so remains, therefore, the redemption of flesh by the flesh of God as it passes through the world.

LEVITICUS 16

Leviticus 16 begins by returning to the death of Aaron's sons. For most interpreters, especially Christian ones, this chapter on the Day of Atonement represents the central climax of Leviticus as a whole. But it is important to see how this climax is achieved: by beginning with a new mention of Aaron's sons and their deaths, the theological substance of the chapter is reached through the history of a family's calling, tragedy, and reoriented hope. If it is a climax, it is only one whose dynamic is designed to be continuous.

I noted at the close of the discussion of Lev. 10 that Nadab's and Abihu's deaths, fraught with moral ambiguity, is rightly grasped as at least an opening to the possibility of atonement in their own persons—atonement, that is, as the coming near of God himself into a place otherwise wholly given over to separation. It is only in the light of this opening that Aaron is given the key to "distinguish[ing]" between the holy and the common, and between the unclean and the clean" (10:10), which he is to teach the people of the Israel. These elements prove to be the distinctions of creation itself, worked out, as the next chapters have shown, among the animals, in human difference (sexual and physical) and in childbirth, mortality, and waste as the historical character of difference. These, in turn, are colored by mourning and loss even though they are embedded in the reality of sacrifice and cleansing, all pointing thereby to some approach by God into the midst of the creation's chasm, so as to overcome it.

The breadth of this differentiation and its character, even as outlined in these few chapters, is deliberately cosmic. This is especially so when we read the chapters as linked to the larger realities of matter and history described in the opening chapters of Genesis.[1] Returning now to the dead sons of Aaron, this differentiation

---

1. This cosmic linkage is explicated structurally in great detail in Beauchamp 1969 (a renovator of typological exegesis in modern France). Beauchamp's classic text was influential on, among others, Ellul 1985.

within life, although centered in filial tragedy and sin, mourning and redemption, is shown to embrace all things. God, through Moses, now gives Aaron a special calling, one he will fulfill "once a year" (16:29, 34), focusing his heart, and all that it carries—its silences and obedience, its concern and hope—upon the whole world through this one moment where God wills his coming near. That is the nature of the Day of Atonement as particularly a ceremony of the sanctuary: it is primarily a "coming near"—in this basic sense an offering—in the most tangible of ways that flirts with the impossibility of the creature's life with God (16:1) even while God chooses to move toward the creature (16:2). Aaron's sons, whether figuring lost righteousness or the fall of human pride, have failed; it is Aaron who shall go instead. But it is the world that is gathered in this passage from one to the other.

The tabernacle and temple were viewed very precisely as such a world, visually marking in their form the pattern of all creation. These were commonplaces of understanding at the time of Jesus, as we know from Josephus's remarks and, more elaborately, from Philo's.[2] But this conviction of the tabernacle as embodying a cosmic pattern derives from the early scriptural record of the building's divine instruction (Exod. 25:40: "See that you make [these things] after the pattern for them, which is being shown you on the mountain"), later renewed in a visionary way by prophets like Ezekiel. Despite Christians, for centuries, maintaining a somewhat ambivalent relationship with the temple's material glory and power, transferring concrete elements of its structure and ceremony to their own ecclesial buildings and ritual, the normative understanding of the temple's significance continued to be founded on this notion of cosmic patterning.[3] The book of Revelation relies on the Jewish tradition here, whereby the heavenly temple of God's dwelling provides imagistic foundations to any earthly forms of its description (Rev. 4:2–6; 8:2–12). This patterning, rather than some purely moral reality, indicated the spiritual character of the temple that Christians consistently asserted, though, unlike Philo's influential version, they tied this character to the tangible realities

2. Josephus, *Antiquities* 3.180–82 (trans. Whiston): "They were every one made in way of imitation and representation of the universe. When Moses distinguished the tabernacle into three parts, and allowed two of them to the priests, as a place accessible and common, he denoted the land and the sea, these being of general access to all; but he set apart the third division for God, because heaven is inaccessible to men. And when he ordered twelve loaves to be set on the table, he denoted the year, as distinguished into so many months. By branching out the candlestick into seventy parts, he secretly intimated the *Decani*, or seventy divisions of the planets" and so on, as noted earlier with respect to the priest's clothing, which represented, according to Josephus, the elements, oceans, earth, sky, and so on. On Philo's similar interpretation, as well as his use of the heavenly/earthly sanctuaries in terms of pattern/image, see Spicq 1952: 1.72–75 (with references); 2.234–37.

3. There are many examples, including, e.g., Clement of Alexandria (*Stromata* 5.9). Christian "temple envy" has long been noted. See the tendentious, but influential, article by Nibley (1959–60). In fact, as Nibley notes in his many references, the Christian tradition regarding the temple is squarely Philonic in this sense, especially in light of its incarnational theology of Jesus (though it is perhaps precisely this that does not square with Nibley's Mormon perspectives).

that are given in the flesh of Christ. Jesus *as* the temple embodies the very pattern inscribed upon creation in its divine origin (John 2:21; Rev. 21:22). If Origen is the key exegete of Lev. 16, it is only because he turns with transparent focus to the letter to the Hebrews ("the whole letter," as he insists, and not just a verse here and there) as the comprehensive expositor of the referents, making the christological and incarnational interpretation in Hebrews determinative: as Aaron enters the temple on this one day of the year, Jesus walks with him, indeed, takes over his duties, his objects, his victims, his purpose, his entire self as he carries with him the taste of his sons' deaths (*Homilies on Leviticus* 9.1).

In his commentary on Lev. 16:4 Origen begins, as it were, by wrapping Jesus up in the adornments of the priesthood, gathering about him some of the various meanings associated with the holy clothing he has already explained earlier in relation to Lev. 8 (*Homilies on Leviticus* 9.2). Aaron's *linen* (i.e., grown from the earth) tunic is more primordially the history of human flesh set in motion through God's providence in Gen. 3:19; it now becomes the actual body of Jesus's life, carried through the world and into God's final purposes and proximity, "draw[ing] all men" to himself (John 12:32). The linen bands that in a literal fashion cover the sexual organs in Aaron's approach of God now veil the "only human act" that Jesus does not take as his own—that is, the sexual act that leads to procreation. This may seem incongruous given, as I have discussed, the central place of such life-creation within the destiny of humankind. Yet there is also a deeper sense in which this act is fulfilled in its own way through Jesus's creation for himself of "many brothers" and "children." This *is*, from one vantage, the "abundant life" that Jesus brings (10:10), but it is given through his own willed and disciplined eunuchhood (Matt. 19:12). Thus, the belt that Aaron assumes is precisely the strength of the Lord's self-control and chastity. Finally, with the tiara Jesus establishes his own position as head of the church's life, which we adorn through our obedience.

In some ways this kind of explication is predictable in its correlation of details. But Origen's outline in fact goes beyond what became the standard Protestant attachment of these details to the exclusively sacrificial character of the cross itself (although still oriented toward it, of course). Rather, Origen takes up the narrative aspect of sacrifice, through his engagement of the historical elements of the incarnation, in a manner whose implications are deliberately broad in their signifying weight. Every aspect provides a concrete reflection of a much larger history that embraces Jesus's passage through the world of time, and, in a way that is more definitive for Origen than in other passages from the book, he clearly comes to Lev. 16 exegetically as a microcosm of the larger macrocosmic reality of God's creation. Rather than reading his comments simply as a list of correlations—something Rufinus's probably paraphrastic version often sounds like—we should therefore see Origen's discussion here as abbreviated notes to be followed through on our own part with a wide imaginative wake.

Origen's direction seems like the right figural approach, given the narrative placement of the chapter itself. Hence, the seasonal character of the liturgy commanded by God is expressive of time itself, a time held in fulfilled summary by the whole life of Jesus. Aaron is told to enter the holy of holies only once each year. Yet, this year or season represents the time of Jesus's ministry in the world for Origen (and for much of the medieval tradition that followed him). It is the "right time" and the "fulfilled time" of Gal. 4:4. After this, he enters into heaven, where he makes intercession for us, only to return at the right time—in this case, the Father's time—for his awaiting followers, who have gathered in the temple in prayer and fasting, just as the people of Israel await Aaron's own return from inside the veil. The temporal scope of the figure, then, extends into a world-historical eschatology, drawing in the prophetic hopes and announcements of Isaiah (e.g., 61:1–4) and leading Israel into the book of Acts and into the creedal assertions that govern the framework of creation's final destiny.

But what of the central sacrifice itself? This has always been seen as the key meaning of the chapter in Christian readings, indeed so much so that the kind of historical reach that Origen implied has been left to the side. Here Origen poses a challenge to traditional Christian exegesis, especially as it has congealed in Protestant terms around the substitionary sacrifice of the cross. For if the cross is somehow revealed in Lev. 16, it can be revealed only in a way that extends the cross's reality into a broader range of historical life than is apprehended in the single transaction for sin that has, rightly or wrongly, proved the popular language of substitutionary atonement theology within the Christian church. Paul himself, after all, in the classic atonement reference in Rom. 5:11, places his discussion of Christ's sacrifice within the context of both personal human history (5:1–5) and of the history of the human race itself (5:17–21). The transaction, as it were, stands at the center, but in a way that informs the shape of human life in its breadth. For Lev. 16, the sacrifices of Aaron on this special day gather up a range of earlier forms of sacrifice—earlier in the sense that they have already been explained—and also extend the realm of distinctions that have been laid out in the preceding chapters as somehow founding the sacrificial life of offering itself. The point is, from a Christian perspective, that this one sacrifice cannot be allowed to overshadow the particularities of life and history already outlined in the range of sacrificial approaches described in the first chapters of Leviticus, in whose midst it rises up with whatever profile.[4]

In Origen's case, for instance, he actually chooses *not* to dwell upon the single sacrifice for sin that Lev. 16 has ended up identifying in Christian exegesis. This singularity is really addressed, as he sees it, from multiple directions within the

4. Origen deliberately avoids a discussion of the blood aspects of the Day of Atonement, largely because they are explicated most fully in the Eucharist, and this, he says, is not something he wants to discuss openly in his lectures (*Homilies on Leviticus* 9.10). The *disciplina arcana* by which the early church shielded the Eucharist from the eyes and ears of the unbaptized no doubt explains some of Origen's reticence surrounding Christ's sacrifice in Lev. 16, since that sacrifice found its illumination in the sacrament; but since Origen is willing to address Jesus as the great victim in many other contexts, we must look elsewhere for a fuller rationale for his silence.

entire book of Leviticus and therefore cannot be reduced to the description given here. Furthermore, as he notes, the whole letter to the Hebrews is also reflected in this chapter and not just those aspects described in the Day of Atonement passages of that letter. Indeed, what most fascinates Origen is precisely the distinguishing reality that the Day of Atonement provides human destiny, embodied most particularly in the scapegoat aspect of the liturgy (Lev. 16:7–10, 20–22). It is to this element that he gives the most—and most varied—attention. And rather than underlining the obvious linkages between the scapegoat and Jesus himself—linkages given in, for instance, Heb. 9:28 or 13:12 or Acts 7:58, and early taken up by the church (*Epistle of Barnabas* 7)—he explicates the *two* goats through a range of possible figures, all of which refer to the differentiation of fate among human beings in general. This may seem counterintuitive, given the sacrificial focus of the chapter and its traditional orientation. But Origen rightly sees that the incarnate reality of Christ's coming into the world and dying in love for sinful human creatures represents, not the erasure of separation, but submission to it of the most ultimate kind. Bede expresses it this way: the sacrifice of Christ is a true crisis in the world, a judgment (John 12:31: "now is the judgment of the world") through which all human beings at last find their freely chosen place in relation to God and the world (Patrologia latina 91.350–51).

And so the two goats represent the two destinies that await those within the Christian body: those who are repentant (i.e., who can die or be sacrificed through their penitential self-offering) and those who cannot, but who are left in the "desert" without Christ at all or who "sin again" after their purification and thereby assume the fate of the scapegoat. But Origen urges his listeners to be imaginative in their application of this historically distinguishing figure, for it represents a whole range of ways in which our lives move toward or stumble before or navigate the great chasm of our relationship with God (*Homilies on Leviticus* 9.4–5; 10.2). For instance, the two goats may well indicate the two thieves on the cross, the bad thief being the scapegoat, going to hell (desert) and leading there the principalities and powers. Or they may indicate the difference between Jesus and Barabbas (the scapegoat), a difference rightly discerned but wrongly applied by the people. Or again, the distinction between the goats may draw in Pilate, or the Jews, or our own evil thoughts that we "chase away." Finally, who is the man who leads away the scapegoat (16:26) but Jesus himself, who then "wash[es] his clothes" in his own blood shed for the cleansing of those who would remain bound to his passage?

Other elements of the sacrificial liturgy become attached to this historical distinguishing, which ramifies through the many possibilities that Origen offers: the fire (16:12–13) might refer to the needed cleansing of our lips, as in Isaiah's vision of the heavenly temple (Isa. 6); but it may also refer to the cleansing of our whole bodies, corrupted by our lack of faith—we must know the particulars of our failings and our callings. The incense embodies the good works that are Christ's on our behalf, though perhaps these works are our own, noted by God as they come before his presence, underlining our own differences in faith. Then again, perhaps these actions of burning illumination point rather to interior realties of the heart as it turns to the word—or perhaps to the negative realities of anger, distraction, or lust. Jesus will take our good fire into the inner sanctuary, to be sure; but God will see whatever it is that unveils the shape of our lives. The notion that it could be this or that seems oriented to the kind of display of realities and particularities of heart and life before the eyes of God that represents the very existence of creation. What appears to be healing about this display, provided through the crisis of sacrifice in its various aspects here, is that the truth is made evident in a way that now penetrates the shadows of normal historical being. The light is made lovable, even as the darkness is set aside as that love's leaving (John 3:16–21).

If the "whole passion is summarized" in Lev. 16, it is because the whole history of humankind is put into the light. The *Rabbah* itself, in its usual understanding of the Levitical recapitulation, makes the same point (especially 21.4–12): as Aaron enters the inner sanctuary, he brings with him the entire sweep of Israel's reality: the history of the priesthood itself, righteous and unrighteous that is taken up before God; the patriarchs and matriarchs from Abraham on, who gather with their merits; Israel's life that is continued in the very festival as it is played out between victim and sacrificer, one cleansing, another cleansed, mingled together in different ways throughout the course of time. Jewish tradition in fact gathered a number of key historical moments to the Day of Atonement: Moses's descent with the second tablets of the law (hence God's forgiveness of Israel's apostasy with the golden calf), the circumcision of Abraham, and the Akedah, or sacrifice of Isaac, the blood from which still speaks to God's atoning desire (*Pirqe Rabbi Eliezer* 29). From this standpoint, this display of Israel itself represents an offering of history to the God who now can mold it for good. Israel *is* Nadab and Abihu, failing, revived, and regiven for the sake of new life from the hand of God. Here the *Rabbah* is explicit: those who sow with tears—that is, offer their very lives—will reap with songs of joy—that is, be taken up by the re-creative touch of God (Ps. 126:5–6), through which the separative power of God's gift of new life begins once again to sort out (distinguish) the confusions of history. The implication is that the Day of Atonement is such a sowing and such a reaping, a notion whose christological extrapolation from the perspective of the church is both obvious and also informing of the sacrificial center of the cross.

For Origen, this christological extrapolation maintains the continuity of the text's Christian meaning with its literal reference. Applying, in a loose way, the traditional view of the tabernacle's structure as an outline of created reality's relation to its maker, he reads the outer sanctuary as the church in its historical existence, that is, as what was once called the church militant. In this temporal world, Christians (the corps of "priests" in their communal meaning as given in, e.g., 1 Pet. 2:9) offer the sacrifices of discipleship, by following Jesus and his cross and bearing the mortifications of this vocation. The inner sanctuary that lies behind the veil, by contrast, represents the heavenly realm entered by Jesus to which we too are granted admission by way of a faithful passage through the world. From one perspective, the correlation of these two portions of the tabernacle constitutes a straightforward application of the text in Hebrews (9:3, 8, 12; 10:19–22), which, furthermore, makes use of the central vision of the ascension to the right hand of God by opening up a way into God's presence for Christ's brothers and sisters (12:2).

From another perspective, the inner-outer spatial distinction here begins to play out the cosmic significance of history as it is displayed in the atonement liturgy taken as a whole, now seeing the earthly form of history as a reflected aspect of the prior heavenly reality. Hebrews 8:5 had already noted the tabernacle's design as being based on a divine pattern handed by God to Moses. The text of Exod. 25:40 upon which this claim was based (cf. also 1 Chr. 29:19 and Wisdom of Solomon 9:8) was a central one for Philo and the Jewish tradition as a whole: the temple reflects a heavenly original somehow and expresses in time something that is going on within the reality of God's own heavenly life.

What was this reality? There is wide debate over how to understand this within the context of Scripture's own explanations, since the hints in Hebrews and elsewhere are tantalizingly few. But it seems clear, as already noted, that the specifically cosmic significance of the tabernacle's ordering, as well as the liturgies within its bounds, was central to its meaning and certainly to subsequent exegesis.[5] What is critical to see here, from within Origen's perspective, is that this cosmic patterning of the tabernacle, through which Jesus passes, is one that marks the distinctions embedded within creation's being as it stands in relationship with God: not only are heaven (as God's dwelling place) and earth different, but the passage from one to the other is given within the tabernacle's sacrificial field. This is marked by the veil that is so crucial to the imagery of Hebrews and that distinguishes Aaron's particular task on the Day of Atonement. The tabernacle spans creation's difference from God, even as Isaiah's vision implies, with the train or skirts of God's presence on high filling the temple on earth (Isa. 6:1) or with the inner tabernacle and ark as his footstool (Ps. 99:5; cf. 11:4). But the veil stands somehow as the very creative purpose by which this spanning is made real. On it are embroidered, in several

5. Barker 1987 was instrumental in encouraging this debate more recently, through a series of arguments aimed at locating the origin of later apocalyptic and Jewish mystical traditions (as well as Christian ones) in the preexilic period. Many of her theories are wildly speculative and have not been adopted by most Old Testament scholars, and the use to which she is willing to allow these speculations to be applied by, e.g., Mormon apologists has raised doubts about the rigor of both her historical analysis and its scholarly purposes. Still, she has amassed a range of compelling evidence for at least a coherent theological exegesis regarding the temple cult and theological cosmology that has undoubtedly proved influential within both Jewish and Christian traditions. For a summary of this material as it pertains to the present texts, see Barker 1998. Scholem discusses some of these elements in 1978: chap. 2; for example, the talmudic notion (Babylonian Talmud, tractate *Berakhot* 55a) that Bezalel, the architect of the tabernacle, possessed the knowledge of the divine letters, upon the combination of which all creation is based and in analogy to which the temple was made a microcosm of creation.

accounts, the very forms of all creatures, the map of the world itself according to God's will, the tracery by which the days of creation in Genesis work themselves out.[6] In 3 Enoch 45 this tracery describes the history of Israel and the nations, much as the Day of Atonement itself gathers these up according to *Rabbah* 21.1–4. Related themes are found in Philo and later rabbinic discussion.

The patterning mentioned in Heb. 8:5, within which the Day of Atonement liturgy takes its place, points therefore to a confrontation and potential approach of created forms by God. That approach is the reality of heaven itself. The very notion of modeling—that all the world and its history follows a heavenly original—is less a philosophical claim analogous to Platonic metaphysics than it is a theological assertion about God's purposes: the divine model constitutes the reality of creative love in that it represents the fact of God's *intention* to create distinctive creatures that can be articulated—traced and mapped—upon the surfaces of time. Love separates; but love also calls and comes, calls and is sent (i.e., approaches one or another). It is marked by God's desire: that is, the veil's universe places all things before God—because God has placed them there of his own will—and calls Aaron to enter them in this approach to God with the offerings of Israel's life.[7]

Origen's unusual interest in the two goats of the sacrifice is properly explained by these distinguishing realities deriving from God's desire that stand at the root of all creation as it relates creature to creature and creature to creator through diversities and choices, efforts and rejections. In their central role within the sacrifice, these distinctions are offered, in the form of the two goats, through the veil and back outside it, as a summary of the approach that their creator has made to them, by drawing them to himself through the work of the Day. The meaning of the name Azazel (Lev. 16:8) has been the source of much debate for centuries. Is it a demon who roams within the realm of the wilderness and who has some analogous role to play in the Babylonian New Year festival? Does it refer simply to the landscape of the desert, to its rocks and crags, as some etymologies explain (with *azaz* meaning "rugged" and *el* meaning "strong") and as some Jewish commentary suggested (Babylonian Talmud, tractate *Yoma* 67b; *Sifra* 177.1)? Is Azazel, rather, a verbal

6. Philo already saw the temple veil and curtains as woven with elements that symbolized the breadth of creation (*On the Life of Moses* 2.88). The view, widely held among both Orthodox and Hasidic Jews, that the Torah itself somehow embodies this cosmic temple patterning upon which creation is ordered is given in Hirsch 1989: 2.425–28, who describes the Torah *as* the holy of holies, whose approach represents the moral calling of Israel (and all human beings eventually).

7. The historical issue of theological continuity around this matter within the books of the Old Testament is interesting: are we dealing with late intertestamental and/or Hellenistic speculations regarding temple and cosmos, or is the archetypal thinking of 3 Enoch, for example, really a maintained and living link with a preexilic perspective? On the one hand, Barker's thesis is far too confident in its own speculations regarding exilic repressions of these themes, and furthermore it is theologically obscure. The point I would emphasize is that Levitical thinking is coherent with the canon, both Old and New Testaments, and also coherent with a range of traditional explications, both rabbinic and Christian. Even beyond this, Leviticus is informative of them. And this is to be expected!

description of the second goat's role, as the one "who goes out," according to the Septuagint translation? There is a mystery to this creature, whose fleeing into the wastes outside the city stands in parallel to the avian sacrifice of atonement for leprosy (Lev. 14:7, 53). The double movement of offering takes in wilderness and camp together, the world in its fullness, Aaron together with his departed sons. In an important strand of Jewish interpretation (also noted in *Yoma* 67b), Azazel is an angel (perhaps identical to Satan, according to *Pirqe Rabbi Eliezer* 46), fallen with its cohorts at the beginning of time and corrupting humankind through intermarriage and temptation (Gen. 6:1–4). This is the view not only of Jewish apocalyptic (esp. 1 Enoch 8–9), but also, in certain forms, of what become authoritative exegesis in, for example, Nahmanides (1974: 217–22). The goal of the sacrifice, in this case, is not only to deal with the sins of Israel, but to draw into the atoning grace of God even the sins of the angels, even of Satan himself as *Rabbah* 21.4 indicates, even of Nadab and Abihu who begin this movement, even of death and loss. For the *Glossa ordinaria* (Patrologia latina 113.341–44), in a strange turn toward this direction of understanding, the desert goes so far as to reach the "bosom of the Father," the gathering of all things, where Christ goes, "outside the camp," to take our sins to their complete consumption in his love—this far.[8]

Here is where the summary character of the Day of Atonement finds its illu-mination: the approach of a family's mourning and diminution, the tabernacle's form, the articulating veil, the separated day each year, the priestly exclusions, the cosmic clothing, the victim beasts, the two goats, the divergent landscapes, the turmoil of angels, the world's unrest—all is laid out as a display by which the great chasm that is creation's grace is overcome somehow by God himself. The letter to the Hebrews describes this "somehow" as the flesh of the Son of God (Heb. 10:20), the very "going through" of the veil, a "living way" that marks the entire movement of Lev. 16 as inscribed upon God's own being that has taken up creation as his own burden and ever renewed love. Azazel's desert cliffs are them-selves rent by this wounded flesh, which, in its own tearing, marks the creation of new life through the resurrection (Matt. 27:51–53; cf. Rom. 4:17). When Origen speaks of the "whole letter" to the Hebrews as the subject of Lev. 16 (*Homilies on Leviticus* 9.2; 12 passim), he means in part this enormous cosmic movement by which the Sabbath rest that is described as the Day of Atonement's form (16:31) is established universally through the re-creative act of God (Heb. 3–4) as shadowed

8. An established Christian tradition that comes into interpretive play in all scriptural dichoto-mies views the two goats in terms of the two advents of Christ, which separate Jew and Christian Gentile: the first goat, covered scarlet, is driven into the wilderness and represents Jesus as rejected by the Jews; while the second, sacrificed upon the altar, represents Jesus as visible in liturgical glory (e.g., Tertullian, *Against the Jews* 14). Rupert of Deutz (Patrologia latina 167.818–20) transforms this into Christ and his evil image, the antichrist (the scapegoat), and the ritual thereby plays out the eschatological history of the world, while also comprehending within it the two fates of humankind outlined by Origen (*Homilies on Leviticus* 10.2).

"in the beginning" (Gen. 2:2–3). Jesus makes new what he has made from the start (John 1:3); and he does this through the assumption of all things in their own limits and mortal incapacities and rejections as they litter the landscape of wilderness and world. His "prayers and supplications," "cry[ing] and tears" (Heb. 5:7), gather the afflicted character of Israel's troubled rest (Lev. 16:31) and draw the Israelites into the heavens of God's own life.

Jewish and Christian exegesis parts ways decisively at this point. The Day of Atonement becomes infused with a radically penitential spirit within Judaism after the temple's destruction, demanding repentance as the effective basis for the Day of Atonement's usefulness and turning the worshiper toward both God and neighbor in search of forgiveness (Jerusalem Talmud, tractate *Yoma* 8.9). But Jesus, through his flesh's own afflictions, becomes the true or perfect penitent, as C. S. Lewis put it in *Mere Christianity* (perhaps only unconsciously drawing on a long tradition brought to a powerful pitch in Bérulle and his followers). Obviously the necessity of true repentance is lodged within the center of the gospel proclamation (Mark 1:15; Luke 13:5). But it is also transposed into the body of Jesus himself: "Father, forgive them; they know not what they do" (Luke 23:34; cf. Stephen in Acts 7:60). And transposition of penitence to the particular person of Jesus is possible only to the degree that this body, like the veil of the sanctuary, gathers to it the fullness of human life and history. This, at least, is what the Jewish ordering of the Day of Atonement points to and therefore provides a pathway for Christian understanding. But the transposition to *this* body is historically limited and becomes, therefore, a single place for all time, the "once for all" of Heb. 9:26, that steps beyond the repeated sacrifices of the Levitical revelation and orders all things through its singular occurrence in this one man.

The mysterious relationship between creation and redemption is laid out here. The Christian tradition, following Hebrews, has tended to see the Day of Atonement's fulfillment in Christ as one of moving from ineffective signs to effective reality, from the indication of sin as a constant in human life to sin's actual purification and removal from the conscience or motivating life of human beings bound to Christ (Heb. 10:3, 11–14). The "blood of goats and bulls" (9:13) that is repeatedly—either daily or even yearly on the Day of Atonement—offered under the old covenant cannot in fact cleanse from sin; it can only point to the need for such cleansing that is possible solely through the act of God in Christ, whose own blood stands as the ultimate breaking through of the separative barrier erected by human sin. Yet just this singular assignment of redemption to the creator alone seems to place the sacrifice for sin in a parallel to creation itself and to creation's miraculous existence at all. What I have called the "chasm of creation" seems to *include* the challenge of sin, not to stand as sin's external object of dissolution: only God can make, only Gold can come close, only God can love; yet is the redemptive love of the "once for all" sacrifice of Christ historically different or continuous with the divine "only" that is God's in any case? Is creation itself a divine sacrifice?

Judaism, especially in its Kabbalistic developments, has answered this last question in the affirmative, as in the Lurianic doctrine of the divine "withdrawal" (*zimzum*) through which creation is, in a sense, given space within which to exist. The tabernacle is itself a physical image of this self-limitation, wherein God's presence is focused in a single location, and thereby the separateness that is creation's very being is granted a kind of visible embodiment, served (and thereby emphasized) by the sacrificial offerings of Israel's people. Christianity has tended to resist these kinds of metaphysical assertions, largely in order to protect the singularity of incarnation and passion. But the question of the continuity of creation and redemption has still pressed itself upon theological reflection, from Duns Scotus's speculations on the incarnation's certain occurrence even without the fall to the grappling with conundra of divine providential foreknowledge fastened to texts like Rev. 13:8, read in the Vulgate as the "the Lamb slain before the foundation of the world" (*qui occisus est ab origine mundi*), and 1 Pet. 1:20, referring to the sacrificial lamb "destined before the foundation of the world." Likewise, debates in the sixteenth through eighteenth centuries on the character of divine grace before and after the fall have similarly been fueled by concerns over what ought to be precise definitions of God's relationship to creation in original and corrupted historical forms.[9] Is the grace of a gracious God—whether creating or redeeming—not one and the same in all of its contexts?

The drift of the present commentary is to answer the question of continuity affirmatively, as the reliance upon the tabernacle's cosmic meaning in this chapter indicates. But the purpose of this affirmation here is not to dilute the singular character of Christ's historical embodiment of God's effective work of salvation on the cross. Rather, the figural direction of the Levitical text's referents must mean that the once-for-all reality of Jesus's sacrifice permeates the breadth of cosmic gathering given in the tabernacle's atonement practice, even as that breadth expands the aim of the cross's occurrence. Incarnation, in its joining of human and divine realities, in its very embodiment of God's creation and coming together, is given in the flesh of sacrifice almost by definition. It is possible to see Origen's ascetic anthropology, then, less in terms of the human work of obedience through which salvation is gained and more as a participatory reflection of the one reality of God's saving work in Christ, which defines in advance the character of creation's existence. Although the Gospels speak of the temple veil as a separating reality between humanity and God, ripped in two by the sacrifice of Christ (Matt. 27:51), Hebrews, as we have seen, rather sees the veil as the incarnate body of Jesus through which we are moved into the precincts of God's presence (10:20), the bridge across the chasm. The rebellion of sin that determines Origen's two-goat dichotomy marking human destiny is thus properly seen not simply as a failure

9. On Scotus, see Cross 1998. Some of the subsequent debates—from Baianism through Jansenism—can be surveyed in Rondet 1966; de Lubac 1998 (his theological defense of continuity); idem, 2000 (his argument versus discontinuity); and Radner 2002.

of will to obey God, but as a rejection of God's own coming and all that it entails for the shape of the world. Sin is not defined independently of the incarnation and cross, therefore, but solely in their light, even "from the foundation of the world." And atonement describes the power of that divine coming to press even beyond such rejecting barriers and take up the human heart struggling with the inadequacies of created self-sustenance.

Creation is old when it is not constantly renewed by the one whose death is his coming; creation is made new when it is taken up in its fullness into the form of the one who comes to it across the chasm of its helpless isolation, glorious in itself, yet nothing in the face of its maker. Those turned to Christ are caught up in this renewal (Rom 12:2; Col. 3:10). "If any one is in Christ, he is a new creation; the old has passed away, behold, the new has come. All this is from God, who through Christ reconciled us to himself and gave us the ministry of reconciliation; that is, God was in Christ reconciling the world to himself, not counting their trespasses against them, and entrusting to us the message of reconciliation" (2 Cor. 5:17–19 Revised Standard Version margin). In this way, the atonement of Christ must, by definition, reach the world; and because it is the atonement *of* Christ, the word by which the world is made, this world's very being is given to it in the form of Christ's sacrifice. There is nothing precisely substitutionary about this: it is rather the character of life itself, of grace, as it touches a creature whose being is never self-sustaining, indeed that is wasting away, yet whose purpose is to be loved and to love in return.[10] The ordering of the world in Lev. 11–15 is thus a commentary upon Nadab's and Abihu's deaths, drawing in all Israel and the Gentiles together, Aaron's loss and Eve's weeping and their common yearning, being oriented toward "the mystery hidden for ages, . . . which is Christ in you, the hope of glory" (Col. 1:26–27).

10. The commentary on Lev. 5 discusses the notion of forgiveness as new creation in the sense of God's engaged entry anew into the life of the alienated creature. Substitution as a theory of atonement attempts to describe the mechanism by which Christ redeems us; but it does not explain, let alone establish, the fact of our concrete destiny in Christ.

LEVITICUS 17

The tradition has always recognized that Lev. 16 is at the center of the mystery of divine love. And now, turning to Lev. 17, we are taken more deeply into the character of this love, that is, the shedding of blood and the offering of self that, understood in the light of the cosmic vision of Lev. 16, is now shown to root the very character of creation. Blood is life, God tells Moses; but blood shed is the wasting of life. Blood shed for sake of wasting creatures is love and life made new. Leviticus 17 takes the reality of atonement and uses it to explicate the unfolding of history itself, and to this extent, it can be rightly understood only as we see creation and history themselves in their full reach. The blood—of Christ—does not solve a discrete problem; rather it is wrapped up with the entire reality of God's creating will in which problems and their responses emerge as the form of his love.

We must recall, then, how Lev. 16 brings creation into the realm of God's initiated approach: "Lo, I have come to do thy will," says Aaron in effect. Yet this exclamation turns out to be the voice of God himself, who comes in the "body prepared" that is Jesus's own (Ps. 40:6–10/Heb. 10:5–7), a "single sacrifice" (Heb. 10:12) by which the veil of created being, its very flesh, is rent and brought into the bosom of the creator, the sacrifice and sacrificer, victim and priest, Abraham who cries out "Here am I!" (Gen. 22:11) and the son for whom and in whom provision is made (22:8, 14). Creation in this way is, in its very origin and being, a sacrificial existent, rooted in offering. This is so in its own fundamental orientation toward God, and the reality of sin in no wise undercuts this foundation: "Worthy art thou, our Lord and God, to receive glory and honor and power, for thou didst create all things, and by thy will they existed and were created" (Rev. 4:11). But there is also—and this is what is revealed in the atoning character of the creator who takes flesh and says, "Lo, I have come!"—a revelation here of God's own self-giving, which allows this song of literal worship that is creation's being to be uttered. God lets creation sing; God gives voice to creation's prayers (his own Spirit praying through it; Rom. 8:18–28); God gives rise to such praise only by giving himself over to the impossibility of such distinction from himself, only by throwing himself into the pit of such difference, even "to [its] end" (John 13:1), even to the depths of its disappearance amid the dead (1 Pet. 3:18–22; Rom. 10:7; Phil. 2:7–8), from which new life is given. Paul speaks of *kenosis* or "self-emptying" in this context, a phrase that has had a significant role in Christian theology, from Athanasius (one of his favorite anti-Arian texts being the hymn of Phil. 2:5–11) to the modern era. But it is important to see this kenotic character of God as lodged within the sacrificial matrix of creation itself, as explicated Levitically. This is why the phrase can be taken up also by a Jewish philosopher like Emmanuel Levinas, in his talmudic discussions of human prayer, wherein he explains the atoning value of intercession as a response to the giving over of God to creation's own need (1994: 114–32 and 1998: 53–60).

Thus, within this Levitical matrix, we can see some congruence between Christian and Jewish understandings of the very nature of divine love. To Heidegger's famous question, "why is there something rather than nothing?" we turn to the self-giving love of God not so much as a satisfying explanation (though it may be that), but as the inescapable movement that turns us toward him in the midst of every destructive aspect of our experience, including the question of our being at all. Psalm 33's linking of creation and divine love (33:5, 18), for instance, is perhaps unexceptional, except that its confession arises from within the reality of estrangement and thereby makes human existence something shaped by waiting and trusting and prayer itself. It is in the context of this estrangement and trust—the consciousness of sin in its theological dimensions—that the true character of divine love emerges. Human need before God perceives God's wrath and judgment (Ps. 6 or 90) as the very basis upon which turning and waiting and trusting can proceed: this is the paradox of "judgment and mercy" joined as one, the paradox by which Pascal, for example, was able to grasp the reality of the cross. Our need is a sign of God's anger, that is, of our turning away from all that gives life; yet our turning back in such need is a sign of God's mercy: if these two aspects are to take shape in history—"Lo, I have come!—they do so in the sacrificed flesh of God's own self. This is the Christian version of *tikkun*, the reordering of a broken world through the reparative acts of righteousness—in this case, God's own, in Christ Jesus, whereby good is brought out of evil.[1] God's anger is a side of God's desire to be with us, to have made us at all to be his. And coming to us, even in this extended difference (extended by our own turning away), death becomes the vessel, not the end, of his drawing near and establishing us with him in his life—what John Milbank rightly notes as the "resurrection being the ground of the ethical" (1999: 38).[2] Resurrection is that new creation that comes from the

---

1. On *tikkun* in the context of Jewish views of repentance—new acts of righteousness that somehow outweigh and reorder the deforming effects of past sins—see Steinsaltz's *Thirteen Petalled Rose* (1985: 125–36), a modern classic on Jewish faith.

2. Milbank's argument (in this case wrongly aimed at, among others, Levinas) is that unilateral self-giving for the other—"pure altruism"—cannot be the highest form of ethical action, for

deepest place of all, not nothingness itself, but the place where the creature stares at nothingness and crumbles.

All this represents a theological context in which the discussion of blood in Lev. 17 must be read, for here we have the only theoretical assertions upon which the previous chapters, in their sacrificial and purity-related discussions, might be explicated: "For the life of the flesh is in the blood; and I have given it for you upon the altar to make atonement for your souls; for it is the blood that makes atonement, by reason of the life. . . . For the life of every creature is the blood of it" (17:11, 14). But we must approach this theoretical clue only from within a discussion of the blood as it is linked to the detailed exposition of created forms given in time that marks the first sixteen chapters of the book. In a sense, we must not allow the blood to be a single theoretical key to the sacrificial system, but must rather insist that it be a reflective element within its larger display of the character of *all* creation as particularly distinct and, in these distinctions, as variously related to God through the reality of self-offering.

Given the encompassing practical reach of the sacrificial system, a singular reliance upon the blood as its interpretive key can easily reduce that system to a kind of ritual choreography or embodied text that is designed to convey a message derivable from its central sanguinary symbol. This has indeed been the tendency within anthropological and related approaches to the matter of sacrifice, which have often sought a kind of translation of the actions—cultural husks—into some core meaning that is extractable from the practices themselves. Obviously, this has been a temptation in Christian exegesis and modern forms of Christian supersessionism especially: the blood sacrifices of Leviticus mean something other than their own embodiments, and this meaning ("unbloody" in the language of the Christian tradition) is more accurately expressed in a different language altogether, the language of the New Testament. But even modernizing Jewish orthodoxies, like Hirsch's (1989: 2.464–74), have followed a similar path. Pursuing his symbological approach to the Torah, he reads the "animal blood" as an expository image of the "animal nature" against which human beings must struggle as they seek to achieve their moral calling in submission to God's elevated demands. The entire chapter (and its prohibitions) is explained in these terms, wherein blood stands for a moral referent. There is something appealing in transforming the directives for the control of bloodshed into the categories of self-control itself, and thereby the preceding chapters of Leviticus into the story of human ethical

---

such sacrifice is in fact unencumbered by the other for whom one dies and abstracts itself from the particularities of interaction and engagement. Citing Robert Spaeman, Milbank notes for example that feasting with the hungry is better than simply giving food away to the hungry. This, of course, represents the very purpose of creation and God's own sacrifice on its behalf—friendship and communion, in Irenaeus's phrase. There is, however, no resurrection apart from that sacrifice, just as there is no creation at all—since creation and resurrection are images of each other—without sacrifice. This is why the Levitical system in fact must signify a very broad history of relationship and not simply a calculus of expiation that can be applied in an ultimate fashion to Jesus's own actions.

transcendence. Still, Hirsch presses for strict observance (within posttemple possibilities), though now the need to practice the kosher laws is explained in terms of simple obedience and ritual pedagogy, two motives less compelling today perhaps than in Hirsch's nineteenth-century German context (leaving aside the question of whether they would have made sense to Moses and the Israelites of whatever period). This is the nature of cultural symbols: their force depends on social factors largely independent of theological provenance.

The interpretive issue raised above is important because it shapes not only the Christian reading of Leviticus, but our understanding of the nature of Christ's sacrifice itself. We are aware of the centrality of the image of blood within both the New Testament and later church tradition as they have depicted the person and work of Christ (e.g., Col. 1:20; 2:14; Eph. 1:7). In general, however, this image has in fact been explained according to its own rather strict symbological code, whereby the Levitical sacrifices have been parsed according to a calculus of meaning that is then applied directly, through the translatable symbol of the blood, to Jesus's own work. Hence, the statement in Hebrews that "without the shedding of blood there is no forgiveness of sins" (9:22) is taken as a comprehensive symbolic definition capable of translating, from the Old Testament, the meaning (and emblematic historical necessity) of Jesus's death. When we are told why this is so—why is there blood rather than nothing at all?—we are sent back to the symbolic character of blood as life within a particular scheme of meaning regarding sin and its forgiveness.

Not all of this is mistaken, but the strict symbological understanding of the blood also creates interpretative problems. As many Jews have pointed out, Jesus's death on the cross fits awkwardly into the Levitical framework taken strictly. And if not taken strictly, where do we in fact locate the symbolic connections most firmly? For instance, the form (crucifixion) and place (outside the temple) of Jesus's death do not conform exactly to the requirements set out in Lev. 17 (and elsewhere). Jews for Judaism, a contemporary Jewish apologetic organization, puts it this way on the FAQ sheet of their website (jewsforjudaism.org):

> Question: What difference does it make if Jesus did or did not undergo serious blood loss while being prepared for or undergoing execution? Answer: . . . In the biblical blood sacrifice offering, a token blood letting is not sufficient nor is mere death sufficient. The sacrifice has to die through the shedding of blood. At no time did Jesus suffer blood loss to the extent of it being the cause of his death. Neither the blood loss due to the scourging (Matthew 27:26, Mark 15:15, John 19:1), the nail wounds (John 20:25), or crown of thorns (Matthew 27:29, Mark 15:17, John 19:2) caused Jesus' death. As a result, not only was Jesus' death not an everlasting atonement for sin it was not even a sacrifice.

> Question: What is the only biblically acceptable means of sacrificial death? Answer: Biblically, sacrificial death could only occur through the shedding of blood exclusively (Leviticus 17:11). Jesus' death by crucifixion cannot be considered a

sacrificial death. His death may have been caused by either asphyxiation or by going into shock brought on by the traumatic physical events of his last hours, before and after he was nailed to the cross. In his case, shock would not have been brought on solely by blood loss. The Gospels indicate Jesus' blood was not shed to a degree that would make blood loss from the body the exclusive cause of death. Death solely by blood loss is the only biblical cause acceptable for an animal's sacrificial death.

Although the spiritualization of the Levitical elements can easily be accomplished, as we have seen (e.g., the prohibition of eating bloody hunted flesh or carrion in Lev. 17:13–15), Origen's fundamental approach to such interpretive adjustment does not employ a careful correlation of symbols, not only because such a correlation is not strictly possible, but because the character of the figures involved—in this case, blood—can be apprehended only from a multidirectional and contextually multiplied vantage (*Homilies on Leviticus* 9.9). Even having said this, however, one must grapple with the central symbolic incongruity of the New Testament application of blood imagery to Jesus's mission and meaning—the call by Jesus, Paul, and the entire Christian tradition grown up around the Eucharist, to "drink his blood": "Truly, truly, I say to you, unless you eat the flesh of the Son of man and drink his blood, you have no life in you. . . . For my flesh is food indeed, and my blood is drink indeed" (John 6:53, 55); "the cup of blessing which we bless, is it not a communion in the blood of Christ?" (1 Cor. 10:16 Revised Standard Version margin). Nothing could be more contradictory to the Levitical discussions of Lev. 17: "If any man of the house of Israel or of the strangers that sojourn among them eats any blood, I will set my face against that person who eats blood, and will cut him off from among his people" (17:10). John tells us that "many of his disciples," when they heard Jesus's teaching, call it a "hard saying" and "drew back" (John 6:60, 66). This is not simply a reaction to "cannibalistic" language. Even more deeply the looming threat of blood impurity that Jesus implies drives them away. So great is the religious affront of Jesus's words that it leads some scholars to treat the eucharistic language as almost purely a Hellenistic influence, derived apart from the scriptural molding of Leviticus altogether. Others prefer to reduce the Christian appropriation of Levitical language to merely conventional usage, an admission that the actual Levitical texts, in Christian terms, have been eviscerated of integral meaning.[3]

Within the Christian tradition, the blood incongruity, if we may so call this particular interpretive problem, has proved a critical line of Protestant-Catholic divergence. Recognizing that the dominical and eucharistic language of drinking blood sits uncomfortably (to say the least) with Levitical and Old Testament commitments, Protestants used the incongruity especially as a basis for their argument

3. See Cahill 2002 for a pugnacious engagement with the critical history of this "extraordinary" and "glaring incongruity," theologically speaking. The notion of "conventional" usage, applied to Christian appropriations of blood imagery, is Wilfred Knox's; see Montefiore and Loewe 1960: xc.

against the doctrine of transubstantiation. With respect to the appropriation of Levitical language by the New Testament, Willet (1631: 415) insisted that we must deploy a twofold application: only the death of Jesus itself, in its historical particularity, can sustain a strict and literal integration of Levitical language; all other usage—even in the Old Testament—of blood imagery and sacrificial tropes must be exclusively symbolic and spiritual in its reference. There is no real tasting or drinking of Christ's blood in the Eucharist, for instance; rather, these phrases of Paul and their parallels in Jesus's discussion in John 6 refer to Christ's word, which is to be "devoured by hearing, ruminated by understanding, and digested by faith," in a famous phrase of Tertullian (*On the Resurrection of the Flesh* 37, in a discussion of Jesus's words that the "flesh profiteth nothing" from John 6:63 Authorized Version).

Apart from the Eucharist, even Catholics tended to agree with this rigorous spiritualization of the blood. Hence, the blood within carrion flesh mentioned in Lev. 17:15, for instance, was read in terms of the evil doctrine of heretics and philosophers—a vivid image in several respects (Bruno of Segni [Patrologia latina 164.440–41]). But the result was to render the historical referents of the text, even where they were necessarily acknowledged, as weak as possible. And so, in the only scriptural case in which a positive Christian approach to the blood laws is mentioned, the literal prohibitions against eating bloody flesh adopted by the apostles in Acts 15 were evaluated as passing cultural adaptations, asserted only temporarily during the time of transition from Jewish to Gentile church—the blurred historical moment when the shadows had not quite yet been dispersed by the dawning light.[4] Contemporary sensibilities, in any case, have seized on these theological views of development and simply thrust aside the bloody sacrifices of Leviticus with the same enlightened disgust, as was early expressed by Heraclitus's disdain of religious devotees of his age: "When defiled they purify themselves with blood—as though one who had stepped into filth should wash himself with filth" (Wheelwright 1959: 69 frag. 78). It is a strange evolution in which modernist sentiments seem to cohere with orthodox Jewish reaction.

Is there a better way to take hold of the almost abstracted discussion of the blood in Lev. 17? As earlier twentieth-century scholars liked to note, the Semitic root for the Hebrew word for blood (*dam*) went through a number of referential transformations, moving through the meanings of "bloodguilt" and "blood-price" to a general sense of "value." To speak of the "blood as the life" rightly points to an underlying qualitative reality, emphasized by the divine interchange with Noah in Gen. 9:4–6, where blood as "life" (*nephesh*) is tied to the creation of human beings in God's image. At its most basic, the precepts regarding blood in Lev. 17

---

4. It appears that Christians in many places continued to follow the Jerusalem injunction against eating flesh with the blood in it for at least a couple of centuries. Curiously, we are told by Eusebius that Christians in Lyons and Vienne countered the calumny of being child-eaters (i.e., cannibals of the kind pointed to by the bare words of Jesus in John 6) by pointing out that they strictly maintained the laws against eating bloody meat (*Ecclesiastical History* 5.1; see also Tertullian, *Apology* 9).

involve turning Israel toward the reality of creation itself, a reality founded in God's own gift of life. The great Anglican evangelical Charles Simeon noted that the reflection upon blood at this point in the book underscores the meaning of sacrifice itself, in that, in the definition of blood's gift as its atoning action (17:11) it turns us toward the "one who atones," that is, who gives life in the midst of death and nothingness (cited in Gray and Adams 1903: 315).

The blood speaks of God as creator somehow. This is important to grasp, since it has been easy for commentators, beginning with Clement of Alexandria, to worry in this context over how the blood, in its reality as physical fluid, relates to the soul by which human beings are counted as creatures. The scientific-metaphysical intricacies of this topic consumed later exegetes. But even Clement realized that, in the end, the reality of the blood within the creature acted as a kind of John the Baptist, pointing away from itself to its maker. The blood itself signifies the word's own work in time of turning us to the creator:

> Thus in many ways the Word is figuratively described, as meat, and flesh, and food, and bread, and blood, and milk. The Lord is all these, to give enjoyment to us who have believed on Him. Let no one then think it strange, when we say that the Lord's blood is figuratively represented as milk. For is it not figuratively represented as wine? "Who washes," it is said, "His garment in wine, His robe in the blood of the grape." In His own Spirit He says He will deck the body of the Word; as certainly by His own Spirit He will nourish those who hunger for the Word.
>
> And that the blood is the Word, is testified by the blood of Abel, the righteous interceding with God. For the blood would never have uttered a voice, had it not been regarded as the Word: for the righteous man of old is the type of the new righteous one; and the blood of old that interceded, intercedes in the place of the new blood. And the blood that is the Word cries to God, since it intimated that the Word was to suffer. (*Instructor* 1.6 [trans. Roberts and Donaldson])

Clement's figuralism is thoroughly historical, as his reference to Abel indicates: the word somehow moves, in time, through the reality of the blood, and the blood thereby becomes a literal actor in the relationship of the human creature to God. Instead of functioning as an instrumental factor within a calculus of substitution—as later Protestant and Catholic exegetes eventually came to understand it[5]—the blood here becomes a living and dramatic character in human orientation to their maker, who is the word become bloody flesh. We have already engaged this way of understanding the sacrificial actions within the earlier chapters of Leviticus:

5. Willet 1631: 404–5 cites various exegetes on this matter: Leviticus sets up a simple formula whereby "animals die for men's sin, out of God's mercy." If this is not done correctly, i.e., in the right place (and with the right intention), there is no effective substitution, and thus the individual is still liable to death or the "cutting off" mentioned in 17:4. In part, it is the liability to breakdown within this system of substitution that makes the singular atonement of Christ's blood necessary—mistakes are too easily made and, in the end, our sins are countless, "more [in number] than the hairs of my head" (Ps. 40:12).

in their various ways they enact realities of human life's history: life given over (Adam), life squandered (Cain), life offered (Abel), life re-creating and re-created (Christ Jesus). The blood is an element within the formulation of human history's shape according to the forms of the scriptural narrative itself that, as Clement indicates, is the word at work in the world's coming-to-be.

Within this context, Lev. 17's particulars must be taken up as markers of this history. What Israel does with the blood traces the contours of its life with God over time. The animals of Israel's common life, for example—the ox or lamb or goat (17:3)—are given by God *as* sacrificial beasts and defined as such exclusively. Their slaughter, God commands, can be accomplished only at the tent of meeting, and thereby the physical relation of the people of Israel to God is constrained and shaped according to the shedding of the sacrificial blood. The entire sweep of the Deuteronomic vision of blessing and dependence, experienced from wilderness to Canaan, is outlined here, as is the exclusive orientation toward God given in the place of sacrifice (17:5, 8–9). The pouring out of all blood upon the ground in other situations engages, as Clement notes, the life and death of Abel and the intricate interplay of sin within the gift of existence. The uncleanness of unsacrificed or unbled flesh marks the trespass into a realm of created difference—given in death—already bound to God's power, much as the later history of Saul and then David demonstrates, in their spirals of vengeance and familial dissolution.

In short, the lifting up of the blood in Lev. 17 unveils the historical interplay of creation (blood as life), sin (shed blood as draining life away), and the acts that embody the particular love that comes from God (blood as self-offering). *Rabbah* 22.1–3 itself moves in this direction of interpretation, taking Eccl. 5:9 as the main elucidating verse to the chapter as a whole: "The superfluities of the earth are among them all" (a particular translation of an otherwise baffling text). The superfluities spoken of by Solomon here signify the vast and multiplied elements of creation and time that God uses providentially to order the universe and Israel's history especially. The application of this scriptural verse to blood sacrifice has puzzled readers of the *Rabbah*. But what the *Rabbah* is after here, it seems, is the drawing of a parallel between God's providential role in all creation—to uphold, distinguish, even alter in distinguishing—and Israel's call to respond to that work of God in its own sacrificial distinctions. These, in turn, become its stumbling blocks in history (through misapplication, disobedience, and perversion), bringing both punishment and proving the occasion for divine forgiveness. "The thing which the LORD has commanded" (Lev. 17:2)—that is, the sacrificial law here in its particularity and detail—is now extended, in its history of fulfillment and rejection, to the story of Israel's and the world's submission to the creative will of God in its historical sweep.[6] It would not be right to call blood, in this reading,

---

6. Lev. 17:2 becomes a proverbial Jewish proof-text for divinely inspired extemporaneous preaching (Newman 1934: 349). More broadly, both Jewish and Christian interpreters saw this foundation of direct command to the laws of blood sacrifice as a helpful means of explaining the historically malleable character of their fulfillment. Why, for instance, were religious heroes of

a symbol of time, to be apprehended as a cipher for a translated referent. Rather, blood here acts as the *marker* of time, the space of history, and thus its physical distinguisher whose shedding in various ways organizes the shape of time. Blood and the fate of blood is the visible demonstration of *created* life and its relationship, via grace, with its creator.

In terms of the Scriptures as a whole, this makes a good deal of sense. Blood imagery within the Bible works generally as an explicator of historical destiny: there are, of course, "rivers of blood" as in the plagues of Egypt; there are also seas turned into blood as in Rev. 8:9—a book within which blood covering the earth to various degrees repeatedly measures the progress of a divine plan (the figures derive from Joel 2:30–31); there is, finally, the "eating" of blood, constituting the engagement of divine wrath. Here especially, in the shadow of Lev. 17, we are faced with the world's complete disordering and caught in the midst of its dizzying dissolution at the hands of sin. In Ezek. 39:17–20, for instance, God's judgment against the nations is depicted as a sacrificial feast at which the blood of God's enemies is drunk and their flesh eaten by "the birds . . . and . . . the beasts of the field," a violent confusion to the orderings of purity and atonement within the distinctions of creation. In this case, the drinking of human blood embodies both the totality of evil and its drastic overthrow. Just here does the blood incongruity, as I have described it above, find its historical profile given in the horrendous fate of sin itself, wherein the enemies of God's people drink blood *because* they are enemies and destroyers of what is good (Rev. 16:6; much like the Egyptians and their Nile, as in Exod. 7:21 and Ps. 78:44); or, debased to the bottom of their pit, they eat their *own* flesh and drink their own blood (Isa. 49:26). It is a strange and numbing victory, especially when triumph is transposed into a comparable scene of bloody ingestion: Jacob is turned into a devouring lion, whose teeth drip red (Num. 23:24).

The discomfort of the Last Supper and Eucharist emerges here in its true character, as the primal affront of God's creative love that shatters every claim to a human order somehow defined apart from the incomprehensible astonishment of God's work. It is not simply that Jesus calls upon his disciples to do something that does not cohere with a fundamental Levitical principle and thus is grossly incorrect. This view, as we have seen, necessitates theoretical histories of liturgical genealogy, a discipline that underlines the constructive task of liturgiology

---

Israel able to offer sacrifices with impunity other than at the tabernacle (e.g., 1 Sam. 7; 2 Sam. 24; 1 Kgs. 18)? Was this not because the sacrificial act, in these cases particularly as in the general law, was engaged via *revelatione divina*, that is, by direct divine command? The sacrifices depended, not upon some moral logic, but upon God's direct and inscrutable demand. For *Rabbah* 22.9 this pointed to the particularistically engaged aspect of divine history; for Christians like Nicholas of Lyra (*Postilla super totam bibliam, in Leviticum*, cited in Willet 1631: 404), it pointed to the sovereign power of God to alter cultic precepts (and hence initiate a new covenant as he chose); while for Calvin (1996: 2.260–61), it underscored the encompassing virtue of human obedience to the bare demands of the divine will.

in its humanly manipulative and domesticated character. But the Eucharist is, by definition of its blood drinking, incapable of being ordered by human history: it is rather constitutive of history as belonging to God. And so Jesus draws his disciples into the fate of Israel and the world. It is a fate, after all, that he has first entered and whose passage he has first traversed, that he has made his own. The Eucharist is a tasting here of the curse that Jesus has become—or rather, a tasting of this very becoming—the sin he has come to embody in his entry into human creaturely existence in all of its disordered freedoms and rebellions (Gal. 3:13; 2 Cor. 5:21). Hence, the Eucharist is tinged with blasphemy from the start. The double sense of the cross—judgment and mercy—is well known. But the same double sense must rightly be discerned within the Eucharist itself, where blood is drunk as the suffusing entry into the world of human sin in love—God's love entered, God's love torn, God's love imbibed (Mark 10:38; 14:36)—and *therefore* the cry, "'Eloi, Eloi, lama sabachthani?' which means, 'My God, my God, why hast thou forsaken me?'" (Mark 15:34, quoting Ps. 22:1), as if Adam's recognition of life given and lost is now the only means of being remade from nothing (Rom. 4:17). All creation shudders at the Lord's Table—and well it should, for here the Lord God of the universe "gives himself" to stains of blood taken and shed. The Eucharist is God's first, before it is the church's. As such, it shakes the foundations of the earth even as it steadies them.

This Eucharist is bound to the cosmic character of the temple offering examined in Lev. 16. Created life is a sacrifice *from* God—God creates, God gives himself away for the sake of life—and this sacrifice is given in the heavenly temple and at the heavenly altar that rises above and towers over all human temples and altars (Rev. 6:9; 8:3, 5; 9:13; 11:1; 14:18; 16:7).[7] What does one behold at the altar of God? One sees the souls of righteous martyrs bound to the Lamb, crying forth, bloodied themselves by the evil ones who shed blood, and covered with the blood of the Son of God (7:9–14), whose life is given most essentially because he has made life and set it over and against himself. Yet they are seen at this altar of God not only because they have died, but because they been made alive once more; they are resurrected. God's own blood is the first life—the Lamb slain "before the foundation of the world" (13:8) precedes all other blood and *is* life itself.

And just as the Levitical blood points to the cosmic Eucharist, so too does the Levitical ordering of the priesthood point to the gathering up of humankind into a cosmic service, swept along into the wake of Christ Jesus, "a kingdom [of] priests" "from every tribe and tongue and people and nation" (Rev. 5:9–10). "Any man of the house of Israel" (Lev. 17:3), drawn by Christ into "the strangers that sojourn among them" (17:8) and from there into "all the world," is sprinkled, even washed, with the blood that daubed the robes of Aaron. What the discussion of

---

7. Bataille's claim (1985: 61–74) that automutilation stands at the root of all sacrifice has some sense from a divine perspective; except that, whereas for Bataille it is a bloodletting of the self exercised in anger and hatred against all things, this sacrifice is given in love for the very being of all things, expressing it, embodying it, inventing it.

blood in Lev. 17 does is to make yet more apparent the understanding that lies behind all the sacrificial actions: the first sacrifice really is God's in Christ, just as the first blood is given there. And all others, both before and after, are taken up into it, approaching God's own approach to them, through the bloody robes that witness martyrially to the truth of God.

"I have given [blood] for you upon the altar to make atonement for your souls; it is it the blood that makes atonement, by reason of the life" (17:11). For God to say this is not to lay out dispensational mechanism, applied mechanistically in a physical way in the Old Testament and symbolic way in the New, for in the Old Testament it has the same symbolic meaning as in the New Testament, and in the New Testament it has the same physicality as in the Old. In both cases, the mechanism, however, is less easily manipulated as human beings might wish, since it is ordered by God's own life, blood, and creative power. When Peter writes that "love covers a multitude of sins" (1 Pet. 4:8, perhaps citing Prov. 10:12), he is using the word "love" as an exact synonym for "blood," although the covering derives from God's own self-giving, not one of human initiative (a distinction implied in the usual application of the two Hebrew words for "cover" and "atone" respectively; Ps. 32:1; 85:2). Love covers sin, because the giving of blood is first God's gift—as life and as the restoration of life. Love is the first and founding sacrifice, whose reality overflows into the self-giving of those who have come near or offered themselves to God (1 John 4:8–12). Not only is this the Christian claim of the gospel, but it coheres (apart from the historical assertion of the incarnation) with the development of rabbinic interpretations of repentance and righteous action, even martyrdom, as extensions of the Levitical blood sacrifices in the posttemple world. Atonement through the shedding of blood is physically continuous with, not only signifying of, the offering of self in love for God and neighbor (Montefiore and Loewe 1960: xci).

The category of expiation in this light is less concretely explained than some have desired. In contrast to a strictly juridical understanding of sin's atonement, whereby justice demands some kind of balancing of disordering sin through a rectifying payment—a life for a life as one might read Gen. 9:5—sin is understood here in terms of its historically rooted exaggeration of creation's cost to God, and therefore its overcoming is given in the heightened transformative reality of re-creative self-expenditure. We cannot logically say that the love by which God creates is different in kind than the love by which God forgives; nor, for that matter, that the love by which the creature worships God is different in kind than the love by which the creature repents. God's love is one, and the love we give in return is called into that oneness. But these loves, divine and human, can be recounted in particular ways whose contours bear differing modes of experiential form. And so to speak of Jesus as "the expiation for our sins" (1 John 4:10; 2:2) "by his blood" (Rom. 3:25) is to speak of the otherwise historically undemonstrable "this" that is God's love: "In this is love, not that we loved God but that he loved us and sent his Son to be the expiation for our sins" (1 John 4:10). It is an uncovering in time by which all is brought into the light (John 8:12; Matt. 5:14–16) and a movement through history (*paresis* of Rom. 3:25) by which sin is dragged forward into a final place of self-giving (1 John 1:7–8). The term "expiation" expresses the specifically *temporal* element of the divine love, much as the blood marks its historical location in the course of time.[8]

Specific practical aspects related to the blood are all to be read in terms of this following of the cross. Indeed, as I shall discuss in the following chapters, this blood "following" becomes the determination, in Christian terms, of the moral law as something derived not by symbolic extraction from Levitical types, but discerned through its embodiment as being physically proximate to Christ Jesus: we truly know the law and its demands only by having Christ take us with him as he lives the law in his body. The blood martyr realism of both Testaments is connected by the tabernacle-Christ realism of the Levitical laws. Only before "the tabernacle of the LORD" may domestic animals be killed and thereby sacrificed (Lev. 17:4–9; cf. the frequent Deuteronomic injunction regarding "the place that the LORD will choose"); only joined to Christ is life given and received in love spent (Phil. 3:7–11; Mark 8:34–35). In this light we can make sense of the patristic view (followed by Calvin 1996: 2.260–61) that exclusive sacrificial locality—the command to sacrifice only at the tabernacle or temple—was part of the divine pedagogy to wean the Israelites away from polytheism (Lev. 17:7) to cleave to the one God, for such exclusive locality bespeaks the physical following that marks the path of the Lord through time.

Hence, the blood injunctions of Lev. 17 directly unveil the Sermon on the Mount's dominical words against anger (Matt. 5:21–26). Not only is Gen. 9:5–6 held in view here, with its general equation of bloodshed as bloodguilt, but Christian interpreters (Hesychius especially, promoted by Rabanus Maurus [Patrologia latina 108.431–34] and the *Glossa ordinaria* [Patrologia latina 113.345–46]) attached every aspect of the blood prohibition to this, from its shedding to its eating, moving from physical murder to verbal or mental denigration of a neighbor (linking Gen. 9:6 with Jas. 3:9) and back again, by emphasizing Jesus's own understanding of hatred as a form of murder itself. For 1 John 3:15—"any one who hates his brother is a murderer"—this bundle of connections is carried by the reality of the Christian life of following. Hating the Christian brother is seen as murder when we have entered the place—the "body"—in which true love is

---

8. See Levering 2005: chap. 2 for an appropriately sympathetic exposition of this. Levering's discussion of Thomas Aquinas's juridical understanding of Christ's sacrifice is subtle and comprehensive and gives the lie to the easy dismissals that moderns make in their rejection of punitive understandings of the cross, which, for Thomas, is located in the creative ordering of God, not in a simple calculus of ledgered balance. Still, some careful conceptual translation of this traditional language is necessary if it is to at least open up the Levitical understanding of sin and expiation in the historical terms outlined here, whereby the narrative continuity of offering and its cost within the temporal forms of Scripture is what is taken up in Christ's death, and not only the abstracted ledger itself.

given through the shedding of one's own blood (1 John 3:16: "By this we know love, the he laid down his life for us; and we ought to lay down our lives for the brethren"). And this act and way of living and dying subsumes the so-called apotropaic (cf. Exod. 12:7, 13; and perhaps various elements in Levitical consecration) and covenantal (cf. circumcision and Exod. 24:6–8) aspects of blood use in the Old Testament.

One might recognize, in passing, the moral pressures exerted by the blood injunctions with regard to animal life. It is pertinent to point out that the question of hunting and the arbitrary or uncontrolled killing of animals was a matter that did indeed concern medieval, Jewish, and Reformation commentators on Lev. 17 (Willet 1631: 413–14 and references). What represented the right treatment of animals and whether hunting was permissible and within what bounds was a matter of serious discussion based precisely on these texts. It is not clear how the topic became marginalized within the church's discourse, so that it now still occupies only the fringe culture wars associated with animal rights activism. Nonetheless, Mary Douglas's work, however one wishes to judge its details, shows how central a place these matters hold in Leviticus (1999: chaps. 6–7). There is no question but that the constraints placed upon killing and eating animal flesh, based upon its blood as life, derives from the animals' status within God's creation as not only analogously dependent upon God's grace along with humans, but as coordinately so within historical terms (Ps. 104). That means, of course, within the terms of redemption as well. At the least, the human instrumentalization of animal life is ruled a profound disorder and even blasphemy by the Levitical vision. And given the breadth of the blasphemy, structurally speaking, that contemporary culture promotes in this regard, it is simply difficult to get a handle on how one might, not to say must, approach this entire topic. Yet the character of imperative is nonetheless unyielding.

The blood injunctions, and in particular their rootedness within the reality of God's gift of life, clearly have retrospective significance for the discussion of childbirth in Lev. 12. Unlike the matters of murder-as-anger or the treatment of animals in the course of human existence, childbirth (and its purity laws) is an oddly specific instance of the character of blood as both life and sacrifice together. I discussed this at length earlier, but it is important to emphasize the way that, through the blood itself, the questions of the actual relations of man and woman in their procreative struggle bridge the too-often-asserted gap between the ritual and moral aspects of Levitical law, much as Augustine and the early church perceived. It is this bridge, through the blood itself, that must mark our attempts in the chapters that now follow to glean the significance of the moral law as the law of God.

Finally, let us return to the Eucharist with a concluding observation. Despite the exegetical efforts of the sixteenth and seventeenth centuries, Leviticus does not tell us what the Eucharist is. The debated distinction between symbol and physical reality is not resolved by Protestant-Roman Catholic arguments on spiritual referent versus transubstantiation. Leviticus does, however, point out the historical breadth of the Eucharist's reality: the life of Christ in its totality, as the eucharistic liturgy rightly orders it in its lectionary and anaphora, goes beyond the singular objects of consecrated bread and wine and points to the reality of the people of God as followers of Jesus in time. That is, the Eucharist unveils the divine creation, in all of its history, of the Christian disciple existing within the church. But this is not to abstract the meaning of the Eucharist. It is, instead, to place the particular within and at the center of time, as formed by time, that is, as marked by blood. The exclusionary nature of tabernacle sacrifice (Lev. 17:5), as I noted, is due to the exclusive nature of God's worship in the particular flesh of Christ, the new temple: follow *this* man, not another. And following—what we might call moral endeavor—is defined only in the terms of this man and his life, not in general ones. Hence blood and flesh are both physical and symbolic—and ever must so remain.

Tertullian, in defending the bodily resurrection, must come to grips with the claim of Paul that "flesh and blood cannot inherit the kingdom of God" (1 Cor. 15:50) and Jesus's own words that "it is the spirit that gives life, the flesh is of no avail" (John 6:63) (*On the Resurrection of the Flesh* 48–50). It is a difficult theological challenge. In meeting it, Tertullian wants to align blood with the Spirit, implying the Levitical claim that the blood (read "spirit") "gives life." But this can happen, he says, only within the reality of bodily resurrection, such as it is confirmed by Jesus's own ascension: flesh and blood, if resurrected and quickened, *do* inherit the kingdom, though not because of their substance as flesh and blood, but as receivers of the substance of God, the Spirit. They represent, indeed they *are*, the created receptors of divine life. The physical body cannot be cast away in heaven; instead, every aspect of it will be used in heaven, including mouths and noses and ears and even sexual organs; we just don't know how yet! But we know that it will all be used, because this is *who* we are made to be, not something else; and this is *who* Christ is, not another. Everything about this created particularity is given in and demonstrated through the blood and its history, which is one of a varied and twisted and finally infinitely focused offering of life and hence of love.

LEVITICUS 18

Leviticus 18 has gained a certain amount of contemporary interest—perhaps beyond any other text in the book—due to its single notation of homosexual sex as "an abomination" (18:22). This verse has become a battleground in the controversy over sexuality. Some of those advocating a revision to the church's traditional condemnation of homosexual sex have rightly sought to read 18:22 as part of a larger scriptural context, and the question of Lev. 18's larger informing character has therefore been raised with much vigor. Is the chapter in fact part of a larger literary scheme, perhaps even one of a certain formal type? Ought we to speak here—or perhaps even earlier, beginning with Lev. 17—of a textual seam that places these regulations concerning sexual liaisons within a separate bundle of laws oriented toward a specific set of cultic concerns? These have sometimes been identified, in the wake of Karl Heinrich Graf's work on Pentateuchal sources and August Klostermann's critical studies in the nineteenth century, as the Holiness Code (Klostermann's term). The so-called code has usually been seen as including Lev. 17–26. Although the present commentary eschews the discussion of textual questions, it is worth noting here this basic hypothesis of a separate literary tradition, integrated editorially at some much later post-Mosaic date by scribes associated with priestly interests within Israel. These kinds of textual distinctions have proven very important to theologians who have sought to derive a special religious character from this section of Leviticus that will somehow, once identified, clarify the subject matter's authority. If, for instance, Lev. 18 can be associated with a subset of laws devoted to ritual purity and if the concept of ritual purity is defined in a way that renders its pertinence anachronistic for the Christian gospel, then the particularities of its sexual prohibitions, especially that of homosexual activity, can also be judged as being scripturally vestigial (a popular example of this general argument can be found in Countryman 1988).

The matter of distinguishing types of law within Leviticus, and in the Old Testament as a whole, and then apportioning to these types varying kinds of

Christian authority, has been an interpretive necessity since the early church. By the Middle Ages, and restated with renewed structural clarity in the Reformation era, a sturdy distinction between ceremonial and moral precepts of the law was firmly in place, along with a theological rationale to support it, which allowed for a relatively easy parsing of legal commandments into the "no longer" and the "still valid" categories. Rapid change in social customs within the past few decades, particularly those dealing with sexual behavior, have raised the question of the distinction's proper application, or even of its usefulness altogether. I will address this matter later in the chapter, but here I want to emphasize that, no matter how one concludes a discussion of the types of law in Leviticus, it is proper to see Lev. 18 as having a particular contextual character that must provide a larger informing sense to the specifics of 18:22 on homosexual activity. The prohibition has only the most limited sense when read simply on its own.

How shall we describe this informing context? In the first place, the common theme of sexual couplings in Lev. 18 follows directly upon the discussion of the blood. This discussion, we saw, had as its core an explanation of the nature of experienced time, of history: life, in its giving and taking, in its care and assault, is the marker of time. Only in light of this discussion is the matter of sexual life now addressed. And it is addressed by returning to the direct speech of Moses to the people of Israel, without Aaron as an intermediary, which was common in the first chapters of the book. Indeed, the speech to the people begins now with a clear assertion by God that "I am the LORD your God" (18:2). It is an assertion that repeats itself throughout the chapter, in the midst of the list of prohibited sexual relationships, emphatically describing the regulations here as the direct commandments of God and as integrally linked to God's own being. The phrase in fact reappears throughout subsequent chapters. But coming here initially in Lev. 18, it hearkens back to the first command at the opening of the book, the command of calling to Moses and through him the people. "I am the LORD." How? In 18:1–5, by the calling of Israel out of Egypt and by God's leading of them into Canaan. The concreteness of this geographical progression is underscored when the land itself is made the discerner of Israel's following, by keeping it or vomiting it out, as the closing verses of the chapter threaten. God calls and God leads; and the commands given here—"I am the LORD"—are given as the form or at least the buttress of this movement that describes the history of a people.

Leviticus 18's own subject matter—sexual coupling and its congruence with the promised land—therefore engages a specific topic: the experiential continuity of a people's identity in time, that is, descendents and their patrimony. It is not that this topic does *not* have anything to do with holiness, in the usual taxonomy. But the emphasis here lies on the way that sexual intercourse is bound to Israel's historical fate within the land given to it by God and less on the way that specific sexual acts do or do not embody a category called "the holy." This observation is in line with the general character of Leviticus as I have already described it. If, in a basic sense, the Bible provides the story of Israel old and new, centered in Christ, and of the world itself through the body of Christ as the church, then Leviticus itself functions as a kind of outline to this history in its breadth. And all its laws signify not so much a body of ethical demands that share a common value system (to be sifted on these terms) as a set of *prophecies* in the technically figurative sense. All of them speak of the life of Israel as it is carried along in God's providence, revealing him and the future that he brings.

The approach of *Rabbah* 23.1–6 to Leviticus moves generally in this sense, as we have repeatedly seen. Its treatment of Lev. 18 in particular is, in this case, relatively thin, but nonetheless maintains its consistent interpretive attitude. Using Song 2:1–2 as an explanatory verse—"I am a rose among thorns"—the *Rabbah* reads the chapter primarily in terms of the destiny of Israel among the nations, as indicated not only in Lev. 18:1–5 but within the entire course of Israel's history as the receptor of the Torah within the world. The Torah given at Sinai to Israel organizes—"saves"—the whole of creation, having been written "in heaven" and come to lodge within Israel itself. Israel's fate, then, is given as it passes through time as the Torah's vessel for the sake of the world. And the sins of promiscuity indicated by the prohibitions of Lev. 18—adultery, prostitution, homosexuality, bestiality—become the enacted chapters by contrast to the law that shape the history of both human race and Israel in particular: from the illicit intercourse of the "sons of God" that gave rise to a race of violence (Gen. 6:1–7), to the flood, to Sodom, to Joseph's temptations in Egypt,[1] to the long list of iniquities in Judges. For the *Rabbah*, the particular injunctions of Lev. 18, in their violation as much as in their fulfillment, represent the course of history that the law will recount even as its content shapes that history's meaning.[2]

If the laws of Lev. 18 are prophecies in this historically formative sense, they are prophecies that refer to the way that sexual union and its connection with the land describes the providence of God. Scripturally, this description falls under the category of genealogy, and evangelically this kind of genealogical prophecy points us to the person of the Christ in Matt. 1:1–17 and Luke 3:23–38. How comes the Christ by his heritage, messianic and otherwise? The *Glossa ordinaria* (Patrologia latina 113.346–48) actually hints at this, when it speaks of Lev. 18 as

1. Joseph is generally viewed as an example of heroic self-control in the face of sexual temptation. But some Jewish traditions attribute either conspiratorial desire to Joseph or even a final succumbing to the allurements of Potiphar's wife—a symbol both of inherent human weakness and of a divine mercy able to use even the fallen for its redemptive purposes. In some versions of Joseph's victorious self-control, the turning point is given by the appearance of his father Jacob in a vision, who warns him precisely on the basis of the promise of his heritage in Israel's future. See Kugel 1990.

2. From a completely different perspective—the history of legal origins—Carmichael 1997 and 2006 argues for narrative priority over codification and attempts to read the Levitical laws as legal commentaries on the stories of Genesis through Kings. In doing so, however, he provides a framework not unlike the *Rabbah's*: each of the laws of Lev. 18 corresponds, as it were, to events in Genesis (Sarah and Abimelech, Abraham and Isaac, Tamar, Reuben, etc.). The notion of such historical correspondence is, from a theological point of view, precisely what is being argued here: the Torah shapes time, and the laws cannot be extricated from their purpose in that shaping.

delineating the heritage of Israel through which we participate in Christ's human reality. The sexual couplings prohibited in Lev. 18 sketch the shape, by contrast, of a proper "union into one flesh" from which the purposed descendents of Adam and Abraham will lead toward the coming of the Christ. They also point to the obstacles that will be overcome in moving to his advent. In all of this, the root shape of the movement is first given in Gen. 2:23–25. Here, from the beginning, "uncovered nakedness" is the primordial gift of man and woman joining in fruitful union.[3] (Hence, in Lev. 18:7–8, e.g., the transfer of nakedness from one spouse to the other, as Rashi notes [Rosenbaum and Silbermann 1932: 82a–83], derives from this creative union almost by proxy. This also underlies the talmudic prohibition of incest between father and daughter, which, although not explicitly condemned here, is implied in 18:10, which prohibits sexual coupling between father and daughter's daughter.)

The gospel genealogies display the historical reality of heritage in terms of grace, obedience, and sinfulness. The lines of descent are, by and large, ones that conform to the practices given in the call of Lev. 18, although they are, at various key points, disrupted by violations of this calling (more on this below). Taken as a whole (via Luke's version especially), however, the lines are held within a container of creation on one side—"Adam, the son of God" (Luke 3:38)—and of incarnate divine presence on the other—Jesus, the Son of God (3:22)—on the other side. Jesus is not, as both versions make clear, physically bound to the line of descent traced in the genealogy; but as the one through whom "all things are made" (John 1:3) he is the basis and end of its historical reality and purpose. Far from being irrelevant to the physical line of descent through which Adam gives birth to a messianic history within Israel, Jesus founds the very possibility of that movement of physical unions through time and upholds its very meaning and promise: we are all born of the union of man and woman, we are formed by its character in time as family, and both of these are given in the prior grace of the "Son of God" as the creator, in, for, and through whom all things come to be and are and to whom they move (Col. 1:15–20).

What then is this possibility and promise, which *because* of Christ is explicated within Lev. 18? Within the container of divine grace that alone is able to call "into existence the things that do not exist" (Rom. 4:17) and bring back to life that "which was as good as dead" (4:19), there is given to the world, in the ordering of human heritage, an entire way of being that roots family within the gifts of landedness. This ordering engages at least three lived elements: the birth of children, their stable rearing, and the bonds of life that are given continuity through time, that is, inheritance. These three elements are bound up in the web of prohibitions in Lev. 18. Procreation, as we know already from earlier chapters,

---

3. That the phrase "uncover nakedness" refers to sexual intercourse is almost universally accepted. Differences have arisen in the nuance of its character: the Septuagint, for instance, translates nakedness in terms of "shame," while the Vulgate goes even further in speaking of *turpitudo*, a kind of evil ugliness. Needless to say, this latter represents an unwarranted and deforming interpretation.

is to be the explicator of sexual intercourse and its life fluids. This is, from the start, the reason that the chapter follows the discussion of blood, which summarizes the previous cosmic promise of creation's grace. But the prohibitions of unions between degrees of family relation and affinity constitute the creation, not simply of life through sexual intercourse, but of a historical context in which the children of life can be raised.

Much speculation has been given as to the reasons for particular prohibitions within this web—some regarding the health of offspring (e.g., the purported infirmity associated with a child conceived with a menstruating woman), some regarding natural rules of familial repugnance. Scripturally, however, only two reasons seem to be compelling. The first is that the union of man and woman creates a single flesh that cannot be dissolved without wounding and destruction. The polygamy of the patriarchs has, in this context, been seen as a problem needing explanation, for both Jew and Christian. But for both, however the interpretive problem was faced, there has been agreement that a monogamous union is founded at creation (Mark 10:6: "from the beginning of creation"), one whose basic meaning brooks no dissolution. For Augustine, this law was not yet articulated in the times of the patriarchs, and their contravention of its demand was permitted only because the author of the command itself chose to do so for the sake of his own providential purposes—procreation for the population of the earth and the genealogical descent of Jesus.[4] This fact, by definition, provides no moral precedent for subsequent ages. As Hirsch (1989: 2.484–85) explains when commenting on these verses, Gen. 2:24 ("therefore a man leaves his father and his mother and cleaves to his wife, and they become one flesh") orders in its implications the *whole* set of prohibitions here: man and woman *leave* their blood families in order to create, through their union, new families ordered by the exclusive and focused love of these two persons. For Hirsch, as for both Jewish and Christian wedding liturgies, Song 8:6 ("love is strong as [i.e., is stronger than] death") illuminates this reality, for this verse points out how the marriage relationship *is* the sign of divine creative grace itself, so fundamental that "nothing else may distract it," especially sexual entanglements that undermine, blur, or otherwise weaken the singular familial relationships that derive from a monogamous union of husband and wife and that protect the exclusive connection of progeny to it. No other love must distract the love of family given as mother, father, sister, brother, and

---

4. Augustine's views about this are not wholly consistent. In some places (e.g., *On the Good of Marriage* 5) he appears to say that polygamy and monogamy are culturally rooted, and in different contexts he says that they are quite independent of some natural law. But his providential framework, as well as the purposeful ordering toward which this framework is built in his eyes, which includes the exclusive and indissoluble sacrament of marriage as it figures Christ's self-giving to the church in Eph. 5, points in a direction other than simple cultural diversity: while the polygamy of the patriarchs was divinely permitted and useful, it was not indicative of the final purposes of God in human creation. Monogamy was more clearly argued for by other fathers (e.g., Ambrose, *On Abraham* 7); and later papal teaching enshrined the (fairly logical) view that monogamy was the original condition and purpose of created humanity.

so on, for by contrast to the life-giving grace of love "jealousy is as cruel as the grave" (Song 8:6). For Hirsch there is far more behind these prohibitions even than this, and their deepest divine rationale must remain "hidden." Nonetheless, an obvious aspect of their demand is the overt need for a deep peace within the household, in which focused love can be given and received in a way that permits the undisputed propagation of the family line.[5] The story of Absalom and David stands as a tragic comment to the Levitical law's deep purpose in this context, where sexual transgression, rivalry, and finally death consume a family that has let love dissipate beyond the family's order (2 Sam. 13–19). When David cries out that he would willingly take the place for his son's death—"O my son Absalom, my son, my son Absalom! Would I had died instead of you!" (18:33)—we hear a dismal hope that only one coming later will be able to assume.

The four prohibitions of Lev. 18:19–23—intercourse with a menstruating woman, dedication of children to Molech (whether literally by a fire sacrifice or, as Rashi (Rosenbaum and Silbermann 1932: 83) and others contended, through a nonfatal consecration to the Molech cult), homosexual intercourse, and bestiality—are of a seemingly different order than the previous directives concerning relations of consanguinity and affinity. But they too fall within the obvious parameters of the family's propagation and security. Moreover, they are all gathered together in 18:24–30 as things that together overturn the land's capacity to receive and nourish Israel's heritage. Together they destabilize the integral promise of people and land that is bound to the exclusive commitment to God and his law and that directs the purpose of Israel's passage through time. Each marks, in its own way, a denial of the possibility of inheritance, the line of descent that will make possible the fleshly coming of the Messiah and that is given over as the body to be renewed. Jesus himself is the true heir (Matt. 21:38), the Son of God—but that is not to do away with the heritage, but to explicate its purpose. As with all figures, their realities are mutually implicating in a historical way: Jesus here shows what is a true relationship of heritage—"I and the Father are one" (John 10:30)—even while the earthly heritage of Israel provides the flesh of this showing. To be a coheir with Christ, calling God "Abba" (Rom. 8:15–17; Gal. 4:5–7), is not to have stepped outside the reality of heritage through the genealogy of the flesh, but to have been "brought near" (Eph. 2:13) to the very blessing by which grace is given *in* the flesh. Much of Rom. 9–11 deals with just

5. The tensions within the patriarchal families among wives and concubines were viewed as indicative of this reality. Still, the possibility of having a legal concubine was much discussed in later Judaism, since it does not appear to be explicitly prohibited in the Torah. Rabbi Eliezer, based on Lev. 19:29 (about allowing daughters to engage in prostitution), forbad it, but although his views were sustained by Maimonides, they were not universally accepted at least in terms of exegesis. But when, e.g., Rabbi Jacob Emden in the eighteenth century suggested the reintroduction of concubinage as a means of carefully controlling sexual passion (versus adultery and fornication, though without the writ of a marriage contract and consecrated union), his views were widely rejected. Despite variations, what became Hirsch's orthodox position (1989: 484–86) represents the standard. See Gold 1992: 82–88 for references and discussion.

this reality, beginning with the affirmation that to the "race [of the Israelites] . . . according to the flesh, is the Christ" (9:5), and the engrafting of the Gentiles is to this *heritage*, not to some relationship abstracted from it. If we are to speak of the "laws of nature" in this context, it is in the sense that Christ orders the nature of human flesh in *this* way by the grace of his own sonship and inheritance, and not in any other way.

But along with procreation, family, and heritage, a fourth element outlined by Lev. 18 is indicated by its prophetic nature: not only the warning of violation but its actual occurrence and the work of God in its face. All of the actions prohibited in the chapter are described as "abominations" (18:26); yet several of them are in fact woven into the genealogy of Christ the Son of God: Tamar (Matt. 1:3), who is impregnated by her father-in-law Judah (Gen. 38); Rahab (Matt. 1:5), who is a prostitute (Josh. 2, 6; cf. Jas. 2:25 and Heb. 11:31; later rabbinic tradition has her as a repentant proselyte; but see Lev. 19:29 for a clearer formulation of the prohibition); and "the wife of Uriah" (Matt. 1:6), that is, Bathsheba, with whom David commits adultery and whose husband he has murdered (2 Sam. 11). In all these cases of specifically sexual violation (along with others in the genealogies involving idolatry, oppression, and murder), Israel is visited with increasing levels of punishment, including finally its spitting out from the land itself in exile. Yet in them, just as we saw with the entire narrative of the spilt blood from Abel on, God also achieves a renewal of life through the suffering of mercy and through the maintenance somehow of the line of descent. It is the coming of the Son of God, even into the seeming conclusion of this line, emerging in the gap like a new creation, that justifies the heritage altogether. The abominations are prophesied even as they are taken up by the one whose heritage is to bring "many sons to glory . . . through suffering" their very future as "brethren" (Heb. 2:10–11). The gospel, which calls to both repentance and new life, is first articulated clearly in these words: "The book of the genealogy of Jesus Christ, the son of David, the son of Abraham" (Matt. 1:1).

If one were to ask what is the overall meaning of Lev. 18 in this light, the answer would have to be that it explicates the peculiar formation of the human race, which comes about as a gift through Israel (to it belongs the Messiah!) and its tortured history, which finally leads all of Adam's progeny into Christ as their alpha and omega. The shape of sexual union given in Lev. 18, both in its fulfill-ment and in its redeemed violation, provides the relational framework, marked by blood, that Christ comes to carry into God's bosom. Robert Gagnon, whose interest is in the Levitical prohibition of homosexual sex, offers four contextual orientations that Lev. 18 provides to this specific injunction, each of which gives an alternative perspective on the chapter's meaning: (1) sexual disobedience as a form of idolatry in conformance with the surrounding nations, in contrast to "an uncompromising devotion to the one god Yahweh" and his will; (2) procre-ation as the purpose of sexual intercourse; (3) maintaining the proper mixing of bodily fluids and their connection with life and death (which homosexual anal sex would violate most clearly); and (4) the created order of sexual relation that is somehow fashioned by God within the original design of human existence as male and female (2001: 128–42). All four of these perspectives must come into play within this larger scheme of historical figure, by which these laws, as they are enacted and disobeyed, become the vessel of human conformance to Christ.

If this is so—if, that is, the sexual laws of Lev. 18 are prophetically figural in this historical sense—then any line between their moral imperative as present demands and symbolic import is very unclear. This conclusion stands some contrast to one line of traditional Christian reasoning. According to Bruno of Segni (Patrologia latina 164.441), for instance, the "whole church takes these [commands in Lev. 18] literally and follows them, and any other interpretation is superfluous." But if they are prophetic in some basic way, they are also fulfilled in Christ and therefore point beyond themselves even as they are obeyed or their violation is punished. Thus, another range of meanings that the tradition has applied to these prohibitions comes into play as Jesus is seen to be their historical referent. Do they not speak of obedience, simply in their utterance from God as a part of Israel's calling? So, then, Jesus speaks of *his* family network of affinity and consanguinity in such terms: "'Who is my mother, and who are my brothers?' And stretching out his hand toward his disciples, he said, 'Here are my mother and my brothers! For whoever does the will of my Father in heaven is my brother, and sister, and mother'" (Matt. 12:48–50). Likewise, when he speaks of his heritage, he speaks in terms of self-subjection to the needs of the "little ones" and of the terrible sin of scandal: "Whoever receives one such child in my name receives me; but whoever causes one of these little ones who believe in me to sin, it would be better for him to have a great millstone fastened round his neck and to be drowned in the depth of the sea" (18:5–6). Inheritance itself is fulfilled in a life of self-giving, suffering patience, and ordered love: "Blessed are the poor in spirit, for theirs is the kingdom of heaven. . . . Blessed are the meek, for they shall inherit the earth" (Matt. 5:3–5). The sexual regulations of Lev. 18, for all their literal directive, actually *refer to* these relations of obedience, subjection, and ordered love that determine the "family" of Jesus.

This inevitably raises the theological issue of the relationship of Old Testament and New Testament with respect to the law. This issue has generated much historical debate and continues to be critical in contemporary discussions and conflicts over especially sexual behavior. Modern scholars, for example, have made distinctions in Old Testament law between laws of purity and laws of morals (Klawans 2000) or between laws of outer purity and laws of inner purity (Kazen 2002).[6] The point of such distinctions, for all their attempted historical descriptiveness, is to provide conceptual categories by which to tease apart those scriptural injunctions from the Old Testament that ought to continue in effect for Christians under the

6. From the Eastern Orthodox side, see Evdokimov 1973 on the way the New Testament interiorizes the law as a new freedom, through our participation in Christ.

new covenant. And in this, they are following a venerable Christian distinction between ceremonial and moral law, such as Thomas Aquinas institutionalized,[7] or even earlier, between symbolic and moral in Augustine's typology (*Reply to Faustus the Manichaean* 6). In every case, the purity (outer) laws or ceremonial/ ritual/symbolic laws all refer to those Old Testament injunctions that are no longer binding on Christians, while the still valid laws from Moses are dubbed interior/moral and in some cases eternal/natural.

Judaism has generally placed the sexual laws strictly within the natural moral category. As noted by Rashi (Rosenbaum and Silbermann 1932: 82) and the tradition on the use of the plural in 18:6, Lev. 18's prohibitions apply to women as well as men, and this indicates their universal validity. The ceremonial/moral distinction is not made here in the same way as among Christians, obviously, but there is an analogy: 18:5 indicates that the laws in question determine human life itself and therefore are pertinent for humanity as a whole. The Babylonian Talmud teaches that, while all other laws may be sacrificed for the sake of saving life, those laws dealing with idolatry, murder, and sexual immorality may *never* be compromised, even when the consequence of this is death itself (tractates *Yoma* 85b and *Sanhedrin* 74a). These are the three moral categories imposed in the Jerusalem declaration of Acts 15:29. For the church also, then, and in general, sexual laws have been seen as falling into the moral, and hence still binding, category of demand.

Whether faithful distinctions or not, this would be pragmatically workable for the Christian church except that it has not been consistently clear what must fall within each category when it comes to particular cases of sexual regulation. Do *all* such cases fall within the moral law? On what basis? Augustine's notion— with respect to, say, polygamy and monogamy—of malleable cultural custom as determining key aspects of sexual behavior complicates this picture somewhat. Similarly complicating have been the evolving differences within the Christian church over elements like sex with menstruating women and now, most prominently, the question of homosexual sex, which some scholars argue are really of a ceremonial, ritual, or outer purity character. Even Jewish theological reflection in more liberal circles has wondered if the reality of sexual orientation as being "unchosen" may place homosexuality and perhaps other tendencies outside the universally applied moral category because of its inescapable character (a category that creates moral exception due to compulsion).

One of the conceptual pitfalls in this discussion, however, has been the application of the reality of abolition to aspects of the law, which implies in a major

---

7. Thomas Aquinas treats the law, richly and comprehensively, in his *Summa theologiae* 1a2ae QQ. 90–108 (the distinction between ceremonial, judicial, and moral begins in Q. 98). For Thomas, it is not as if the ceremonial law is somehow unattached to the moral law; indeed, it is derived directly from it and serves the general purpose of all law in ordering human life to its just fulfillment. But it is historically limited and with Christ is abolished (a word he will use, along with many early fathers).

fashion a distinction now between valid and invalid. And although the concept of abolition was commonly used by Christians, it was neither uniformly applied nor congruent with Jesus's own words in Matt. 5:17: "Think not that I have come to abolish the law and the prophets; I have come not to abolish them but to fulfil them."[8] The notion of fulfillment here pointed to the historical *force* of the laws in general: their meaning lies in their enactment in time, which is to lead toward a fullness of embodiment and happening (5:18). Augustine had worked with this character of the law in great detail in his controversy with the Manicheans (especially *Reply to Faustus the Manichaean* 6, 19). Distinguishing between symbolic and moral (or eternal) laws, Augustine characterized the former in terms of their predictive quality. These were the ceremonial laws of the Old Testament, whose purpose was to show forth the life and work of Christ in the future even as they were obeyed in the time of Moses and Israel. Once fulfilled with the coming of Jesus, they are therefore no longer observed. History is the issue, of course, and the purpose of reading the symbolic laws of the Old Testament is to "see Christ" in them, Christ as he in fact lives and acts in time and space. One reason that the laws of sexual behavior, in this scheme, were rarely viewed as symbolic or ceremonial is because they were not seen as predictive, in any obvious way, of Jesus's life. And when they were so viewed, as we saw in the case of menstruation and childbirth in the later Western church, they were in fact set aside as legally binding upon Christians.

Judaism also moved in the direction of historicizing distinctions, although on a very different basis. Rashi (Rosenbaum and Silbermann 1932: 81) and Maimonides (*Moreh Nebukim* 3.2) and the later Christian Arminius, *Private Disputations* 29 [1853: 2.71–75]), for instance, distinguished between ceremonial and moral laws in terms of their relative rationale: those laws for which no reason could be given were properly ceremonial, and their character demanded a purer form of simple and raw obedience. For Jewish commentators, however, there was no question of this difference mitigating the force of the ceremonial law. In fact, as Hirsch (1989: 2.477–83) writes, these kinds of law required even *greater* care in obedience, since they could not be encouraged through natural instinct and knowledge. (For Arminius, via Calvin, this kind of unmotivated obedience was of a lesser sort and served more of a pedagogical purpose.) Hirsch went so far as to claim that the purity laws, for instance, although without a natural universal claim upon all peoples, provided the foundation for all natural societies. In a real sense, therefore, the distinction between ceremonial and moral was irrelevant in terms of demand, but came into play only in terms of parsing the history of God's revelation among Israel and the nations. God shapes time through the various ways in which he reveals his law; but the law itself inevitably ends by determining the final form of divine justice within human society.

8. For a common form of the contrast between old and new in terms of abolition or annulment, see Cyprian's *Testimonies against the Jews*, esp. book 1. Yet even here there is no clear-cut distinction between moral and ritual law (see esp. the list of "heavenly precepts" in book 3, which contains many seemingly ritual concerns).

The distinction between ceremonial law and moral law is therefore not immediately obvious. It is not made in Scripture itself, unless one wishes to explain the notion of the legal shadow in, for example, Heb. 10:1 in these anachronistic terms. Markus Bockmuehl (versus Countryman 1988) convincingly shows that concepts like purity continued to have an essential connection with morality, through the wider reality of holiness, within the New Testament and that, however one wishes to deal with the binding character of particular Old Testament laws, it cannot properly be done on the basis of sifting injunctions out according to such a template (Bockmuehl 2005). All laws are prophetic and all laws are taken up in Christ. They remain "until heaven and earth pass away" as they are "filled up" in him. The issue is our own relation to them through Christ, what we have been discussing in terms of our following of him proximately within the time and space of our lives as we are drawn close to the one who has filled up these very injunctions and who, rather than putting them aside, carries them with him. As we are close to him in the form of our following, the laws, therefore, of Lev. 18 will be given their substance for us. We must, then, look at how Christ fulfills the laws of sexual coupling, a question that has not generally been broached explicitly by the tradition, but that has, nonetheless, been answered pragmatically within the history of discipleship.

We have already observed above how the laws of Lev. 18 refer directly to the "obedience, subjection, and ordered love" that are embodied in Jesus's own life and teaching. Within this larger framework, there are innumerable details that are properly figured in Christ from this chapter. Here is but a small list:

- The figure of procreation is fulfilled in the peculiar fruitfulness that is Jesus's own: "Truly, truly, I say to you, unless a grain of wheat falls into the earth and dies, it remains alone; but if it dies, it bears much fruit" (John 12:24). This marks the most paradoxical of Lev. 18's projections: life is given in the "servant" who loses his life "in this world" (John 12:25–26).
- The figure of familial relations, as we have seen, is fulfilled in the community of obedience to the word of God that Jesus gathers (Matt. 12:48–50). This communal reality is given in the common life of mutual subjection in the church of Christ: "When Jesus saw his mother, and the disciple whom he loved standing near, he said to his mother, 'Woman, behold, your son!' Then he said to the disciple, 'Behold, your mother!'" (John 19:26–27; cf. Acts 1:14; Phlm. 10–16). It is also fulfilled, in its human passion and commitment, in the parents who bring their children to Jesus to be healed and in the sacrifices of heart or body they offer (Mark 5:22–24; 7:24–30; 9:17–29), as well as in the sharing of faith that this embodies (2 Tim. 1:5).
- The figure of prostitution implied in the prohibitions generally and made explicit in Lev. 19:29 is fulfilled in repentance and forgiveness, shown in the

woman of Luke 7:36–50, traditionally associated with Mary Magdalene:[9] "Therefore I tell you, her sins, which are many, are forgiven, for she loved much; but he who is forgiven little, loves little. . . . And he said to the woman, 'Your faith has saved you; go in peace'" (7:47, 50).

- The figure of prohibited adultery (Lev. 18:20) is fulfilled by means of confession, self-recognition, forgiveness, and conversion in the Samaritan woman (John 4:16–18) and in the woman caught in adultery who is brought before Jesus (8:2–11).
- The implied figure of chastity, understood in terms of sexual self-control (Gal. 5:23) in all relations, is fulfilled in the teaching on divorce and eunuchhood "for the kingdom" (Matt. 19:3–12), matters that are commented upon in practical ways by Paul (1 Cor. 7).
- The particular figure of the union of man and wife is fulfilled in Jesus's own self-giving for the church in a full and exhaustive manner, a reality that draws together his own teaching on marriage (Mark 10:2–12) with the character of sacrifice as it is given in the mystery of human marriage (Eph. 5:21–33). This reality of exclusive union is, as I have noted, common to both Christian and Jewish teaching on Lev. 18 and carries with it the Levitical implications of exclusive devotion to God as his landed people (Isa. 62:4–5).
- The figure of the prohibited giving over of children to Molech (Lev. 18:21) is fulfilled variously in the massacre of the innocents of Matt. 2:16–18, in Jesus's warnings regarding scandal (18:6–9), and in his exhortation that "the children come to [him]" (19:14), for to them "belongs the kingdom of heaven."
- The figure of prohibited homosexual sex is fulfilled in the warnings of judgment upon those who reject him and his messengers (Luke 10:12–16) and in the predictions of final judgment (17:29). The clear link between Sodom and the sin discussed in Lev. 18:22 has been recently disputed, but has also been conclusively shown to be present within Scripture and consistently within the milieu of Jesus and after (Gagnon 2001: 71–91). More to the point, the contrasting character of personal relations that Jesus embodied and gave over to his disciples is one of a peculiar kind of friendship that finds its form in self-sacrifice on the one hand (John 15:13) and in the community of shared faith and witness on the other (e.g., the beloved disciple and Mary). Paul explicates this graphically in terms of bodily union that crosses over between human sexual coupling and membership in the "body of Christ"—the figure is palpable. The "one body" union that sexual intercourse provides (Gen. 2:24) is, when misplaced—and this would include within a homosexual relationship—considered a form of idolatry (1 Cor. 6:15–20; Rom. 1:24–27),

9. *M'gadd'la* ("hairdresser") was a common term for prostitutes, and the Western tradition associated the sinner of Luke 7 with Mary Magdalene, as well as with Mary of Bethany who anoints Jesus in John 12:1–8. The Talmud also calls Mary Magdalene a prostitute.

according to the Levitical scheme of union-by-proxy (Lev. 18:8, 10: "their nakedness is your nakedness"). And since the Christian is the possession of Christ through being joined to Christ, any union of flesh or spirit that draws away from the fullness of that joining to Christ is a worshiping of that which is not God (1 Cor. 10:13–22). Participation—or union—with Christ draws us into the peculiar friendship that is his, which is the actual following after his cross in its comprehensive passage.

- The figure of prohibited bestiality is fulfilled in Jesus's own dwelling with the beasts (Mark 1:13). But this, as with the entire chapter, is granted its grace through his resistance in the wilderness to the temptations of human and especially divine power and his reliance in faith upon God. Isaiah 11:6–9's vision of the "peaceable kingdom" under the rule of the "little child" bespeaks a complete transformation of heart that, in the Christian tradition, found its fullest human expression in the penitent poverty and love of Francis. All this stands in stark contrast to the bestiality of the cruel Nebuchadnezzar (Dan. 4:10–33) or the tempted and idolatrous Israel in Egypt (Ezek. 23:19–21). What Augustine (Patrologia latina 42.152) and Hirsch (1989: 1.300–319) together describe as the "animality" of human instinct here warned against becomes the instrument, when confronted in faithfulness, of redemption: "Behold, I send you out as lambs in the midst of wolves" (Luke 10:3). This entry of witness into the land of the beast, still unresolved, constitutes "the kingdom of God ha[ving] come near" (10:11).

- The figure of the land's vomiting is fulfilled both in fuller prophecies of the world's (and not only Israel's) end, now reaching all people (Mark 13:8–37), and in the more cosmic release of life by the mortal earth that is provided in Jesus's suffering on its behalf and breaking through the bondage of death: "The earth shook, and the rocks were split; the tombs also were opened, and many bodies of the saints who had fallen asleep were raised, and coming out of the tombs after his resurrection they went into the holy city and appeared to many" (Matt. 27:51–53). This is perhaps the most startling of prophecies from Lev. 18: the death of Jesus, in which all the wastage of Israel's failed unions of flesh and blood are spewed, alters the fluid of creation into one remarkable and miraculous act of renewal. It is the "sign of Jonah" (Jonah 2:10; Matt. 12:39–40) in all its fullness.

It is in this overall figural direction given by Lev. 18 in Christ Jesus that we must seek to discern the particulars of obedience to its legal demand: into what land has the proximate following of Jesus carried the discipled church in this regard? The place to articulate an answer to this question is in the pattern of social change, initially given impetus by the apostolic church and then taken up in the succeeding centuries: sexual continence, monastic and ascetic discipline, care of widows and orphans, chaste marriage, a new hospitality of self-giving communities, the rise of orphanages and hospitals, of schools and formational cultures. While it is possible to see changes taking place in this pattern, they are changes that contributed to a specific development, of what today is in fact a contested patrimony: what is called the "Christian civilization" of the West (Ratzinger and Pera 2006). One of the great failures in present debates regarding cultural construction and diversity, particularly on the topic of sexuality and family, is not taking seriously the historical weight of figural fulfillment in the light of the church's own offering and fate. What may appear to the social historian as but the ad hoc fulfillment of the sexual laws given in the Christian reading of Lev. 18 becomes in a figural apprehension of their shape a coherent tradition, as given in the life of the church in its fullness of self-giving and following. And because of the church's integral and unbreakable relationship with Jewish Israel, bound as it is in its own way to Christ's body, genealogically in the deepest sense, the development of Jewish sexual culture is rightly a part of this figural direction and discernment.

Another way of making this point is this: Lev. 18 constitutes an instrumental description of how the history of that communal life that grows with and follows God will and must unfold. The prophetic character of its regulations represents the obedience of time to God's will here. In this light, the highly charged discussion over the meaning of abomination as applied both to homosexual acts in particular and to the chapter's entire set of prohibited acts (18:22, 26, 29–30) can easily get bogged down on the question of its regulative specificity (details in Gagnon 2001: 117–21, but his discussion lapses into this quagmire). Rather, we ought to see the abominable as including all that rebels against the shape of God's coming into and passage through the world. And this rebellion is overwhelmed *by* the coming and passage of God. This is the key: God *comes* in *this* particular way, as described in Lev. 18. And this is the nature of the injunctions' figural weight: the world is shaped by this coming. This is the life that the laws provide (18:5).

If we are to look for the final fulfillment of these figures, that is, an image of the actual shape of the world to which they lead, we will rightly turn to Rev. 19:1–22:5. Here we are given the description of a world conformed to God's passage through it in Christ Jesus, which includes the shaping of Lev. 18 and which takes the church as God's own bride. The ethical questions over sexual and familial relations are answered in the "Bride [who] has made herself ready" through "fine linen" and "the righteous deeds of the saints" (Rev. 19:7–8); in the "bloodied" word of God (19:13); in the overcoming of a harlotry that has led to death across the world and the oppression of Christ's disciples (19:2); in the destruction of death (20:13–15); in the exclusive union of God with his beloved (21:2–5); in the heritage of a new kind of life that is cleansed of abomination (21:7–8, 27)—that is, life itself (22:2). The ethical questions over sexual and familial relations are answered here by asking how our lives with regard to these matters are conformatively congruent with this final "fulness of time."[10]

10. On the nuptial figure of Revelation as governing the form of human history, see Radner 2004: 121–38.

In response, it is difficult to see how contemporary behavioral contradictions to Lev. 18 further in time the very figures of the text, except in terms of calling forth their own judgment. Still, it is this way of raising the question of discernment that properly arises from Lev. 18, in contrast to using the text according to a simple rule of its meaning. The difference between the sexual laws of Lev. 18 and the laws of clean and unclean flesh in Lev. 11 cannot simply lie in their respective relation to the category of ceremonial character. The difference lies in the way Jesus himself carries these realities in his body and in the body of his church. With respect to the animals, we saw via Peter's address that they are gathered up by Christ as reconciled creative distinctions that he bears in his own death. But with respect to the laws of sexual relation and family, we see the legal particulars, much as in the Sermon on the Mount, taken up by Christ and passed on to his church in an almost exaggerated fashion, renewed and refocused. We see both these things, however, not according to a logic of categorization, but according to the discernment of time as the Scriptures have molded them in God's good will. The Scriptures are the book of God in the same sense as Revelation speaks of "the Lamb's book of life" (21:27)—they form the shape of life as God's creative purpose. The word/words distinction in this case is as potentially misleading as the ceremonial/moral distinction is unhelpful. Jesus as the word fulfills the words of the text by carrying them in his own flesh through time: word and words are one, and the bonds of blood and life are thereby made strong.

LEVITICUS 19:1–2

Leviticus 19 is generally viewed today as forming the *theological* center of the latter portion of the legal codes of Leviticus. And the substance of this center, as most readers of the text agree, is the call to holiness: "Say to all the congregation of the people of Israel, You shall be holy; for I the LORD your God am holy" (19:2). Obviously, holiness is a crucial reality for Leviticus as a whole, but as the purposively directing theological principle for the entire book, or at least for that textual core known as the Holiness Code, it is only now in Lev. 19 that many commentators see its full force as being unveiled. And that force has generally been evaluated in terms of the overwhelming power of moral purity. My reflection on 19:1–2 is an attempt to engage this widespread view and, on the basis of Leviticus itself, to recast it in terms of the historical reality of God's approach to Israel and to creation. Holiness is less a quality or character attributed to God— and reflected in creatures—than it is a description of how God *in fact* temporally wills to act with respect to his creation, by *coming to* it with his whole being. By giving special consideration to just these two verses, I am responding more to the critical tradition of reading Leviticus than to the text itself (which does not separate these verses out). But it is a necessary consideration, given the orienting importance of the verses themselves.

Leviticus 19:2 takes what almost seemed a passing divine exhortation in 11:44—"be holy, for I am holy"—and turns it into the summary description of the entire ethical law of the book: "You shall be holy, for I the LORD your God am holy." As commentators note, God asks Moses to speak these injunctions "to all the congregation of the people of Israel," an audience traditionally seen here as gathered together in one large group, addressed directly and without mediation, requiring a miracle of vocal projection from the otherwise halting Moses. They are thus called as a people to the core of their vocation (compare Exod. 19:6 and 1 Pet. 2:9). What could be more central, therefore, than this opening directive toward holiness?

But it is the previous articulation of this vocation in the midst of the discussion of clean and unclean animals (11:44) that warns us against privileging the laws of Lev. 19, as if these represent the highest moral vision of Moses's instructions. Distinguishing (and not eating) the swarming things of the earth as, if not a central, at least a broadly characteristic embodiment of holiness means that the presentation of the holy in Leviticus cannot at any rate be made equivalent to modern definitions of the ethical. Ought we to see holiness as a quality? If so, how is it consistent among both the laws of animal distinction and caring for the poor (as in 19:9–10)?

Leviticus 11:44's context of distinction coheres with the standard conception of the Hebrew term for holiness, *qedusha* (sometimes spelled *kadusha*), which has the connotation of separate and distinct. The difference between the Sabbath and other days is marked by the making of *Kiddush*, the "sanctifying" blessing offered over the cup of wine on Friday nights. *Kiddushin*, the wedding betrothal that marks the reality (if not the consummation) of a marriage (and is impossible for concubines), is granted the "sanctified" character because through it the two individuals are distinguished from all others in their commitment to one another. If bound to the reality of distinction, then holiness is distinction for the purpose of creative substance, of the gift of traversing distance, with all its cost and glory. That is what we saw in the original discussion of this reality in Lev. 10–11. If holiness is about separation, then it is a separation for the sake of granting life and the giving over of oneself as the basis for its very being. The holiness of the marriage betrothal is constituted just there, not simply in a bare distinction of two grouped individuals, but in their coupling, their one fleshedness. In this light, the preceding chapter's discussion of sexual intercourse and genealogy is foundational to a discussion of holiness.

The link between distinction and costly closeness is illustrated by a common Jewish interpretation of the root relationship between the words for holiness (*qedusha*) and prostitute (*qadasha*), which use the same Hebrew letters. Rather than seeing the word translated in the story of Judah and Tamar in Gen. 38:21 as "prostitute" in some technical term, some Jewish commentators understand the description of Tamar's status in a broader way, as a woman living "outside the distinctive limits" of marriage and its rules and forms. That there are such limits and rules is a given; that there is a passage beyond them, for good or ill, is also assumed. The link with holiness in this, however, is that with God the limits and distinctions are both given and overcome at once. The boundless one creates limits; yet he creates them only by going beyond them in his own self.

If we are to speak of holiness in terms of separation, then, we must not do so only in a negative sense—separation *from*, for example, the world, sin, impurity. It is rather a separation of distinction that draws us into a relationship with the one who alone can make distinctions and reconcile them. Holiness is somehow about locality, proximity, and passage. Thus, when Origen comments on this passage (*Homilies on Leviticus* 11.1), he stresses that holiness marks a separation from what is evil, yet he emphasizes even further that this is only because of a prior "dedication *to*" God. Since the word "holy" can qualify "dumb beasts" and physical utensils and not only human beings and spirits, it can only mean that holiness refers to a kind of "exclusive use" by God, a movement away for the sake of another movement toward. Origen cites, for instance, Phil. 3:20, which points to the corrupted reality of "earthly things," yet only because Christians are being drawn *toward* a "heavenly commonwealth." This movement toward God finds its term, finally, in an ultimate closeness. Hence, holiness as separation actually comes to mean union with God, for both Christian and Jewish interpreters.[1]

If holiness can describe a movement toward God's proximity, it is therefore a kind of approach. As I discussed earlier, such an approach is of the nature of sacrifice itself, the offering of the self as, and with the end that, one comes near God in the midst of the great chasm of creation that defines our distinction as living beings. Actions then can be holy to the degree that they act as this offering, both as a means and as the very act itself. The relationship between holiness and the law becomes more evident in this light, and the immediate flow of commandments from Lev. 19:3 on, without explanatory connection to the initial call, seems absolutely natural: the keeping of the law is, in every aspect, an act of offering by which we draw near to God. And the laws themselves are gifts from God, distinctive practices by which we are made close to him. "We thank God because, through the commandments that He gave us, our bodies become holy, even though they are flesh and blood," writes the great Sephardic Torah commentary *Me'am Lo'ez* (Kaplan 1982: 12.7). In this, it echoes the prayer a Jew might recite before fulfilling a religious duty (*mitzvah*): "Blessed are you, Lord God of the Universe . . . who has made me holy through the commandments." The unbounded God provides his creatures time and space in which to distinguish his gifts through obedience to his commands, thereby granting them the intimacy of his otherwise inaccessible being. "A Jewish definition of holiness," says Rabbi Hayim Donin, involves "developing one's sense of discernment as to be able to distinguish and choose the right from the wrong, the true from the false, the good from the bad, the sacred from the profane, the pure from the impure, and the clean from the unclean. The greater the sense of ethical-moral-religious discrimination, the greater the holiness of the individual" (1972: 36).[2]

From a Christian perspective, the gift of God's commandments and the means of discrimination that provides the approach to God is given in God's own embodied self as Jesus, who *is* the word of the law and whom we attend, obey, and follow. In doing so, we are drawn close to God. He is our divine proximity in time and beyond time. And so he calls out, "Come to me" (Matt. 11:28), a coming that is enabled by the response to the invitation, "Follow me" (4:19). Holiness is

1. Hassidic interpreters like Schneersohn make this a central focus; but so too, both explicitly and implicitly, much of the Christian mystical tradition of both East and West.

2. Donin provides in this small volume what is essentially an introduction to precisely the kinds of laws outlined in Lev. 19.

a calling to be with God where God is and where God goes—and his own going, to us in our creation and redemption, is all that *is* holy. The version of Lev. 19:2 used by Jesus in Matt. 5:48—"be perfect, as your heavenly Father is perfect"—is cited to his disciples as an acknowledgment of this passage into greater and greater maturity, a perfected completeness that is given as they attend closely to the call of Jesus to go with him. As the Lord "called Moses" (Lev. 1:1) and thus the entire book of Leviticus comes under this calling, so he calls, in Jesus Christ, followers who will be holy in the walking of his way in its length and breadth, height and depth (Eph. 3:18–19).

Leviticus does not define holiness, either God's or our own, in an abstract way, as a quality or an essence. The direction of the present reflection moves toward a common Christian way of looking at God's holiness as that which is the coincidence of his very being and act. In the context of Christian revelation, this is something that is fully and exhaustively real in the temporal life, death, resurrection, ascension, and coming again of Jesus Christ—no more and no less. Even if this is not wholly comprehensible by human beings, this is truly *who* and *how* God is without remainder, and our approach into this exhaustive mystery constitutes our own sanctification. There are different patterns of conceptualizing this in the Christian tradition, some more abstractly, some more scripturally ordered.[3] But all attest that a human creature might itself *be* holy, even that an entire people can be called into such holiness, through acts ranging from sacrifice to haircuts to discriminations among animals and finally through a relationship in time to a particular historical individual's life and death.

What is important to note, however, is that this general way of looking at the holy stands in considerable contrast with widespread modern understandings of holiness as a manifested element within the world's own structure that we encounter as power or terror or blinding force. These modern conceptions have more recently entered the standard language and sensibility of the Christian church—for example, in the hugely influential work of Rudolf Otto (1958)—mainly through an energetic amalgamation of romantic ideals and anthropological analysis that has today become part of our cultural presuppositions.

It is worth tracing how this happened, since it goes in a direction so different from the thrust of Levitical holiness. The natural religion of Catholicism and deism had been developed, in part, to deal with a widening encounter with religious pluralism, both in a world of missionary and colonial engagement and locally in nations where the virtues of toleration were necessarily being advanced. Some of the theological fruits of this exploration of a universal religious human character were developed in the subjective direction of romantic naturalism, deliberately Christianized by Friedrich Schleiermacher. Schleiermacher's posited "God-consciousness" was based on the now-famous claim to a fundamental human

3. For a substantive systematic treatment, involving some historical material, of the theology of holiness from a more Reformed perspective, see Willis 2002: esp. chap. 3.

sensibility of "absolute dependence." Within this framework, he defined God's holiness in terms of the absolute demands felt within such consciousness—that is, conscience itself. This feeling, in turn, implies a range of constituent elements: sin, as anything that hinders the fulfillment of such demand; and justice, as representing our sense, via divine causality, of the "penal desert" that underlies all of our social and civil law by which we live. This nexus of sensible understanding is never taken away from the human person, but forms a universal aspect of our religiosity as it gives rise to social order. It is not simply that holiness and punishment somehow go together. Schleiermacher in fact explicates the entire reality of holiness as that which gives rise to the ethical ordering of society (1928: 341–54 §§83–85). This will become one developing strand of rationalist religious explanation: holiness *is* the moral imperative at work in human hearts and society. At the same time Schleiermacher also charts the path for what would become another very common modern way of dealing with the reality of religious life and observance, that is, as something that provides the physical markers for some deep and complex shape to human spiritual experience: holiness *is* the experience of an incomprehensible and external power pressing in upon human existence.

As comparative cultural reflection became organized in terms of anthropological science in the course of the nineteenth century, and later as religious sociology in the early twentieth century, both the rationalist and romantic elements of Schleiermacher's analysis were deployed in the study of actual religious practices. This involved shedding Schleiermacher's own attempts at maintaining the specificity of Christ in favor of some universal human substratum of the religious that could help correlate the worldwide variety and similarity of documented sacred actions, particularly sacrifice, observed in far-flung and diverse cultures. A real question, after all, had presented itself to the Christian West, for the first time perhaps since antiquity: almost all religions have sacrifice as a part of their base, with categories seemingly similar to the Old Testament ones of holiness and demand; what could this possibly imply? It was in this context that a number of theories regarding the sacred and sacrifice itself were developed, many of which traded on increasingly similar views about holiness.

In the characteristic approach of Gerardus van der Leeuw, Reformed theologian and scholar of comparative religion, theory was spurred by a search for some common truth regarding God experienced—that is, encountered in some form of manifested phenomenon—as power (1963: part 1). Here van der Leeuw used the categories (e.g., *mana*) of South Sea and Melanesian cultures, recently made famous through on-site investigators. For van der Leeuw, the real subject of experience is a religious object, the other from which all else depends, including ourselves. The only and natural response to this source of life is that of awe or amazement, something akin to Schleiermacher's "consciousness of absolute dependence," a concept in fact explicitly taken up by van der Leeuw. The object of awe is always some unexpected (i.e., unnatural) power, generally impersonalized, but not always. It can be tied to human bearers or places or things, but it is never understood in a spiritual or ethical sense, but rather as an empirical reality, constituting the way the universe and the world is actually structured. Behind all things is the holy, breaking in.

The evolution of an ordered human society based on some common sense of powerful otherness is something theoretically traced by more recent religious sociologists. In this general perspective, Jewish and Christian scriptural social orderings have been interpreted as developed means of dealing with the specifics of manifested holiness.

The anthropological concept of the taboo—which marks out the presence of sacred power and its threat, like a sign announcing "danger! high voltage!"—has been used to delineate the laws of Leviticus in particular: they are at base completely nonethical and seek simply to maintain the boundaries between what is powerful (sacred) and what is powerless (profane). What appears to be a divine punishment—for example, Uzzah's death in touching the ark (2 Sam. 6:6–11) or, for that matter, the death of Aaron's sons in Lev. 10—is tied, in this view, not to a moral transgression, but to the *imprudent* trespass upon the realm of divine power, an unfortunate fall into the uncontrollable currents of cosmic ordering. Thus, the Levitical "observances" do not constitute an ethics in the rationalist sense, but are rather the articulated means of dealing with divine power—for example, sacrifice, purity, sacred days—as a kind of original, though also sublimated, categorical imperative. They embody feelings of awe in response to power. When these observances cease to do so—when they become formalized—the taboo aspect falls away, and human beings are released into the aweless world that, indeed, becomes the evolved realm, finally, of the ethical.

On the basis of this general theory, a range of theological programs is easily (if not necessarily accurately) explained as reflecting the transition from primitive sacred worlds of intrusive holiness to ones of increasingly sophisticated moral consciousness. This transition marks, for instance, the early Christian movement from abrogated ceremonial to moral law; the rationalistic tendencies of modernizing Jewish Orthodoxy seen in Hirsch (1989: 2.713–15), with all of its struggle to maintain observance as a buttress to moral character; and the dismissal by contemporary liberalism of Levitical sexual injunctions as now surpassed primitive systems of control. The theory also explains reactions to these transitions, for example, the counterliberal renovation of holiness-as-power seen in certain forms of modern evangelicalism[4] and Pentecostalism. The vision of the overwhelming (if uncontrolled) power of God, phenomenally given (hence capable of being captured by camera) in the ending to the film *Raiders of the Lost Ark* (1981),

---

4. This trend began already in the eighteenth century, among evangelical romantics as much as among deistic ones, for both of whom the numinous and the sublime were a kind of encounter with the holy whereby "we feel ourselves alarmed" and "wrapped in silence and inquisitive horror" (quotation from James Usher's 1769 *Clio; or, a Discourse on Taste*; see Stock 1982: 106–9). More recently, R. C. Sproul's bestseller *The Holiness of God*, though firmly orthodox in its Reformed character, trades heavily on the modern objective character of holiness as power.

represents both a modern cultural assumption of religious primordialism as well as its perceived anachronism within the realm of civic morality. Holiness *is* power (and Aaron is a shaman); but we must also be willing to leave behind this aspect of existence like a disturbing memory, so as to engage a higher form of consciousness. The double purpose of much modern historical-critical work on Leviticus follows this path: unveil the naked character of primitive religiosity within the book and then consign it to a lower historical form of existence, always mindful of its helpful relativization of traditional theology.

No matter the popularity of the theory and its cultural currency, however, the theory itself is profoundly misleading and has contributed directly to the marginalization of Leviticus as a book of Christian Scripture. From the perspective of Scripture and of Leviticus as a constituent part of Scripture, an objective power that we can call the holy does not pervade the cosmos, nor is our religious existence—of whatever kind!—a carefully ordered attempt to navigate this dangerous world of *mana*, in which we can trace a progression of increasingly efficacious methods for controlling and perhaps finally eliminating its disruptive intrusions. "You shall be holy; for I the LORD your God am holy" is a calling uttered in love by God that leads us *into* and forms the very character of time as we traverse it toward him and in fact with him. The passage is costly, in the world of difference and its exaggeration through sin, and this seems to be the import of the terror implied in Exod. 19:16–24 or Isa. 6:1–5. But the terror is not inherent in God, for it is not because God is holy—too dangerous in himself to be approached— that God cannot be seen (Exod. 33:20; John 1:18). *It is because God is seen by mortal creatures that God is holy* and hence known to be glorious (1:14). We have looked at sacrifice as the offering of difference, that is, of creaturely being. This is the movement of love, and the holiness of God is the fundamental divine movement of that love, which is creative, redemptive of sin, restorative, renewing, and transformative. If the trinitarian life of God is, in theologian Klaus Hemmerle's phrase, "motion and relationship" (1976: 140) as centered in the historical reality of Christ Jesus, then holiness is rightly defined *as* God's self-offering in Jesus who *is* "the Holy One of God" (Mark 1:24; cf. Acts 3:14) in a way that is described in the form of his life.

Holiness as a human reality, conversely, is responsive to this act of divine offering—"*for* I the LORD your God am holy." Indeed, it is finally derivative of it. When Paul has sung the hymn of this great act in Phil. 2:5–11, he goes on to describe this response and derivation: "Therefore, my beloved, . . . work out your own salvation with fear and trembling"—this is the "same mind" as Christ's (2:5), with all of its communal self-offering implied—"for God is at work in you"— this is the first offering of Christ himself—and this offering draws its objects of love into the very midst of its own movement: "both to will and to work for his good pleasure" (2:12–13). Only God himself *makes holy*, in the sense that it is his own coming that brings close. This is why he says of his law: "Keep my statutes, and do them; I am the LORD who sanctify you" (Lev. 20:8). The famous "love commandment" of 19:18, quoted by Jesus (and other rabbis—e.g., Rabbi Akiba, according to *Rabbah* 24.5; Rabbi Hillel, most famously) in his "summary of the law" (Mark 12:31), is an expression of this. As the Baal Shem Tov noted on this text (2005: 3), each person's very creation is given through the self-offering of God and is hence a "portion" of him (working from Job 31:2): to love another person is to enter the realm of God's participatory coming-close and coming-within. It is to love God (Deut. 6:5), quite literally, by being made a part of his love given and received together.

The laws of holiness, then, are intimately bound to the nature of God's self-coming to his creatures in time: they constitute a participation somehow in that very coming. This means that one traditional Christian approach to their meaning—that they derive from the natural law in a way that is distinct from other ceremonial precepts—is too narrow and static a view. The notion that the laws of Lev. 19 represent a restatement of the Ten Commandments is, in itself, an ancient one. We find it among Jewish exegetes (*Rabbah* 24.5 mentions Rabbi Levi as the main expositor this position) and among Christians, beginning with Origen (*Homilies on Leviticus* 11.2).[5] But for these last, the Decalogue came to represent a kind of republication of the natural law in a manner that was both culturally shaped and also now set within particular civic penalties (Lev. 20). The interpreter, in this perspective, is called to extract from the text's historical peculiarities, the universal truths that should guide our behavior. The diverse precepts of Lev. 19 were grounded in nature in such a way, then, that it was possible to gather from its text not simply parallels to the Decalogue, but the kind of practical advice that today's widespread commitment to the Scripture's moral allegory has called "life application." Willet (1631: 490–93), for instance, will summarize the chapter simply through a list of moral exhortations: honor your parents, give to the poor, do not lie, do not swear, judge justly, avoid soothsayers and witchcraft, mourn the dead with moderation, reverence the house of God, hallow the Sabbath (in good Puritan fashion), honor the elderly. Although we find Cyprian treating injunctions in Lev. 19 as, to the modern eye, haphazardly applicable to the Christian (he includes, for instance, the prohibitions in 19:27 on the shaving of hair as a still valid moral directive; *Testimonies against the Jews* 3.81–85), by and large there has been a general sense in the Christian tradition that Lev. 19 makes sense largely to the degree that it fits some broader scheme of basic and universal moral discourse.

But if Lev. 19 is indeed a restatement of the Decalogue, not already defined in terms of a prior natural law, but as the revelation of God to Israel first and foremost, this restatement should be viewed as continuous with the character of its original receipt: God's costly approach to the human creature, given its flesh in the law fulfilled

5. Calvin's case is somewhat different, since he saw much of the Pentateuch, and Leviticus especially, as ordered toward the explication of the Decalogue in general (1996: 1.xv). This re-ordering governs the otherwise confusing and piecemeal system by which he sets out the central portion of his commentary.

in Christ Jesus, who draws the world to the Father in his obedient love. The law here is not some timeless ordering of life, but the actual movement of life through time, across the divides of creative being. To speak of God as the absolutely other in this case would make sense only within a context in which what is absolutely other has actually and in fact created that which it can love, move toward, and touch and be touched by. This is, in part, the peculiar character of its Levitical context, noted by many commentators, that the Decalogue is promulgated as tied to *penalty* (Lev. 20) and not simply as an abstracted code. The struggle for obedience passes through the historical realities of consequence and response. The law in Leviticus is historicized in the sense of being described as a passage within space and time. And the passage is given in the shape of provision, its loss, and its costly rededication.

Rabbah 24–25 offers a complex perspective on this vision. Beginning with a discussion of the holiness described in Lev. 19:2 as of the nature of separation, it then discusses this in terms of God's primary work of distinguishing reality in the creation of the world and of thereby marking off the line between life and nothingness. Job's assertion that "naked I came from my mother's womb, and naked shall I return; the LORD gave, and the LORD has taken away; blessed by the name of the LORD" (Job 1:21) becomes a key explicator of the way that creation is intrinsically bound to divine justice and mercy, the distinctive indicator of life as it arises miraculously out of nonexistence. Israel in its vocation is distinct and holy; but that is because it stands as a witness to the fact of God's justice and mercy as fundamental to existence itself: Zion (*siyyun*) is special to God on account of its embeddedness in this creative distinction (*siyyun*) marked out from other nations. But the witness it offers is always to something greater, to God's surpassing holiness that lies at the root of and beyond anything Israel might embody.

But what shall Israel embody nonetheless? *Rabbah* 25.1–8 sees as the key section of Lev. 19 the laws of *orlah*, the injunctions regarding planting in 19:23–25. This will strike Christian readers as tendentious, given the centering weight of 19:18 within the church's tradition. But the *Rabbah* focuses the nature of Israel's obedience in the character of the laws of planting as being the most revealing of God's own holiness, that is, of bringing life. The tree of these verses refers first to the Torah and the wisdom that it brings in its study and in the sharing of its study; this is so because the law itself constitutes the summit of, even the founding blueprint, of created existence. But if God's holiness is beyond Israel's in every way, how shall Israel be holy, except by engaging in the creative provision of the law's distinctive ordering of the universe? Deuteronomy 13:5 calls Israel to walk after God. But where? In the seas, as God does (Ps. 77:19)? Through the fire (Deut. 4:24)? These regions are too far outside our reach. Only by *planting* can Israel cleave to its Lord's presence. The laws of *orlah* therefore figure the primordial work of creation in the garden, which encircles the tree of life. Plant life, just as life itself, follows the outline of the Torah. God gave manna and quail in the desert. So now must Israel plant its trees and follow God's work of provision within its own life and the world's. "You shall be holy; for I the LORD your God am holy."

Holiness rightly defines the law—but holiness understood in terms of the dynamic work of God who comes, whose creation is his coming toward that which he makes for himself. Holiness as this divine fruitfulness, then, becomes the center of the law in Lev. 19, indeed of the law as a whole. This is why this chapter follows immediately upon Lev. 18 regarding sexual coupling and the power and history of genealogy and heritage. For *Rabbah* 25.1–8, the great mark of Israel's distinction, circumcision, is really a call to fruitfulness. The Hebrew of 19:23 actually speaks of the first three years of a tree's fruit, not as "forbidden" (as in the Revised Standard Version) but as "their uncircumcision" (Revised Standard Version margin). Yet what is circumcision (the fourth and fifth year's "fruits") but the blood (life) of the genitals (procreation)? Hence, the law here is focused primarily upon the vocation of Israel to provide seed for the nation, the calling to labor for children and posterity according to the distinctive offerings that the community's life together—including sacrifice, the works of justice, the relationships of family—must provide as part of God's own movement of creative self-giving. Holiness *is* the work of creation, the giving of life. By the same token, the works of creation—which are bound to the ordering of fluids and family, of mutual care and trust—are, in their derivation from God's self-offering, sanctifying.

Whereas *Rabbah* 25.1–8 turns to explanatory scriptural verses dealing with divine creative action and the works of fruitful planting, Willet (1631: 452) turns to Hos. 11:9 as his summary illumination: "I will not execute my fierce anger, I will not again destroy Ephraim; for I am God and not man, the Holy One in your midst, and I will not come to destroy." The prophetic context here is Israel as God's wayward child: "How can I give you up, O Ephraim! . . . My compassion grows warm and tender" (11:8). But there is a congruence between the *Rabbah* and Willet, in this sense of God's procreative love as the mercy that overcomes the death dealing of sinfulness: God has a child whom he loves so deeply as to forgive its rejection of the one who made it. So the first commandments given to the people within this discourse concern respect of parents and keeping the Sabbath (Lev. 19:3). The creation of life physically from the man and the woman and more primarily from God constitutes the revealed foundation of divine love as exposited in previous chapters. And almost all commentators have seen this initial connection between one's physical parents and one's heavenly parents (God and, in Christian terms, the church) as deep and wide ranging. Physical parents bring us to faith, teach us the commandments, show us how to live (Deut. 6:7; 2 Tim. 1:5; 3:15), in addition to sharing their own bodies in the unitive act that, by God's grace, brings forth new life. These actions, recognized in the reality of respect (Matt. 15:4–5), themselves derive from the creative action of God recognized in the keeping of the Sabbath (Gen. 2:3; Exod. 20:11), spoken of in the plural in Lev. 19:3 because here it subsumes all the festivals of praise (23:32) that pour out to God for his goodness—and his alone (19:4).

While not all the laws in the chapter represent this human embodiment of divine provision so explicitly, yet all should be read in these terms, particularly as they contribute to the ordering of a community of such creative provision. The discussion of the eating of the peace offering (19:5–8), for instance, refers to the discipline of trust in God's giving (something that is holy in itself) and the refusal to save for the future: no eating of the sacrifice on the third day. In this, it is parallel to the calling of Israel to gather only for the day from the gift of manna and not to hoard (Exod. 16:19–30), since God's promise was to feed his people: "Give us this day our daily bread" (Matt. 6:11). The peace offering itself was an act of thanksgiving for God's creative blessing, and so its consumption would represent that reality as far as possible. Though later Christians would count the days in this injunction as the ages of life, pointing out that the third age of death and judgment would be too late to offer the fruit of repentance (Hesychius in Rabanus Maurus [Patrologia latina 108.443] and *Glossa ordinaria* [Patrologia latina 113.449]) this reading strays from the clear import of the context, which is that of trusting dependence, rather than limited opportunity.

The law regarding leaving gleanings for the poor (Lev. 19:9–10) follows from this base. Both Jewish and Christian traditions have read this command less in terms of some abstract justice, but rather as an important instance of receiving the providential love of God as a community. This is not always expressed in ways that modern social policy finds comfortable. Willet offers a very typical seventeenth-century Puritan claim, for instance, that the command shows that "the poor you always have with you" (John 12:8) and that the division of rich and poor is itself providentially ordered (1631: 483). Although this sets up what is clearly a static social disparity of classes, his point is actually that the charitable responsibilities of the better-off are always pressing and can never be avoided. More pointedly, *Sifra* 196–98 (Neusner 1988–: 91–102) comments extensively on the reasons for God specifying the edges of field: this was to provide clarity for the poor and public visibility and scrutiny that prevents cheating on the part of the fields' owners. Why? Because the kind of care demanded for the poor derives from the larger reality that poor and rich alike receive all things from God and hence are required to live together within a dynamic community of provision that flows from God's own offering. *Me'am Lo'ez* (Kaplan 1982: 12.14–17) therefore underlines God's providence in terms of the historical switching around of rich and poor at any time (noting the alternating use of the second person plural and singular within these verses). The command ends with an assertion of God's reality for the whole community, rich and poor together (19:10), which emphasizes that *all* the harvests belong to God and from him are shared with *both* rich and poor: to fail to leave is to steal from the poor what *God* has given them. It is the connection between rich and poor, indeed between the entire community here, as commonly dependent upon God's life that is in view here.

And that life, furthermore, is one whose commonness—passing beyond the boundedness of creative distinction to reach us—is given in assuming the form of the most needy. The *Glossa ordinaria* (Patrologia latina 113.349–50) therefore reads the law of gleaning on the basis of 2 Cor. 8:9: "For you know the grace of our Lord Jesus Christ, that though he was rich, yet for your sake he became poor, so that by his poverty you might become rich." God's self-offering draws our own self-giving into its current, including the concrete life of giving to the poor. In this way, God's gift transforms us into persons of mercy, and his provision becomes, not merely sustenance, but new life itself.

Many of the more obvious laws enumerated here—obvious in the sense of their assumed moral substance—fall within this same current of divine sharing of life, which once embraced becomes a profound change in the character of the obedient follower of God. Injunctions against stealing, lying, and profaning God's name, as well as dealing justly with laborers and watching over the deaf and the blind, are all gathered together as entailments of the one offering of life. *Sifra* 199.1, for instance, speaks of the inexorable and intertwined movement from stealing to lying to cursing God, a movement that ends in "devour[ing] the earth and its inhabitants" and leaving the land scorched and depopulated (Isa. 24:6). This sense of enmeshed entailment in sin is common in Jewish exegesis: lying (and covering up lies) leads to slander and tale-telling, as does cheating and its justification (Lev. 19:15), which leads to bloodshed through anger and revenge, as well as leads people to disdain their neighbors even when in need (19:16; see *Me'am Lo'ez* [Kaplan 1982: 12.26–28]). Each of these sins ends by casting a larger and larger net of accomplices and victims (in a famous talmudic assertion, the tale-teller commits murder against his own self, the person spoken to, and the person spoken of—not to mention a sin against God who hears all; Babylonian Talmud, tractate *Arakhin* 15a). All this represents the contradiction of God's own coming to bring life, a coming that is bound to giving away the truth not taking it, to uncovering the truth not obscuring it, to enacting one's own being not contradicting it.

Christian medieval commentators saw this entailment in the widest sense in terms of the church. The sojourner or stranger of the gleaning law in 19:10 is linked to sinners mentioned in the subsequent laws as figures of those opposing the faith in general. Yet these are then understood in terms of the deaf and the blind of 19:14, whose condition is to be *cared for*, not rejected outright. This is, it should be said, an anomalous position when compared with most medieval discussions of heresy and sin, which generally counsel separation and destruction. But Bruno of Segni (Patrologia latina 164.442), for instance, takes Rom. 14:13 as the explanatory verse here—never to scandalize fellow believers or pass judgment on them—as a call to treat sinners kindly and to win them back with love and a spirit of welcome (14:1), for this is the path to repentance and life itself provided in the welcome of God in Christ to us (15:7). Others will read these verses in connection with Lev. 19:17, on reasoning with one's neighbor, which is viewed as a part of church discipline in its deepest sense (Matt. 18; cf. Prov. 28:23; Ezek. 33:6) and which mysteriously moves in the direction of including all human creatures, even enemies (Matt. 5:44) who are made neighbors.

The ecclesial context of this discussion is important, for although both Jewish and Christian commentators are agreed that the prohibitions of stealing and lying and so on are absolute and cover every conceivable case (much as Augustine argued in his treatise *On Lying*), the implied question of penalty addressed here in terms of welcome is given a direction of response that is governed by the health or life of the community understood as body. Individual concerns regarding right and wrong are thereby relocated to this wider body. The neighbor and the stranger are actually brought together in this body (Eph. 2:12–22), and therefore the love commandment of Lev. 19:18 is reiterated in terms of the stranger also, on the basis of God's own gathering up of his people who *were* strangers and exiles (19:34). From a Pauline perspective, the divine imperative behind all is now "what builds up" as opposed to what "tears down" (1 Cor. 8:1; 14:12, 26; Eph. 4:16, 29), for God's very act is to grow (1 Cor. 3:6). To obstruct such growth and upbuilding in *any* way is itself a profanation of God's name.

If the holiness of separation or distinction is, as I have been arguing, the same as the holiness of following the Lord of creative distinction as he gives himself to distinction's reconciliation, then we would expect that the laws of this chapter would demonstrate their place in this dynamic. This is not, however, always easy to discern, as we can see with the laws against mixing (19:19) and the laws regarding shaving of the hair (19:27). According to Jewish exegesis, these laws are of a special kind, the *khuqqim*, often translated "statutes" (Revised Standard Version) or "decrees." The *khuqqim*, as I noted earlier, were viewed as those laws for which no rational justification was obvious. They are to be treated as "decrees of the king," to be obeyed simply because they come from God. This represents, at best, a pure following of God's will, at worst a kind of blind obedience. Holiness here is a cleaving to God, but not one imbued with a coherent understanding. In general and in tacit recognition of this unexplained quality, Christians have simply spiritualized these laws in terms of their indication of separation itself from sin and faithlessness: "What accord has Christ with Belial?" (2 Cor. 6:15) was a common refrain in this context.

However, where a reason *is* given by Jewish exegetes for these mysterious laws, it roots the command in the creative blessing of God. For instance, Nahmanides (1974: 295) points out that the prohibition of mixing animals or seeds derives from the distinct forms of each creature as God made them. These come in an albeit mysteriously fixed number within the world, each species of which is governed by a heavenly angel, so that earth and heaven mirror each other. Mixing, in this sense, is a tampering with life itself—a judgment with obviously broad implications for the kinds of genetic engineering now common in both agricultural and medical fields (Wolff 2001).[1] The distinctions, as I have stressed, *are* life itself, not something opposed to it.

But God's own love, which creates these in their discreet character, also seeks to bring them into the fullness of proximity with him. There are at least two contexts in which this reality is engaged in the New Testament. First is Jesus's parable of wheat and the tares (Matt. 13:24–30). Jesus himself attributes the mixed sowing to the work of an enemy. The goal of the enemy in this case is to bring about the ruin of the good seed by having all taken up together. Instead, the householder in the parable agrees that the good and bad seed should grow together until such time as their true distinctions become not only apparent, but capable of being separated out. Common growth, in this case, leads to a fuller life for those who will, in fact, live, and the act of separation is suppressed during history for the sake of that life with God later. This is "compared to the kingdom of heaven."

Paul goes further with this and actually implies that the kingdom may involve not only a divine patience with the transgression of difference, but even somehow its divine reconciliation through contradiction. While there has been some debate over the actual horticultural basis of Paul's discussion of grafting in Rom. 11:17–24, it would appear that the process to which he refers—grafting wild olive branches onto a natural olive tree—is indeed highly unnatural and under normal conditions incapable of bearing true olives.[2] In other words, this would be a case of manifested contradiction to the law of *kelayim* ("mixing") as later elaborated talmudically with respect to grafting (*harkavah*), a conclusion that Paul's use of the terms "natural" (*kata physin*) and "unnatural" (*para physin*) would seem to underscore. Yet it is what God, in his mercy, actually does: a contradiction

---

1. Based on the Levitical notion that life derives from the mixture of sexual or reproductive fluids, there has been a strong (though by no means uniform) permissive attitude among Jewish halakic scholars regarding more specifically genetic mixtures. From a theological perspective, however—like Nahmanides' (1974: 295–97)—there is an even stronger sense that such mixtures are probably contrary to the purposes of divine creation (Hirsch 1989: 2.530–37). The issue is not simply maintaining the distinction of the fluids, but upholding the ordering of creation itself.

2. Sir Thomas Browne's 1683 *Certain Miscellany Tracts*, tract 1: "Observations upon Scripture Plants," refers to Theophrastus's *De causis plantarum* 1.7 and the anonymous *Geoponica* 10 in a way that enlightens Rom. 11:17–24.

fulfilled—distinctions drawn together—by being borne in his own flesh upon the cross (Eph. 2:15–16). If this represents a divine provision and upbuilding, it is of a strange kind. This should alert us that the character of the laws of Lev. 19 is not simply one that follows a single principle that can be extracted and then applied, as desired, in new ways and within new cultural settings. The laws of mixing are Pentecostal in their gathering of tongues; they are also Golgathic in their cost. If this is a following, the path for the church goes through unimaginably difficult terrain. This points forward to the history of stoning in Lev. 20.

With respect to the specific rules concerning the mixing of fabrics as clothing, exclusively applied to linen and sheep's wool on the basis of Deut. 22:11 (*shaatnez*), Jewish mystical exegesis was forced to go further afield. There was, for instance, speculation that the separation of the fibers effectively figured the separation of good and malevolent spirits in heaven, which God had put in place to preserve Israel from overwhelming satanic accusation. The person who mixes the fibers actually gives an opening to the evil spirits to enter into Israel's realm, so pulling down the nation. Furthermore, such a person renders it difficult for prayers to reach God—the Hebrew text of Lev. 19:19b literally reads not "putting on," but "going up," as in one's petitions to heaven. Because of the communally destructive power believed to be inherent in the failure to obey the law of *shaatnez*, and also the ease with which one might transgress, elaborate instructions were offered regulating clothing (*Me'am Lo'ez* [Kaplan 1982: 12.41–49]). But the central issue remained one of maintaining the proper configuration of the created order, in this case between earth and heaven, Israel and its enemies, the human soul and God—an order by which life itself is given birth and upheld. Furthermore, the mixed fabric in this case is not in itself considered "unholy"—*shaatnez* was permitted for coverings of the ark itself—only the use of it in any way as a form of human clothing. That is to say, the humanly willful intent to disorder the distinctions of creation for one's own benefit, out of a prideful self-regard, renders the mixed-fabric sinful. The respect of *shaatnez* is, by contrast, a discipline of the will, an offering of one's own desires to the purposes of one's creator (Hirsch 1989: 2.530).

But having said that, and in a way similar to violation of *kelayim* in the church of Jew and Gentile borne by the body of Christ, Jesus himself bears the mixed fabric as the burden of his own self-giving. While we cannot be certain, the scarlet robe placed by the Roman soldiers upon Jesus during his passion (Matt. 27:28) was probably *shaatnez*. The *chlamys*, as it is called, was a Greek cloak, made of wool, but generally seamed and embroidered on its borders with threads of different origin. The careful description of Jesus's stripping, his clothing with the *chlamys*, his mocking and abuse, and then a final stripping and reclothing emphasizes the degree of degradation to which these pagan soldiers drag their Jewish victim, hailed as king yet profaned through a symbolic subjection to the insult of his coverings. Later Christian discussion of the two fabrics, which derive from plants and animals respectively, emphasized the distinction God made between the parallel sacrifices of Cain and Abel (fruit and flock) and the history of their separation within the fate of humankind. Yet here the Lord's own passion brings them together again, thrust upon him by the rejection of humankind as a whole, Jew and Gentile together.

Finally, the laws regulating the shaving of the temples and beard (Lev. 19:27)—corners to the hair on a man's head known as *peyoth*—also fall within the general dynamic of the chapter's stress upon divine provisioning, if also gleaned only in a figural way. In general, both Jewish and Christian commentators have viewed these rules as aimed against the ritual practices of pagan priests and devotees who shaved their hair and beards in particular ways (cf. Letter of Jeremiah 6:31). This was the main rationale given for most of the *khuqqim* for which deeper meanings could not be found (Maimonides uses this argument also for *shaatnez* in *Guide to the Perplexed* 3.37). But hair was always viewed as, more primordially, endowed with or as an expression of vital power—this quite universally, but in a special way with Israel. The cutting of beards from defeated leaders was a form of final insult (2 Sam. 10:4; Isa. 7:20). There was, notably among martial heroes like Samson, an identification of hair with physical strength (Judg. 13:4–5; 16:17–22) or with masculine prowess and beauty (Absalom in 2 Sam. 14:26). And, most importantly (and related to this), there was the custom of the Nazirite vow, which Samson himself had taken, which included the refusal to cut one's hair at all during the period of the devotion and offering it back, after shaving it off, to God at the end of the vow (Num. 6:5, 18). The Nazirite vow (which included men and women) involved the devotion of one's whole self to God, and with the distinctive offering of an unfettered growth of hair, this included giving over one's full vital strength to the Lord. Hence, the shaving of the leper indicated a kind of return to infancy and to the moment of one's first creation (Lev. 14:9). Similarly, shaving of the hair among mourners and penitents marked a kind of vulnerable self-exposure and self-offering before the Lord of the universe (Job 1:20; Jer. 48:37; Amos 8:10; Hirsch 1989: 2.551–54).

While it is not clear how the regulation of Lev. 19:27 specifically functions, its general thrust seems clear: the particularities of life, as given by God, are represented in the hair, and therefore its ordering is tied to these particularities. Most especially, they appear to be the particularities of fruitful vitality, as the laws of hair for women and men differ according to their own distinctions. Despite this general sense of the hair's importance, it is not clear what the particular law here refers to. Later Jewish tradition made much of women covering their hair, which itself was not to be cut—a sign of her procreative role as well as her unitive tie to her husband alone. Some of the still mystifying logic of Paul's advice in 1 Cor. 11:3–16 at least fits within this outlook: the man's hair is to be publicly ordered, not left to grow, as a sign of personal control; while a woman's hair, allowed to grow, is to be left covered in what would become (if it had not already become) a standard rabbinic practice (Bronner 1993). These realities, as with later discussion on *shaatnez*, are related to the order of the heavenly beings, which display the creative purposes of God in their fullness. Leviticus 19:27 is congruent with this call to a kind of subjection to the order of life-giving, sexually rooted, in this regard; and Hirsch (1989: 2.551–54) is surely right in seeing these laws as specifically geared to the maintenance of *attention* to this reality within the course of daily life.

But just as the prophets symbolically enacted the full brunt of the law's transgression—as seen in Ezekiel's corporeal display of God's judgment through his own shaving of himself (5:1)—so the breadth of the law's actual significance is carried within the body of Jesus's own life and is fulfilled. In its mirror converse— the ordering (and covering) of woman's hair—the laws of *peyoth* are both defiled and their disordering taken to himself in the penitent woman's (Mary's) weeping and washing of Jesus's feet with her hair (Luke 7:38–50; John 11:2; 12:1–8). In an exploding of the law's distinguishing function, Mary violates the line between man and woman, married woman and other men, by uncovering her hair, letting it down, and actually using it physically to touch the feet of a rabbi.[3] She does this, seemingly, as someone overwhelmed and emotionally broken by her own sins and by their forgiveness at the hands of Christ's divine love. But what is in fact unveiled in this act? Not only divine forgiveness and love drawing out repentance, but the link between these and the reality of Jesus's death, that is, his embalming and burial: "Let her alone, let her keep it for the day of my burial" (John 12:7). The distinction is not done away with, as we have seen; rather, the disordering of its life-giving reality (Mary's sinfulness as well as her transgression before Jesus himself) is borne by a divine self-offering that overcomes it through its extent, a reach that embraces the very end (13:1). So Paul's Nazirite vow, hair and all, becomes the means of his self-giving into the hands of his own people and finally into the hands of Rome, which will send him to his own sacrifice (Acts 18:18; 21:24; 2 Tim. 4:6).

The rest of the laws in Lev. 19—including those against consulting mediums and wizards, against self-mutilation, and demanding the respect for old age and the welcoming of strangers—are more obviously linked to the character of exclusive trust in God and in his own gift of life and heritage as a creative provision according to which Israel's life is to be shaped. They can be readily understood as such in both their purpose and weight. Jesus himself links law keeping with fruitfulness in this way, at the end of the Sermon on the Mount (Matt. 7:17–20), the immediate context of which is the Father's loving provision for his children who are always to be ready and open in their asking (7:7–12). But it is not so much that fruitfulness is a principle that should then be used to judge, in various situations, what is to be done or not, as if the laws themselves were epiphenomenal expressions of this deeper reality. It is rather the case that the laws *are* the historical forms that embody this fruitfulness that derives from

3. On uncovering and loosening the hair of an adulteress, see Num. 5:18, a verse that became the scriptural basis for the talmudic prohibition of uncovering a married woman's hair; see Mishnah, tractate *Ketubbot* 7.6, and Babylonian Talmud, tractate *Sotah* 8a.

God's own work of creation, which is itself the great work of self-offering in time that holiness describes.

Therefore, in all of these particular laws, the distinction between moral and ceremonial, in the traditional Christian sense, is not clear, nor should it be (on the question of the judicial law, see the next chapter). It might indeed be helpful if a strict template could be applied by which modern Christians might know which laws of the Old Testament were still binding upon them—laws against murder, but not against planting of mixed seeds; laws against lying, but not against the shaving of one's beard. But in fact, because all of these are laws of holiness, that is, of following God in proximity, their significance is never abolished but rather borne in the body and fulfilled more and more as we become one body with God's body in Jesus. The laws against homosexual sex are fulfilled in Jesus's own eunuchhood for the sake of the kingdom; short of that, they remain exactly as they are stated here. The laws against shaving the beard are fulfilled in the self-giving forgiveness to repentant sinners; short of that, they remain exactly as they are stated here. The question is what Jesus bears, and how he does so, and what he calls his followers to carry as they walk with him. To bear the penalty of a law no longer followed is precisely to fulfill it, perfect it, make it a part of the life one lives as a follower of God, "always carrying in the body the death of Jesus" (2 Cor. 4:10), that is, the law's rejection. This carrying itself takes the law close to oneself. If one does not do this, the law remains valid in its bare form—demanding and perhaps ultimately burdensome and crushing.

The key text here is the whole of Rom. 2, where circumcision is appealed to externally and internally as the description of the law keeper. This is sometimes read in terms of the contrast between the keeper of the revealed law and the keeper of the natural law, with the emphasis on keeper rather than on the means of knowing this ultimately single law. However, Paul is clear that the keeper of the law, in this sense, is the one whose own *heart* is circumcised (2:29, following Deut. 10:16), though in a way that is coincident with "bear[ing] on [the] body the marks of Jesus" (Gal. 6:17). The obedient heart shows itself in a corporeal conformity with Christ. Those who do not follow Jesus are bound to the law as it is given—in its distinction between Jew and Gentile—still unfulfilled and awaiting the subjection to its details. The question of binding/no longer binding is perhaps, then, not resolved consistently or definitively for Christians, the ultimacy of whose following of Christ is rarely achieved and is, in any case, constantly waxing and waning in its proximity to the Lord. The fulfillment of the law in Christ for us and subjection to the law in its details are mirrors of each other in different locations of time and space. This also means that the weight of the law, the sin it unveils and in this unveiling empowers (Rom. 7:7–12), is felt over and over again in different ways throughout our individual and corporate histories. So we tell the stories of our incompleteness, our falls, our renewals, our desperate needs. These realities themselves are what the Lord takes to himself as he passes through and with the world to his Father.

LEVITICUS 20

Because the law embodies the shape of God's coming to us, that shape encompasses our rebellions and rejections to this proximity, and the issue of penalty, treated in Lev. 20, is an essential part of God's holiness and of our own following. And just as Jesus ends the Sermon on the Mount with the parable of the foolish man, whose house built on sand falls, "and great was the fall of it" (Matt. 7:27), so the procreative actions of Lev. 18–19 give rise to the concatenation of disasters that befall the transgressor of this pattern of life, here clearly mixing together the particular injunctions on sexual coupling with other laws as if they both pertain to the same realities and give rise to the same consequences. When the Lord speaks of "beatitude"—in however strange a way—he speaks also of "woe" (Luke 6:20–26; see below on Lev. 26). Sin opposes and runs from life and therefore effectively embraces death. Hence it is its *own* punishment (Ps. 7:15; 57:6; the *paradosis* or "giving over" of Rom. 1:24–32), and the reality of the penalty is not so much a discrete response to sin as it is sin's inherent self-expression, death itself. How the power of this self-expression is broken is indeed the message of the Christian gospel and the work of God in Christ.

The exposition of the penalties for the law's transgression is not systematically presented within the Scriptures as a topic in its own right. Rather, discussions of punishment appear only here and there, scattered within the major groupings of legal material (Exod. 21–24), traditionally known as *mishpatim* ("laws"). Still, the penalties themselves do have common features. Some involve restitution and multiplied restitution; others involve corporal punishment; others involve death. But together there is a sense behind these punishments that the law's creative provision has been assaulted and a call is made to respond, if response is still possible at all.

To give a prominent example: Deut. 25:2–3 became the basis for the common penalty of thirty-nine lashes (to which an entire section of the Talmud—tractate *Makkot*—is devoted). Eventually 168 offenses were defined as liable to this punishment, and Paul refers to having received it five times (2 Cor. 11:24). They were applied to the many defined offenses of the Torah for which specific punishments are not given in the scriptural text. The interpretation of how the number thirty-nine was established, since Deuteronomy actually says "forty" was extensive: was it a matter of scriptural rounding of numbers? did it relate to the days it took Moses to receive the law? and so on. But theologically, an interesting view took hold: a human embryo was seen as becoming an actual person on the fortieth day, that is, fully living; therefore, to limit the number of lashes to thirty-nine was a way of saying that this punishment (and the crime it met) was not life destroying, but was in fact constrained by the life-preserving mercy of God (see Midrash Tanhuma, tractate *Bamidbar* 23). The crime and its penalty are bound up with God's creative purposes, both as the object of rebellion and the underlying motive of response.

In this light we should look at the stark character of punishment described in Lev. 20, where the specific crimes outlined are all described as capital offenses. In fact, the only punishment explicitly mentioned here, usually extended to all the others, is death by stoning (though 20:14 gives burning as the penalty for one form of incest; see also 21:9). The figural import of this method of execution is broad. It allows for a communal participation in the execution, one that enacts the sense of wider assault involved in the crime (24:14; Deut. 17:7). More importantly, its form—crushing—represents a kind of *interior* disintegration of the created life, one that mirrors the effects of the sin itself in dismantling what God has put together. (Lev. 20:11 is sometimes, for instance, seen as implying the interior hemorrhaging that comes from being crushed by rocks.) Crushing by stones is linked by Jesus himself to the complete reversal of God's creative purpose, whereby "things that are" are "br[ought] to nothing" (1 Cor. 1:28): "Daughters of Jerusalem, do not weep for me, but weep for yourselves and for your children. For behold, the days are coming when they will say, 'Blessed are the barren, and the wombs that never bore, and the breasts that never gave suck!' Then they will begin to say to the mountains, 'Fall on us'; and to the hills, 'Cover us'" (Luke 23:28–30; cf. Hos. 10:8; Rev. 6:16). Death by stoning manifests in its very materiality the return to dust and commonness that the creature's very being hovers over at its core, now fulfilled through the perverse wishes of human beings who prefer death to life (Gen. 3:19). As we saw in the discussion of Lev. 11, this return to the dust of death stands as the slippage into indistinction, the loss of difference as the gift of God in forming that which is other than himself.

That most of the capital crimes mentioned in Lev. 20 are either related to the laws of sexual coupling from Lev. 18 or to the matrix of heritage otherwise implied clearly demonstrates this character of the penalty itself. Willet, for example, rightly sees the cursing of parents (20:9) as a blasphemy against God's created blessing, that by which we exist at all through the gift of our procreated being (1631: 499). (In good seventeenth-century Anglican fashion, however, he extends its application to the magistrate and all authority, ecclesial and civil.) To curse one's parents is to curse God in the deepest sense for the infinite miracle of being (Job 2:9). That homosexual coupling is singled out in this list (Lev. 20:13) has proved a source of much modern embarrassment; but its subjection to the penalty of stoning is precisely a reflection of its rejection of the created and creative purposes of God by which life is received, nurtured, and passed on. It is not coincidental therefore—nor simply a subject for predictable moral allegories concerning sin and sinfulness—that the chapter closes (20:25) with a reiteration of the distinction between clean and unclean beasts. Such distinction is something that is, as we saw earlier, at the very basis of what it means that God creates at all: the setting up in existence of something other than himself and, in the engagement of these distinctions, the furtherance of created life itself.

It is from this fundamental creative work of God that what is called his wrath proceeds. Divine wrath manifests itself as that creative work that is held back through its twisting and denial (Rom. 1:18). The wrath of God, which is tied to sin and to the transgression through sin of the law (4:15), receives its historical dynamic from the divine movement of creation and its purpose. This is the truth of God mentioned in 1:18, and it is also a truth that is visible in the very realities of the world that are formed by God (1:19–21). There is no avoiding the reality, in any dispensation of history, of death as the "wages of sin" (6:23), for such death, as in Jesus's remarks concerning those who will wish they had been barren and never born, is literally the historical tendency of all that cannot and will not follow God as he both creates time and moves through it. *There is no life apart from God.* And although life is the gift that God gives distinct from himself, its origin and sustenance demand God's self-giving love at the center of its being. The sins of Lev. 20 qua sins are death dealing (Rom. 1:32)—they deserve death in the sense that they are fitted and conformed to death—and in themselves are opposed to God, regardless of the status of their legal definition even within the life of the church. Sins are the pits into which their perpetrators fall, as by the gravity of death (Ps. 7:15). Stoning, then, is a scriptural figure first of all, with all of its perduring theological and historical substance, and not simply a passing cultural custom.

But it is a figure, nonetheless, and not simply a command, for it is borne up by Christ Jesus and approached therefore only through him. While "those who do such things deserve to die" (Rom. 1:32), it is also that case that "God shows his love for us in that while we were yet sinners Christ died for us" and "since . . . we are now justified by his blood, much more shall we be saved by him from the wrath of God" (5:8–9). Somehow, God himself enters and reaches out beyond the death-dealing movement of human rebellion against the reality of our own creaturely glory. In the one incident in which a penalty of Lev. 20 comes into play within the Gospels (John 8:2–11), the capital offense of adultery is presented to Jesus in the person of the "woman caught in adultery," and an actual stoning as called for by the law is turned aside. Why is this? On one level, Jesus simply forgives the woman, sending her away with a grant of new life for the sake of amendment of life (8:11). On another level, he also spreads the forgiveness out to all the bystanders—for they, in their abandonment of the penalty, have admitted their own sin (8:7, 9). As in Lev. 20:4–5, the net of guilt is cast wide among the people. Yet in this case, Jesus's refusal to condemn stretches just as widely. There is a deeper reality at work here than an act of individual mercy.

The status of the Levitical penalty in this incident has been a subject of debate. Willet proposes the principle that penalties themselves are culturally bound, though not the nature of the (moral) sin for which the penalty is given (1631: 502–3). Hence, he speaks of "Moses's judicials" as inherently malleable, though only in a certain direction: no more than Moses, but not necessarily less. The gospel can temper but does not abrogate. Had Jesus wished to allow the stoning of the woman, he might legitimately have done so, without contradicting his own nature, and his clemency was of a purely local kind. Similarly, the church in different times and cultures may choose to impose or uphold a variety of judicial responses to sin, so long as it does not exceed the explicit limits of scriptural possibility, with Moses and Jesus as the markers on either side. Thus, should a penalty of death by stoning (or perhaps some other means) be imposed on those committing adultery, the Christian church would be well within its theological permission to support such a penalty. All judicials are ad hoc by their very nature within this scope and applied on a discretionary basis within the forms of particular communities.

This view, however, appears to be inadequate within the perspective of Levitical figuralism, for the nature of punishment for sin is explained in Leviticus in terms of the movement of God's creative life in relationship to creaturely reality. And that movement finds its fullest form, historically, within the life, death, and resurrection of Jesus. In this light, the nature of punishment is rightly explicated by the cross of Christ, solely and exclusively, and not by the variables of historical or cultural change within human societies, even the society of the church. "Surely he has borne our griefs and carried our sorrows. . . . He was wounded for our transgressions, he was bruised for our iniquities; upon him was the chastisement that made us whole" (Isa. 53:4–5; cf. 1 Pet. 2:24). Stoning itself involved a sacrificial transfer of guilt by the community (Lev. 24:14) through the laying on of hands by witnesses, and in the cross this transfer is perfectly completed through the long handling of Christ among Jew and Gentile alike that finally raises him to his death. The sinfulness of Mary is forgiven through the proleptic action of touching that marks his death and burial (John 12:7), and so too all forgiveness, all taking away of penalty, is really a gathering up of penalty by and upon the body assumed by God in the midst of degraded time.

The relation of God's sin-bearing to the civil law's concrete penalties visited upon the guilty provides the theological challenge to Christian social ethics regarding punishment. Why do we still punish in the wake of the cross? The unsystematic character of civil society's response to crime gives a clue, for it is difficult to see how the civil law's ad hoc character can be attributed to anything other than the still uncompleted history of human life before God, that is, its assertion of its own unredeemed independence from God's self-giving. Willet (1631: 514) and Calvin (1996: 2.90), for instance, can read Lev. 20:20 or 20:27 as perfectly appropriate penalties for the state to impose precisely because of their conviction, not of the fallen character of human societies in the face of God's traversal of the world, but of the morally weak and intrinsically susceptible character of *women* to become witches. It is misogyny, in this instance, that is ad hoc, not the divine appropriateness of variable penalties, and because of this, a testimony to the still-rebellious nature of human social life. This observation is not mitigated by Paul's insistence that the civil power or governing authorities are instruments of God's wrath upon wrongdoing (Rom. 13:1–7), as if all penalties are thereby essential manifestations of God's own punishing will. The issue that Paul addresses here is subjection, rather than the nature of the punishment itself—a subjection that is primarily Christ's own to the injustices of the world's life, which may include even those of the governing authorities. We are called to follow the same path "in him." This is, as Peter writes, a question of "trust in [God] who judges justly," not the approbation of the ad hoc judicial structures themselves of the world (1 Pet. 2:18–23).

Origen at least struggled with the obvious *differences* of form between the penal laws of Lev. 20 and the gospel's own description of Jesus's call to and modeling of mercy. His resolution of this problem was to see in the Mosaic punishments the very mercy of the gospel proffered to the sinner, for the law's penalties make possible a repentance in this world that bears fruit to eternal life, while the gospel's mercy is granted only to those who rightly fear eternal punishment (*Homilies on Leviticus* 11.2). Working with Nah. 1:8–9, Origen's concern is to see punishment in this world as a warning figure of the far worse fate that awaits those who remain impenitent: lapidation, after all, pales in comparison with everlasting damnation. Ambrose, however, went further (Sermon 23) and saw the Sermon on the Mount and its call to "nonresistance to evil" as given in the cross itself and therefore as presenting more than a sign to stir up a proper sense of concern over sin. It is now a banner of sorts, raised up to be followed by the Christian as the one who stays close to Christ Jesus in his own self-giving path within the world. The adulteress cannot be killed *because* of the cross, and therefore the Christian's approach to punishment is not ad hoc at all, but bound to the very forms of Jesus's own teaching and embodied existence.

Ambrose, the former civil governor, thus intimates that a historical change in penal form has taken place with Christ: capital punishment on the part of God's people is inconsistent with the cross, where Jesus himself gathered up and fulfilled this form of wrath. So too is warfare, it would seem, because of the relationship between nonresistance and Jesus's own being. But nonresistance is not the same thing as nonviolence, since it is Jesus's body that *draws* violence to himself. If the world is gathered to him and by him and finally in him, this unleashing of violence that is received and not given constitutes a kind of fury that is not without its terrible suffering (Luke 12:49–53). Forgiveness is costly to the body of the forgiver and perhaps to the bodies of others nearby. Forgiveness is not the destruction of wrath, only its transformation. The whole process by which sin stirs up its own violence within the world, which is then embraced by God, is a part of history's conformance to its maker, of God's own continuing punishment of the world, into which his followers are drawn as he bears it himself. The deep mystery of this is not resolved by a simple parsing of political realities or of pacifistic alternatives. If there are two kingdoms, as Luther imagined, they cannot be so easily distinguished one from the other, since the passage of Christ's kingdom is through and within the world's, and the violence of God's wrath lies in their meeting, one way or the other. Though Christian efforts to transform the kingdom of the world are appropriate, they cannot be pursued simply in terms of imposing a new (Christian) legal system upon another. The nature of the cross is given partly in the two kingdoms having wedded somehow in this sacrificial body—the differences taken up in God's own self-giving. Indeed, the follower of Christ enters the place of death, the place of stones heaped upon stones, in order that therein life may be given by the power of God's miraculous and creating love. To be drawn into such a place is not the same thing as bearing what Christ bears; but it *is* a participation in the way of the cross upon which we are led (Col. 1:24). There is no place wherein the death that sin grasps after is escaped as a reality. But there also is no place, even such a place as sin's crumbling into dust, that God's own power cannot reach. Hence, we "die to sin," truly and concretely, by being bound to the Lord's own life and death, within which God creates anew (Rom. 6:1–11). The adulterous woman of John 8:2–11 is asked to sin no more, but if she is to do this, she must die in Christ, and in this sense she *does* in fact come to bear her punishment, though only in him and through following him.

The wages of sin are paid by God's own Son and self. Yet the world exacts this payment, through its voracious desire for death. The follower of God, the Christian disciple and church, stands at the intersection of this meeting, where God steps through and beyond. The forms of this following cannot therefore be precise, nor are they the stuff of policy reform, since they derive from cross and resurrection before all else, the historical insistence of the chasm of creation's being and reconciliation that is divine love. Leviticus 20, therefore, finds its communal fulfillment in Stephen, accuser and forgiver (Acts 7:51–60), upon whom the stones of many fell—individuals, people, those standing and approving such as Saul (7:58; 8:1), the wide net of human depravity taking in even apostate disciples (Mark 14:66–72), for "all have sinned and fall short of the glory of God" (Rom. 3:23). Yet this man "gazed into heaven and saw the glory of God, and Jesus standing at the right hand of God" (Acts 7:55). "Will the dust praise thee? Will it tell of thy faithfulness?" asks the psalmist (Ps. 30:9). And Stephen, the one stoned for blasphemy, answers yes. With Jesus, he answers yes, for "the very stones would cry out" before the coming of the humble king (Luke 19:40). There is life and glorifying of God even from the rocks and stones, from the trembling mountains that "praise the LORD" (Ps. 148:9). And the temple, torn down stone by stone through sinful human hands (Mark 13:2), is transformed into the offering of life by which the church, now gathered as Christ's own body, carries the world to God (1 Pet. 2:5).

LEVITICUS 21–22

In the course of reading Lev. 19, we began with a discussion of holiness. We looked at holiness not so much as a quality or objective essence, but as the historical trajectory of God's creative approach to that which God has made and loved. Holiness is a word that describes the reality of that making and that approach, and as such it describes God's way of being in time and for creatures. This is not to say that God is holy only in relation to creation; it is rather to emphasize that God's creative acts and historical actions are the perfect expression or instantiation of his holiness. We also saw in Lev. 19 that the holiness of a person or people, conversely, describes the human creature's participation in this historical relationship, embodied primarily in the engaged responsiveness to God of law keeping or law breaking. It is a response that is transfigured in the bearing of the transgressed law's penalty by God himself—God moves to the place where human movement withers and dissipates; God takes the place of the creature's own disappearance into death or coming-to-life out of nothingness through God's own love. This particular transfiguration of human holiness is the reality taken up again in Lev. 21–22, which I shall treat as an ensemble, despite the locutionary distinction within the text. It is now explored, however, from the Christian perspective most profoundly in terms of the story of how divine holiness can indeed draw into itself human creatures. In these chapters human holiness is explained, more generally, as a way of life, delineated in terms of the priesthood of the church as Christ's body given in the form, as we saw with Stephen's stoning, of the martyred witness. What is crucial to grasp in these chapters is the manner in which all human coming is a following and a gathering with respect to Jesus.

The content of Lev. 21–22 speaks to several categories of approach to God, in continuity with the great Levitical theme of sacrifice as a "coming near." Here, the approach to God, still sacrificially described, is discussed with respect to the tabernacle, as it touches several classes of the priesthood: first "the sons of Aaron," next Aaron himself, and finally all the Israelites as a kingdom of priests

(Exod. 19:6). The elements discussed for each in terms of this approach include the touching of the dead, proper sexual relating and coupling, the physical form of the priests, and the character of and constraints upon the priestly ingestion of the sacrifices as food as well as the physical form of the sacrificial animals themselves. But just as the Christian reading of Leviticus as a whole locates the human approach to God in terms of the incarnation of God in human flesh, so too the outline of a priestly approach within the tabernacle is rightly recast in these incarnational terms. These two chapters, therefore, constitute an answer to the question: how can *God's* own approach to us become *our* way of life? And the answer is given through the Levitical insertion of Israel's life into, and its explication within, the story of the incarnation, death, and resurrection of Jesus, for is not the story of Jesus Christ's approach and movement one of marking out a way that becomes our way? "Prepare the way of the Lord," proclaims the Baptist (Mark 1:3), speaking not only to Israel but to all whom Israel itself, in its prophets (e.g., Isa. 40:3), addressed to "all flesh" within the world's range. This way is given in the one who comes and declares that "I am the way" (John 14:6). And in so declaring, in this pointing out of his own path and self before their eyes, he directs his disciples into an apprehension of his holiness: "You know the way," he tells them (14:4). And knowing it in this fashion, by seeing it and being drawn into it, they become the followers of the way (Acts 9:2; 19:9), not only for a moment, but as their destiny. Leviticus 21–22, more clearly than any other sections in the book, therefore, underlines the participatory character of reality within the Levitical revelation.

To some extent, this aspect of Lev. 21–22 was recognized by early Christian interpretation, though with some obscuring limitations. Jesus marks the way to the Father, in John's famous phrase. But for the great exegetes of the early church this way is indicated by the life of perfect virtue that Jesus himself embodies, as indicated in the Levitical descriptions of priestly holiness and self-offering. Christians may indeed follow this way by conforming to the virtuous pathway marked out in advance by the Lord. This is Origen's general reading of these chapters, and his resolute ascetic framework provides an uncompromising unidirectional application of the scriptural referents of the priests' sexual purity and unblemished sacrifice, enumerated in these verses. Jesus stands for the perfection of human virtue, in this reading, and the movement of holiness that Origen sees in these chapters is that of Jesus to the Father, schematizing in his flesh the movement of human virtue to God. To be sure, Jesus as the high priest in Leviticus (e.g., in 21:10–15) is absolutely unique. Yet his uniqueness in this case is one of degree: it lies in the perfection of his sinless life as it is lived before God. All the references in these chapters to contamination by corpses or to physical deformities and sexual distortions to be avoided by the servants of the temple, then, refer to human sin and vice. As high priest, Jesus enters beyond the veil, as Hebrews puts it (9:11–14) and so approaches God through the purity of his will and being; yet the approach is one he lays out for all human priests—Christians and Christian leaders—to follow, demonstrating to them, as it were, the efficacy, reward, and even possibility of a virtuous life (especially *Homilies on Leviticus* 12.1–2).

With this framework in place, medieval exegesis simply read off the Levitical prohibitions and warnings in these chapters as diverse elements that might signify the variety of potential ills attributed to priests. Each was explained through a malleable allegorical template. Hesychius, normalized in the *Glossa ordinaria* (Patrologia latina 113.358–59), for instance, takes the list in Lev. 21:18–21—blindness, lameness, mutilation, deformity, skin problems—and applies each defect to a particular vice or spiritual weakness (pride, ignorance, lassitude, indiscriminate moral perception, carnality, etc.). The constraints on marriage in Lev. 21 or the levels of familial approach to the food of the altar in Lev. 22 follow a similar line of application. Reformation interpreters did pretty much the same, often focusing acutely on the more general responsibilities of Christian leaders by means of a broad-brushed moral allegorical application of the priestly blemishes: the service of God demands a perfection congruent somehow with its divine object, and the physical wholeness required of the Old Testament priesthood is properly taken as an inclusive indication of the whole range of moral virtues that might contribute to this. Willet (1631: 520–40) does a good job in demonstrating the Jewish concerns behind such attitudes, at least as they are later elaborated in rabbinic exegesis, and to this extent shows how Christian and Jewish exegesis of the priesthood's form ends by converging on a common standard of conduct for religious leaders. Such an approach to the text is sound as far as it goes: goodness and perfection are of God and are therefore to be embodied in those whose lives would reflect the God to whom they minister.

But who *is* the God served by the priesthood of Israel, that Israel's life should reflect him? The virtues articulated by a moral allegory of physical shapeliness in Lev. 21–22—for example, purity and goodness—seem to point to the almost platonic forms of a being only partly visible in the history of Israel. They are static in a metaphorical sense, because they are bound to the single apprehension of being primarily and not to its temporal explication. Where is he who calls and acts from the very opening of scriptural time and, of course, the opening of Leviticus (*Vayikra* ["calling"] in 1:1) itself? Whose name is revealed as the one who *will be* in terms of the one who *will do* as being and doing in fact occur (Exod. 3:14–22)? Where is he who himself *comes* to Israel (Isa. 35:4; 40:9–10)? Origen's unidirectional movement of human virtue as it goes toward God simply does not do justice to the coincidence of Jesus's uniqueness with his intractably human sexual origins, which are so enmeshed in the Levitical description of human differentiation and coupling, as we have seen. This coincidence raises the issue of God's coming *to* us: he who is infinitely different from us, who most certainly *is* pure and good, also comes among us.

How do we describe this coming, and hence *this* holiness? The framework of human virtue when unidirectionally applied to the priesthood prevents *God* from being exposed in the reading of Leviticus, and not surprisingly God drifts eventually into a far realm, an object of approach that remains distant, holy, and otherworldly in the evolved romantic orientation of modern gnosis. In the course of this religious evolution, the access to God becomes a problem to be solved by the correct method of human movement, one that derives, in Origen's case, from his mediatory Logos Christology, with all of its openings for later transformations in the hands of, for example, Arius. The violence of religious opposition comes to focus on who knows the "proper way." For Origen, thus, it is simply the fault of the Jews that they do not grasp the proper path—of Christian discipline—to this God whose shape was given in the types of Scripture; they are blind, not in failing to see God rising up beyond the horizon as the goal of human life, but in refusing the right way to come close to his image, one provided solely in the priestly mediation of a being greater than Israel's creaturely sacral office (*Homilies on Leviticus* 12.1). The effect of this judgment, when emphasized over time, has made of Leviticus a book of hoary divine transcendence, containing a now anachronistic religious discipline, in contrast to which the Christian gospel is meant to offer a leaner and more amenable approach.

The central concern with God's name in these chapters (21:6; 22:2, 32) points in another direction. This divine name is itself holy, and, when placed as the framework for the discussion of the priests' physical form, it ends illumining the prior character of God as the one who acts. This character, bound to the divine name, is given in the self-revealing nature of God's relationship with Israel, one that refers specifically to his initiating work of deliverance in time: "You shall not profane my holy name, but I will be hallowed among the people of Israel; I am the LORD who sanctify you, who brought you out of the land of Egypt to be your God: I am the LORD" (22:32–33). Whatever the priests do and are, and whatever Israel as a nation of priests must be in their holiness, they are such to the degree that they expose *this* God and that they speak *his* name within the forms of life they embody. God sanctifies by delivering Israel and establishing his covenant with them. Without fixing this claim as the interpretive key to these chapters, their meaning evaporates into either the detritus of religious history or the platitudes of ethical exhortation.

The traditional notion of sanctifying the name of God, within Jewish witness, points to just this reality. In Rabbi Jonathan Sacks's view, Lev. 22:32 is the key example of this sanctification-of-the-name, known as the *kiddush ha-shem*; and this text is to be read specifically in concert with Ezek. 36:19–23. According to this textual linkage, the context in which God's name is either made holy or is profaned is that of the nations; and sanctification or profanation of God's name is achieved by reference to Israel's own life in their midst (2005: esp. 57–70). God's name, as Sacks puts it, is his "public reputation" within the world, a reputation founded upon the witness of his authoritative domain. If Israel's holiness in keeping the law successfully testifies to this domain, it does so because this law—and in Lev. 21–22's case, it is a law of priestly purity—mirrors or expresses the delivering agency and initiative of God.

But how does this take place? The Jewish tradition of the *kiddush ha-shem* follows a significant line of development in this regard, as it came increasingly to be identified with a particular kind of witness, that is, the testimony of death for the sake of the law, what today we call martyrdom in its technical sense. Initially, this appears as a humanly initiated action. Although the law is designed to give life and not be source of death (Lev. 18:5), by Maimonides' time dying for the law was demanded at least in relation to the three categories of idolatry, unchastity, and murder. In times of persecution, a Jew was called to die for any element of the law as a witness to God in the face of idolatry in general. The sanctification of God's name, therefore, came to be viewed as an act taken in the face and midst of sin's death dealing. But the deathliness that is sin's character envelops Israel too, even prior to its martyrial vocation. As Ezek. 36:24–25 goes on to say, God sanctifies his own name through the work of *delivering* Israel, not only from its enemies but from the sins by which it itself has profaned its deliverer. And thus, in the end, Israel's witness to God's name is given through its own receipt of his work, as an object of divine grace. This proves a paradoxical assertion, in which God's holiness is exposed through the sinner's embrace of God's action on his or her behalf. Indeed, there is a sense in which the martyr's upholding of the law in this context is an acknowledgment of his own complicity in the law's transgression.[1] And God, by delivering sinful Israel, sanctifies his *own* name even in the midst of Israel's failure to uphold the law among the nations and its sins. God alone is his own witness even before Israel can be his. If there is such a thing as *kiddush ha-shem* within Israel (Lev. 22:32), must one and dare one speak, therefore, of the martyrdom of God?

This is in fact the Christian claim, and it directly elucidates the Levitical ordering of priestly purity. The Christian martyr bears witness to the word and does so by dying for the word's sake. But there is a double meaning to the notion of "the witness of Jesus" that marks this martyrdom (Rev. 1:2, 9; 6:9). The Christian bears testimony to the word, yet the word itself is bound up, not to the reputation of God as distinguished from that word, but to the flesh of Jesus come among us, to this one who is named (Phil. 2:10). Jesus *is* God's reputation assumed in godly flesh. And *this* name that is exalted above every name, Jesus himself, is the great witness, the martyr to whom God himself testifies even as God is witnessed to in

1. The common conviction that a true martyr is one who also acknowledges his or her own sinfulness before God and the world is wonderfully expressed by Trappist monk Christian de Chergé, who was killed (along with colleagues) by Islamic terrorists, after being kidnapped from his monastery in Algeria, on May 24, 1996. His last testament, written during a time of imminent threat and with his family not long before his death, included the following paragraph: "My life has no more value than any other. Nor any less value. In any case, it has not the innocence of childhood. I have lived long enough to know that I share in the evil which seems, alas, to prevail in the world, even in that which would strike me blindly. I should like, when the time comes, to have a clear space which would allow me to beg forgiveness of God and of all my fellow human beings, and at the same time to forgive with all my heart the one who would strike me down" (quoted in *First Things* 65 [Aug./Sept. 1996]: 21).

the death of his only Son, the Lord and God of all (John 8:18; 1 Tim. 6:13; Rev. 22:20). God is thus his own witness and his own martyr, a testimony offered in the middle of the world itself. If Lev. 21–22 appears to outline the way to God, then, this way is now unveiled as God's way to us, not as a path of virtuous living, but as the actual journey in time of God's own self into the midst and heart of his own creatures' distance and death. To approach God is somehow to stand within the prior movement of this God. The Levitical exposition of approach, therefore, outlines such a movement primarily and before all else.

When Origen stresses the meaning of the priests' holiness in terms of a framework of human virtue on its way to God, perfectly revealed in Jesus, his views are not so much false as misleadingly constrained (*Homilies on Leviticus* 12.1–2). Writing *after* the destruction of Jerusalem, it may have seemed obvious to him that the Jews needed to look more deeply at their former cult and its now disappeared map for coming close to God: without a temple to uphold its signifiers, Leviticus itself was withering as an instruction in human sanctification and required a new set of moral referents if it was to function as Scripture for a people in search of God. That new set of referents, Origen argued, was to be found in the example of Jesus's victory over the passions of sinful human nature, read out allegorically from the text of Leviticus. And to refuse such rereading, as the Jews were doing in Origen's view, was a mark of obstinate self-delusion.

But *was* it? Origen centers his reading of these chapters on the Hebrews vision of a high priest who is different from the Levitical paragon (Heb. 7:11). It is true that Hebrews asserts a new covenant of priestly service that supersedes the Aaronic priesthood. Yet Hebrews also insists that the Levitical priesthood still refers somehow to this priestly reality embodied in Christ (10:1). To this degree the coming of the "better" high priest who is Christ Jesus was already given in Israel somehow. It is not so much a question, therefore, of whether the Levitical system works any longer as an effective approach to God, but how it has *always* displayed that approach that in fact is given in Jesus. And if that approach turns out to be fundamentally not a human approach to God but God's own coming to fallen creation, then Leviticus must also point to this even in its discussion of priestly form.

From this perspective, the *Rabbah* grasps what is at stake more clearly than Origen and the tradition he initiated. When the *Rabbah* turns its attention to the character of the sacrificial victims discussed in Lev. 22, its interest moves directly to the relationship of these victims as figures of the golden calf to Aaron's sin in Exod. 32, and this event becomes the explanatory lens for all of the Levitical material (*Rabbah* 27). Every bull or calf bespeaks the blasphemous transformation of animal creation's praise of God into idolatry, and every priestly act immerses itself in the venal fears and reckless self-promotion of the slide into pagan power. Every sacrifice described in Leviticus, therefore, partakes of this primordial sin of the people against God's promises, a sin that tinges the very nature of the priesthood that Aaron embodies, only because it first tinges the whole of creation, of "man and beast" together, whose disintegration into the homogeneity of death is stopped only by the salvation of God (Ps. 36:6). These Levitical chapters therefore describe, in their detailing by a reverse description, Israel's *failures*—not its virtues. What then does it mean for Israel to continue its sacrifices? The *Rabbah* asks this in order to indicate the nature of the God who *accepts* the sacrifices of a sinning people and priesthood. From the *Rabbah's* point of view the Levitical discussions of the cult's purity have nothing to do with the call to a virtuous ministry (although, of course, such a call is not contradicted) and have instead everything to do with the reality of a God who *forgives* radically. It is all about new life, the life of resurrection in fact—the *Rabbah* actually uses this word—wherein the nothingness of sinful Israel is made into a living thing through the sheer grace of God, once typically and over and over again historically.

Here is an astounding vision of the sacrificial cult that, if not exactly resolving the classical opposition identified especially by Christian exegetes between Levitical sacrificial efficacy and its prophetic critique (e.g., by Jeremiah and Isaiah, not to mention the Psalms), nonetheless goes beyond that opposition: sacrifice and its offering, which is exemplified in the priesthood, *in fact* enacts weakness and sinfulness in need of redemption. Therefore sacrifice (by human beings) is not an action that, in its own right, can be evaluated as either good or bad, or as necessary or unnecessary, or as pertinent or obsolete. Rather, sacrifice acts as the historical occasion for the coming of God as Israel's miraculous and unmerited deliverer. Similarly, when Jesus speaks of the *kiddush ha-shem* in the Lord's Prayer, the driving element of the "hallowing of God's name" is the forgiveness of sins, and he goes on to stress that this is about God's own nature as a gift giver, as the one whose gracious relationship to his creatures goes beyond anything we might imagine, for it finally includes the giving of his very self in the Holy Spirit (Luke 11:1–13). Whatever yearning it is to which Jesus responds here—"teach us to pray"—his answer is based on the action of God *already*; and therefore whatever Christ is doing, as high priest in this case, he is doing it in complete continuity with the Levitical text: "If you, then, who are evil, know how to give good gifts to your children, how much more will the heavenly Father give the Holy Spirit to those who ask him!"

We return again to the question of whether the form of the priest's approach to God in Lev. 21–22 is what is paramount (what kind of human priest should we have?) as opposed to the form of Christ's approach to and within the world, an approach that embodies God's act of resurrection from sin (what kind of God do we in fact have?). Certainly the attempts to make Lev. 21–22 center upon the holy character of the *priest* primarily in terms of the priest's access to God end by devolving into treatments of the character of the religious leader. This was true, as we have seen, for Origen, the *Glossa ordinaria* and its tradition, and even much Jewish interpretation.[2] It is also true of much Christian reading from today (follow-

---

2. The *Rabbah's* exegesis was not definitive in any way here. More characteristic is the *Me'am Lo'ez's* interest (Kaplan 1982: 12.103–4) in using Lev. 21:13–15 (on the high priest's more exigent

ing Calvin 1996: 2.239–40), wherein the application of Leviticus on this score is seen to be most readily accomplished through standard moral allegory, by which the priest-pastor figure is explained in terms of the high demands for integrity of life and spirit. Yet, the awareness of God's prior approach as fundamental to a reading of these texts resists such allegorization. Rather, is not the description of the holiness of the priesthood here a matter of tracing how the priest (and kingdom of priests!)—and hence the church—is drawn into Christ's own life as it is given to the world, the only true offering God himself might accept? In this light, Col. 1:24–29, regarding Paul's joyful "divine office" of suffering for the body, represents an outline of Israel's prayer to God for forgiveness, now embodied in the life of discipleship.

The blemishes and deformities of the priest, in this case, are transformed by Christ in their offering—that is, as flowing from our joining in faith with him—into marks of holiness, and the Levitical text is rightly read (as *Rabbah* 26.1–8 begins to do) in a paradoxical reversal of referents. One could take as a remarkable example of this reading the enactment given the text's physical reordering in the career of Isaac Jogues, the canonized seventeenth-century Jesuit missionary among the Iroquois. Cruelly tortured and disfigured at one point by his captors, who bit and ripped off parts of his fingers, he escaped and returned to France as a priest physically deprived of his means of celebrating the Eucharist, unable, for instance, to hold together his mutilated thumb and forefinger as required during the consecration. Jogues, however, received a papal dispensation in 1644 that released him from being constrained by this physical blemish (as he would otherwise have been canonically bound by the church's law from at least the thirteenth century). The pope's dispensation was based on the *mark* of holiness that had been given Jogues in his conformance with Christ's suffering, received at the hands of his Iroquois tormentors. Indeed, Pope Urban VIII provided Jogues with a faculty to say Mass despite his deformities, uttering a judgment that became proverbial: *Indignum esset Christi martyrem, Christi non bibere sanguinem* ("it would be unjust that a martyr for Christ should not drink the blood of Christ"). In fact, the account of Jogues's tortures was quickly disseminated and, in many versions (including later the famous writings of Parkman), took on the role of a perverse Levitical drama of priestly holiness

---

marital constraints) as a springboard to enumerate the qualities demanded of a religious leader to perform his tasks effectively (stature, strength, wealth, intelligence, appearance). Christian exegetes, as we have seen, did the same from their own perspective of ascetic virtue. Hirsch, on the other hand, elevates the moral demand upon the priests' conduct to comprehend the entire high calling of Israel's life as the epitome of the human creature's unique personhood. In a way, this ratcheting up of the moral vocation bypasses the entire question of approach to God and simply explicates these chapters in terms of Israel's ethical purpose as whole. In contrast to paganism, says Hirsch in the context of 22:6 as a larger explanatory verse, "Judaism teaches us how to spend every moment of a life marked by moral freedom, thought, aspirations, creativity and achievement, along with the enjoyment of physical pleasures, as one more moment in life's constant service to the everlasting God" (1989: 2.590–91). This is the meaning of a hollowed life.

through martyrial deformation.[3] Jogues obviously contradicted Lev. 21:18–19 quite explicitly; yet it was *he* who proved the priest capable of offering true testimony, thus sanctifying the name of God among the nations!

If the *Rabbah* turns to Aaron's and Israel's fall into idolatry as its lens for Lev. 21–22's ground base of divine mercy, the Christian gospel thus transfigures this through the lens of the Suffering Servant of Isa. 52:14–53:5, who redefines the sense of forgiven disfigurement into the beauty of sacrificial service: "As many were astonished at him—his appearance was so marred, beyond human semblance, and his form beyond that of the sons of men. . . . He had no form or comeliness that we should look at him, and no beauty that we should desire him. He was despised and rejected by men; a man of sorrows, and acquainted with grief; and as one from whom men hide their faces he was despised, and we esteemed him not. . . . [Yet] he was wounded for our transgressions, he was bruised for our iniquities;

3. Jogues's graphic account of his actual torture stands in a strange relation to the Levitical text and, from a Christian point of view, its astonishing fulfillment: "Seeing, then, that I had not fallen by accident, and that I did not rise again for being too near death, they entered upon a cruel compassion; their rage was not yet glutted, and they wished to conduct one alive into their own country; accordingly, they Embrace me, and carry me all bleeding upon the stage they have prepared. When I am restored to my senses, they make me come down, and offer me a thousand and one insults, making me the sport and object of their reviling; they begin their assaults over again, dealing upon my head and neck, and all my body, another hailstorm of blows. I would be too tedious if I should set down in writing all the rigor of my sufferings. They burned one of my fingers, and crushed another with their teeth, and those which were already torn, they squeezed and twisted with a rage of Demons; they scratched my wounds with their nails; and, when strength failed me, they applied fire to my arm and thighs. Having ascended that scaffold, I exclaimed in my heart: *Spectaculum facti sumus mundo et Angelis et hominibus propter Christum*—'we have been made a gazing-stock in the sight of the world, of Angels, and of men, for Jesus Christ.' We found some rest in that place of triumph and of glory. The Hiroquois no longer persecuted us except with their tongues,—filling the air and our ears with their insults, which did us no great hurt; but this calm did not last long. A Captain exclaims that the Frenchmen ought to be caressed. Sooner done than it is said,—one wretch, jumping on the stage, dealt three heavy blows with sticks, on each Frenchman, without touching the Hurons. Others, meanwhile drawing their knives and approaching us, treated me as a Captain,—that is to say, with more fury than the rest. The deference of the French, and the respect which the Hurons showed me, caused me this advantage. An old man takes my left hand and commands a captive Algonquin woman to cut one of my fingers; she turns away three or four times, unable to resolve upon this cruelty; finally, she has to obey, and cuts the thumb from my left hand; the same caresses are extended to the other prisoners. This poor woman having thrown my thumb on the stage, I picked it up and offered it to you, O my God! Remembering the sacrifices that I had presented to you for seven years past, upon the Altars of your Church, I accepted this torture as a loving vengeance for the want of love and respect that I had shown, concerning your Holy Body; you heard the cries of my soul. One of my two French companions, having perceived me, told me that, if those Barbarians saw me keep my thumb, they would make me eat it and swallow it all raw; and that, therefore, I should throw it away somewhere. I obey him instantly. They used a scallop or an oyster-shell for cutting off the right thumb of the other Frenchman, so as to cause him more pain. The blood flowing from our wounds in so great abundance that we were likely to fall in a swoon, a Hiroquois—tearing off a little end of my shirt, which alone had been left to me—bound them up for us; and that was all the dressing and all the medical treatment applied to them" (quoted in Thwaites 1898: 43–45).

upon him was the chastisement that made us whole, and with his stripes we are healed." "Marred" and without "form or comeliness": God's approach to sinful people bears the image of a sinful human approach to God, yet now willingly carried as a burden for another rather than dragged about as a lie on one's own behalf. Yet in this is revealed "the fairest . . . of men" (Ps. 45:2), for whom the "tongue fashions" songs of praise. What kind of priest and what kind of people shall approach God? It is as if Nadab and Abihu (Lev. 10) call out and plead for an answer to their own failure: who, then, shall it be? "And I wept much that no one was found worthy" (Rev. 5:4). Then who? That one who follows the God who approaches an incapable priest and people: "'Behold, the Lamb of God, who takes away the sins of the world! . . . Behold the Lamb of God!' The two disciples heard [John] say this, and they followed Jesus" (John 1:29, 36–37).

It is important to see how the whole of the Levitical description of the priestly approach is assumed in its fulfillment by divine contradiction in Jesus as Suffering Servant: God's name is profaned (Isa. 52:5), purity is spoiled (52:11), the people scatter each according to their own way (53:6), and the place of the wicked becomes the resting place of all (53:9). Yet in visiting all these transgressions of the Levitical call, in entering, confronting, and bearing each, the Servant somehow is received by God and thereby approaches him (53:10–12). It is a strange path. It is an alien way. Yet it turns out to be God's own way into the midst of the very law he proffers: "Therefore, my people shall know my name; therefore in that day they shall know that it is I who speak: here am I" (52:6). Just as the Servant announces, "Here am I, and the children God has given me!" (Heb. 2:13, quoting Isa. 8:18). God is his own martyr, when he "share[s] in flesh and blood . . . and part[akes] of the same nature" (Heb. 2:14). The Servant's way is not an overturning of the Levitical laws, but their assumption, *in transgression and final purpose both*, thereby revealing and demonstrating the fullness of holiness and purity as the act of God's own coming-close. This is the law's "perfect history," begun in creation, bound to Israel's release and rebellion, drug through the dirt in the camp at Sinai's foot, taken into the heart of God. This is the nature of the figure: true beauty and physical perfection is given the form of Jesus, who "did not count equality with God a thing to be grasped" (Phil. 2:6).

We are to read the Levitical details of the priestly approach, then, as signals of a divine history adopted *sub contrario*—that is, in the form of human incapacity— and humanly received in this literal posture, as Jogues's ministry demonstrated. This does not contradict the calling given to Israel, so much as make it effective. Called to sanctify God's name, Israel is itself sanctified by God's own self-giving in the midst of its profanations (Lev. 21:23). And these chapters are to be read as the visage of the Son of God's coming according to the gospel outline, as the sanctifier Jesus as the high priest (Heb. 2:17) coming close as the one who, connected to the people he serves, is one of them in bearing their flesh. Yet this bearing is exactly what heals the flesh (Mark 2:17, 23–28) and fulfills the Levitical call to unblemished offering. "He who sanctifies and those who are sanctified have all one origin" (Heb. 2:11). God offers to Israel the form of its own beauty, called out of it as God has entered among it and shared his form with it (1 John 3:2). This is the "new man" of reconciled humanity, given in the body of Christ Jesus to Jew and Gentile together (Eph. 2:15–16), but bearing the shape of *his* flesh: "Put on the new nature, created after the likeness of God in true righteousness and holiness" (4:24).

The concern of the Christian and Jewish traditions with religious leadership as a focus for these chapters needs to be reframed in light of the reality of this divine history of approach and the consequent creation of a "new man" that Jesus's life, death, and resurrection provides. Religious leadership does not take us to God. It does not pioneer. It does not, in the first instance, clear the way or cleanse or even build what does not yet exist. It receives, confesses, and follows.

If we were to take the details of pure priestly form and action outlined in these chapters, they would now need to be read in terms of this turning "upside down" (Acts 17:6) of their referents in the body of Jesus and hence making of the human leader the "last of all" (Mark 9:35), because bound to the "first of all" (Rom. 8:29; 1 Cor. 15:23; Heb. 2:10) as he comes near and gives himself. So the first and last are joined. Jesus, for instance, touches the flesh of cadavers (Lev. 21:1–3) in order to heal them and resurrect them (Mark 5:41; 9:27); Jesus distributes, analogically, the bread of the presence to his disciples in order to bring life (Mark 2:23–28; Luke 6:9) and indeed finally does so through the distribution of his own flesh as food for the world (John 6:51; 1 Cor. 10:16); the regulation of sexual coupling for the priest is finally included in the death of husband for wife, Christ for the church, the one flesh that subsumes the whole history of agonized self-offering struggled over in the union of husband and wife outlined in the Levitical law (Eph. 5:25–31);[4] the relationship of familial responsibilities and proximities accessible to the Lord are gathered in the hearers and doers of the word (Luke 8:19–21), who themselves are taken up in the one who comes to do God's will through the offering of his flesh (Heb. 2:11–14; 10:7–10). The issue is not that priestly blemishes are somehow good and that God affirms that which is imperfect and indeed sinful. That would be an argument, in this context, for priestly automutilation. Rather, God comes to the deformed, assumes their distinctive agony, whether moral or physical, and drawing them with him to his goal, *trans*forms them.

In each element, the Levitical history of creation and humankind, such as we have been reading it in previous chapters, is swept up into the approach of God

---

4. Many of the marital elements in Lev. 21–22 point, therefore, not simply to a generalized or eschatological figure of spiritual union with God (e.g., the unblemished character of the bride in Rev. 19:7–8 or Eph. 5:27), but backward to the way in which the struggles around human coupling engage faithfulness to the gift of God's creative self. The marriage figure here is crucial and takes in the actual carnal character of the relationships discussed in Lev. 21–22: hence the framework of corpse touching allows immediate family, including (as rabbinic discussion makes clear) the wife herself. The human struggle for one fleshedness points to and is finally perfectly given in the one body of Christ both offered for and receptive to human life.

himself to a kingdom of fallen priests, the shape of whose own life of regulated difference encloses all things in their contingent being. Human holiness itself (1 Pet. 2:5, 9/Exod. 19:3–6; Rev. 1:6) is not so much separateness from the world as it is the *result* of God's *coming near* and approaching the world. Holiness marks the difference traversed, suffered, and embraced, thus uncovering the way of the Father, who gives his Son and thereby displays that way to all the world. When the church follows along this way, it calls down upon itself the form of Jesus Christ and the beauty of his blemishes. It is a prayer to "bear . . . the marks of Jesus" (Gal. 6:17), the "stigmata" of the thirsting disciple (à la Jogues). "The Spirit and the Bride say, 'Come.' And let him who hears say, 'Come.' And let him who is thirsty come. . . . 'Surely I am coming soon.' Amen. Come, Lord Jesus!" (Rev. 22:17, 20). These are words of proclamation and praise, not only of petition. They are also words of confession. And the priestly movement here, the following of this way, as with all of the Levitical details, represents a veil slipping aside as it displays a half-caught vision of the "plan for the fulness of time, to unite all things in [Christ], things in heaven and things on earth" (Eph. 1:10).

LEVITICUS 23:1–24:9

God himself traverses a way, as we have seen in the two previous chapters. It is a way that leads toward his own creation, moves into its center and down to its depth, and carries it forward. It is the way of Jesus. But Jesus's way is not foreign to the world. After all, the world takes its form from him (Col. 1:16–17). Jesus's way molds the world, bends it into the shape of his own path, thus ordering creation in its purposed form, as it takes its place in love across the divide of its own being. Hence, the world provides a kind of chart to the wake of God's purpose and passage. This chart is given, in Levitical terms, through the temporal lines of the festivals of the law.

In a well-known Hassidic parable, attributed to Yechezkel Panet (chief rabbi in early nineteenth-century Karlsburg [Transylvania]), famous for his advocacy of women abandoned by their husbands, a king travels through the desert, accompanied by his entourage. His son is thirsty, and the king responds to his child's need by calling in his engineers and slaves and having them dig wells along the route. These he marks for future travelers. The fable becomes an image for the significance of the great festivals among the Jewish people: each is a gift of nourishment, provided by God to his people on their historical journey, through the use of which God's historical provision for Israel is regrasped somehow. Passover marks the liberation and historical creation of a people; on Shavuot the law is given at Sinai as the articulation of this people's form; God is crowned king and master of all things by his people on Rosh Hashanah; while Yom Kippur, focusing on God's forgiveness of the people's apostasy with Aaron before the golden calf, becomes the way station of atonement for all time; the Feast of Booths/Sukkoth marks the protection of Israel by God on its journey through the wilderness. Add to this Hanukkah and Purim, and the calendar of Israel is completed in the shape of a map through time, according to which moments of the year are revisited as sources of divine renewal.

The parable has often been retold as a kind of homiletic gloss on Lev. 23. This chapter, after all, lays out the shape of the festivals that God reveals to Moses as the appointed times (23:2, 4, 44) by which the year is to be ordered. As Hirsch (1989: 2.644–51) explains, while the sanctuary and its laws (epitomized, in his view, in the previous chapters of Leviticus) represent the spatial character of God's meeting with Israel—the center of human moral action—the festivals provide a temporal or horizontal framework for such encounter. "Each year, as they recur, God expects to meet you in renewed reunion." They draw the nation, over time, into the localized focus of their moral duties (precisely by bringing them at regular intervals to the sanctuary). As the Sabbath stands to the ordinary round of temporal existence, so the festivals stand to the seasonal rounds, not by sanctifying these natural recurrences, but by leading them into the moral universe that God's law embodies. Hirsch is clear that festivals calculated according to the new moon, and through it the dating of other holidays, have nothing to do with turning one's religious attention to the times themselves and to their natural basis—what he calls a base "nature worship." Rather, through the festivals time is opened up to the God of Israel and is thereby subjected to *him*. This, for Israel, is a way of giving itself over to God, and it stands in contrast with the slave's human subjection of every minute of his or her day to a brutal master, a contrast that rightly pits the purpose of the exodus against the destructive horror of Egypt.

Given the way that Lev. 23 is framed, however, Rabbi Panet's parable provides an odd analogy. It is odd, not in that it interprets the festivals as times of remembrance, whether as openings to divine encounter in Hirsch's view or as moments of anamnesis in Christian terms. Clearly they are at least that, in a limited way (although only the last feast mentioned, the Feast of Booths, is actually tied by the text to an explicit historical memorial, in 23:43). Indeed, discussions elsewhere in the Old Testament, as elaborated in the tradition, reinforce the festivals' character as remembrances of God's deeds and Israel's receipt of grace in the past. Rather, Rabbi Panet's analogy of regularized nourishment is odd in that it locates the festive rest, the foundational character of the feast days as Sabbaths (23:3, 7, 8, 21, 25, 28, 30, 32, 35, 36, 39), in the midst of the wilderness journeying. What is odd is that, through the festivals pictured as oases, rest is given only *within* and *as* the history of struggle. Israel's movement to and from Sinai provides the form of this history, narrated immediately in Exodus and Numbers, but extended from Abraham, and even before and out to the exile and return. Because the festivals mark this history, they do not, in their sabbatical character, constitute a respite from the movement, but rather claim the movement itself as the very rest that Israel is given.

The implications of this way of looking at the festivals are immense, for they point to the history of Israel being itself that within which and through which God engages his creation for life in its breadth. Since Israel's history is the shadow of Christ Jesus's own pathway as he moves across his own domain, from creation's beginning through its fall and deathward spiral, and into its renewal, the notion of a rest amid the wanderings of Israel is taken up and transformed into the markers of Jesus's own journey to Jerusalem (Luke 9:51). "Come to me, all who labor and are heavy laden, and I will give you rest" (Matt. 11:28). What rest? A time of no servile labor and of rejoicing? No; rather of "fire upon the earth," of "division" and "constraint" (Luke 12:49–53), of "setting one's face" and "not looking back," of "no place to lay one's head," of going from "village to village" (9:51–62). The festivals as markers of Israel's history with God cannot constitute oases in a popular sense, but are rather arrows pointing beyond themselves, the sum of which outlines the image of Christ. If the festivals are temporal encounters with God, they are an encounter with *this* God in his movement through time.

That the festive rest of the Levitical feasts actually constitutes the battered and transfigured form of Christ, the wash of history, has been rarely understood by Christian exegetes. We shall look positively at the relation of festival and Christ's form below. But first we must take a moment to consider why that relationship has been so difficult for the church to grasp. Fundamentally, the problem arose from making a principle out of the distinction between ceremonial and moral aspects of the law. (This is a problem that, in various contexts, we have seen as a root cause for misreading Leviticus.) In light of this principle, the evident distance between the two that Christians quickly established pressed them decisively to locate their reading of the Levitical festal appointments within the realm of moral allegory. And in doing so, the horizontal character of the festivals, that is so obvious from a Jewish and plain-sense perspective, was swallowed up.

The early church, as we have seen, made use of the prophetic denunciations of Israel to contrast the empty formalities of ritual from a life of moral purity. This set the stage for the firm distinction between types of law. Classic proof-texts like Isa. 1:13–17 on God's rejection of Israel's Sabbaths and festivals in favor of a call to "cease to do evil" or like 58:6–9 on the nature of "true fasting" as a moral endeavor in pursuit of justice were all brought to bear in the argument against the requirement of the scriptural festival. Justin provides what became a standard Christian trope in this regard: the Sabbaths and festivals, taken literally, are an excuse for immoral self-indulgence in debauched celebration; their true significance, in light of Jesus, is as *universalized* metaphors for *constant* moral righteousness:

> The new law requires you to keep perpetual sabbath, and you, because you are idle for one day, suppose you are pious, not discerning why this has been commanded you: and if you eat unleavened bread, you say the will of God has been fulfilled. The Lord our God does not take pleasure in such observances: if there is any perjured person or a thief among you, let him cease to be so; if any adulterer, let him repent; then he has kept the sweet and true sabbaths of God. If any one has impure hands, let him wash and be pure. (*Dialogue with Trypho the Jew* 12.3 [trans. Roberts and Donaldson])

The idea of festive perpetuity thence becomes the regularized Christian approach, whereby the temporally limited forms of fleshly ritual observance are meant to fall away in the Christian's comprehensive change of life: "Even for the solitary, the whole of life is a continual festival, insofar as it is entirely consecrated to God in an act of thanksgiving" (Clement of Alexandria, *Stromata* 7.7). Actually, the difference between Justin and Hirsch is not so vast, except that the latter, for obvious reasons, will not allow his symbolic moral reading of the law to escape the tether of time and place itself.

It is important for us to grasp the direction of interpretation here. Not only does it end up in a place far different from the time-anchored vision of Leviticus, wherein history is unfurled for God's own *qorban* toward his creation; it also comes to shape Christian approaches to time as a whole. By pressing the atemporality of Christian service or liturgy, the actual shape of incarnation was increasingly veiled. Of course, this is only a tendency and a danger, not a determining necessity. The early church, after all, had its own solemn assemblies. Origen had to defend Christian holidays to Celsus, given the antiritualistic presuppositions already well grounded in the church's apologetic. He mentions the Christian observance of the Lord's Day, Passover, the Preparation, and Pentecost. The last seems to comprehend Easter and the ascension, at least in its meaning, but also the gift of that power capable of transforming the Christian into a new creature capable of living "all his days as the Lord's Day." Each of these observances, for Origen, actually signifies the work of God in Christ to *free* the Christian from time-bound (and hence physically limited) obedience to and life with God: Passover, in Christ's death, is a continual eating of the word in a life in which there is "ever a hastening to the city of God"; the Christian life of resurrection and exaltation is a continual living in the "season of Pentecost." Why then the temporal observance of any of these occasions in particular? Origen addresses this question head on: given that none of us are completely free of the fleshly pull upon our natures—we are all divided creatures, with the spirit struggling against the material aspects of our being—we need help to point us toward our goal. The establishment and celebration of particular holy days and feast days provides a "sensible [i.e., physically palpable] memorial" for the weak, so that they might at least keep their attention on the larger spiritual requirements of the Christian life. At any rate and however much a mark of divine condescension to our nature, Origen points out, Christian holy days are to be characterized by contrition and self-humbling, rather than by indulgence and debauchery, the attitudes normal to festive celebrants (*Against Celsus* 8.22–23). This represents *some* small step toward eternity. And even if the idea of holy days as aids to the weak disappeared within the liturgical elaborations of Catholicism, it reappeared with vigor in Calvin, where the Sabbath and the festivals are described, foundationally, as props given by an indulgent God to encourage divine worship on the part of the infantile Israelites (1996: 2.455–64).

But if useful for the weak—and Christians themselves remain weak—why not retain the Levitical festivals themselves? Here the need to distinguish the Christian church from Judaism took over, fueled often by quite energetic hostility (a hostility transferred by Protestants toward their Roman ritualistic and hence "judaistic" neighbors): Jews, after all, constitute the "carnal man," mired in temporality, whereas Christians have left such self-regarding limitations behind. The problem of the Sabbath was paradigmatic of this claim. Given that the Sabbath was a part of the Decalogue, at least from a commonsense perspective, it would seem to demand continued obedience on the part of the Christian church. Yet the church *did* displace the Sabbath, and with it went all the Jewish festivals. The connection between Sabbath and festival was obvious, as Calvin shows in discussing the festivals only under the rubric of the fourth commandment (1996: 2.455–56). A key interpretive text in his eyes here was, for instance, Col. 2:16–17: "Let no one pass judgment on you in questions of food and drink or with regard to a festival or a new moon or a sabbath. These are only a shadow of what is to come; but the substance belongs to Christ." The law of the Sabbath disappears with Christ and with the "fulness of time" that is his, according to Calvin; any attempt to continue its celebration veils the reality of the death and resurrection of Jesus. Thus, the Sabbath falls into the same bin of used ceremonials that are now given a new life through their moral scriptural apprehension as the call to self-renunciation. And the festivals are useful only to the degree that in reading about them we are reminded of our own vocation to spiritual renewal of one kind or another.

It was not easy to displace the Sabbath quite so peremptorily, however, and various strategies were adopted by Christians to justify both its place within a still-valid Decalogue even while worship on Sunday was to become the Christian norm (Greene-McCreight 2004). In general, these attempts took the form of arguing that Sabbath keeping is a figure for some deeper principle that alone retains its force. Thomas Aquinas was able to claim the Sabbath as part of the Decalogue (under the rubric, according to the common Catholic enumeration, of the third commandment) because the command itself has both a moral and a ceremonial element. It is only the moral aspect—the demand to set aside some kind of time to give thanks to God through worship—that remains fixed, while the ceremonial aspect—specifying that the day be the seventh during the week—is figurative and is properly rescheduled by the church's institution to the Lord's Day (*Summa theologiae* 2a2ae Q. 122 A. 4). In this way, the Sabbath turns into a theological principle that ironically ends by *deconcretizing* time. Indeed, in large swaths of the Christian tradition, the Sabbath becomes itself a kind of antitime, the promise and reality of some relationship to God that has escaped time altogether in order to find a perfect and therefore unconstrained rest with the Lord. This was Augustine's seminal vision, articulated among other places in the glorious final chapter of his *City of God* (22.30). Here he describes how the saints' ultimate destiny is given in the seventh age of complete repose for body and spirit, which opens up onto the timelessness of God's own self: "There we shall rest and see, see and love, love and praise. This is what shall be in the end without end. For what other end do we propose to ourselves than to attain to the kingdom of which there is no end?"

(trans. Dods).[1] Practically speaking for Augustine, however, Sabbath keeping in the present age meant living a life of sinlessness and cleaving to God. The notion that there are temporally specified days that could be set aside as legally binding upon the service of the Christian was to him a regress into fallen Judaism.

That time and rest should stand in such violent contrast became axiomatic in Christian theology in the face of the Levitical festal injunctions. The most stark example was perhaps John Chrysostom, who, in his less pleasant sermons "against the Jews" goes through a lengthy attack on the very idea of a festival or Sabbath, wildly swinging back and forth in his logic regarding the Old Testament (*Discourses against Judaizing Christians*, esp. 2, 7). Evidently, there were many Christians in Antioch who frequented the synagogues at festival time, attracted in part by the music and pageantry, as well as drawn by the religious connections with their faith through the Old Testament people of Israel. But Chrysostom warns his flock that those who attend Jewish feast days are playing with the fires of apostasy. The Jewish festivals are possessed by demons and akin to the pagan contamination that Paul associated with non-Christian worship. God destroyed Jerusalem and the temple, Chrysostom argues; hence he destroyed the festivals themselves. Jesus kept them all, to be sure; but he did so in order to supplant them, and with the fall of Jerusalem he fulfilled God's curse upon the Jews. Chrysostom makes much of the festivals being appointed for the tabernacle and the temple and notes that the Jews in exile never kept these liturgical rites, knowing full well that they were not permitted; but now, he says, they pointlessly and illicitly keep them outside of Jerusalem, so that the very existence of Jewish feast keeping marks a continual blasphemy. In fact, God *never wanted* the Jews to sacrifice in the first place—a now-common Christian claim through which Chrysostom here moves to reject the whole of the Old Testament ceremonial—and the Jews were and are therefore "dogs" to whose weakness God only condescended by letting them do a few sacrifices in a controlled manner. The Sabbath, and with it all Jewish festival keeping, is profaned for all time by the Jews having killed Jesus (on the Sabbath?). The whole ordering of these rituals is disgusting. And what of Christian holidays? Chrysostom relies on the standard trope of perpetual obedience: for the church, the Pasch refers to the cross of Jesus and to the Eucharist that represents it; it is for "all the time, if we wish," not once a year; and if the Christian fasts at Lent it is only to prepare him or her for the Eucharist, no more, no less. Chrysostom finally dismisses the entire concern with timekeeping and worrying about the exact dates of this or that religious assembly or custom. Who cares about such things? All that matters is that we have a spirit that is willing to live in peace, all the time.

But does "all the time" and "beyond time" and "no time" cohere in any way with the "fulness of time" (Gal. 4:4) or with the "right time," the "moment" (Rom. 5:6), the very "days of Jesus" (Heb. 5:7), the "time of Christ," let alone with the

1. For a full discussion of this and other related patristic material, see Daniélou 1956: chaps. 14–16.

"appointed times" of Lev. 23? If God traverses the world's time, then such ingathering has its own time, its own calendar. The Christian church did, in fact, wrestle with this fact, especially as its own liturgical life took form. And it did so by transferring these appointed times to the time of Jesus's own life, through whom they cascaded down again into the times of the church. Origen and others will take the specific feast days—Passover, Firstfruits, Sabbath, Booths—and allow the shift in ceremonials to land within the moral or ascetic framework of Jesus's embodied example; soon these forms will take shape in a kind of eschatological vision, where the fulfillment of the Christian life finds its partial significance in the way in which the figures of the festivals conjure up the promises of transformed humanity. Passover reflects the deeper reality of Easter; Pentecost and its memorialized gifts point to the Holy Spirit's self-giving; Sabbath to the Lord's Day of resurrected life; Booths to the transfiguration of human flesh.[2] Even the nativity found a connection with Firstfruits (Rupert of Deutz [Patrologia latina 167.826]). Spurred by the fourth-century rediscovery of the Holy Land and its landscape as offering tangible signs by which to grasp these figures, appointed liturgies grew up around them and began to mold the calendar of the church's own life, a calendar that, through Jesus's time, emerged from the times of Israel.

Historians of the Christian liturgy have struggled, with enormous subtlety, to trace this emergence. But its foundation appears to lie in the movement by which the church sought carefully to correlate transformed festivals with the Christian eschatological symbolism that evolved out of the more primary paschal work of Jesus. This meant always that, on a theological level, the temporal character of the feasts was secondary. To be sure, great weight was placed on exact calendrical calculation, as we know from the astonishing conflicts over the date of Easter in the early church and beyond. But the need to anchor all within a framework that was wrested away from the Jewish Sabbath and relocated in the Lord's Day (this was the explanation for the counting of the Christian Pentecost from Sunday, in Lev. 23:15), with all of that day's atemporal connotations, as we saw with Augustine, pointed to a great transfer of interest from the process of mapping time. Instead, the focus grew increasingly upon the task of outlining the image of Christ iconically through the liturgy. Even an effort by Bruno of Segni (Patrologia latina 164.451–55), who sought to place all the Levitical festivals into the temporal container he called the "age of the church" only partially obviated this temporal mitigation, for the age that he identifies for the church's historical life is that of Christ himself, and so he interprets each Jewish festival as being a kind of simultaneous image of new life and sinless discipleship before God that is given in the single act of living as a Christian. "All your life is a Sabbath" or a "Pentecost" or a "firstfruits offering," for history itself has been subsumed into the risen Christ's *eternal* life.

2. Daniélou 1956 provides the fullest and most accessible account of these figural correlations with eschatological promise in the early church.

By this point in the Middle Ages the Levitical festivals, as moral figures, have little connection with the church's own liturgical practice, and the latter's temporal character (though not its meaning) is important more in terms of its institutional expectation than as a central aspect of its significance. Although Orthodox theologian Alexander Schmemann uses the phrase "liturgy of time" to describe one of the essential aspects of the church's calendar of worship (in contrast to the Eucharist's sacramental nature), he describes this liturgy's temporality in a very modern way as "an affirmation of time as a history within which this kingdom [of the new eon, the age to come] must grow and 'be fulfilled' in the faith and practice of men."[3] This seems less to describe the early church's liturgical perspective than that of a contemporary reappropriation of its Jewish background.

It is a modern phenomenon, in fact, that Christian readers of the Gospels have recently realized to what degree the narrative of Jesus's own life is there presented as shaped by the festivals of Israel. Obviously, as my summary of John Chrysostom noted above, no one denied that festivals like Passover and Pentecost appear in the Gospels; but such observations were usually a prelude for a judgment of "fulfilled and therefore dismissed" with respect to the holy days themselves. In the last century, however, Roman Catholic thought especially has apprehended the festal markers of Jesus's own ministry as being deeply illuminative structures for his life. Some of this has been tied to an elaborated theology of sacrament, in the wake of the influence of Odo Casel (1999), now expanded to the breadth of historical and religious existence.[4] Anglican interest, since the early twentieth century, in the Jewish particularities of Jesus's ministry and teaching has also borne fruit in a new recognition of the specifically cultic rootedness of his gospel, giving rise more recently to whole-cloth theories regarding the literary origins of the Gospels themselves within, for example, Jewish-Christian cultic lectionaries.[5] *La Bible de Jérusalem*, issued in 1956 out of the Dominican École Biblique, ordered, in their paragraphing of John's Gospel, the initial ministry of Jesus according to the

3. See Schmemann 1977: 69; also 31–38. Schmemann insists that the true character of the *ordo*, the traditional framework of the church's worship, is a coordination of sacramental (eucharistic) and nonsacramental and calendrically structured prayer, in which the first's eschatological reality is somehow engaged through the second's temporal outplaying. The distinction is one that even Schmemann realizes is often difficult to make and possibly misleading. Chilton 2002—a work deeply informed by the scholarly retrieval of the New Testament's Jewish framework—argues from a quite different (and in fact political) perspective for the importance of Jewish and Christian festal ordering of the year (each in quite different ways) as necessary for the preservation of the moral imperative to "take history seriously."

4. But see Schmemann's critique (1977: 37) of this kind of englobing projection of sacramental reality into the history of both Christian and Jewish worship. Casel's seminal *Mystery of Christian Worship* continues to dominate the Christian theology of the sacraments.

5. Liberal Jewish scholar Claude Montefiore's *Synoptic Gospels* (1927) had a tremendous influence in this regard on British Christian New Testament interpretation. The group of Christian scholars most associated with developing a theory regarding the genetic relationship of the Gospels themselves and the Jewish-Christian liturgical calendar include Carrington 1952; Guilding 1960; and Goulder 1974 and 1978. A critique of the whole approach is given by Morris 1964.

festivals mentioned in the narrative, giving way to the long Passion Narrative as a week of preparation for a new Passover. This proved a novel editorial move that has, for example, in Raymond Brown's magisterial Anchor Bible commentary on John become standard in especially Catholic circles. The conclusion given by this new festal marking of John's Gospel is, however, a standard Christian trope, at least as expressed in the Jerusalem Bible's introduction to the gospel: "This division suggests that Christ not only fulfilled the Jewish liturgy but by doing so brought it to an end."[6] Despite the still-traditional sweeping away of Israel's time, the new sensitivity to the ongoing festal calendar within the Gospels at least places the festivals squarely back within the temporal reality of Jesus's, and thus Israel's, *theological* history.[7]

But what then is this history? An emerging element of our reading of Leviticus is that the time that is Israel's is not only *also*, but is *first* Jesus's time. It marks his gathering up of creation. It is Israel's time only because God has first desired to walk this way. And so, if Israel's way is in fact Jesus's, the map of this way is given in the path that Jesus himself walks through time. Time and history look like the festal form of Jesus's narrative. "Fulfillment" and "ending," in the Jerusalem Bible's view, represent the *priority* of Jesus's life and journey to the Father through Israel and the world; it does not point to the dismissal of either Jew or Greek because of Jesus's historically particular coming.

Leviticus 23, as we have seen, begins with an instruction on the Sabbath and orders all the festivals in accordance with this foundational day—they are all, as it were, recapitulated within the Sabbath itself. As Rashi (Rosenbaum and Silbermann 1932: 104) notes, in citing *Sifra* 228.2, Sabbath and festival are brought together so that Israel might know that festival keeping is "as if" keeping the Sabbath, and festival desecrating is "as if" desecrating the Sabbath. And the Sabbath itself is bound to and, in its summation, explains the story of God's creating. Sabbath—and festivals also—are thus descriptive somehow of that creation, which undergirds the character of their ordering. The linguistic network of the opening verses points to the Sabbath and festivals in the breadth of this creative orientation. The "feasts" (*moed*) are gatherings of the congregation, and these represent "convocations" (*miqra*, generally used of a "reading" that is appointed for an occasion of assembly, including the whole of Scripture) that are "proclaimed"; this last word is used in the sense of "called" out to the people and takes us back to the opening of the book itself, *Vayikra*, the "calling" of God to Moses and Israel. Only here, this calling is the same calling that God speaks out to the created beings as he forms them and grants them identity in Gen. 1. Indeed, the *moed* or "feast" of Lev. 23:2 is bound to the *moed* of Gen. 1:14, the seasons marked by the created

---

6. The New Jerusalem Bible has let go, in its introductory comments, of the festal ordering of the gospel, even while keeping these divisions within the paragraphing of the gospel text.

7. Conservative Protestant exegesis, particularly of a premillennialist kind, has always maintained this vision, now fueled by the interests of evangelical messianic Christian Jews. See Chumney 1994.

lights in the firmament, which organize what we are able to perceive as time itself. Hence the frequent addition in English translations of the word "appointed" to qualify "feast": they are appointed to the extent that they are created as the infrastructure of temporality. What follows, as Sabbath and festival, are therefore manifestations in time of the very character of God's original and essential creative being; they are signs of his creation and of what creation is.

The Sabbath, of course, has always been viewed as such, and Gen. 2:1–3 and Exod. 20:11 speak to this. Calvin reckons that the Sabbath was kept by the patriarchs precisely because its marking as a day derives from the same intrinsic character as God's creation of the human form itself, with its breath taken from the mouth of God (1996: 2.434, 439–40). (Calvin's displacement of the Sabbath from within this created time of God's derives, therefore, from a deep theological motive, as we have seen, and not from "plain reading.") While Leviticus gives no explanation for the Sabbath, its binding of the Sabbath with the festivals (and they with the Sabbath) points forward to Deut. 5:15's own description of the day's meaning: God's saving of Israel from Egypt by his mighty power. Creation takes its form in the time of Israel, whose calling or historical identity is given in the exodus and its long journey of wandering and redemption. If the Sabbath appears as the mark of creation's perfection (Gen. 2:2), then the festivals detail this perfection as the work of God within time as he continues to move with and toward that which he has made: "My Father is working still" (John 5:17).

This linkage of Sabbath and festival, perfection and history, is brought out by *Rabbah* 28.1, whose initial discussion of Lev. 23 moves to the Firstfruits of 23:10 and immediately raises questions of meaning with respect to human labor: "What does a man gain by all the toil at which he toils under the sun?" (Eccl. 1:3). The question, however, reflects upon the unmentioned texts concerning both Sabbath and Passover (Lev. 23:3–8), perfection and history together, for in raising it, the *Rabbah* acknowledges the deep fissure of the fall and of the curse (Gen. 3:17–19), whose effects turn the seasons of time into a wearisome march, too long in its burden, too short in its promise. "My Father is working" because time has become the place of his life, creation taking the form of his coming and deliverance. Hence the rationale of the chapter, according to the *Rabbah's* implication, is that perfection and rest are implanted within the fall *into* time. Their proclaimed convocations and gatherings point to the histories of creaturely life within time, as it is the object of God's own coming and redemption. The festal calendar, to this degree, signals the full gathering up by God, the calling of God that sweeps up Adam to Adam, nation to nation, Genesis to Revelation.

Beginning with the Sabbath's establishment by God as something comprehensive of his creating act, Lev. 23 ends with a discussion of the Feast of Booths/ Sukkoth whose liturgical use of the branches and boughs of trees returns the actions of Israel to the embrace of all created things. The bulk of *Rabbah* 30 focuses upon just this aspect and draws into this closing section of Lev. 23 the psalms of creaturely praise (e.g., Ps. 96:12–13), where the new song of the "trees of the wood" and of the "fields" refers back to "all creatures" and to the "earth" as being the "LORD's" in every respect (*Rabbah* 30.4). This, in turn, is woven into an interpretation of the trees under consideration that sequentially treats the referent as God (clothed in glory), the patriarchs and their wives, the work of the law, Israel in its history, and finally the human creature itself, where the palm branch and other plants used in the feast are seen as images of the human body, with spine, mouth, eye, and heart (30.14). The recapitulation, in a Christian sense, of all the world is thereby given in the festal grasp.

Jews have generally seen this comprehensive historical movement at work in their calendar. The Passover feast, linked with the week of Unleavened Bread (Lev. 23:5-8) has its obvious location in the deliverance from Egypt. This is briefly indicated in 23:5, through the description of the Passover as being "the LORD's"; that is, it is his own work that is primarily given in this festival. The weeklong observance of the Unleavened Bread is described by the term *hag* (23:6; as is Sukkoth in 23:34, 39), a word that may imply a more public celebration, which has sometimes been seen as distinguishing it as a pilgrimage feast (to the temple), rather than a domestic one. But in Leviticus, the stress in all of the festal calendar is that these are times for the people *as a whole*, and they describe popular histories, not individual ones. Very early in its interpretation, this season of calling, initiated in the Passover, was enmeshed in the longer passage to Shavuot/Feast of Weeks. The offering of a sheaf of firstfruits (23:10-11) on the day after Sabbath sets in motion a period of counting, for seven weeks, until the Feast of Weeks arrives (23:15-16). The Feast of Weeks, in turn, marks the main celebration of Firstfruits (23:17), later known as the *hag-ha-bikkurim*, the Feast of Firstfruits itself. But as Deut. 26:1-11 points out, this passage *from* and *to* the Firstfruits—from Passover to the Feast of Weeks—is primarily the story of Israel's wanderings, from deliverance in Egypt in the midst of the death of the firstborn to a promised land where all that is enjoyed is given by God. Indeed, the "counting of the omer," the "measure"—time itself—for the weeks between Passover and Shavuot comes to stand as the story of God and Israel unveiling creation itself. Israel is purged in the wilderness, sinning and suffering punishment, and its history becomes one of rebellion, grace, forgiveness, and transformation that reveals the very nature of God.

Thus *Rabbah* 28.4-5 reads "harvest"—of both Lev. 23:10 and, by implication, the Feast of Weeks—as a symbol of Israel's and the world's history, with all of the kingdoms of the nations coming under God's sovereign judgment, and the "waving" of the offering referring to the four directions of heaven and earth. Within this encompassing reach, Israel lives its life as the gatherer of human sin and redemption. The *Me'am Lo'ez* (Kaplan 1982: 12.165) pictures this as a "menstruating woman" in the desert, counting the days of her purification as week by week she is released from the defilement of Egypt and life is restored to its purpose. The later linkage of the Feast of Weeks to the giving of the law on Sinai became rooted in both Jewish and Christian traditions.[8] But the meaning of this linkage seems to derive from the reality that the law was a form of nourishment (hence its harvest character and the later customs of refraining from meats on that day, as for a growing infant) and thus the occasion of Israel's consistent disobedience and God's difficult mercy. Later talmudic connections between the Feast of Weeks and the first sacrifices of Cain and Abel grow out of this wider understanding, wherein the very nature of the human rejection of life and the sacrificial character of love and its divine affirmation take form. The movement from Passover to the Feast of Weeks, in all of its symbolic accretions, is none other than the movement in time of Israel in the world, and the world in Israel, as God comes to redeem them.

Leviticus itself does not spell this out in its own terms. But the foundational character of Lev. 23 as the marking out of time *for Israel* makes its history the central focus. Later traditions regarding the New Year/Rosh Hashanah (23:23–25), Yom Kippur (23:26–32), and Sukkoth/Feast of Booths (23:33–36, 39–43) follow the same pattern. The *Rabbah* describes how the Feast of Trumpets, or New Year, marks the day when creation began, explicated by Ps. 119:89—the word by which the heavens and earth are established. As a result, it is also associated with the redemption of Jacob, with God's judgment of the angels and nations (47:5), with God's forgiveness, with works of mercy (based on the preceding Lev. 23:22 regarding gleaning), and so on. The binding of Isaac (Akedah) is also brought into relationship with the New Year, as the date is identified with the oath (*shaba*/swearing, viewed as cognate with *sheba*/seven of the calendrical computation) made by God to Abraham (Gen. 22:16–17) to bless his descendents. This event, as it is recalled each year, makes atonement for the "toils of transgression and bad deeds" committed by Israel in the course of its life. Creation is thus explicated by Israel's history and the history of the nations, wherein, in every detail, God's nature and purpose are embodied in his actions of judgment and mercy. Rabbi Tahalipa of Caesarea is quoted as expressing the following divine summary of the New Year: "My children, since you have come before me to judgment and gone forth with a pardon, I credit it to you as if on this very day you were made [afresh] before me, as if today I created you as a new creation" (*Rabbah* 29.12). The placement of the Day of Atonement, ten days after, reveals yet another crucial element of this history, centrally bound up with the sin of the golden calf, as we have seen. Leviticus 23 explicates its significance now with regard especially to the sacrificial drawing near of God. In general, observant Jews would begin their prayers of confession and afflictions on Rosh Hashanah (or even before) and carry them through to a culmination on Yom Kippur, demonstrating how the day itself was but a part of a larger history, reflecting the movement of time as a whole before God.

8. See St. Leo, *Sermon 1 on Pentecost*. Jerome, Augustine, and others pick up the theme, contrasting the old with the new covenant and spiritual law given by and through the Holy Spirit to the apostles on the Pentecost of the church.

This history is one of continual struggle and grace, the toil of time as it is also the toil of God's own labor. But the festivals in this temporal exposition are not so much interludes from that history itself, as they are illuminative exposures of the events and their meaning as they unfold in that history. Thus Rabbi Panet's parable, with which I began, cannot simply point to the refreshing character of a holiday in the modern sense of the word, a day of rest as an oasis within time, by which one "gets away from" time. The sabbatical character of the festivals opens Israel to see how God's creative engagement, temporal at its roots, of the world and of Israel itself constitutes the perfection and fulfillment of his purpose from the beginning: Israel finds its rest *here* as enmeshed in this history of engagement. Its ceasing from servile labor during these days, which represents the marking off of their seasonal nature, gives Israel over to God unfettered (to use the intended imagery of freedom from Egyptian bondage). But it is not thereby released from *time*: it will see God clearly in his work, though it will be the same work as he has done year by year and day by day. How will this happen? Through the prayers and sacrifices that mark these years and days, the life of God's coming is given in their appointment, is exposed or revealed in judgment and mercy, realities that are ever unveiled.

It is crucial, therefore, to see the historical nature of the festivals, their revelation of history as it *is* in fact; for otherwise, the paradoxical bite in the prophetic critique of the cult is lost. The justified polemic against the cult by Isaiah is a part of the same creative action as the cult's celebration and finds its place in the same movement from Passover to the Feast of Weeks, Adam to Adam, as God confronts Israel in its sinning and in his redeeming. Like the Eucharist in 1 Cor. 11, the festivals work for life and death at the same time (also 2 Cor. 2:15–16), as God draws near in their midst, and they come to signal the single body of judgment and mercy together. The vision in Amos 8 of the basket of ripe fruit presents just this reality: the festivals and Sabbaths become places of "mourning and lamentation," not because they themselves are useless or simply the vessels of Israel's hypocrisy eventually to be discarded, as some of the early Christian interpreters claimed. *Rather, the festivals expose the actual history of God's work with Israel, as he judges, destroys, and resurrects.* The Sabbath and festival are, from this perspective, centrally places of God's creative judgment. Far from thereby demonstrating their secondary character in the face of some more ultimate timelessness, both Sabbath and festival manifest the necessary character of created time, wherein God moves to his creatures and gathers them. And such created time is God's in all breadth.

When Jesus is described as our "rest" in Hebrews, such a dominical Sabbath refers to this time of God in the world, not to some otherworldly referent. It is true that Hebrews speaks of a rest (*katapausis*, based on the Septuagint of Ps. 95:11 and Gen. 2:2) that is yet to come (Heb. 4:1, 9). This is the rest tied to the Sabbath of the seventh day itself as it marks God's creation (4:3–4), yet that somehow remains for those who today maintain faith and obedience to God. But it is this "today" that, according to Hebrews, itself embodies our "share in Christ"

(3:14). And this "today," as it constitutes a participation that embraces even the creative rest of God, is given in God's *own* participation in the life of struggling obedience, in which he is "tested" in "every way" within this world (4:15). Paradoxically, then, the rest of the Christian remains tethered to the world of Christ's passage through time.

The structuring of the gospel narrative of Jesus's ministry, within John, according to the sabbatical festivals of Leviticus follows this course of connection. As the Jerusalem Bible lays it out (it was the first to organize the text this way), these festivals are interwoven even among themselves. The Passover recurs three times (John 2:23; 6:4; 11:55–19:42); within this framework appears what seems to be the Feast of Weeks (5:1), in connection to which there is a discussion of the Sabbath (5:10–18), and also the Feast of Booths (7:1–10:21) and the Feast of Dedication/Hanukkah (10:22), obviously not mentioned in Leviticus. Some clear thematic elements in Jesus's deeds and words are associated with these festivals:[9]

- The Passover is linked to (a) the cleansing of the temple and prophecy of its destruction and Jesus's resurrection; (b) the new birth of the Christian (if John 3:1–21 still lies within this first section); (c) the gift of heavenly provision and manna through the body and blood of Jesus (Lev. 6); and (d) the passion and crucifixion.
- The Feast of Weeks involves a discussion of the law of Moses (John 5:30–47).
- Sabbath is linked to works of healing what is deformed and God's continuing work of creating life through resurrection (John 5:1–17).
- The Feast of Booths involves a discussion of the nature of the Christ as the bringer of water (John 7:37), light (8:12), and a promised people (8:31; 10:1).

Most of these aspects are bound up, in their historical recital of Israel's life, with the festivals as understood in their Jewish context. Constellated around Jesus, they point to the continuing engagement of God, in these elements, through his own grasp of human life in judgment and mercy, in creation, sorrow over sin, and re-creation.

If the sabbatical rest represents the perfection of creation, it is a creation fulfilled in Jesus. Fulfillment, however, cannot mean primarily the transcendence of time, if indeed the creative judgment of Israel's festal life is taken up by Jesus. Rather, this fulfilled perfection is manifested in the temporal participation of God that enacts new creation explicated in the festal form of the Son, given in the gospel

9. Nonfestal events in Jesus's life—e.g., the transfiguration—engage elements drawn from the feasts and associate them, through his person, with the kingdom. But these events and their thematic coloration do not engage the specifically *calendrical* aspects of the festal ordering of time and in this sense are not directly connected with the Levitical concerns of this chapter.

as a whole: "Lo, I have come" (Heb. 10:7, 9) are the words that proclaim that "God is still working," that new birth comes from above, that sin is cleansed, that the "crooked [is] made straight," that dead bodies are resurrected to new life. "Go and tell John what you have seen and heard" (Luke 7:22). This is the great calling of the convocation that Jesus himself embodies as he approaches God, and in him God approaches the world, in the one sacrifice of love that crowns creation's purpose. Perfect worship (Exod. 3:18; 5:1, 3)—the purpose of Israel's liberation—the "serv[ice of] the living God," is given in this offering (Heb. 9:14), through which the people are gathered in this one movement and sin is taken away through the shedding of blood (10:1, 4).[10] The festal form of Jesus passes through Holy Saturday, the quiet and rest of the cross as the Sabbath of all things within God's arms.

> The great silence took hold of the earth on the Friday of the passion. After the death of God is proclaimed, it appears as if the whole world has entered into the silence of the great Sabbath. According to the fathers, before hearing the words of the word, one must learn first to hear his silence, "this language of the world to come" according to St. Isaac. And here the silence means simply "finding oneself in the midst of the word." It is only on the level of this particular silence that a human being can do this. And it is in such a silence as this, in the royal liberty of his spirit, that a human being is invited to respond to a very simple question "who is God?" To which Gregory of Nyssa allows a simple answer to slip from his lips: "You, who love my soul." (Evdokimov 1973: 38–39)

The time of Christ is this season whose festal shout is given the deep resonance of quiet by the Sabbath rest of the cross. It encompasses Passover to the Feast of Weeks to the Feast of Booths. "How I am constrained"—even now!—Jesus says of the pressures of the moment, a moment whose fulfillment is given in the now (Luke 12:50). Time has been shown as *his* time, and *our* today—"today, when you hear his voice, do not harden your hearts" (Heb. 3:7–19 [quoting Ps. 95:7–8]; Heb. 4:7)—is his now. Within it and embodied as it, lies "the judgment of this world" now (John 12:31) and life together "in Paradise" (Luke 23:43) today.

The Christian attempt to thrust aside the festal form of Christ has confused thereby the very notion of his body, which is the convocation or assembly of his Sabbath offering given in time and molding time to his image. That form is his gathering of all things (Eph. 1:10), but first and foremost it is the gathering of

---

10. See Kilmartin 1994: 427–28: "In modern Catholic theology the sacred character of the Eucharist is grounded on more than the Christological basis. Its sacredness is not merely based on the fact of originating in a historical act of institution by Christ. Rather what grounds the holiness of the Eucharist is the initiative of the Father: the self-offering by the Father of his only Son for the salvation of the world. Here we touch on the unique New Testament understanding of the 'true sacrifice' as that which is based on the movement of God to us. The death of Jesus is ultimately the expression of the turning of God to us. The love of the Father is the origin of the self-offering of Jesus."

his people, the body made one and, in this making one, offered up. "Proclaim [the] holy convocations" (Lev. 23:2) is a way of saying "this is my body" (Mark 14:22) or "the church . . . the fulness of him who fills all in all" (Eph. 1:22–23). Augustine seized upon this identity, precisely in terms of the reality of the sacrificial cult as it takes its form in the church, when he said, "This is the sacrifice of Christians: we, being many, are one body in Christ" (*City of God* 10.6). The church's common life, much as Israel's in the festal passage of its movement out of Egypt, becomes the creation-comprehending path of God's offering given in the universal cry, "Take up [your] cross and follow me" (Mark 8:34). This is the king's sabbatical oasis: "Take my yoke upon you . . . and you will find rest for your souls. For my yoke is easy, and my burden is light" (Matt. 11:29–30).

The early Christian claim that "every day is a Sabbath" is not wrong, therefore, if by the words "Sabbath" and "every day" is meant the history of the church's common life of creative judgment, which is given in the mutual self-offering to God of the body's members: "Present your bodies as a living sacrifice, holy and acceptable to God, which is your spiritual worship. . . . Love one another with brotherly affection" (Rom. 12:1, 10). Yet Christian worship, as we saw, has too often been siphoned off from this history and laid alongside the transcendent bond with God in Christ as its provisional prop or aid or, from another perspective, appropriated and reformatted for participation in a timeless reality beyond history. But the festal form of Christ demonstrates at the least that such distinction between material and spiritual worship cannot be made. Worship is more than a token of the atemporal praise of God. Rather, as we see in Colossians and Ephesians when such praise is encouraged, worship *is* the very historical context out of which such praise arises and takes form, that is, the body of Christ and the sacrifice of forgiveness that reflects the origin of creation itself: "As the Lord has forgiven you, so you also must forgive. And above all these put on love, which binds everything together in perfect harmony. And let the peace of Christ rule in your hearts, to which indeed you were called in the one body. And be thankful. Let the word of Christ dwell in you richly, teach and admonish one another in all wisdom, and sing psalms and hymns and spiritual songs with thankfulness in your hearts to God" (Col. 3:13–16; cf. Eph. 5:15–33).

The key to this entire passage is indeed Col. 2:17, as Calvin wrote, but in a very different sense than the text's usual interpretation: "These [the festivals, new moons, and Sabbaths] are only a shadow of what is to come" (1996: 2.435). Yes, in the same sense that they are shadows cast by something real whose image they bear as that reality passes by through time. The problem is that the translation of the next phrase of Col. 2:17 can and has often given the impression that this reality is something that stands beyond time: "the substance belongs to Christ" (Revised Standard Version); "the reality . . . is found in Christ" (New International Version); "the reality is the body of Christ" (New American Bible); "but Christ is real!" (Contemporary English Version). Paul's phrase, however, is clear enough: "the body is Christ's" (*to de sōma tou christou*). The body of Christ is that which casts the shadow on the world and on its time. The body in every and all its aspects: coming to birth, born in blood, changing over time, hungering and weeping, eating and laughing, touched and touching, hurt and bleeding, immersed in created mortality, dying and rising, shining and ascending, gathering and gathered. If Paul rejects the festivals, new moons, and Sabbaths, it is not because they are somehow false means of righteousness; it is because the body of Christ in the church of Jew and Gentile is the historical marker of God's righteousness in creating and redeeming the world to which he comes in love.[11]

It is not so much, then, that the Eucharist and the Christian liturgical calendar take the place of the festal sequence of Israel. They explicate the festal form of *Jesus's body* that walks the very path of Israel—because it marks that path in advance, as it were—through God's creative judgment. They are not forms of alternative worship for Judaism, but derive their own form from within the reality of "life together," the "holy convocation" of the actual body of Christ laid out within the world and moving through it to the fullness of God's embrace. Dom Gregory Dix's famous saying that the "Eucharist is nothing else but the eternal gesture of the Son of Man toward his Father as he passes into the kingdom of God" (1945: 266) captures this reality so long as one bears in mind that the gesture is not given by Jesus privately and independently of his body as the church. The gesture is in fact sensible only to the degree that it is given *as* the body is taken up by Jesus in his movement to the Father through world: there is no Eucharist without the church; there is no church without God's time; there is no time without the passage of Jesus through the world that he has made, through, for, and in himself (Col. 1:16–17).

There is no fundamental reason that Christians, as is done by so-called messianic Jews, should *not* celebrate the festivals of Lev. 23. But unless these festivals are now bound to the body of Jesus, they themselves do not constitute Christian worship. How might this be done? More properly, the passage of Israel is given in the body of Christ through his life, signified within the Christian calendar of the Gospels and their reading according to the seasons of his ministry, but engaged in the church's representative participation in these temporal realities of their Lord. Sixteenth-century French theologian Pierre de Bérulle provides perhaps the most sophisticated and elaborated discussion of this in the course of his many meditations upon the "states" of Jesus, those aspects of his life's experiences (birth, flight, growth, baptism, ministry, etc.) that embody the truth of his

11. In N. T. Wright's phrase, Paul's argument over justification "wasn't so much about soteriology as about ecclesiology; not so much about salvation as about the church" (1997: 119). My reading of Leviticus in fact resolves some of the competing ideas at work in the debate over the so-called new perspective on Paul, in that it seems clear from this context that the primary reality of God's redemptive action—*sola gratia*—is at work in the Levitical outline of history. But because Leviticus makes a historical claim that is comprehensive of creation itself, the corporate character of this grace as embodied in the self-offering of Christ and gathered into the church as that body clearly describes the righteousness of God in the ecclesial terms of Jew and Greek reconciled by God as they serve within this body. The imputed righteousness of the individual is, from this vantage, at best a secondary concern.

eternal life within time itself and that the church and the Christian are drawn into so as to be formed by, through, and in them. Bérulle could seize upon Exod. 12:2's description of the month of Passover's celebration, a month that "begins all months," and see how this month is Jesus's month in every way and was taken by him to be used for his work (conception and death together); he could therefore grasp the particularities of time as Jesus's time into which we too must be drawn to expend our lives.[12] The Passover and its season become a motor of the Christian life, precisely because it is the temporal form of Jesus's own. It is not clear that there is a feasible way to mimic Jesus's own use of the seventh month, for instance, or even his celebration of the Feast of Weeks, which became the locus of his opening up of the Scriptures of Moses to his own being. However, it is *his* use of these times, and the shape of this time as it has already been framed for Israel, that is the Christian's path; not simply the following of a liturgical practice. In a sense, the full range of the Levitical festivals themselves is now refracted (not discarded) through the prism of his life, and the festivals themselves are therefore grasped by, or grasp, the Christian only as that life is subjected to the body's history. This is an ecclesial matter, in its widest (i.e., catholic) sense and not a matter to be left to individual or even congregational tastes.

The liturgical forms of such subjection are, perhaps, only to be apprehended as they unfold in the passage of the Son to the Father through the Spirit. They have been given to the church, as it were, in its own time and have developed in their own way, neither as parallels to the Levitical festivals nor as their replacements, but simply as the outgrowths of Jesus's own life and times, with all their festal character as it forms the body of the church. Odo Casel's mystery sacramentology was, after his death, the subject of debate and, from one perspective, censure.[13] But

12. See the celebrated discussion of this in Brémond 1923: 43–79, with its focus upon the incarnation, the material world, and the states or conditions of Jesus. Brémond seems to miss some of the significance of Bérulle's attempt to draw a binding connection between the earthly and heavenly intratrinitarian states of Jesus, asserting that this reflected Bérulle's abstracted and nonmaterial vision. To be sure, some of Bérulle's Neoplatonic presuppositions led him into formulations of matter that imply a denial of the mystery of God's establishment of a creature, other than himself, as in fact *real*; but the effect of these emphases is not so much to denigrate temporal reality as to assert its divine character within the reach of God's essential purposes. The nothingness of the human soul before God that Bérulle stresses and that became a hallmark of the French school in this context articulates most fundamentally the chasm of creation, and hence the nature of divine love, far more than it denotes creation's superfluity in relation to God.

13. Pope Pius XII's 1947 encyclical *Mediator Dei* raised this issue and in particular singled out for rejection the view (associated with Casel) that the sacraments in themselves acted to re-present the christic mystery, or Christ himself, rather than functioning as instruments of grace to communicate the effects of the mystery (§165). The debate over the mechanism of such communication may be appropriate. But it seems that the festal form of Jesus actually shapes and comprehends the time in which we live, rather than acting upon or within it from a distance, as from a separate temporal location. We are to celebrate the Passover of Christ, according to St. Leo, as a "presence rather than commemorate it as a past event" (*Sermon on the Passion* [Patrologia latina 54.358a]), a phrase he uses of other liturgical feast days as well.

his notion that the fullness of Christ's being and action—"the mystery"—takes hold of the Christian and the church in the course of its liturgical orientation to his "mysteries" (in the plural), his "times" in their history-shaping grace, properly reflects the reality of Jesus's traversal of the world and its sweeping ingathering of our own lives, the "making his" of temporal reality. "So then, whether we live or whether we die, we are the Lord's" (Rom. 14:8). The church's service and mission among its members and to the world now becomes the locus of this festal form, by definition; for time itself, as the vessel of God's creative judgment, now serves the church and world, reshaping it according to the self-offering of God's Son. The *history* of the church itself is the "liturgy of time."

The book of Revelation is built around the vision of this liturgy, using the image of earthly history as the outplaying reflection of a comprehensive heavenly reality, familiar to us from Jewish meditation on the temple. Jean Corbon points out that the heavenly liturgy that takes place within the presence of the ascended Lord, behind the veil of time, is nonetheless bound to the repeated cries of sought-after vindication and praise by the martyrs, those whose lives are shaped by their temporal passage in the wake of their Lord, who still stands in the midst of the heavenly host as a "Lamb [that] had been slain" (Rev. 5:6) (Corbon 2005: esp. chap. 4). History is "en route," in Corbon's words, to this place of worship. Yet it is also the temporal face of this same worship, "dead time" being taken into the "vast reflux of love in which everything turns into life." Leviticus 23's tracing of the temporal festivals of the people of Israel as the shape of their receipt of God's coming founds the mission of the Christian church: rather than transforming history into Sabbath, it marks the transformation of Sabbath into history, Jesus's history as carrying Israel's way into and through the world. The end is veiled; now, there is only the miracle of time, this carrying by Jesus into his Father's bosom from which life itself is given. This "today" is already the end, "the acceptable time" (2 Cor. 6:2).[14]

So the final aspect of the *moadim*, the festivals, turns to dailiness as it is ordered according to the continual passage of Sabbaths—the lamp inside the tent of meeting and the weekly bread of the presence or showbread (Lev. 24:1–9). These two elements of the worship of God are given for their quotidian "continuousness" (24:4, 8) and "perpetual due" to the priests (24:9). Today becomes the acceptable time, the time of receiving God's receipt and of loving the one who loves, because all time has assumed the form of this offering. *Rabbah* 31.7 notes that the daily and perpetual light of the temple, which represents the influx of God within the world, marks out the final reconciliation of the lights of creation. Brought together now are lights experienced in the lower world of human existence (Gen. 1:14–19) and

---

14. The notion of an "eternal Sabbath," understood eschatologically in a way parallel to Augustine, can be found in Judaism too (e.g., Schneersohn 1986: 160). But here the Sabbath that is God's is comprehensive of creation itself; it marks God's single and eternal "creative vision," and the return to the Sabbath at the end of time is a return to the fullness of God's purpose that is not so much opposed to time as inclusive of it.

the light of God's heavenly realm within the higher world. God who *is* light has made the day and night alike (Ps. 139:11) through the sharing of his glory. When "the dwelling of God is with men" (Rev. 21:3), then "the Lord God will be their light" (22:5). The oil lamps at the tabernacle are therefore the signs of the festal form of Jesus as he comes into and goes through the world (John 1:9, 14). They do not end time, but manifest time's form as God's self-offering in Christ. It is a form that it holds from its beginning to its center to its end. And this draws in the whole of creation's meaning, for the one who draws in is the one who enters in. "Said the Holy One, blessed be he, to the fetus, 'During all those nine months that you were in your mother's belly, who gave light for you? Was it not I? . . .' (cf. Job 29:3)" (*Rabbah* 31.7). Yet, "I am the light of the world . . . the light of life" (John 8:12). The "eternal covenant" that the lamp signifies, while it is surely specific to Israel's calling from one perspective (Hirsch 1989: 2.714–15), becomes the calling of all creation precisely in its form as temporal creature. Sabbath perpetuity does not stand in contrast to history, as we saw early Christian interpreters claim; rather it underlines the significance of each day as God's day of passage in Christ, as light to light draws each day into the other (Ps. 19:2, 6).

The bread of the presence, in this context, is properly read as a sign of the miracle of creation itself, as various Jewish interpretations point out: the bread stays warm (it was said) for the entire week, and only a bean-sized portion for each priest would nonetheless satisfy their hunger "as would an entire meal" (*Me'am Lo'ez* [Kaplan 1982: 12.233–34]). This is the perpetual grace of God's sustenance of creation in its formation and existence and points to the basis of trust upon which the Jubilee provisions are founded in Lev. 25. But, as Jesus underlines in his discussion with the Pharisees over Sabbath keeping, this same grace constitutes the movement of God to that which he has made. The bread of the presence is itself given as a gift of life by God, and it is *this* that binds it with the Sabbath itself: "The sabbath was made for man, not man for the sabbath" (Mark 2:27); yet, because "the Son of man is lord of the sabbath," it embodies mercy at its core (Matt. 12:7), the divine mercy of God's self-offering, the "bread which comes down from heaven" to be eaten as his own flesh and self (John 6:50–51). What the *Me'am Lo'ez* calls the "influx of the divine" upon creation, represented by the bread of the presence, is this "coming down" and "being eaten" (Kaplan 1982: 12.233–34).

"Give us this day"—every day, today, the acceptable day—"our daily bread" (Matt. 6:11). Thereby the Lord's time feeds the time of his creatures, as the two are measured by the same standard of divine action and gift.

LEVITICUS 24:10–23

From the light of eternity as it embraces the world, we now move to the second and final explicit narrative of Leviticus. It is a short and violent counterpoint to the long festal section that precedes it. In fact, it seems to turn back to the previous legal chapters as a whole, dangling its angry and punitive weight over the entire law, as it summarizes in one bitter and explosive episode the whole character of creaturely life, family, nation, and devotion to God. Like Nadab and Abihu's role as historical embodiments of the sacrificial life in all of its emotional struggle, the nameless mixed-race son of the Israelite woman Shelomith seems to gather into his deathly resentment the whole burden of human obedience and faithfulness within the actual arena of temporal engagement. It is not surprising, then, if here, in this brief story of the law's discerning weight, we perceive the shadow of Christ Jesus as he stands and walks behind the torn family allegiances of Israel's flight from Egypt and the tangle of remorse and retaliation that follows it. The measure of God's daily gift of bread with which the last chapter ends, is now, in a sense, explored and shown to be the measure of the body eaten, the cross become a fruited tree.

This section of Leviticus contains one of the most famous verses of the book, 24:20, concerning the so-called *lex talionis*, "eye for eye, tooth for tooth," cited by Jesus in the Sermon on the Mount (Matt. 5:38; cf. 7:2). But by and large the narrative of Shelomith's son has generally pushed aside this key verse in Jewish interpretation, as if the ethical principle enunciated there has meaning only as emerging from the tortured argument over consanguinity and blasphemy that the story describes. This stands in contrast to Christian exegesis, which has shown little interest in the story itself, preferring to concentrate on the moral principle and at most its seeming perversion as retaliatory restitution. We shall see that, from a Christian point of view, narrative and principle are properly held together precisely by Jesus's own historical embodiment of their meaning.

The Shelomith story, propelled into the midst of the legal text, is, in its very unexpectedness, a disturbing intrusion: the son of a Jewish mother (Shelomith) and an Egyptian father has a quarrel with an Israelite and blasphemes God's name; on God's command, Moses has him stoned to death outside the camp. Jewish interpretation rapidly enfolded it within the drama of Moses and Israelite people, as if its only raison d'être could be found in its elucidation of a primal aspect of the nation (Ginzberg 1911: 3.689–91, with extensive references to talmudic and rabbinic material). These simply could not be random characters in Israel's story, useful only in illustrating in passing the consequences of brazen sin (a moral mostly amenable to rather lazy Christian exegesis). Rather, the rabbinic tradition indelibly fastened the human characters of the narrative to the central dynamics of the exodus. Who was Shelomith? She turns out (according to rabbinic tradition) to have been the wife of the Hebrew man whom Moses discovers being beaten by an Egyptian, an Egyptian whom Moses then murders and hides in the sand (Exod. 2:11–15). Indeed, the whole drama of sin, oppression, election, and vocational obedience is focused microcosmically in this story as elaborated by the tradition. After Shelomith was raped by an Egyptian, so the traditional narrative explained, Shelomith and her husband were threatened with their lives by the violator, and Moses saves the offended Hebrew man from the Egyptian's murderous rage. But Shelomith nonetheless gives birth to the rapist's progeny, a mixed-race bastard, who appears as an adult now in Lev. 24. His demand to be received into his mother's tribe—a detail from the tradition, which is meant to explain his fight with an Israelite that refigures the events of Exod. 2—sets in motion his rejection by Dan, giving rise to his blasphemous cursing and eventual execution by stoning, judged by the very man (and saint!) who killed his Egyptian father long ago. In its rabbinic elaboration, the story is graphic and lurid.

Rabbinic tradition saw in this story an example of the strange paradox of sin and deliverance. On the one hand, Shelomith is remembered as the *only* Israelite woman to have had sexual relations with an Egyptian until that time. Why else would the Scripture recall her name? In this, the sin of her Egyptian violator is stressed—a figure for all time of the Jewish nation's oppression—but so too is Shelomith's own unique subjection to his advances—another figure of Israel's future idolatries and debasements. Was not the exodus itself a reward for the persevering and heroic chastity of the Hebrew women under bondage, until this sole exception?[1] But Moses too was seen as tainted in this tangled history, as Scripture itself indicates through its account of the taunt of his fellow Hebrew (Exod. 2:11). "Look[ing] this way and that" before killing the Egyptian, Moses demonstrates his own dilemma: who was there to help this assaulted woman but himself? Yet in helping, did he not take human life into his own hands (an aspect stressed by *Rabbah* 32.4)? To be sure, deliverance for both the Hebrew husband

---

1. Hirsch 1989: 2.719–24 vigorously stresses Shelomith's role as a figure of sinning Israel, who rejects her own moral vocation under God.

and, through the figural chain, Israel itself derives from this episode. Yet far from simply recounting the courageous intervention of Moses into a situation of injustice, the story of Shelomith's rape and its consequences opens up the ambiguous mystery of moral struggle within Israel's history, where choices are made in the midst of competing evils, rather than in the light of obvious goods. Much as Nadab and Abihu's story unveils the shadows of love and desire, Shelomith's corridored past with the murdering Moses manifests the way that good and evil confront the human will in contexts of conflicted judgment and outcome.

Broadly diverse interpreters have recognized that this section of Leviticus, briefly told and starkly dramatic, concentrates upon the reality of an ordered existence under God's sovereign hand. Hirsch (1989: 2.725–29), for instance, fastens it solidly within his soaring ethical vision of human destiny, arguing that the very shape of the latter part of this chapter reflects the scope of God's moral calling to humanity through Israel. Leviticus 24:15–22 concludes with a comprehensive set of commands that move from blasphemy against God to human murder to the killing of animals to the injury of bodily parts—a series of injunctions that applies to Israelite and sojourning foreigner alike. This series, for Hirsch, is a deliberate construction that locates all human choice within the framework of the personal God, who founds the free exercise of the will through his own acts of grace, imparted to human beings through the created image that they share with him. Without such a personal God, there is no such thing as an intrinsic human dignity, and apart from the giving of the law and the distinctions in kind among all creatures, the moral structures of the world through which this dignity is expressed would collapse. The possibility of blaspheming God and the consequences of its reality thus embrace the chain of categories that here actually concretize the coincidences of creation's diversity and moral demand: for God to create freely *means*, according to Hirsch, that human beings must make choices that bear consequences from within their rich relations within the world, including human and animal flesh.

Origen hints at something similar from a more limited Christian perspective, when he compares the struggle between Shelomith's son and the Israelite in 24:10 to a paradigmatic moral struggle within each of us (*Homilies on Leviticus* 14.1–4). As in Exod. 1–2, the Egyptian and Hebrew quarrel expresses the rootedness of sin within even the Christian and hence explains the need for continual penitence and cleansing on the part of the believing follower of Christ. For Origen, Lev. 24:15–16 becomes the focal interpretive verses of the passage, since they imply, he says, that there is a gain to dying in the flesh as opposed to "bearing one's sin" for eternity, to mortifying the flesh in repentance as opposed to suffering in hell (Luke 12:4–5). But even from this typically ascetic perspective Origen also sees the story of the blasphemer as one that exposes a broader reality of moral struggle in general. And, as implicating the entire created world, from the sanctified heart to the wide intention of God's creatures in nation and history, this struggle is not to be simply resolved by the hope of some divine influx signified by the lights of the altar (Lev. 24:1–9). We are not freed from moral struggle simply because God is gracious and comes to our aid.

The presentation of the *lex talionis* as a legal consequence to the blasphemer's actions seems to respond to this reality, as it provides almost an ideal summary of the struggle's outcome, a kind of moral stability in which balance is restored among competing—and injuring—parties. "Eye for eye, tooth for tooth" (24:20) uncovers, at the base of the moral struggle at work in the world, an intense striving after equality of life, and it pulls our attention to the primordial figures of Cain and Abel, of Jacob and Esau, of the prodigal and his elder brother seething under the weight of seeming paternal distinctions, of the importuning sibling who demands that Jesus "bid [his] brother to divide the inheritance" with him (Luke 12:13). Still, though the *lex talionis* may bespeak the urge for this equilibrium, its very figures (such as those just enumerated) within the history of Scripture point to its incapacity to render whole the perceived distortions. "Who made me a judge or divider" among the people (12:14)? Is the moral order of the world, hoped for and grasped after by human agents, in fact attainable?

In any case, the issue of equality, in a literal sense, was judged as being impossibly applied by the tradition, both Jewish and Christian. The Babylonian Talmud pointed out with respect to Exod. 21:22–27 that "eye for eye" cannot apply to eyeless people, nor can "tooth for tooth" apply to those who are without teeth (tractate *Bava Qamma* 84a). The issue is rather one of fittingness and dignity within the larger demands of the law, according to Exod. 21:21 with respect to slaves. Personal retribution is prohibited (Lev. 19:18), and therefore the challenge of justice in the face of injury and even evil is resolved only through some measurement higher than the exact proportion of material harm. It is that measure that the moral struggle of the world illuminates.

We see this in Jesus's use of the *lex talionis* in Matt. 5:38–42 and Luke 6:27–38. Jesus does not reject the character of fittingness in the historical outworking of moral struggle: "measure for measure" retains its descriptive force (Luke 6:38; Matt. 7:2). But here the measure itself is redescribed, now in terms of nonretaliation, forgiveness, and the actual love of enemies. This *is* a true measure of sorts, but the measure becomes God's own self, whose goodness toward the ungrateful and the evil (Luke 6:35) is a good measure precisely because it overflows specifically *human* measuring. All the inequalities of the world, which feed the violence and reactive uncertainties of Shelomith's blaspheming son, set into the midst of a people toward whose history his own status is an affront, are filled in and overwhelmed by the gift of God's self-giving grace, which draws along with it the flailing efforts of the morally calculating and perverse hearts of his people. So Jesus would have it.

And Jesus would have it thus because he has taken for himself the very form of the struggle that Shelomith's blaspheming son engages: the form of the *mamzer*, the mixed-race bastard. This is the link that joins the pointed drama of Lev. 24 with its abstracted ending: Jesus *joins* the son of the violated Hebrew woman.

Although the exact definition of the *mamzer* within Jewish tradition changes over time, its general meaning finds its fulfillment in Jesus (Chilton 2006). While originally the status of the *mamzer* may have designated solely those born to adulterous or incestuous unions (Lev. 18:20; Deut. 23:2, following on 22:13–30), it also came to identify those from mixed marriages (Babylonian Talmud, tractate *Qiddushin* 70a). The Deuteronomic exclusion from Israel of the *mamzer* up to "ten generations" (Deut. 23:2) was perhaps one spur to the eventual definition of matrilineal descent as the bearer of Jewish identity. Shelomith's son was, in this light, born before this legal elucidation, and his status as a *mamzer* was seen by the rabbis as an integral part of his conflicted relationship not only with Israel but with God.

The *mamzer* in this case blasphemes (a word indicating a wound or piercing); he "curses the name of God," as Rashi explains it (Rosenbaum and Silbermann 1932: 111). What does this signify? For many, the curse arises from and reflects the identity of the one who curses: born of evil roots—the first Hebrew adulteress (despite also being a victim), remembered by name for eternity in her sin—his words simply mirror his origins, the sins of parents visited upon their children. His is a story almost too wretched to tell, but morally instructive in its ghastliness, as the *Me'am Lo'ez* remarks (Kaplan 1982: 12.236–37). To *be* a *mamzer* is itself a curse, a blight upon human creaturehood and a mark speaking to the universe of the reality of human sin as it drags down generations. Yet this cannot be the end of the story for its immediate participants, anymore than it is for Israel as a whole in its own history. Is not Israel itself engaged in the whoredom of Shelomith, however one wishes to parse the blame? So *Rabbah* 32.7 here injects a long note of regretful hope. In line with a previous tradition (Tosefta, tractate *Qiddushin* 5.4), it turns to Ezek. 36:25 ("I will sprinkle clean water upon you, and you shall be clean") and applies this verse, via Israel, to the *mamzer* himself: the *mamzer* will be purified one day, in the age to come, and will join fully in Israel's own restoration. If we hope at all, we must hope for the *mamzer*. And Shelomith's son and his cursing and sordid end—an end that Moses himself had a hand in making possible—becomes a strange figure of *redemption* for the *Rabbah*, born out of the compromises of human moral decision and the holiness of God in its face.

But how born? Born just as Jesus is himself born, of a virgin. The question of Jesus's own birth status was raised by detractors of the Christian faith, both pagan and Jewish, from the early centuries. Was Jesus himself not the bastard son of a woman, Mary, whose own loose living demanded strange tales of divine intervention to explain it away?[2] Traces of the origins of these charges can still be found in John 8:41, where those arguing with Jesus over true descent from Abraham accuse him of being a child of "prostitution" (*porneia*), no doubt building on the tales surrounding his birth. Although modern scholars have

2. See Celsus's charge, apparently commonly made, in Origen's *Against Celsus* 1.2. On the talmudic claims of Jesus's parentage, see Chilton 2006.

once again taken up some of these ancient snippets of prurient gossip, there ought to be little room for doubt as to the Christian *theological* significance of the charge, quite apart from discussions on how Mary's relationship to Joseph might be defined according to the Mishnah on this question. Leaving all these details aside, on the basis of the New Testament's and the church's own claims regarding Jesus's virgin birth, Jesus was most definitely a *mamzer*, a divine *mamzer* to be sure, born of a woman without a human husband as the child's father. Jesus inserts himself into Shelomith's story as another, analogous son, taking upon himself the separations and chasms caused by sin itself, the chasm of sexual disorder and genealogical division and incompleteness, starting with the angels themselves (Gen. 6:1–4) and entering the depths of the only chasm by which life is given and not simply lost, the chasm of God's own creative act: the word became flesh (John 1:14). Hence, there is hope for Shelomith's son, for Israel, and for all flesh together.

To be sure, the New Testament does not dwell on this means by which hope is born, anymore than Shelomith's son becomes a byword for the nations. Israel *itself* becomes the latter, and Jesus, the *mamzer*, is swept up by his fate into currents that go beyond the anger and distaste over descent. Yet his strange genealogy stands at the threshold of the gospel (Matt. 1:16), and his death for blasphemy stands at the gospel's end, upon a cross whose palpable expression of God's self-giving breaks down the whole reality of mixed-race bastardy altogether (Eph. 2:11–18). Indeed, the blasphemy of Shelomith's son hangs all about the cross: Son of God or Son of Man?—blasphemy! (Matt. 26:65). Destroyer or rebuilder of the temple? Savior of Israel?—cursed! (27:39–43). Fulfiller of the law and all its moral demands?—anathema! (Gal. 3:10–14). Bearer of God?—sin itself! (2 Cor. 5:21). Driven outside the camp (Lev. 24:23; Heb. 13:11–12), the divine *mamzer* makes all good in the other world, the place where thieves and sinners find their hope, for they discover how God alone is able to pass to such a place (Luke 23:43). Although the divine *mamzer* declares that there is "neither Jew nor Greek" any longer (Gal. 3:28), it is a declaration made only on the cross. Redemption is not affirmation but re-creation.

In this sense, the cross alone embraces and makes clear the nature of the moral struggle, in all its ambiguities, that Shelomith exhibits, pulling Moses and Israel, children and violators, into its grip and displaying the true measure of God. This measure sweeps up the long division that runs from Cain and Abel to the end of Malachi (2:10–12) and finds its resolution in the one new man, in *his* form and being, given on the cross (Eph. 2:15). Root, branch, and graft are now joined (Rom. 11:16–24) in the new home for which Cain himself sought from the beginning (Gen. 4:12–13), the home of God (Eph. 2:19–22) wherein the children of the *mamzer* have become heirs again (Rom. 8:15–17) with the children of the true Father. It is a broad and deep measure (11:33–36), beyond sounding, by which all that is fitting and just is ordered. Every claim to a portion, every demand for restitution, every clamor for return resonates with God's response, the divine blasphemy of launching his own being into and beyond the grip of human measurement itself.

The final matter of blasphemy in Jesus's death is paramount within this context. Jesus himself points only to a mysterious sin "against the Holy Spirit" as the un-forgivable "blasphemy" (Mark 3:28–29; Luke 12:10). But what blasphemy could this be? Is it not the turning away from the divine giving and sacrifice itself? Jesus's own death is this work of the Holy Spirit, an offering of himself (Heb. 9:14) by which God's measure is placed upon the world. The medieval commentators (e.g., *Glossa ordinaria* [Patrologia latina 113.366–67]) often linked the vanity referred to in the third commandment of the Decalogue (Exod. 20:7) to a particular sin, namely, the rejection of Jesus's two natures, the basis not only of his status as a *mamzer* but the embodiment of God's work of re-creating love, in which death is given and resurrection taken. To deny *this*, the pneumatic conception of the cross, is to deny the redemptive outcome to the moral struggle of subjection and self-offering to God, a struggle whose deep secrets and failures find their own healing in this one act of God's.

This is the great question and hope posed by Moses's killing of the Egyptian, in its own way a teasing apart of the inexplicable murder of our primordial frat-ricide, whereby Moses looks for aid, finds none, except the unexpected coming of God into the midst of the morally corrupting oppression of which he is a part. Karl Shapiro, in his poem "The Murder of Moses," meditates on the shadowed background from which Israel's leading arises: "You and your black wife might have been foreigners," the Hebrew narrator reflects; "we even discussed your parentage; were you really a Jew?" (2003: 113). Were you perhaps *also* a *mamzer*? Yet, in retrospect, after all the suffering and heroism and simple devotion and compassion of Moses has been exhausted and the people have made their way to Canaan without him, they look back on the remarkable consequence of this man's ambiguous struggle, offered to God:

> At the end of it all we gave you the gift of death.
> Invasion and generalship were spared you.
> The hand of our direction, resignedly you fell,
> And while officers prepared for the river-crossing
> The Old God blessed you and covered you with earth.
>
> Though you were mortal and once committed murder
> You assumed the burden of the covenant,
> Spoke for the world and for our understanding.
> Converse with God made you a thinker,
> Taught us all early justice, made us a race. (2003: 114–15)

This is possible: the head of Israel pokes out into time from the dust of the wilderness, because God's own love not only calls within this tangle. It binds its own power to it, so that the ambiguities of Israel's moral lives need not drown and so mark our own moral failures finally, but might even become a sort of measure for history's larger flailings. Israel teaches the nations as it points us to God's blasphemy. And God's blasphemy is this: the face of Shelomith's son, now assumed by his own Son, does not open its mouth in a curse (1 Pet. 2:23), though banished from his own people (John 1:11; Heb. 13:13–14). To deny this is to deny love. It is to deny God.

LEVITICUS 25–26

Leviticus 24 explicates the blasphemous measure of the cross, by which Israel's moral struggle is allowed to stand within the world's history as a guide. The discussion of the Jubilee in Lev. 25 concretizes this divine measure for human life in temporal terms (just as festal reality, described in Lev. 23, does this for sacrifice): the measure is that of "allness," God's all in all (1 Cor. 15:28). The measure is not one of self-sufficiency, however, whereby God somehow "returns to himself." The measure is rather one of created communion between God and the world he has set into existence from nothing apart from himself. The Jubilee is about the things God has created as they make their way back to their Father, like prodigals. In historical terms, it is the *apokatastasis*, or "restoration" of Israel's created life, mentioned by the apostles in Acts 1:6 and communally embodied after a fashion in the early Jerusalem community (on the model of Deut. 15:4, but also of the Jubilee) in Acts 3:21 and 4:34. But because it is the measure of the cross as it organizes the entire world—and this is the weight of Lev. 26 in particular—the Jubilee points more substantively to the "plan for the fulness of time" that marks the mystery of God's will in Eph. 1:9–10, not as a *reditus*, a "return" of fragmented divinity into the wholeness of God's being, but as an *anakephalaiōsis*, in Paul's term, as a "gathering" into coherence under an ordering reality of the head, a gathering in fullness, of land, families, produce, human freedom and work, in Lev. 25's terms. This is the fullness of God's creative intention returned to God's own redemptive sovereignty. The Jubilee is the final measure of time itself, as the offering of all things is made possible by the offering of the maker of all things.

Homecoming

The very meaning of the term "Jubilee" is indicative of this joining of history and creation under God's redemptive sway. And in examining the word and its referent(s) we realize that its reach goes far beyond the calendrically regular reorganizing of property, inheritance, and servitude described directly in the text. First mentioned in 25:10 and then acting as the touchstone for the rest of this second longest chapter in the book (after Lev. 13), the Jubilee is never itself explained as a word. In the modern age, since the seventeenth century, it has been generally assumed that the word *yovel* refers to the trumpets used to signal the beginning of the Jubilee year (25:9). Exodus 19:13 and Josh. 6:4 speak of the *yovel* in such an instrumental context. But in these cases, the horn itself is referred to more explicitly as the *shofar*, and it is rather the sound that the *yovel* designates than the instrument itself to which the word refers. Is it in fact the sound of celebration, such that Lamech's son Jubal (Gen. 4:21), the "father of those who play the lyre," is made the ancestor to the sounds of praise that finally mark (via Latin etymology) the work of "jubilation"?

Nahmanides (1974: 436–38), however, established an alternative explanation, one that read *yovel* as the source of a movement, a sense that can be seen in the river of Jer. 17:8. The Jubilee here, he cryptically explained, is tied to the secret of creation, of creating itself, and to its origins. Kabbalistic interpretation, in which Nahmanides himself was engaged, took this up in discussions according to which the seven-year sabbatical (*shemittah*) of Lev. 25:1–7 and the Jubilee existed as two principles of creation to be resolved only in the new age. Rabbinic views, in any case, maintained the etymology with some consistency, refining the explication of *yovel* in terms of a movement *back* to its source, as the *Me'am Lo'ez* (Kaplan 1982: 12.249) remarks with respect to Ps. 76:11. Hirsch (1989: 2.739), finally, takes this tradition and makes sense of it, describing the causative form of *yovel* as an act "of suitable bringing, to bring a person to where he is suited to be, or a thing to whom it really belongs." Thus, he finally translates *yovel* as "home-bringing" and the Jubilee as a returning home, a returning to the source of all things who distributes them, a restoration to God's own true purpose. The meaning of Lev. 25 falls into place within this context.

As a measurement of time, the Sabbath year and Jubilee therefore describe how history finds its home with God and reveals its true purpose. The seven-year sabbatical (25:1–7) is designed to provide a "sabbath for the land," during which fields are not sowed and vineyards dressed, but rather the people and animals, domestic and wild, sustain themselves from the natural yield of the land itself. Here, the land returns to its created abundance, and creatures receive from it as in the original purpose of Gen. 1. The Jubilee year, which follows a Sabbath of Sabbath years, that is, forty-nine years, and so falls on each fiftieth year, takes up the rest of Lev. 25 and extends the elements of the Sabbath year to a range of human relations. Not only is the land given its Sabbath from agricultural labor, but families return to their inheritance, debts are forgiven, and slaves are freed. The detail of the chapter involves in part the application of the Jubilee year's arrival to the valuation of property and service, and the fiftieth year becomes the marker according to which payments for redemption are calculated in the intervening period. Social measurements, thereby, are shaped by the Jubilee measurement of time, which imposes a deeper meaning upon all transactions, labor, movement, and economic possession, through its final enforcement of a return to some more fundamental set of arrangements and reality.

The commandment of the *shemittah* was first given with the original revelation of the law in Exod. 23:10–11. Why is the law of the Jubilee year given only now, presumably with the second revelation to Moses on the mountain (hence the special mentioning of the words of "the LORD . . . to Moses on Mount Sinai" in Lev. 25:1)? Christian interpretation tended to read the reference to Sinai here in terms of Paul's allegory in Gal. 4, placing the entire discussion within the shadow of the law's slavery and thereby, in a fundamental way, rejecting the chapter's theological pertinence altogether as another example of an overcome past. But the reference to the Jubilee year's beginning according to the celebration of the Day of Atonement (Lev. 25:9) points in another direction, as rabbinic exegesis made clear: the law of the Jubilee is given only in light of Israel's *sin* and, in particular, the sin of the golden calf, which is such a prominent reference point to the whole of the narrative location of Leviticus. Only *after* Aaron and the people slide into apostasy is this law revealed from Sinai in the second revelation to Moses. And in this way, the law's meaning is tied to the forgiveness and restoration that lies at the center of God's work with Israel and thereby with history in general. Beyond the Sabbath, given in the first revelation of the law, God now points Israel and the world to the Sabbath of Sabbaths.

The Homecoming of the Ages

Hence, the Jubilee year becomes a traditional measurement of the ages. One sees this most clearly in the book of Jubilees (second century BC), actually a part of the Ethiopian church's canon. Here, the entire history of the world from creation to exodus, given through a specific revelation to Moses on Sinai, is retold according to a scheme of "Jubilees," or sets of forty-nine years. This history itself contains a shadow for the future. Daniel 9:20–27 had already presented this form of historical calculation, through a prophecy regarding the history of Israel's coming life, from exile to restoration, to the world's final conflagration. This prophecy is given in "seventy weeks of years," that is, seventy *shemittahs*, and thus ten Jubilee years—a complete round of God's creative engagement with Israel, in this case with its sin, through the full "finishing" of its transgression and the "atoning" of its iniquities. Rightly speaking, then, the Jubilee emerges within the context of Israel's *failures*, precisely the moral struggle of Lev. 24 by which God's measure is offered for its transformation. Sin and redemption are made the essence of historical experience, the very way of God's fashioning of time. The central Jewish tradition regarding the length of the captivity reflects this insight, according to which the seventy years of the captivity were due to seventy missed *shemittah*s, from the entry into the promised land to the destruction of the temple (490 years) (Mishnah, tractate *Avot* 5.9). Indeed, there is little or no evidence of the laws of Lev. 25 ever having been enacted. And the only clear reference to them elsewhere in Scripture—Jer. 34:8–22—is to Israel's failure to follow through with this covenant. The seven-fold punishments for Israel's transgression of the law detailed in Lev. 26 mirror this temporal scheme and demonstrate the measuring character of the preceding explanations of the Jubilee in their *negative* judgment.

Christians also took up this historically schematizing application of the Jubilee as a means of uncovering God's purposes. By the fourteenth century, the Roman Catholic church had initiated an ecclesial version of the Jubilee year, proclaiming the first "plenary indulgence" for the year 1300 and formalizing (in the 1342 bull *Unigenitus dei filius*) the figural meaning of the penitential implications with the second Jubilee of 1350.[1] These were taken up in chiliastic projections of an imminent future age of forgiveness, delivered by the Spirit and identified in advance through the calculation of Sabbath years according to Daniel's instructions. Even though the Reformers rejected the contemporary practices associated with this new revival of Jubilee thinking, they maintained the measure as the mark of God's forgiveness in history. Hugh Broughton, a Puritan and biblical chronologist of enormous sophistication and detail, in his highly influential *A Concent of Scripture* (1588) argued that Christ's passion falls upon the Jubilee and hence that his suffering and death fulfills the Jubilee's typical meaning. Both Jewish and Christian interpreters took hold of the Jubilee measurement as a means of structuring an array of dispensationalist speculation, which flourished not only in medieval (*Glossa ordinaria* [Patrologia latina 113.368–71]) and Reformation periods, but also evolved finally into modern Christian Zionism.[2]

The Homecoming of Mercy

The point here is not simply to note the imaginative sway that the Jubilee has held on interpreters, but more specifically and deeply, the way that, even at their most fanciful, interpreters have sensed at a deep level how the Sabbath years and Jubilee, precisely in their concrete demands for the measurement of Israel's time, are to reflect the *work* and purpose of God. And that work, at its base, is one of mercifully reordering creation's dislocating forces. *Rabbah* 33.1–5, not surprisingly, gets to the heart of this fundamental purpose of the Jubilee. Concentrating first on Lev. 25's interest in *forbidding* certain actions on the Jubilee, the *Rabbah* focuses upon the kinds of sins that Israel itself commits: lying, gossip, fraud, robbery, even public humiliation of others. The chapter therefore opens up a vista upon

1. This was built on the already elaborated scholastic theories of indulgences and linked to the developed offer of plenary indulgences tied to the Crusades.
2. See Finkel 2003 and Sizer 2005. For a more detailed look at the seventeenth-century English background, see Glaser 2007.

Israel's own responsibility before God in time, which ends up by structuring its own fate: the liberated slave of Lev. 25 becomes exiled Israel awaiting God's mercy as it languishes among the nations. Interestingly, it is not Dan. 9 but Dan. 3 that is brought in by the *Rabbah* to illuminate this reality: the call to faithfulness in martyred suffering. Israel's own place among the nations is difficult, subtle, and intertwined, as an appeal to Deut. 32 makes clear. Leviticus 25, in this light, encloses not just a promise of deliverance, but the fullness of Israel's own disordered life with the world's arena. The land of Israel—within which the particulars of this drama are described in Lev. 25—becomes, not a protected corner of the globe, but the topological figure of the world as a whole. Sin is exposed as upsetting the order of individuals, Israel, and nations. And the measure of this process is one by which God pulls the world, in the reflected experience of Israel, back into its created form—the ultimate act of mercy upon that which God has made.

The common Christian reading of the Jubilee in terms of Jesus's vocation, outlined in Luke 4:16–21, needs to be read in this light. As Jesus refers the "acceptable year of the Lord" from Isa. 61:2 to himself, he is describing (as is generally understood) the fulfillment of the Jubilee year's provisions.[3] But this must be understood not simply in terms of specific actions by which Lev. 25's details are finally made good, as if Jesus's claim added up simply to a renewed political manifesto to be promulgated among his followers. "Today this scripture has been fulfilled in your hearing" refers more broadly to the larger history of God's dealing with Israel's failure as it mirrors the life of creation and evokes God's own response. His claim is much closer, that is, to the prayer he teaches by which God measures the world through the conformance of our lives to God's own act of mercy: "Forgive us our debts, as we also have forgiven our debtors" (Matt. 6:12), which becomes the image of all transgression (6:14–15). This is the *aphesis* ("release, forgiveness"), not only of Luke 4:18, but of John the Baptist's preaching (3:3) and, more inclusively, of the cross and its "riches of . . . grace" for all of creation (Eph. 1:7). It is also the name used in the Greek Septuagint to translate *yovel* in its literal form (e.g., Lev. 25:12). If the Jubilee is fulfilled in Jesus, it is only because it remains *un*fulfilled in Israel and in the world, and the particularities of God's self-offering in response become its true expression.

What comes to the fore in Lev. 25, therefore, is the way that God's mercy—embodied in the historical acts of salvation (25:38, 42, 55)—represents a drawing close again of God's foundational purpose for our lives in the midst of our

3. That Isa. 61:1–2 refers explicitly to the Jubilee is doubtful. Rather it takes up, metaphorically at best, a number of elements associated with the Jubilee, especially the proclamation of liberty (or release) in 6:1, that are a part of the general promise tied to the Servant's mission (49:8–9). The promise here, however, is less structured according to the temporal measurement that the Jubilee implies and is more depicted in terms of a new age altogether. If in fact the Jubilee in particular is fulfilled in Jesus, it is its temporal measure that finds its embodiment in his life, not simply the principles of reordered social life. This measure involves his own time, his own walking, his own ordering of his actions and life in terms of offering.

rejection of it, a communion given by God's own self within the specific history of our departure and alienation from it. The freight borne by the chapter is its own history of enunciation and rejection, which unveils God's own performance of its meaning and that in *this* unveiling marks the way we live in *God's* own land (25:23): God is our host, who shares *his* home with us. *Yovel* is *this* kind of homecoming, a drawing back into something that is not ours and cannot be ours in any way but through the infinite offer of grace.

The Servitude of Homecoming

The paradox involved in such a homecoming has always been obvious to commentators: God frees us to be his guests; he gives us a home that is not ours at its root. This paradox is lodged concretely within the social character of the chapter, which has proved Lev. 25's central interest since early modern times, but an interest often limiting the chapter's actual meaning. Joined with Luke 4, this social thrust has more recently formed the basis of an entire modern liberal and radical political theology. Within this modern perspective, the question of ownership of property has been prominent, with arguments in the seventeenth century already centering around whether the "Anabaptistickal" claim to a community of goods could be upheld by the Jubilee laws.[4] The economic assertions of Christian socialism continued this debate. In general, the traditional answers, both Jewish and Christian, tended toward a dispensationalist response to the challenge: the provisions of the Jubilee, according to rabbinic exegesis, pertain only to Israel's tribal allocation of the land and hence become moot following the destruction of the temple and the dispersion; in Christian reading, the provisions are fulfilled in the expiatory poverty of Christ (so Willet 1631: 654) and lose their exemplary and legal status. But the question of ownership is nonetheless rightly central to Lev. 25, although perhaps in a nonstructural way, since God as "owner" does not easily parse into stable social structures. Inequalities of wealth are obviously presupposed in the chapter, otherwise there would be no return to family heritage and forgiveness of debts to be regularly followed according to the measurements of unfolding time. Indeed, where it comes to the walled cities of 25:30, such inequalities are actually positively maintained. And even when addressed, their abolition is not so clear as to provide a blueprint for an ongoing reordering of social ties.

What *is* clear is that both Sabbath and Jubilee years regularly place rich and poor in the same position as to the source of their sustenance, who is God alone. Rashi (Rosenbaum and Silbermann 1932: 114, 116–17) and the entire rabbinic tradition point out that "the sabbath of the land" (25:6, 20–24) means that all live off the same divine provision from the fields' natural fruit, that all become

4. Article 38 of the Anglican Thirty-Nine Articles of Religion focuses explicitly on this issue.

gleaners after a fashion. And if, as is generally accepted, the Jubilee year *follows* the forty-ninth year's sabbatical injunctions, this would mean two years in a row of such common receipt. Every seven years, and double on the forty-ninth and fiftieth, the rich learn "worry," such as the poor always have (Deut. 28:67); but they also learn complete and utter dependence upon God, which is the practical purpose of the laws. "God is the master of the Universe," the *Me'am Lo'ez* (Kaplan 1982: 12.245) concludes when discussing this particular topic. And the specific moral commands regarding just dealing (Lev. 25:35–55) derive from this reality that everything reverts to God as the true owner of all things: "The land is mine" (25:23). Hence one can never succeed in truly or permanently stealing anything, and the very notion of "cheating" is ruled out as a lasting stratagem for human behavior. *Rabbah* 34 indicates that the chapter's interest is less prescriptive and turns more to the narrative realities of social interaction within time, such as those given in Jesus's parable of the rich man and Lazarus (Luke 16:19–31). Here the issue is mercy ignored and the literal chasm that mercy's foiled purpose creates: unless a bridge across is found, mercy melts into a darkness that overwhelms the land.

That the provisions of Lev. 25 are meant to touch even the animals and beasts of the land (25:7) points out the reach of this merciful dependence that the Sabbath year and Jubilee offer. Not only does it reveal the actual goal of creation in its paradisiacal form, but it also indicates God's historical assertion of this form, renewed in time through the submission of Israel to its reality again and again precisely because of its failure, again and again, to be grasped by its truth. The poor are to be "maintained" as "brothers" (25:35–55), as Abel and Cain before the seizure of murderous envy, because all people belong only to God, as "strangers and sojourners," like Cain himself. Usury is forbidden (25:36) because all money and all goods belong to God and will return to God willy-nilly, dust to dust. Servitude and slavery are to be regularly expunged from the land and from lived relations (25:39–41, 47–55), for the people of Israel as a whole are servants to God (25:55), whom God alone orders and redeems.

None of this is easily resolved in practice—hence the historical measurement of its implementation, repeatedly demanded over time, as if God were pressing Israel into a place of truth it always resists and whose resistance itself informs the character of the calling. What does it mean to free those in servitude for the sake of asserting the entire people's servitude to God? Israel's resistance to the Jubilee becomes plain in the context of Jesus's own discussion of slavery and freedom (Mark 10:43–45): his mission is to *be* a slave to all, a slave in a very palpable manner—for example, the washing of feet and finally the giving up of his life—precisely *because* of the human rejection of God's demanded liberty. This becomes Jesus's very being (Phil. 2:5–11), and it gives rise to Paul's own discussion of power, whereby rights are given up for the sake of the gospel's truth, that is, the truth of Jesus's own liberating self-offering (1 Cor. 9). The slave of God—and, for God's sake, the slave of others—is the only truly free person because he or she is bound to and by the mercy of God. Pilate claims to have the power to release Jesus (John 19:10–11), but Jesus instead claims the power as God's, and therefore his own failure to be released becomes the Jubilee of the world's own redemption.

This paradox of God's slave as the free person who makes others free lies at the historical root of slavery's only slow dissolution within the Christian church and culture, a delay that many have taken as a brazen repudiation of the Jubilee's evident significance. It is a tardiness that has much vexed idealists, with the practical tension over it firmly lodged in the Scriptures themselves (e.g., the discussion of slaves and masters in 1 Pet. 2:13–25): to be a slave of Christ and in the form of Christ must necessarily put one in a position of powerlessness before the rejecting social powers of enslavement. At the same time, there is an obvious sense that human slavery's conscious disappearance was inevitable from the start of Jesus's self-offering for the sake of the slave himself, something that the letter to Philemon indicates.[5] To be free is to give oneself to God; to grant freedom is to die for those who are enchained. The contorted justifications of slavery in rabbinic law, as well as in Christian circles during the revival of slavery in the sixteenth–nineteenth centuries, do not undercut this inevitability; they only demonstrate its particular locale within the complete—and therefore humanly difficult and frightening—self-giving of Jesus, a truth that sets free only within the infinite and thus incomprehensible act of divine mercy to the fallen. As both Jewish and Christian exegesis of Lev. 25 insists over and over, freedom can only be *for* God, never *from* God.[6]

The Shape of Home

In the end, the descriptive character of the Jubilee release and its social details are given less fully in the stories of free people than in the parable of tenants. Here the issue is, as Leviticus stresses in its repeated assertion that the land is God's and that Israel is but a sojourner within it, the behavior due to the true owner. God asks for what is his, and the tenants reject the offer, to the point of killing the offerer. This outcome becomes the center of focus in Lev. 26. But without the injustice of ingrate and cruel tenancy, the redemptive power of the killing of the owner's son would have little traction, for it is both the killing by those who by rights own nothing and the merciful offer by the wronged owner itself that provide freedom, the mark of mercy that allows for tenancy at all. Like the prodigal son, the *social* order envisioned by the Jubilee is one of mercy and finally forgiveness—which

5. See the stimulating, if debated, discussion of early Christianity in Patterson 1991.

6. One interesting reading of the temporal measure of the Jubilee, in this context, is given by the *Me'am Lo'ez*: for the first fifty years of adult life (the first ten years of childhood do not count in this calculation), a man works according to the standards of earthly toil; but at age sixty, he is to be freed from this curse and become a slave to God, giving himself over to the study of the Torah in the Jubilee of his old age (Kaplan 1982: 12.249–50).

does not order life in a utopian manner, but rather gathers history (ordered in a variety of ways potentially) in the direction of God's own coming to it and suffering for it. Mercy presupposes self-giving in the face of rejection. The Jubilee provisions—details that, when groped after in actual time, can bring only social anguish for all the resistances brought against them—shine the light of mercy upon the reality of rejection.

So Origen interprets the Jubilee in terms of the history of penitence (*Homilies on Leviticus* 15.1–3). Struggling to understand the various kinds of dwellings that Lev. 25 details—houses in the country, houses within the city, houses of the Levites—he reads each as a figure of the human soul mired in earthly sin, as it attempts to survive the reality of God's holy demands: will it stand (Matt. 7:24–27)? And the Jubilee provisions of redemption refer, he argues, to the different degrees of fallenness that each type of house represents, that are transformed through the turning of the house-dweller to God in repentance (the Levites representing the soul of the saints). The point for Origen is that the measure of time given by the Jubilee is the measure of sin's history of redemption, in its variety. The true home of Christians, after all, is in heaven (2 Cor. 5:1), and earthly homes are in fact withheld from them (Mark 6:9), to whom possessions are forbidden. The chapter's social reorderings, then, point to the struggle to let go of and be released from what drags us down in sin. This proved to be the general reading of the chapter by Catholic exegetes for centuries (e.g., Bernard and Bossuet). It should not exclude the social challenges of the Jubilee; but it ought to locate them within a history that is far more complex than policy articulation. This is so especially when Lev. 25 is read in conjunction with Lev. 26: the reordering of social and economic ties called for by Lev. 25 is a struggle carried on in the face of human refusal to accept its complete dependence upon God; it is therefore a struggle whose full resolution comes only in the form of martyrdom.[7] In this context, the house that is assumed in Lev. 25 is both creation's (Ps. 84) and that built upon the rock that is Christ's life, death, and resurrection. Origen's call is to the home—and thus the home-bringing or *yovel*—that emerges within this temporal conjunction of creation and Christ, that is thus time's fulfillment in cross, suffering, and charity.

It is important to see this conjunction clearly, for the true *yovel* is the "going back" to a specific reality, the creative act of God himself and all that this act implies. Because it is God's act to which true tenancy testifies, the very act of making from nothing something outside of God's self, its human response is one without anxiety, where all is joyful dependence: "Fear not, little flock, for it is your Father's good pleasure to give you the kingdom" (Luke 12:32); "by grace you have been

7. The "city of God"—figured by the walled gatherings that Lev. 25 exempts from the Jubilee provisions (a distinction that much exercises Hirsch 1989: 2.758–59)—points to a realm beyond this struggle. The provisions themselves, on the other hand, point to temporal struggles of individual vocation and historical destiny that necessarily find the fulfillment of the calls to social justice only within the self-offering of discipleship.

saved" (Eph. 2:5, 8); "what have you that you did not receive?" (1 Cor. 4:7). This is the story of creation as given in Col. 1:15–20, where family and land, fruit and plants, beasts and cattle—all stand before God in their purposive fullness. But it is a fullness given as Christ Jesus himself "goes to the Father," in the second creation of making all things new (2 Cor. 5:17; Rev. 21:5), taking all back to the Father, in its moral integrity and discreteness (Eph. 1:10). The Jubilee measures time, not according to points of achievement, but as a movement, wherein all the animals and people and relations are brought together again through the fullness of the gospel's temporal expression. When Jesus says in the Nazareth synagogue that "today this scripture has been fulfilled," he means the "today" of temptations, preaching, healing, hungering, feeding, healing, weakening, dying, and rising, the "today" of *his* existence. Rather than laying out "Sabbath time as utopian time"— the new age yet to be embraced—Jesus's Sabbath becomes his own life, no more and no less. And the creation of all things "through him and for him" (Col. 1:16) is fulfilled in suffering for the sake of others (1:24), not as a partial aspect, but as its very temporal embodiment. Against any fully articulated dispensationalism, the *yovel* into which all things are gathered, the head (Col. 1:18; Eph. 1:22; 4:15), is the head crowned with thorns.

The Shape of Coming

Leviticus 26 follows naturally from this insight and so must be read in direct conjunction with the Jubilee (as the text itself indicates by not providing it with a new divine locutionary sign) and not simply as a general set of warnings about the law. Traditionally known as the *tokhachoth* ("admonitions") in rabbinic Judaism, this section (likewise the admonitions in Deut. 28:15–68) demanded special regard in public reading, for the cantor was forbidden to break off the reading in the middle of the curses.[8] This was to emphasize both the gravity of the warnings and also the completeness of its explication, for which no abbreviation was permitted. As Lev. 26:18 points out, there is to be a sevenfold punishment for Israel's sins in breaking the law, a numerical qualification that links its divine imposition to the sabbatical character of the law itself, as just articulated in the previous chapter (see *Sifra* 266.1). The admonitions are thus drawn into direct relationship with the Sabbath year and the Jubilee, and the latter's promises are likewise tied to potential (and real) divine curses. The Jubilee provisions are bound to God's ownership of Israel, expressed in the first table of the law (26:1–2) and embodied in a promise of blessing (Deut. 28:3–13), which then blossom into a much fuller elaboration of punishment. Blessing and curse go together, then, as the outworking of time's measure. And the blessings, no more than the curses, can stand alone as simple explicators of God's character and act.

8. See *Orach Chaim* section of Jacob ben Asher's fourteenth-century *Arba'ah Turim* 428.

The proper context for understanding this is Luke 6:20–26, where Jesus pronounces his beatitudes and woes. Together, they refer to God and to the revelation of God in time: beatitude and woe is what it is like, even what it is, to find God in the world. But God is the "God . . . of the living" (Mark 12:27), he is the "life-giving spirit" (1 Cor. 15:45), and he brings "life from the dead" (Rom. 11:15). Hence, the admonitions are indeed a promise about the future, but bound to promised blessings, and both blessing and admonition represent the work of the living and life-giving God. "If you do this" (Lev. 26:3) refers back to the fullness of the Levitical revelation, and this *is* the form of life that God promises through his unbreakable covenant (26:44). But the much longer woes refer to the *historical* reality of *finding* this life, the reality of encountering and confronting and assimilating the fullness of this revelation. They refer to a history of sin, not in complete distinction from the blessing, but as the historical outworking of the blessing, which is taken up in the history of God's own coming in Christ (also revealed in Leviticus as the secret movement of the whole). God fulfills his promise—the offering of blessing—by taking on the woes as the form of his own history in the world of his creation, his own coming, his own bridging of the chasm.

This is shown in the way that the admonitions are structured as the historical outworking of Lev. 25's call to *shemittah* and *yovel*. They mark the actual bridge between the call and the blessing: 26:43 (and earlier) speaks of the land's own Sabbath, imposed upon it as both a grace and a payment, and through this Sabbath of the land, the Jubilee rest finds its embodiment through a kind of desolation (25:35). On the one hand, this is a simple prophecy of Jerusalem's fall and of the exile, mirroring the summary of 2 Chr. 36:21 and Jer. 25:11–12. This kind of linkage leads historical critics to view Leviticus as a postexilic priestly retrojection of Israel's fate. But Jerusalem's fall is that which is precisely fulfilled in Jesus (his body is the temple destroyed and people exiled; John 2:16–22). And so transcending the historical-critical question altogether, we must see in the bulk of Lev. 26 the outline of the passion of Christ, the gathering head of the Jubilee through which the body brought together finds its redemption. Like the *Rythmica oratio* attributed to St. Bernard and made famous by Buxtehude in his cantata *Membra Jesu Christi*, Lev. 26 becomes neither a simple punitive expostulation nor a judgment disguised as a prediction; rather, it unfolds as an adorative display of the body of Jesus in whom all is fulfilled.

The structure of the admonitions of Lev. 26 is fourfold and can be seen as corresponding to the four woes of Luke 6:24–26. The correlation is not exact—nor is it meant to be, as interrelations between Leviticus and the Gospels here reach a point of simple overflow and intermingling that is unfathomable—but in fact the latter cover much of the same content as the Levitical material. The Lukan woes are themselves fulfilled in Jesus's person (rich/poor; full/hungry; laughing/mourning [e.g., as Jesus mourns over Jerusalem]; spoken well of/persecuted [e.g., Nazareth as it leads to Good Friday]). The correlation is theologically necessary, in that it is demanded by the central Christian claims about Christ: Jesus becomes

Israel's fulfillment, and as the *verus Israel* he provides Israel its true Sabbath, a reality that must include the Levitical laws regarding sabbatical time made so prominent in Lev. 25–26. Each admonition contains a sevenfold punishment, the Sabbath of suffering, which finally attaches itself even to the land (26:34–39) and draws its desolating destiny into the words of Jesus's own vision into the future (Mark 13:14; Matt. 27:45).

If we look at each of the admonitions, then, we see reflected within them an array of passional forms taken up by Jesus. First, in Lev. 26:14–20, the predicted woes include terror (the crucifixion in Matt. 27:54 or the entire enveloping dismay in Luke 21); the diseaselike withering of hope (much like the disciples at the crucifixion); the barrenness of the land (like the fig tree in Jesus's final week; Mark 11:12–21); the breaking down of pride (as predicted in the *Magnificat*; Luke 1:51–52); the striking down by enemies and the scattering of courage (the evident form and outcome of the crucifixion; Matt. 26:31 and Luke 22:52), and the final extinguishing of strength (John 19:30).

The second admonition (Lev. 26:21–22) is the shortest and draws into its orbit the fullness of creation, touching upon the reversal of natural order and the overrunning of human sovereignty by its own trust, the animals and beasts. Jewish tradition saw this as a kind of transformation of peaceableness into unnatural barbarism, where domestic animals themselves would turn into flesh-devouring beasts and where the walls of the city would no longer protect humans from the depredations of prowling man-eaters. All the hopes of, for example, Isa. 11:6–9 are broken, and the glimpse of Eden's possible renewal in Mark 1:13 is wiped away. Instead, like the vision of Jerusalem in Lam. 5:18, the body of Jesus lies exposed to the vultures (Luke 17:37), and again the crucifixion is unveiled, this time in a context that pulls at the whole world and its creatures.

The third admonition (Lev. 26:23–26) continues with the images that take form in the passion, only this time there is a focus upon hunger and the lack of bread, a detail that ushers in not only the famines of the last days (Mark 13:8), but more importantly, in the face of the disciples' question where they will get bread (John 6:5), the very gift of the bread of life, of Jesus's body broken (Mark 14:22; John 6:35, 51).

And the last admonition (Lev. 26:27–33) dwells upon the destruction of the city, with its famine, cannibalism, barrenness as blessing, and rubble—a city that is at once Jerusalem and also Jesus himself (Luke 21:23–24; 23:28–30; Mark 13:2).

The evocation of the book of Lamentations here is hardly coincidental, nor is it merely tied to the historical connections of the text with a later reflection upon Jerusalem's demise, for the reading of Lev. 26 is properly pursued in the same context as the reading of Lamentations during Holy Week.[9] In some ways the service of

9. This theological intuition, *mutatis mutandis*, is shared by Jews, in relation to the destroyed temples of their history, in their later celebration of Tishah B'av (the "ninth day of the month of

Tenebrae (a lay version of several monastic Holy Week offices) marks the pinnacle of the Christian integration of the two Testaments, as Lamentations, the gospel *responsoria* of the passion, and readings from the fathers are woven into a single penitential plea before the display of Christ's self-offering on behalf of the entire world. The worshiper and the whole church is drawn into this reality and literally taken into its unfolding, as the church becomes Israel itself within the measure of God's time: *Incipit lamentatio Ieremiae prophetae. Aleph Quomodo sedet sola civitas plena populo: Facta est quasi vidua domina Gentium: Princeps provinciarum facta est sub tributo. . . . Ierusalem, Ierusalem, convertere ad Dominum Deum tuum* ("here begins the Lamentation of the Prophet Jeremiah. *Aleph*: How [lonely] sits the city that was full of people! How like a widow has she become, she that was great among the nations. She that was a princess among the cities has become a vassal. . . . Jerusalem, Jerusalem, turn again unto the Lord your God").

The cry of Jerusalem becomes the cry of the church and thereby the cry of all humanity, Jew and Gentile alike, the cry of the complicit, of Abel's blood and Cain's fear, of Lamech's self-hatred, of angels fallen and astounded, of psalmist and Messiah. Leviticus 26's meaning here, in its own context within the book, is given through the same adorative transposition of reader and church as Israel within the historically exposed body of Christ. The concluding verses of the chapter, 26:40–46, draw us back into the sabbatical reality, caught up in this temporal reconfiguration of the true sabbatical measure, that rest is penance, that it is through the assumption of penance by the true penitent, Christ Jesus, that the heart is "circumcised"—not through the human will, but through the cross and the Spirit that offers up the Son (Heb. 9:14) into the quiet of death and the hands of God's creative remaking. *This is God's promise keeping*, the vow fulfilled. And Holy Saturday is made the womb of Jubilee.

The admonitions in Deut. 28 make this clear: the punishment of Israel takes the form of a return to *Egypt* and to its original slavery and the plagues afflicting the land. God's mercy effects a kind of rewinding of the promise to its beginning of smallness and fewness and affliction, a return to the moment of covenant making itself, of the raising up of a people from their nothingness and misery. This marks the revelation of beatitude, whereby in Jesus's woes the mighty are brought low for the sake of their own lifting up in renewal: here Israel returns to its true home, the true *yovel*, to God's life giving (hence blessing), by being taken up *by* God into the place of his grace. It is the movement of Jesus himself, in Phil. 2:6–11, that, of its own power, creates from nothing the humble and contrite heart that God accepts and exalts (Ps. 51:10, 17).

Although we do not have Origen's discussion of the admonitions, his long treatment of the blessings of Lev. 26:3–13 (his last surviving homily on Leviticus)

Av" [August 11]). The day is meant to lift up, in summation, all of Israel's woes, past and future, bound up in the mournful and penitent prayer of the sinner and the sinning nation before God. The primary reading here for Tishah B'av is the book of Lamentations as the container of all of Israel's history.

points to their emergence from, as fruit of, the kind of penitential reformation of the soul that has been humbled before God and rendered open to divine re-creation (*Homilies on Leviticus* 16.1–7). Rain, harvests, vineyards and wine, trees, flocks and herds, fertility, peace and security—all these represent (in Scripture's own terms) the spiritual gifts of the blessed, the beatitudes uttered from Jesus's mouth. They describe the fruit of his own life, life given across the chasm of cre-ated difference into the hands of the one who creates from nothing. Who is this God who "will walk among you" (26:12)? The word who "became flesh and dwelt among us" (John 1:14), whom we "crucified and killed," but whom "God raised . . . up, having loosed the pangs of death" and having overcome "corruption" (Acts 2:23–27), the corruption of lies and murder, of life's fertile waters tossed upon the ground, of leprosy and abandonment, of grief and sin, of resurrection.

LEVITICUS 27

The final chapter of Leviticus is often read as a compositional addendum, tacked on in a late editorial move. The book, after all, seems to end at 26:46, a verse repeated again, somewhat superfluously, at the final ending (27:34). To be sure, the contents of this last chapter appear to fall flat, with their return to the minutiae of calculating contributions to the cult, after the sweeping historical vision with which Lev. 26 concludes. But is not such a return to the world's detail before God just the meaning of the preceding prophecy? Are not the details of offering—deliberated, measured, determined, and promised—exactly the stuff of historical existence and the stuff from which its fulfillment is woven? Rather than being an appendage, the final chapter of Leviticus provides the book its tether to the world of created form it has described over the previous twenty-six chapters.

"When a man makes a special vow" (27:2) speaks back to the created form of *adam*, the *ish* who represents the actual mortal frame of human life in the world, rendered male and female (Gen. 2:23) and called out to the coupling of childbearing (2:24). The call to *adam* that opens the book of Leviticus has now settled its shape into the vocation of each man and woman in their sexual difference and relation within the world, a vocation that takes each, their children, their beasts, their fields and homes and binds them to God in a special way, that of offering.

The chapter as a whole focuses upon the vowed offering by which a person would make a free contribution to the tabernacle or temple's life (see 1 Kgs. 15:15 for an example of royal votive gifts for the temple and Exod. 36:2–7 for the original votive offering through which the tabernacle was itself built). This could be done, obviously, by simply giving money or some other possession directly to the temple for its use or monetary value (and this applies, it seems, to the section on houses and fields in Lev. 25:14–23). But it could also be done through the offering of the equivalent *value* of a person or animal, part of a house or field, or an object. Either on the front end of the offering, or later through the redemption of an object (e.g., land) already offered, the monetary value could be given in the place of the thing offered. The chapter provides ways of valuing (*erek*—hence the name of a talmudic tractate that deals with appraisals of this and other kinds: *Arakhin*) persons, animals, and things and also lays out the framework of commitment that binds the offering of such value (the vow itself). The chapter answers the question, "What is the value of a life or of a gift already given by God and now offered back?" The answer given, in terms of the vow, which renders unbreakable the possession of God in terms of its holiness, is of course, everything.

Leviticus 25 has already made this clear, in its explanation of true tenancy and God's essential ownership of all persons and things. The book, therefore, ends here with the call of Moses, shared now with the people, given its specificity: to gather all things to God, because of the unbreakable reality of God's own possession of all things as their creator. But, in the context of Lev. 26, this possession is historically stated in terms of God's own coming and God's own self-offering. What is a life worth? It is worth the life of God. "But he charged and commanded them to tell this to no one, saying, 'The Son of man must suffer many things, and be rejected by the elders and chief priests and scribes, and be killed, and on the third day be raised.' And he said to all, 'If any man would come after me, let him deny himself and take up his cross daily and follow me. For whoever would save his life will lose it; and whoever loses his life for my sake, he will save it. For what does it profit a man if he gains the whole world and loses or forfeits himself?'" (Luke 9:21–25). To vow is to confess God's gracious sovereignty over all life—sovereign because it is total, gracious because it is God's and is enacted in God's total self-giving. To vow, therefore, is to live or follow such a reality. When Jesus speaks of the character of one's word he speaks in terms of what belongs to whom and what can be done by whom (Matt. 5:33–37), noting that all belongs to God and all is done only *by* God.[1] This is the truth, and there is no equivocation or nuance to it. If this is indeed what we follow, we are true, and we reflect that which is true and therefore trustworthy.

The actual duties of valuation outlined in the chapter might seem to contradict this confession of divine gracious sovereignty. After all, how could human beings measure and distinguish that which is God's? But, in fact, it is the divine measure itself, given by God to Moses, and the manner in which it is applied that demonstrate how appraisal in Leviticus has been taken out of human hands altogether. Tractate *Arakhin* in the Talmud, and the rabbinic tradition associated with it, makes this point over and over: according to Lev. 27, in any given category of being, all are equal, whatever their apparent qualities may be. When it comes to human beings the value of the gift attached to the vow (27:2–8) does not note differences in talent, social rank, achievement, or even holiness. These are all meaningless before God's own estimation of value, which is measured by

---

1. Hence the added fifth attached to votive property subsequently redeemed: their value is not stable with each transaction; once given over to God, God's ownership, now illuminated publicly, asserts itself as over and beyond the established value (Lev. 27:13, 15, 19).

his sovereign grace: God makes value and preserves it. "For God so loved the world that he gave his only Son" (John 3:16). The rabbis concluded that the offering itself could never be either good or bad when the intent of the giver was simply oriented toward the great valuer, God, who makes the sun's light and rain's moisture fall on evil and just alike (Matt. 5:45). Hence, the reason for the difference between offerings explained at the opening of the book, among the rich and the poor or among different social roles (e.g., Lev. 4:13–35; 5:7–13), appears evident: these do not represent the different values of each person, but rather the mercy of God for all persons. So we note in 27:8 that the poor man's vow is valued according to his ability to pay and to live (the later talmudic laws limiting offerings for the sake of preserving livelihood are very specific). In this way, divine mercy enables human intent to flourish equally: all sacrifices are "sweet smelling" in their offering. Later rabbinic and Christian commentators understood this to be extended to the fullness of human offering itself: whatever the object or deed, if offered to God as his own, it is sanctified by his coming close and taking it. It is the same sentiment expressed by George Herbert in his famous 1633 poem "The Elixir" (from *The Temple*), where "thy sake" is the sake of the giver who is God and represents something more than a pious recollection, but points to the very glorification of God's name, through the complete offering of Jesus's self (John 12:28):

> Teach me, my God and King,
> in all things thee to see,
> and what I do in any thing
> to do it as for thee. . . .
>
> A man that looks on glass,
> on it may stay his eye;
> or if he pleaseth, through it pass,
> and then the heaven espy.
>
> All may of thee partake;
> nothing can be so mean,
> which with this tincture, "for thy sake,"
> will not grow bright and clean.
>
> A servant with this clause
> makes drudgery divine:
> who sweeps a room, as for thy laws,
> makes that and the action fine.
>
> This is the famous stone
> that turneth all to gold;
> for that which God doth touch and own
> cannot for less be told.

There is, according to Leviticus, a difference in valuation according to age and sex, with males and adults appraised at a higher value. This reflects, it would seem, a social perspective based on the measurement of physical labor. In fact, as the rabbis noted, the passage of time begins to equalize this difference, as the woman's value increases with age relative to the male's. An old man is a "nuisance" in the home, while an old woman is a blessing and a "treasure," her love more steady and constant in action as time goes on than a man. Puritan Matthew Henry in his famous scriptural *Exposition* claimed that the Israelites were misogynistic and that it took Christ to proclaim and so establish the equality of the sexes (e.g., in Gal. 3:28). But the issue here is not the actual human sum accorded to each person for their gift, but rather that God has measured it and receives it as his own. God, after all, takes the mite of the widow as more than all things (Mark 12:41–44). Why is that? Because, in the nature of God's own love, God became poor (2 Cor. 8:9), and the small sum is rendered infinite. God becomes a widow. God is each offering, for it is offered by God first and fundamentally in the very act of creation and redemption—a word now given to God's own act on behalf of us (Mark 10:45). There are no exchanges (Lev. 27:10), for each offering is unique—that is, distinct, separate, loved—in its possession by God, in his receiving of its particularity, and in his own offering. God knows each by name (John 10:3), and knowing them he can therefore offer himself for them (10:15) and in this way gather them together as one (10:16).

Jewish law seems to point to a tension between human offering and divine offering in this respect. Though God's sovereignty is total, and his grace infinite in its creative reach, nonetheless there is no sense that God asks human beings somehow to mirror this in their own offerings. There is a consistent prohibition, in talmudic law, against giving everything away as an offering to God (Babylonian Talmud, tractate *Arakhin* 28a).[2] The general rule was that no more than a fifth of one's resources should be contributed as a votive offering, not for selfish reasons, but so that one might have the means to continue to help fulfill one's responsibilities to the community, including the charitable help of the poor.[3] Jesus, on the other hand, makes it clear that, at least in terms of the perfect response to God, selling all for the care of the poor is to be desired and sought after (cf. the rich man in Mark 10:21). Here, however, the emphasis is precisely on what it means to follow God's own coming close, God's own *qorban* and offering. The vow of sacrifice that reflects *this* divine promise must include all things.[4]

2. Hirsch 1989: 2.833 emphasizes this point strongly, perhaps in contrast to Christian teaching.

3. Maimonides seems to have struggled with this, and he finally determined that no limits could be placed on the offering of sweat and effort on behalf of God and that in cases of immediate need by others, one might exceed the measure of one fifth (see his commentary on the Mishnah, tractate *Peah* 1.1).

4. Jesus does argue against using the law of the votive gift as a way of avoiding charity to others, in this case, parents (Mark 7:9–13). The situation seems to envision a case where assets

The reality of holiness enters here, as certain votive offerings, like animals or houses or even a monetary gift from a valuation, become holy through the vow (Lev. 27:9, 10, 14, 23, 32). The offering itself is termed a "sanctification" or "rendering holy" (*qadesh*, often translated "to dedicate"). There is a sense, in this closing chapter of Leviticus, that the particular items of the world, within and by which human beings live and including their own selves in certain cases, are being offered up into the realm of holiness, bit by bit through the passage of time. And, as the attracted expression of God's own self-offering, this movement must issue in the offering, and therefore holiness, of the whole world. Is not this the prophetic promise given by Zechariah in 14:9, 20?

But how shall the entire world be offered? Through the taking up of life by God's own self and, carried with him, like lambs (Isa. 40:3–5, 9–11). Only God carries the lambs (Luke 15:3–7), but he does so by becoming a lamb (John 10:11; 1:29, 36). What becomes holy is not simply what is given to God, but what God takes; and God takes by coming. This, as we have seen, is the meaning of holiness itself: the passage of God through the world he has made, for the lambs and other animal offerings in Lev. 27 are not chosen at random. Rather, they follow the ordering laid out in 27:32, by the counting of tens under "the herdsman's staff." Maimonides explains that the lambs are not pulled out by hand from the pen, but are lured out by the mother, who has been placed outside and whose voice calls them forth (commentary on the Mishnah, tractate *Bekhorot* 9.1). In this way, God calls and thus chooses. "The sheep hear his voice, and he calls his own sheep by name and leads them out" (John 10:3).

The dynamic of a votive offering goes beyond monetary values and property. It touches upon human individuals, in the fullness of their lives and deaths. Samuel stands as the type for this fullness of offering (1 Sam. 3:1), and the vows of the Nazirites do so similarly in a more limited way (Num. 6:1–4; Acts 18:18; 21:23–26), and it is related to the offerings at childbirth, as seen earlier in the book. Thus, it opens us to the presentation of the infant Jesus himself in the temple (Luke 2:22–38). And, with this in mind, we realize that the vowing of a person's value, even in a purely monetary fashion, evokes the offer of salvation given with the sword (2:30, 34–35), which, as I noted in Lev. 12, embraces the maternal giver of life, whose own bloodshed and pain Jesus himself takes with him. To offer up is to give oneself over to the cost of offering, with all of its mystery.

---

are "vowed"—perhaps land—that can later (after the parents' death?) be redeemed, according to the dictates of Lev. 27:19–25. The general strategy was perhaps common enough. The Jerusalem Talmud, tractate *Arakhin* 6.2, 5 insists that redemption of a votive offering requires giving back from the proceeds what was owed to someone before the vow taken (e.g., a dowry, debt to creditor), so as not to use the votive gift as a means of escaping a responsibility. Similarly, even the priests who received unredeemed votive gifts at the Jubilee (Lev. 27:21–22) were required to pay for them, so that their own lives might not simply profit from the gifts of others, without giving in return (*Arakhin* 7.4).

And the converse to this mystery, only hinted at this ending to the book, is the condition of being "devoted" (*kherem*), a term usually associated with things dedicated to being destroyed (Lev. 27:28–29; cf. Josh. 6:19; 1 Sam. 15). As in Exod. 22:20 and Num. 21:2, Israel could vow to destroy something as a form of offering. Such destruction relates to the sanctification of an object in the same way that unclean things relate to clean things: they are both reflective of the sovereign creating that distinguishes God, but the former bespeak in their own and clearer way its horrible character within the chasm of created being. But, as the description in Lev. 27:21 of a devoted field—a field that does not return to its family owner at the Jubilee—makes clear, its character is as something *already* seen as wholly God's. Indeed, the connection between such devoted things and the Jubilee measurement of time is hardly accidental: what is devoted, even and especially in the exhaustive character of its wrenching out from the world of human possession, is what has completely returned to the owner, and true tenancy and the sheer giftedness of life—life as the essence of gift, and vice versa—is exposed. Jesus becomes a curse in this sense (Gal. 3:13). The intermingling of the votive offering and the offering of destruction—not so different, in any case, from the whole burnt sacrifices—is a reminder here of the exhaustive character, with respect to creation, of offering as a whole.

But offering is also shown as a way of life, in its particular duties and actions that mark out the times of human life and of the birth and propagation of animals and families, homes and duties. Leviticus 27 places the entire preceding book back into the step-by-step walk of Israel and its members, which echoes throughout time and defines the shape of history. Leviticus here ends by showing "the way," as described earlier, Jesus's way, the "way to the Father" that brings us to the one who would have us as his own (John 13:1; 14:1–6, 12, 28; 16:10, 17, 28). This perspective is foundational to the Christian sense of sacrifice as offering, and it derives its first extended exposition from Irenaeus (*Against Heresies* 4.14–19). As the book of Leviticus closes, it is appropriate to allow its unfolded vision to illuminate its own Christian meaning, as Irenaeus articulates it.

Irenaeus's view of offering derives from understanding creation as the essential statement of God's nature: creation shows God as the one who loves and who seeks love in return, what Irenaeus calls "friendship." Thus, the God who needs nothing encourages free friendship among his creatures through the law, and sacrifice provides the expressive motive of this human love, nurtured and grown through the law's specific rituals (*Against Heresies* 14.1; 16.4–5). Sacrifice becomes, in Irenaeus's eyes, a consistent feature of God's creative purpose for humanity from the beginning, one that binds Christians with all peoples and with the Jews in particular. "The class of oblations in general has not been set aside," he writes (18.2): Jews, Christians, indeed all peoples offer sacrifice. Not only that, but the basic forms of sacrifice are constant too: the offering of the firstfruits (common among many peoples), the giving over of the things of this created world in some fashion or another, all out of affectionate regard for the creator's mercy. But only

Christians in the church catholic do so with the fullness of liberty—that is, out of conscious love, which is the fruit of true thanksgiving.

If, at the end of Leviticus, we return to the daily offerings of Israel, this means we also return to the Eucharist, for, as seen in the discussions of Lev. 17 and Lev. 23, the Eucharist marks out time as it is lived in its offering; it expresses the "how" of our temporal lives, both in its gifts and in its sufferings. And the Eucharist for Irenaeus is the great Christian sacrifice, and in a very peculiar way (*Against Heresies* 18.4–5): it both epitomizes the essence of sacrifice through its purified character of offering the elements of creation in thanks—bread and wine, as well as the offerings of one's possessions—with no other motive or even form than that of love for God. But the Eucharist also, through its embrace of the "body and blood" of Christ in its transfigured elements, somehow instantiates the very fullness of the whole creation taken up in the incarnation as it is drawn through time into a heavenly communion with God. Jesus himself, summing up all the dispensations of the past—of sacrifice and offering among other things—in himself and taking up the very created flesh of humanity into a heavenly grasp, draws all things into an offering of love to God (*Against Heresies* 19). And here in the Eucharist, this is performed before our eyes.

All this represents the great Irenaean vision of *anakephalaiōsis*—the "heading up" of creation in Christ for God. It is a vision that is well known to students of the history of doctrine (see the epilogue below). Only here it is expressed precisely in terms of sacrifice; and it is articulated most fully, from a human perspective, in terms of the Eucharist:

> We have given nothing to him previously, nor does he desire anything from us, as if he stood in need of it; but we do stand in need of fellowship with him. And for this reason it was that he graciously poured himself out, that he might gather us into the bosom of the Father. . . . And just as a cutting from the vine planted in the ground fructifies in its season, or as a corn of wheat falling into the earth and becoming decomposed, rises with manifold increase by the Spirit of God, who contains all things, and then, through the wisdom of God, serves for the use of men, and having received the word of God, becomes the Eucharist, which is the body and blood of Christ; so also our bodies, being nourished by it, and deposited in the earth, and suffering decomposition there, shall rise at their appointed time, the word of God granting them resurrection to the glory of God. (*Against Heresies* 5.2.1–2)

The point to be emphasized here is that sacrifice, variously and quite specifically, is made the very articulation in history of this process by which every element of creation through time is brought, by Christ through the Spirit, into its final communion with God. All is offered up—and offering is the same thing, for Irenaeus, as friendship and love—in Christ to the Father.

This is surely a complex and also shifting semantic system. It founds the deepest of eucharistic pieties, taken up within aspects of Eastern Orthodox spirituality especially and in a way that goes to the side of the kinds of crude "victim" devotionals of certain aspects of sacrificial sacramentology in the West. But Irenaeus's vision also provides a kind of metaphysical history of the world in theological terms—something sweeping, but in terms of Leviticus, hardly novel. This represented history is one in which the concrete Levitical actions have both a necessary and a profoundly expressive and revelatory place, not only as types within a set of evolutionary stages, but as the always demanded lens through which the very elements of the "great Eucharist," as it were, are explicated. Through it, we see the whole array of created existence, brought before God as a universal act of love. Here, at the end of Leviticus, we are reminded of how the book as a whole takes in the breadth of the scriptural history that is God's way of enunciating time. As we have seen in the previous chapters, it embraces time itself, which begins with what is clearly a universally human sacrificial impulse and action, in Abel and Cain, and it ends, in the book of Revelation, with an explicit disappearance of the temple's palpable existence, even while the temple's purpose is given in the actual presence of God (21:22) and a sacrificed Lamb who is the Lord. The eschatological gathering of sacrificial actions and signs here is itself, canonically as much as anything, an assertion of some historically universal claim about their meaning that is larger simply than the individual forms of sacrifice that populate the Levitical text as a single document and that are cast back onto the ground of daily existence in this final chapter.

But nonetheless, these forms embody this greater meaning as they only can be embodied in the moment of our living and aging, in the values of our time, as the initial verses of Lev. 27 indicate. Turned toward God as persons who vow and offer, time becomes its own self. This is how time is walked through by human beings and all creatures, where tithes and firstlings, from the steady offering that sustains God's gift of life, mark out the passage of fecundity. That the Jubilee measurement is applied, as the book closes, not to the large swaths of Israel's history or to the great dispensations of the nations and the church, but to the choices of this or that person as they bring the value of their homes and property to the Lord in an act of quotidian self-giving (27:21–22)—this describes the shape of a normal future, in which God's self-giving is mixed into the soil of time. Love is always measured by time, because it derives from the separation of beings and the labor of limits that creation embodies. Offering has a history.

Finally, God's own covenant—with creation, with Abraham, and with Israel—is fulfilled, made full in his own self-offering, whose history is given in Christ Jesus. And we therefore understand that this is what is in fact happening *when* God makes his covenant with creation, Abraham, and Israel: the history of Jesus is being given. This is why each covenant is bound with sacrifice and why each is bound by a vow (Heb. 6:16–20; 9:15–22; 7:21, 28), a term that indicates both self-offering and love, even into the midst of creation's and humanity's and Israel's—and therefore the church's!—embrace of its own death-dealing autonomy, its sin. Even here, God offers himself and so redeems the times. "All the promises of God find their Yes in him"—in Christ Jesus—in the offering of God (2 Cor. 1:20). When Jesus says "amen," even on the cross, God looks into his own heart and beholds the world he has made, gleaming.

EPILOGUE

A Christian Vision of Sacrifice

The body, what is it, Father, but a sign
To love the force that grows us, to give back
What in Thy palm is senselessness and mud?

Karl Shapiro, "The Leg" (2003: 56)

Leviticus ends, in its brief chapter 27, with a loose outline of the laboring shape of human history, the vow and the offering, the giving over and the being swept up that is in fact God's own creation of time in his Son, Jesus Christ, that is God's own patience and suffering of that which he loves. Moving through the text of the book as a whole, I have tried to follow the order and interests of Leviticus as they have presented themselves. But without doubt, theological perspectives extraneous to the text have intruded along the way. They are at one, so I hope, with the larger church's own vision, but nonetheless they may seem alien to the text's own hopes. In order better to assess the character and value of this possibly perceived tension, it is worth now drawing back and summarizing the particular Christian perspective that I have argued is fundamentally offered by Leviticus precisely in terms of its great theme of creation's offering. Leviticus is not the place to articulate a full-scale systematic theology of offering. But it does provide an essential and always corrective form to such a theology.

The History of Christ's Universal Fulfillment of Sacrifice

To attempt a more normative summary of how we are to take the Levitical sacrifices as definitive of the truth of our Christian life, in the church as much as in anything, we must return to what is, after all and in some fashion or another, the constant claim of the Christian gospel, that Jesus fulfills the whole of the law in its forms and purposes. This comes from Jesus's own mouth: "Think not that I have come to abolish the law and the prophets; I have come not to abolish them but to fulfil them. For truly, I say to you, till heaven and earth pass away, not an iota, not a dot, will pass from the law until all is accomplished" (Matt. 5:17–18). And Jesus's words are confirmed quite explicitly by Paul, for example, in Rom. 10:4: "Christ is the end [fulfilling] of the law."

The connotation of the English word "fulfillment" is, of course, not immediately evident, nor is the connotation of the reality "in Christ." The Greek indicates a kind of "bringing to perfection" as well as a kind of "coming to an end." Fulfillment thus implies both a historical action or process as well as a finalizing. That this should be understood with respect to the concrete particulars of the law—every *iota*—suggests something more than an abstracted ideal whose only temporal effect is legal abrogation. Somehow—to keep to the sacrificial topic that dominates Leviticus—the holocausts and offerings, the very beasts and their blood, find their perfect place in Christ. On this score, we must at least accept Irenaeus's (or later Augustine's) insistence that sacrifice engages the material world, even within the Christian scope of experience.

This it must do if the "in Christ" aspect of its fulfillment makes sense, for whatever its whole meaning, fulfillment in Christ involves his own blood in a literal way. Thus, Hebrews rightly sees the prefiguring work of the Old Testament in terms, not of some spiritual reference in an allegorical fashion; but, in the more typological sense of one thing indicating historically another thing as concrete as the first. So, Jesus's response to the sacrificial calling of the law is to present his own *body*: "Lo, I have come to do thy will," something accomplished "through the offering of the body of Jesus Christ once for all" (Heb. 10:7, 9–10). The animals and their blood refer, in the sense of historically instantiating to their own degree, to the bloodied body of Jesus.

The Christian tradition of typological exegesis, however, is built around the primary reality of the antitype, not the type. Thus, Jesus's body and blood is the originator of the beasts (and the harvests and cakes and so on) and their offering. He creates them in some basic sense. This is the sense of "once for all": not that they were once without meaning; nor that they were ever useful in themselves. Rather, were it not for the death of Jesus in his flesh and blood, there would be no sacrifices of animals and grain at all, anywhere. They speak of him; they tend toward him; they exist only because of him (Col. 1:15–20).

This is why, from a Christian perspective, the only way to approach the sacrificial system of Leviticus is through the *christological explication of creation* itself. And this is why, in turn, Irenaeus's more general theological vision is precisely where the matter should be located: the *anakephalaiōsis*—the "summing up" or "regathering" of all things in Christ—the central scriptural explicator of which is Eph. 1:10. The purpose of God, Paul writes, was "set forth in Christ as a plan for the fulness of time, to unite [or sum up] all things in him, things in heaven and things on earth." The term *anakephalaiōsis* is a rhetorical one (cf. Heb. 8:1), where topics are gathered together under a main category (or head); and this is how Paul uses the related verb in Rom. 13:9: all "the commandments [against adultery, killing, and so on] are summed up in this sentence, 'You shall love your neighbor as yourself.'" "Love," he goes on to say, is thus "the fulfilling of the law." In Ephesians, however, the rhetorical term is granted cosmological reach: God orders the whole creation, as history itself is filled up "in Christ." And this ordering, or gathering, represents a renewal: God does it again, that is, he restores what was in the beginning. The meaning of this is reiterated in Col. 1:16–17, 20, where Paul explains that "in [Christ] all things were created, in heaven and on earth, visible and invisible . . . all things were created through him and for him. He is before all things, and in him all things hold together. . . . And through him [he] reconcile[s] to himself all things, whether on earth or in heaven."

The term *anakephalaiōsis* is sometimes translated "recapitulation," from the Latin. But this gives the misleading impression today, from the word's modern musical and rhetorical application, that we are talking about a kind of "repetition," rather than an active dynamic of comprehending movement. For Irenaeus, therefore, Jesus holds within himself all of history and all of its forms—fulfilled time and fulfilled creation. This includes, of course, the various dispensations of Israel's history and of all of Israel's actions. All of this, in Christ, is brought into its reconciled order under and in unity with God. And in this sense, Israel's history and actions, which have as their meaningful goal the movement into communion or "friendship with God," themselves enfigure the whole of creation's belonging and movement to God with them. In the understanding of both Irenaeus and a good portion of the Christian tradition (and even aspects of the Jewish tradition), this *is* the act of sacrifice itself.

Thus, Augustine will explain Jesus's sacrifice on the cross precisely in terms of both Eph. 1:10 and Col. 1:19–20: "Wherefore the apostle says, that 'all things are gathered together in one in Christ, both which are in heaven and which are on earth. . . . And thus, through that single sacrifice in which the Mediator was offered up, the one sacrifice of which the many victims under the law were types, heavenly things are brought into peace with earthly things, and earthly with heavenly. Wherefore, as the same apostle says: 'For it pleased the Father that in Him should all fullness dwell: and, having made peace through the blood of His cross, by Him to reconcile all things to Himself: by Him, I say, whether they be things in earth or things in heaven'" (*Enchiridion* 62, trans. Oates 1948: 1.694).[1]

The sacrifice of Jesus, then, is a divine action of gathering the whole of creation to God. And the sacrificial actions of Israel, and even of the nations, are themselves a kind of indicating aspect of this ingathering, taking hold of the very elements

---

1. A good place to study Augustine's more fundamental interpretation of sacrifice is *City of God* 10.5–6, 20, 22. See also Young 1979.

of creation that are offered up to God and having them drawn, however unbe-
knownst to them, into the reconciling movement of Christ. The images of this
movement are not only given in the primary descriptions of Jesus's mission—as
in John, where he speaks of his "going to the Father" and bringing his disciples
with him (14:28; 16:10, 28). They are crystallized, from a sacrificial point of
view, in the directional dynamics of the depiction in Hebrews of Jesus, the priest
and victim, who fulfills this role in explicitly cultic terms—going into the holy
of holies as the pioneer who enters into the realm of heaven, "taking many" with
him (2:13; 6:19–20; 7:27; 9:11–14; 10:19–20; 12:1–2). Finally, Ephesians itself
makes use of the cultic context's directional movement in its use of the language
of access to the presence of the Father: "Through him [and through the blood
of the cross] we . . . have access in one Spirit to the Father" (2:18; 3:12; cf. Rom.
5:2; 1 Pet. 3:18), and through his death "for us" he allows us to "live with him"
(1 Thess. 5:9–10).

That Jesus's own sacrifice of himself is variously described in terms of Levitical
types is therefore to be expected:

- Passover lamb (Lev. 23:5; 1 Cor. 5:7)
- covenant (Mark 14:24; Heb. 8; 9:15–22)
- scapegoat (Lev. 16:27; Heb. 13:11)
- thank offering (Lev. 7:12; Mark 14:23/1 Cor. 11:24; Rom. 1:8; 7:25)
- libation (Lev. 2:1; Mark 14:3)
- burnt offering (Lev. 1:9; 2:9; 3:5; Eph. 5:2)
- expiation (Lev. 4:20–26; Rom. 3:25; Heb. 2:17; 1 John 2:2; 4:10)
- redemption (Lev. 25; 27; Mark 10:45; Rom. 3:24; 1 Cor. 1:30; Titus 2:14)
- firstfruits (Lev. 23:17; 1 Cor. 15:20, 23)
- vicarious replacement (John 13:15)

The theological meanings of these different sacrificial characters are hard to apply
in a unitary way to the cross itself, unless they are seen as comprehended by it.
And the comprehension—or gathering—of these particular acts of sacrifice, each
performed in a particular situation, is the overarching act by which each of these
meanings and their historical participants and objects are brought near to God.
My attempt to tease out these particularities is but an aspect of allowing their
specific reality to be taken up within the dynamic framework of Christ's own
specific form of infinitely comprehensive self-offering.

There are clear ethical or devotional implications to this reality for the church,
whose elaboration would require a separate treatment. Here I can simply stress how
this approach to the atonement is decidedly impervious to attempts at organizing its meaning according to a single logic—whether that of guilt or inspiration

or triumph, as the standard histories of doctrine still lay it out. It is precisely the wooden particularities of Leviticus—and their particular contexts of wealth, need, violence, fecundity, sin, joy, illness, repentance, hope, and sorrow—that prevent this, insofar as they are not reduced to a principle, but gathered up in a movement—the movement that Leviticus calls holiness, which refers to the movement of God's own coming in Christ and the path of his life, death, and resurrection. This movement is one that, furthermore, encompasses and orders the passage of time—the dispensations discussed by Irenaeus and many others—and therefore acts as a kind of interpreter of time itself. And our attention—however we frame it—to his one sacrifice of Christ will open us, so we ought to expect, to the richness, depth, direction, and character of history and its many forms. If it does not, but rather limits such an opening, we have missed the mark in our apprehension of the atonement's reality.

Sacrifice as Compassion

This understanding of the framework in which to approach Levitical sacrifice presents, in a larger Christian framework, some analogies with Mary Douglas's theories about Leviticus in *Leviticus as Literature* (1999). While she maintains her general sense that religious language and practice represent in a symbolic and vital way the forms by which social groups navigate the world, she now reads Leviticus in a more cosmic fashion than in her early groundbreaking book that first discussed the Levitical codes of cleanliness: *Purity and Danger* (1970). First, she approaches Leviticus as a fairly unified presentation of the world's created order from a divine perspective. Next, she interprets the regulated coordination of cultic practices according to the particulars of plants and animals, bodies and their carcasses, as a grand organizing tableau by which God cares for his creation, through a variety of carefully controlled regulations that deal with what can be killed and what must be left untouched. The distinctions between these classes, according to Douglas, are not based on rationalized forms of moral, let alone medical, concerns. Rather the distinctions between clean and unclean that underlie both the sacrificial and dietary (as well as other) laws derive solely from an imposed divine method of provision for the world. This is given in the covenantal mercies of a creator who would hold Israel and its permitted possessions—edible plants, flocks, and herds—in a controlled relationship of worshipful obedience to God, while holding the rest of the creation—the unclean world—in a direct relationship of immediate dependence upon God, protected from the incursions of Israel's human rapacity.

The taxonomy of the Levitical code is therefore seen as the depiction of a vast creation as it is ordered and preserved by God. Sacrifice in particular stands as the enacted means by which particular bodies are set aside as instruments for Israel's own preservation—one eats only what one has sacrificed, if Leviticus is taken strictly. The whole structure of sacrifice itself represents the character of God's own relationship to his people, the body of the animal victim, for instance, being sectioned and offered in a way that figures the hierarchy of Sinai and then the spatial ordering of the tabernacle or temple itself. In this way, the cult, the dietary laws, and an array of other taboos—which finally includes the Gentiles themselves—function as a kind of reinforcing and enacted symbolization of God's ordering of the entire world.

Douglas writes as a social anthropologist (even though she has been a devout and somewhat conservative Roman Catholic all her life). But her reading of Leviticus can easily be transposed theologically within the recapitulative gathering of Christ's self-offering that I outlined above. It is precisely the comprehensive subsumption of created being and human action—whether one chooses to see it ordered Levitically according to Douglas's interpretation—within the movement of Jesus to the Father that expresses an adequate Christian understanding of sacrifice in general and in particular. In this case, however, a movement—that is, Leviticus seen as part of a history directed by God through time—and not a kind of static ordering is central.

And for this reason, a Christian understanding of Leviticus will make use quite openly of the kind of general explication of sacrificial meaning that Douglas skillfully *rejects* on a purely anthropological basis, for the theological mind will see in the movement of Christ through time the outworking of a *particular purpose* of God. And this purpose will be specified in a universal way, much as Augustine felt impelled to do. We cannot afford to dispense with the prophetic critique of sacrifice as itself regulative for our understanding of sacrifice. But rather in acting as the negation of Levitical sacrifice, the call to a "contrite heart" or a "thankful heart" as the only "sacrifice" pleasing to God functions as the unveiling of the meaning of all sacrifice, much as the theory of offering given by the early church insisted. In the blood of a creature is its life, we are told—the only, if cryptic, theological statement afforded by Leviticus (and the Old Testament as a whole) for explaining the action of sacrifice (Gen. 9:4; Lev. 17:11, 14; Deut. 12:23). Taken as a purely descriptive assertion, it fails to illuminate either the motive or the effect of sacrifice. But taken within the context of a divine motive centered in the acts of Christ, the blood, as Augustine insisted, once offered is the embodiment of love itself, located historically within the critical and miraculous act of divine creation, the permission of and movement across the chasm of God and created being. Sacrifice—if it is anything real at all in Christian terms—*is* the act of love done for the sake of God, within the place of God's love, the body of Christ, the place where creation is unveiled in its origin and purpose. And this fact becomes the force by which the elements of creation are ordered as for their gathering: love for all things for the sake of God, who loves all things, and loves them in the very suffering of their being as created forms assertive of their distance from God. And we shall read Leviticus as the enumeration of this world dangling by this love; it is a kind of psalter of tangible creatures as they are brought to God by God's own bringing of their reality into being and drawing that being back to himself.

If atonement for sin must inevitably remain central to this outline, it is only because sin represents the reality of obstacle to the creative ingathering of all things, a mark of the creature's desire to press against the fundamental sacrifice of God that gives it life in the first place. The cross becomes the center of this act of the creator's triumph, but the act itself is one of love, and therefore the cross inserts itself within the world in *these* places (in loving all things for the sake of God) not in another. The cross is continuous with God's creating (John 5:17). Thus, although we can underline the Levitical assertion that there is atonement primarily in blood (Lev. 17:11); and although this is, in a different way, underlined again by Hebrews—there is no forgiveness without shedding blood (Heb. 9:22)—we need not have recourse to an obviously alien metaphysics such as Jacob Milgrom would surmise (1991–2000: 1079–84), by which blood is viewed as a kind of "attractive cleanser" for pollution in and of itself. Nor do we need to posit a kind of universal "bloodletting" for the sake of balancing out sin, as did Joseph de Maistre in his spectacular revival of a Christian sacrificial metaphysic in the late eighteenth and early nineteenth centuries.[2] Rather, the shedding of blood—offered through an animal in the right spirit or through one's own self as a summit of giving (John 15:13)—is, by the nature of the thing, the most concrete enactment of love possible in this or that circumstance wherein sin's recalcitrance obviates the movement of the heart to God.

Hence, the proper Christian explication of the Levitical comment and the paraphrase in Hebrews regarding blood in particular is that given in 1 Pet. 4:8, itself quoting Prov. 10:12: "Love covers a multitude of sins." Blood is love offered, it is life (and bound to the other fluids derivative of its meaning) in the sense that God's creation of a free being other than himself and apart from himself is the expenditure of self. This is clearly sacrificial language. It ties up with a number of christological implications regarding sacrifice (in 1 John 4:10–12 God's love is defined in terms of the sending of his Son as a sacrifice for sin). In Peter, however, the context is one precisely of the life in the body of Christ, with all of its grace and gifts, to be used and offered within the common life of service. That is, the body is a—if not *the*—place of offering. And bound to this is the central reality of Israel as the historical explicator of this reality of sacrifice, the temporal form of how a body of human creatures delineates the movement of Jesus's own physical life through time.

The Ecclesial Character of Sacrifice

Levitical sacrifice in particular constitutes the "telling of the story" of relationship and action—Christ's, within the world—from the divine perspective. In this light,

---

2. Joseph de Maistre's *Traité* was written in 1809 and his (unfinished) *Soirées* in 1810; both were published together in 1821. See Bradley 1999: chaps. 2, 3, 7.

we can note the Augustinian stress upon the implications of sacrifice for ecclesial life that find their foundation here. Augustine describes sacrifice as this: "This is the sacrifice of Christians: we, being many, are one body in Christ" (*City of God* 10.6). In this, he refers to the "form of a Servant," that is, the "sacrifice of Christ," now embodied mutually within the church (and, I would add, defined by the history of Israel). Origen, although he may have failed to integrate his exegesis as a whole, was certainly not off the mark in repeatedly turning to the sacrifices of Christians as appropriate referents for the Christian calling. Building on 1 Pet. 2:9's assertion that the Christian vocation is that of "a royal priesthood," Origen writes (on Lev. 16, but drawing in previous elements of the cult):

> Therefore "you must offer to God a sacrifice of praise" [Heb. 13:15], a sacrifice of prayer, a sacrifice of mercy, a sacrifice of purity, a sacrifice of justice, a sacrifice of holiness. But to offer your sacrifices rightly, you need pure clothing, different from the clothing shared by other men; you need a divine fire, not one that is foreign to God, but the fire given by God to men, [the fire kindled by the Son of God]. (*Homilies on Leviticus* 9.1)

Leviticus, even in its details—properly and not allegorically—refers to the actions of Christians to each other, within the world. This ought to be a fundamental Christian claim, given that the language of sacrifice, as linked with Jesus, is attached to the Christian vocation with pointed explicitness throughout the New Testament: "I appeal to you therefore, brethren, by the mercies of God, to present your bodies as a living sacrifice, holy and acceptable to God, which is your spiritual worship" (Rom. 12:1)—nothing could be more concrete. "Therefore be imitators of God, as beloved children. And walk in love, as Christ loved us and gave himself up for us, a fragrant offering and sacrifice to God" (Eph. 5:1–2)—again, a drawing in of the Christian person, in bodily terms, into the dynamic of a very particular set of sacrificial acts and forms. "I am already at the point of being scarified [i.e., poured out as a libation]," Paul writes to Timothy (2 Tim. 4:6; cf. 1 Pet. 2:5). "For we are the aroma of Christ to God among those who are being saved and among those who are perishing, to one a fragrance from death to death, to the other a fragrance from life to life" (2 Cor. 2:15–16; cf. 6:4). God has given Paul grace "to be a minister of Christ Jesus to the Gentiles in the priestly service of the gospel of God, so that the offering of the Gentiles may be acceptable, sanctified by the Holy Spirit" (Rom. 15:16).

These are not just metaphors by which aspects of the Christian life are spoken of meaningfully through the application of diverse images. It is precisely in their typical relationship with the antitype of Christ and even more so in their incarnate character as the body of Christ, whose types in Israel order its form, that the sacrificial actions of the Christian in and with others in the world are bound to the historical acts of the cult. Leviticus actually describes this body of Christ and does so through a welter of details whose forms—from death to burning to eating, through the character of thanks and sin, of self-giving and payment, in the relations of sexual coupling and the agony of its fruit, in the shape of the ordered creatures of the earth—are themselves carried into and contained by Jesus Christ and shared with this church of which we are a part.

The Ethics of Sacrifice

Therefore, the Christian arena in which this works itself out is and must be the fullness of creation itself: in Christ, as it were, the ordered and partitioned universe presented by Douglas as the Levitical vision is opened up to the Gentiles and thus to the whole range of God's dominion. The relation of Jew and Greek and their reconciliation in Christ becomes a determining lens. Leviticus, read in Christian terms, describes a movement in which creation itself acts, as I have said, as a kind of psalter through sacrificial discourse. It is the movement of the Christian life's passage with Jesus: drawing the world, from Adam to Adam, with us toward God, rather than denying it or leaving it behind.

The moral occasions of contemporary division in our churches are therefore not properly approached in terms of whether this or that Levitical prescription is still valid as a law, but in terms of how the imperatives of the New Testament, morally and otherwise, both incorporate and are framed by the Levitical details, as the former carry us through the "plan of Christ," in Ephesian terms. Or, more pertinently, as we have seen in the commentary, they need to be approached in terms of how they have been carried by Jesus himself in his passage through the world, into which he gathers us. This may or may not involve the retaining of Levitical laws (e.g., John 13, 15, 16), as something that even Jesus would have us do. More to the point, the details of Leviticus, taken within the sacrificial movement of Christ, demand that we draw into a *direct relationship of responsibility with God* the range of elements upon which our love, ordered to God, is to be exercised. These necessarily include prayer, disease, sexual relations, moral usage of money, animals, crops and plantings, the poor, civic life, and accountability. Thus, Leviticus provides the theological underpinnings—along with some other texts, but in a uniquely focused way—for understanding the material world of creation in which and through which and for which our Christians lives are to be led: the environment, labor, the use of the human body, property, and so on. It does so by naming these things, but also by placing them particularistically in a relationship to the incorporating love of God—in the character of giving/offering rather than of taking; in the character of cherishing for the sake of God alone rather than for our own sake or for the end of their own denial. That all these things are bound up with the sacrificial acts of the people of God before God means simply that they cannot be rendered subordinate to other ethical matters. They are unavoidable matters of faith.

To this degree, Leviticus is among the most challenging of the Bible in a way that addresses the weaknesses of both evangelical and liberal theologies together, as each, with respect to different realms of reality to be sure, are tempted into various forms of "letting go of the world." In our day, this "letting go" is part of the compartmentalization of Christianity and secular life, which has gone so far as to banish the corporeal character of Christian life altogether. Paul's notion of "glorify[ing] God in your body" (1 Cor. 6:20)—"the body is for the Lord" (6:13)—has become foreign to us. Yet without a grasp of this notion that we worship God with the offering of our most palpable, because life-embodied, created substance—and of course Leviticus as a whole wallows in the realm of this substance—how shall we even begin to understand the meaning of John 17, where Jesus glorifies God through his self-giving and prays for us to be drawn into this?

Here, finally, is where the danger of Christian spiritualization of Leviticus lies. That is, when such spiritual readings are detached from the material character of the figures and discourse of Leviticus, which after all are about real things, we lose a grasp upon the call of God into the world that is one and the same with God's call to Moses in the desert, which founds the Levitical revelation. In Augustine's notion of language, the Levitical details—animals, blood, grain, oil, and the rest—are "real sounds," within a continuum of meaning in which Jesus is the final sound or word by which God indicates himself. Medieval interpretation moved steadily in the direction of moral allegory, which ended by achieving a near marginalization of these sounds. Significantly, by contrast, where such allegory was transposed back into the terms of creation's own primary relationship with God, the world reappears as the object of God's vocation.

Jewish exegesis was steadier in maintaining this sense of the world's tangible placement, in temporal terms, within the Levitical framework. But Christian examples also exist, sometimes of remarkable clarity, and their theological accent is usefully noted in terms of a particularly Levitical orientation. Yet it turns out to be one beset with theological and ethical dangers. We can take, for instance, the so-called French school of spiritual theology initiated by Pierre de Bérulle (1575–1629), founder of the Oratory. One of Bérulle's central themes was the proper worship of God, which he described in terms of adoration. He developed a rich trinitarian theology that attempted to describe God's being as a kind of interior adoration within which creation itself is drawn, through the grace of the incarnation (Thompson 1989: 112). Jesus, Bérulle says, is a world himself, containing all things (112)—this a kind of outworking of Ephesians and Colossians (Bérulle also worked from a fundamental Neoplatonic sympathy). But in Christ, creation is now renewed through the originating Holy Spirit (133) as a "new heaven and new earth"; he is the "end point" of God's emanating love for creatures, but also their starting point creatively and redemptively, bringing them all to unity (134), joining God and earth together (141).

In this grand movement that is the history of God's work as Trinity within the world, divine love constitutes the act, not only of establishing creation across the divide of God's being and nonbeing, but of turning creation toward God and, from creation's side, being so turned (Thompson 1989: 145–46, 148). Love is a kind of divine separation (155), by which God makes clear and particular, distinguishing creation as a sphere separate from himself, and himself as one with whom creation can delight; and this separation takes place for the sake of loving in return and joining God. This becomes our own adoring crucifixion (126–29), of which Jesus is the originator. He is the only "perfect adorer" of God, embodying the essential being and purpose of creation itself. His passage through time both hallows and also thereby provides places for our own adoration.

The notion of adoration as separated love, tied to a kind of self-distinction within the world toward God (to which we have referred earlier in the commentary), was taken up by Bérulle's followers and explicated in specifically sacrificial language. "It is through sacrifice that adoration is offered," wrote Madeleine of Saint-Joseph (Thompson 1989: 200), commenting on the notion of adoration as the necessary response of creature to creator (201). True adoration can be accomplished only in Jesus's self-offering as a victim, an assertion she buttresses by reference to Phil. 2:6–11: have the same mind as is Christ Jesus, whose worship of the Father (and by creation itself) is given only in the obedient form of a self-offering slave. Adoration is sacrifice, and as such is love itself (203).

The essential linkage between sacrifice and worship, however, was taken further by other followers of Bérulle, the most famous of whom was Jean-Jacques Olier (1608–57), the founder of the Sulpicians and their great seminary in Paris. Olier saw the sacrifice of Christ, and our own in him, as a death to all creatures that are not God, for the sake of elevating God alone. The motivating principle here was the destruction of all idolatry, which he located within too strong an—indeed within any—attachment to created things. The result is that true adoration must involve the consuming of all creation (Thompson 1989: 219, 249 [due to the fall]) in the Christian life, something he speaks of in terms of complete detachment (220, 225) from the world, via mortification and the like. The key image lifted up was that of "annihilation" (*annéantissement*; 222–23), by which the Christian soul is "completely devoured and lost in God," in conformance with Jesus's "exterior mysteries" appropriated to our "interior crucifixion."

Annihilationism with Olier and his colleagues became the dominant lens for much of French Catholicism over the next three centuries through which to interpret the Christian life. Olier himself evidenced a tension between seeing Jesus as one who brings all creatures into true worship (Thompson 1989: 278) and seeing him as the one for whom we must sacrifice all creatures. It is a tension embodied in his writings, which veer between sanctifying every aspect of the daily round (from food to the sound of birds to sleep and to cleaning) and rejecting the world and everything in it as seducing. And after Olier, it took little time, for the spirituality of annihiliationism—sacrifice as creation's death to the self—to unhinge the church's self-understanding from its engagement with the world's forms altogether.

Louis Bouyer, raised in the midst of this devotional context, comments on the resulting theological and ethical chaos that such an orientation can bring, calling it a "ridiculous logic":

> The perfect homage which only Christ was capable of giving to His Father tends to be confused with the annihilation of all humanity and creation with it, beginning with Christ's own humanity. . . .
> If this is true, then must we not go further and say that creation was God's first mistake? Irenaeus had said that we are the glory of God, but for these strange theologies it seems that the only glory that we or any creature could give to God would be not to be. . . .
> As if the reality of the world and especially of man clashed with that of God—in other words, as if creation somehow diminished God. . . .
> God [in this view] is not the center of all. He is only an abyss where everything disappears into nothingness. (Bouyer 1979: 388)[3]

The church as the adorer of God is a central motif of the New Testament and stands at the heart of the various sacrificial passages to which I have already referred. But the receipt of this motif has been historically beset—if hardly, today, within the dynamic of self-denial we see in the French school, perhaps!—by much the same outcome: God ceases to order all *creatures* to himself, and in such a way that either God fades before a disordered world or a disordered world is left behind for the sake of a disembodied God. The rediscovery of Leviticus as Scripture for the church is a primary imperative in the escape from this now entrenched religious dilemma that has left little to be gained by choosing at all.

It is true, of course, that we cannot read Leviticus like any other book of the Bible: it has virtually no stories from which we can draw examples of life and response; it offers no moral exhortation within a developed theological framework (unlike many of the letters or the prophets); it barely refers to the events of God's life with Israel (although it itself *is* such an event); there are no reflections upon God within it. More than any other scriptural book, then, it is for the Christian a lens rather than the object of vision itself. It can be read only as a filter for other books, as it were. Certainly, as Mary Douglas argues, it must be read with Genesis. But other books too *must* take to themselves the Levitical spectacles—not just Ezekiel or Hebrews, not just a passage here and there of Paul. We must apply it to Ephesians, to the eyes of Philippians, to the Psalms as a whole, and in part to the book of Acts.

Leviticus represents, especially through its sacrificial framework, a kind of structure for the whole story of Scripture and its historical meaning. Its details

---

3. Bouyer rightly worries over the loss of creation's integrity in this vision. But when he comes to his own positive theology of creation, Leviticus curiously disappears, except as a compelling lens for understanding mythic elements of sacrifice within the history of religions. Far more important to Bouyer is the wisdom tradition (see Bouyer 1988). Alas, without Leviticus as a limiting foundation, granting revelatory and redemptive status to God's history itself, the wisdom tradition's interest in creation easily falls into a new paganism, as we see in much contemporary creation spirituality.

are not given heteronymously as in the Qur'an, laws to be followed simply because they come from the mouth of God; nor even, according to some rabbinic
interpretations, as stand-alone elements of revelation; nor are they to be seen in
terms of Moses Mendelssohn's rational morality or universal ethics of the body,
divorced from the particularities of the divine story. Rather, the nuanced contours
of Leviticus lay out, in terms of their historical shadows, the very story of Christ's
passage through all creation—and therefore of the church's passage with him. In
this sense, it is not so much a code, with bits of information to be deciphered, as
it is a form of divine speaking itself, to be incorporated through its actual details
into the message of salvation as that message's moral object. As its Hebrew title
suggests, the book is a calling. The book leads us back into the world—which may
seem a strange thing to emphasize as a peculiarly *Christian* calling. But since that
world has, for so long at the hands of Christians, been forgotten, manipulated, or
abused simply *for lack of love for God*, that is, for the negligence of sacrifice, the
call is absolutely essential.

BIBLIOGRAPHY

Anthony of Padua. 1979. *Homilies of St. Antony*. Translated by Paul Spilsbury. Mansfield, MA: Franciscan Archives.

———. forthcoming. *Sermons for Sundays and Festivals*. Translated by Paul Spilsbury. Padova: Messagero.

Arminius, James. 1853. *The Works of James Arminius*. Auburn, NY: Derby & Miller.

Baal Shem Tov. 2005. *Thirty-Six Aphorisms of the Baal Shem Tov*. New York: Chabad-Lubavitch Media Center.

Balthasar, Hans Urs von. 1968. *Man in History: A Theological Study*. Translated by William Glen-Doepel. London: Sheed & Ward.

Barker, Margaret. 1987. *The Older Testament: The Survival of Themes from the Ancient Royal Cult in Sectarian Judaism and Early Christianity*. London: SPCK.

———. 1998. "Beyond the Veil of the Temple: The High Priestly Origin of the Apocalypses." *Scottish Journal of Theology* 51:1–21.

Bataille, Georges. 1985. *Visions of Excess: Selected Writings, 1927–1939*. Edited and translated by Allan Stoekl. Theory and History of Literature 14. Minneapolis: University of Minnesota Press.

Baudrillard, Jean. 1998. *Simulacra and Simulation*. Translated by Sheila Faria Glaser. Ann Arbor: University of Michigan Press.

Beauchamp, Paul. 1969. *Création et séparation: Étude éxégétique du chapitre premier de la Genèse*. Paris: Desclée de Brouwer.

Bockmuehl, Markus. 2005. "'Keeping It Holy': Old Testament Commandment and New Testament Faith." Pp. 95–124 in *I Am the Lord Your God: Christian Reflections on the Ten Commandments*. Edited by Carl E. Braaten and Christopher R. Seitz. Grand Rapids: Eerdmans.

Bonar, Andrew (ed.). 1978. *Memoirs of McCheyne*. Reprinted Chicago: Moody.

Bouyer, Louis. 1979. *The Eternal Son: A Theology of the Word of God and Christology*. Translated by Simone Inkel and John F. Laughlin. Huntington, IN: Our Sunday Visitor (orig. 1974).

———. 1988. *Cosmos: The World and Glory of God*. Translated by Pierre de Fontnouvelle. Petersham, MA: St. Bede's Publications (orig. 1982).

Bradley, Owen. 1999. *A Modern Maistre: The Social and Political Thought of Joseph de Maistre*. Lincoln: University of Nebraska Press.

Brémond, Henri. 1923. *Histoire littéraire du sentiment religieuse en France*. Paris: Bloud & Gay.

Bronner, Leila Leah. 1993. "From Veil to Wig: Jewish Women's Hair Covering." *Judaism* 42:465–77.

Cahill, Michael J. 2002. "Drinking Blood at a Kosher Eucharist? The Sound of Scholarly Silence." *Biblical Theology Bulletin* 32.4:168–81.

Calvin, John. 1996. *Commentaries on the Four Last Books of Moses Arranged in the Form of a Harmony.* 4 vols. Translated by Charles W. Bingham. Reprinted Grand Rapids: Baker (orig. 1852).

Carmichael, Calum. 1997. *Law, Legend, and Incest in the Bible: Leviticus 18–20.* Cornell: Cornell University Press.

————. 2006. *Illuminating "Leviticus": A Study of Its Laws and Institutions in the Light of Biblical Narratives.* Baltimore: Johns Hopkins University Press.

Carrington, Philip. 1952. *The Primitive Christian Calendar.* Cambridge: Cambridge University Press.

Casel, Odo. 1999. *Mystery of Christian Worship.* Edited by Burkhard Neunheuser. New York: Crossroad (orig. 1932).

Chilton, Bruce. 2002. *Redeeming Time: The Wisdom of Ancient Jewish and Christian Festal Calendars.* Peabody, MA: Hendrickson.

————. 2006. "Recovering Jesus' *Mamzerut*." Pp. 84–110 in *Jesus and Archaeology.* Edited by James H. Charlesworth. Grand Rapids: Eerdmans.

Chumney, Edward. 1994. *The Seven Festivals of the Messiah.* Shippensburg, PA: Treasure House.

Cochrane, R. G. 1963. *Biblical Leprosy: A Suggested Interpretation.* London: Tyndale.

Cohn, Jeffrey P. 1989. "Leprosy: Out of the Dark Ages." *FDA Consumer* 23 (Sept.): 24–28.

Confraternity of Christian Doctrine. 1954. *Collectio Rituum.* Milwaukee: Bruce.

Cook, F. C. 1953. *Biblical Commentary: Exodus–Ruth.* Reprinted Grand Rapids: Baker (orig. 1871).

Corbon, Jean. 2005. *The Wellspring of Worship.* Translated by Matthew J. O'Connell. Second edition. San Francisco: Ignatius (orig. 1980).

Counihan, Carole M. 1999. *The Anthropology of Food and Body: Gender, Meaning, and Power.* New York: Routledge.

Countryman, L. William. 1988. *Dirt, Greed, and Sex: Sexual Ethics in the New Testament and the Implications for Today.* Philadelphia: Fortress.

Cross, Richard. 1998. *Duns Scotus.* New York: Oxford University Press.

Daniélou, Jean. 1956. *The Bible and the Liturgy.* South Bend: University of Notre Dame Press.

Davies, G. Henton. 1962. "Tabernacle." Vol. 4 / pp. 498–506 in *The Interpreter's Dictionary of the Bible.* Edited by George A. Buttrick. Nashville: Abingdon.

Davis, Ellen. 2005. *Wondrous Depth: Preaching the Old Testament.* Louisville: Westminster/John Knox.

Dix, Gregory. 1945. *The Shape of the Liturgy.* London: Black.

Donin, Hayim. 1972. *To Be a Jew: A Guide to Jewish Observance in Contemporary Life.* New York: Basic Books.

Douglas, Mary. 1970. *Purity and Danger: An Analysis of Concepts of Pollution and Taboo.* London: Routledge & Kegan Paul.

————. 1972. "Deciphering a Meal." *Daedalus* 10:61–81.

————. 1999. *Leviticus as Literature.* New York: Oxford University Press.

Elliger, Karl. 1966. *Leviticus.* Handbuch zum Alten Testament 12. Tübingen: Mohr.

Ellul, Jacques. 1985. *The Humiliation of the Word.* Translated by Joyce Main Hanks. Grand Rapids: Eerdmans.

Evdokimov, Paul. 1973. *L'amour fou de dieu.* Paris: Seuil.

Feuerbach, Ludwig. 1841. *The Essence of Christianity.* Translated by Marian Evans. New York: Blanchard.

Fieldhouse, Paul. 1995. *Food and Nutrition: Customs and Culture.* New York: Chapman & Hall.

Finkel, Asher. 2003. "Millennium, Jubilee, and Human History under God." Pp. 312–23 in *"Ich bin ein Hebräer": Gedenken an Otto Michel.* Edited by Hugo Lindner. Basel: Brunnen.

Gagnon, Robert A. J. 2001. *The Bible and Homosexual Practice: Texts and Hermeneutics*. Nashville: Abingdon.

Ginzberg, Louis. 1911. *The Legends of the Jews*. Translated by Paul Radin. Philadelphia: Jewish Publication Society of America.

Glaser, Eliane. 2007. *Jews without Judaism: Philosemitism and Christian Controversy in Early Modern England*. London: Palgrave Macmillan.

Gold, Michael. 1992. *Does God Belong in the Bedroom?* Philadelphia: Jewish Publication Society of America.

Goulder, Michael D. 1974. *Midrash and Lection in Matthew*. London: SPCK.

———. 1978. *The Evangelists' Calendar*. London: SPCK.

Gray, James Comper, and George M. Adams. 1903. *The Biblical Encyclopedia*, vol. 1. Cleveland: Barton.

Greene-McCreight, Kathryn. 2004. "'Restless until We Rest in God': The Fourth Commandment as Test Case in Christian 'Plain Sense' Interpretation." Pp. 223–35 in *The Ten Commandments: The Reciprocity of Faithfulness*. Edited by William Brown. Louisville: Westminster John Knox.

Gregorios, Paulos Mar. 1987. "New Testament Foundations for Understanding the Creation." Pp. 83–92 in *Tending the Garden: Essays on the Gospel and the Earth*. Edited by Wesley Granberg-Michaelson. Grand Rapids: Eerdmans.

Grossman, Richard. 1990. *The Animals*. St. Paul, MN: Graywolf.

Guilding, Aileen. 1960. *The Fourth Gospel and Jewish Worship*. Oxford: Clarendon.

Hanson, R. C. P. 1988. *The Search for the Christian Doctrine of God: The Arian Controversy, 318–381*. Edinburgh: Clark.

Hemmerle, Klaus. 1976. *Thesen zu einer trinitarischen Ontologie*. Einsiedeln: Johannes.

Hirsch, Samson Raphael. 1989. *The Pentateuch: Translated and Explained*, vol. 3. Translated by Isaac Levy. Gateshead, NY: Judaica.

Isaacs, Ronald H. 2000. *Animals in Jewish Thought and Tradition*. Northvale, NJ: Aronson.

Jacobsen, Thorkild. 1987. *The Harp That Once . . . : Sumerian Poetry in Translation*. New Haven: Yale University Press.

Jammes, Francis. 1976. *Selected Poems of Francis Jammes*. Translated by Barry Gifford and Bettina Dickie. Logan: Utah State University Press.

John Paul II. 1997. *The Theology of the Body: Human Love in the Divine Plan*. Boston: Pauline Books & Media.

Kannengiesser, Charles. 1991. *Arius and Athanasius: Two Alexandrian Theologians*. Collected Studies 353. London: Variorum.

Kaplan, Aryeh (trans.). 1982. *The Torah Anthology: MeAm Lo'ez* (vols. 11–12 on Leviticus). New York: Maznaim.

Kazen, Thomas. 2002. *Jesus and Purity Halakhah: Was Jesus Indifferent to Impurity?* Coniectanea biblica: New Testament Series 38. Stockholm: Almqvist & Wiksell.

Kellogg, Samuel Henry. 1988. *Studies in Leviticus: Tabernacle Worship and the Law of the Daily Life*. Reprinted Grand Rapids: Kregel (orig. 1891).

Kenny, Anthony. 2006. *What I Believe*. New York: Continuum.

Kilmartin, Edward J. 1994. "The Catholic Tradition of Eucharistic Theology: Towards the Third Millennium." *Theological Studies* 55:405–57.

Klawans, Jonathan. 2000. *Impurity and Sin in Ancient Israel*. New York: Oxford University Press.

Kugel, James L. 1990. *In Potiphar's House: The Interpretive Life of Biblical Texts*. Cambridge: Harvard University Press.

Leeuw, Gerardus van der. 1963. *Religion in Essence and Manifestation: A Study in Phenomenology*. Translated by J. E. Turner. New York: Harper & Row (orig. 1933).

Lessing, G. E. 1910. *Literary and Philosophical Essays*. Edited by Charles William Elliot. Harvard Classics 32. New York: Collier.

Levering, Matthew. 2005. *Sacrifice and Community: Jewish Offering and Christian Eucharist*. Oxford: Blackwell.

Levinas, Emmanuel. 1990. *Nine Talmudic Readings*. Translated by Annette Aronowicz. Bloomington: Indiana University Press.

———. 1991. *Otherwise Than Being; or, Beyond Essence*. Translated by Alphonso Lingis. Dordrecht: Kluwer.

———. 1994. *In the Time of the Nations*. Translated by Michael B. Smith. London: Athlone.

———. 1998. *Entre Nous: On Thinking-of-the-Other*. Translated by B. Harshav. New York: Columbia University Press.

Levine, Baruch A. 1989. *Leviticus*. JPS Torah Commentary. Philadelphia: Jewish Publication Society.

Lubac, Henri de. 1998. *The Mystery of the Supernatural*. Translated by Rosemary Sheed. New York: Crossroad.

———. 2000. *Augustinianism and Modern Theology*. Translated and edited by Lancelot Sheppard. New York: Crossroad.

Maegher, Robert. 1978. *An Introduction to Augustine*. New York: New York University Press.

Milbank, John. 1999. "The Ethics of Self-Sacrifice." *First Things* 91 (March): 33–38.

Milgrom, Jacob. 1991–2000. *Leviticus*. 3 vols. Anchor Bible 3. New York: Doubleday.

Montefiore, Claude G. 1927. *The Synoptic Gospels*. London: Macmillan.

Montefiore, Claude G., and Herbert Loewe. 1960. *A Rabbinic Anthology*. Philadelphia: Jewish Publication Society of America.

Moore, R. I. 1987. *The Formation of a Persecuting Society: Power and Deviance in Medieval Europe, 950–1250*. Blackwell: Oxford.

Morris, Leon. 1964. *The New Testament and the Jewish Lectionaries*. London: Tyndale.

Nahmanides (Ramban). 1974. *Commentary on the Torah*, vol. 3: *Leviticus*. Translated by Charles B. Chavel. New York: Shilo.

Neusner, Jacob. 1986. *Judaism and Scripture: The Evidence of Leviticus Rabbah*. Chicago: University of Chicago Press.

———. 1988–. *Sifra: An Analytical Translation*. 3 vols. to date. Atlanta: Scholars Press.

Newman, Louis. 1934. *Hasidic Anthology*. New York: Scribner.

Nibley, Hugh. 1959–60. "Christian Envy of the Temple." *Jewish Quarterly Review* 50:97–123, 229–40.

Oates, Whitney J. (ed.). 1948. *Basic Writings of Saint Augustine*. 2 vols. New York: Random.

Origen. 1981. *Homélies sur le lévitique: texte latin, introduction, traduction et notes*. Edited by Marcel Borret. 2 vols. Sources chrétiennes 286–87. Paris: Cerf.

Otto, Rudolph. 1958. *The Idea of the Holy*. New York: Oxford University Press (orig. 1917).

Palmer, G. E. H., Philip Sherrard, and Kallistos Ware (eds./trans.). 1979–95. *The Philokalia*. 4 vols. London: Faber & Faber.

Pascal, Blaise. 1966. *Pensées*. Translated by A. J. Krailsheimer. London: Penguin.

Patterson, Orlando. 1991. *Freedom*, vol. 1: *Freedom in the Making of Western Culture*. New York: Basic Books.

Pelikan, Jaroslav. 1978. *The Christian Tradition: A History of the Development of Doctrine*, vol. 3: *The Growth of Medieval Theology (600–1300)*. Chicago: University of Chicago Press.

Pontifical Council for the Family. 2006. "The Family and Human Procreation."

Radner, Ephraim. 2002. *Spirit and Nature*. New York: Crossroad.

———. 2004. *Hope among the Fragments: The Broken Church and Its Engagement of Scripture*. Grand Rapids: Brazos.

Ratzinger, Joseph, and Marcello Pera. 2006. *Without Roots: The West, Relativism, Christianity, Islam*. New York: Basic Books.

Rondet, Henri. 1966. *The Grace of Christ*. Translated and edited by Tad W. Guzie. Westminster, MD: Newman.

Rosenbaum, Morris, and Abraham Maurice Silbermann (eds./trans.). 1932. *Pentateuch with Targum Onkelos, Haphtaroth, and Rashi's Commentary*, vol. 3: *Leviticus*. London: Routledge & Kegan Paul.

Sacks, Jonathan. 2005. *To Heal a Fractured World: The Ethics of Responsibility*. New York: Continuum.

Sahlins, Marshall. 1990. "Food as Symbolic Code." Pp. 94–101 in *Culture and Society: Contemporary Debates*. Edited by Jeffry Alexander and Steven Seidman. Cambridge: Cambridge University Press.

Sanday, William. 1903. *Inspiration*. Bampton Lectures 1893. London: Longmans & Green.

Schleiermacher, Friedrich. 1928. *The Christian Faith*. Edited by H. R. Mackintosh and J. S. Stewart. Edinburgh: Clark.

Schmemann, Alexander. 1977. *Introduction to Liturgical Theology*. Translated by Asheleigh E. Moorhouse. Second edition. Leighton Buzzard, UK: Faith Press.

Schneersohn, Menachem. 1986. *Torah Studies: Based on Excerpts of Talks by the Lubavitcher Rebbe, Rabbi Menachem M. Schneerson* [sic]. Adapted by Jonathan Sacks. London: Lubavitch Foundation.

———. 1997. *Beacons on the Talmud's Sea*. New York: Dwelling Place.

Scholem, Gershom. 1978. *Kabbalah*. New York: Meridian.

Seitz, Christopher. 2005. "The Ten Commandments: Positive and Natural Law and the Covenants Old and New—Christian Use of the Decalogue and Moral Law." Pp. 18–38 in *I Am the Lord Your God: Christian Reflections on the Ten Commandments*. Edited by Carl E. Braaten and Christopher R. Seitz. Grand Rapids: Eerdmans.

Servain-Riviale, Frédérique. 1999. "Physionomie et paléopathologies des populations precolombiennes de l'occident du mexique." *Centre d'étude et d'histoire de la médecine de toulouse* 27 (Jan.) (online at cehm.toulouse.free.fr).

Shapiro, Karl. 2003. *Selected Poems*. Edited by John Updike. New York: Library of America.

Sibony, Daniel. 2000. *Don de soi ou partage de soi? Le drame Lévinas*. Paris: Jacob.

Sizer, Stephen R. 2005. *Christian Zionism: Roadmap to Armageddon?* Downer's Grove, IL: InterVarsity.

Smith, William Robertson. 1886. "Sacrifice." Vol. 21 / pp. 132–38 in *Encyclopaedia Britannica*. Ninth edition.

———. 1888. *Lectures on the Religion of the Semites*. Edinburgh: Black.

Spicq, Ceslas. 1952. *L'épitre aux Hébreux*. Sources bibliques. Paris: Gabalda.

Spinka, Harold M. 1959. "Leprosy in Ancient Hebraic Times." *Journal of the American Scientific Affiliation* 11 (Sept.): 17–20.

Steger, J. W., and T. L. Barrett. 1994. *Textbook of Military Medicine: Military Dermatology*. Washington, DC: Office of the Surgeon General, Department of the Army.

Steinberg, Leo. 1996. *The Sexuality of Christ in Renaissance Art and in Modern Oblivion*. Second edition. Chicago: University of Chicago Press (orig. 1983).

Steinsaltz, Adin. 1985. *The Thirteen Petalled Rose*. New York: Basic Books.

Stock, R. D. 1982. *The Holy and the Daemonic from Sir Thomas Browne to William Blake*. Princeton: Princeton University Press.

Thomas Aquinas. 1905. *Of God and His Creatures*. Translated by Joseph Rickaby. St. Louis: Herder.

———. 2002. *The Commentary of St. Thomas Aquinas on the Book of Job*. Translated by Brian Mullady. Oakland, CA: Western Dominican Province.

Thompson, William M. (ed.). 1989. *Bérulle and the French School*. Translated by Lowell M. Glendon. Classics of Western Spirituality. Mahwah, NJ: Paulist Press.

Thwaites, Reuben Gold (ed.). 1898. *The Jesuit Relations and Allied Documents Travels and Explorations of the Jesuit Missionaries in New France, 1610—179: The Original French, Latin, and Italian Texts, with English Translations and Notes; Illustrated by Portraits, Maps, and Facsimiles*, vol. 31: *Iroquois, Lower Canada, Abenakis, 1647*. Cleveland: Burrows.

Vérut, Dominique. 1973. *Precolumbian Dermatology and Cosmetology in Mexico*. Translated by Barbara Andrade. New York: Schering.

Wellhausen, Julius. 1885. *Prolegomena to the History of Ancient Israel*. Translated by John Sutherland Black and Allan Menzies. Edinburgh: Clark (orig. 1883).

Wheelwright, Philip. 1959. *Heraclitus*. Princeton: Princeton University Press.

Wilken, Robert L. 1997. "Leviticus as a Book of the Church." *Consensus* 23:7–19.

Willet, Andrew. 1631. *Hexapla in leviticum; that is, A Six-fold Commentarie upon the Third Booke of Moses*. London: Printed by Aug. Matthewes, for Robert Milbourne, at the signe of the Greyhound in Pauls Churchyard.

Willis, David. 2002. *Notes on the Holiness of God*. Grand Rapids: Eerdmans.

Winnig, Hasso von. 1986. *Portrayal of Pathological Symptoms in Pre-Columbian Mexico*. Springfield: Southern Illinois University Press.

Wolff, Akiva. 2001. "Jewish Perspectives on Genetic Engineering." *Jerusalem Center for Public Affairs: Jewish Environmental Perspectives* 2 (Oct.) (online at jcpa.org/art/jep2.htm).

Wright, N. T. 1997. *What St. Paul Really Said: Was Paul of Tarsus the Real Founder of Christianity?* Grand Rapids: Eerdmans.

Young, Frances. 1979. *The Use of Sacrificial Ideas in Greek Christian Writers from the New Testament to John Chrysostom*. Cambridge, MA: Philadelphia Patristic Foundation.

SUBJECT INDEX

Aaron, 31, 81, 89–95, 100, 103, 130,
140–41, 143, 161, 225
   Grief of, 99, 104
   and his sons, 79–81, 85, 89, 92
Abel, 286
   blood of, 55, 178–79, 192
   death of, 110, 197
   offering of, 44–45, 46, 47, 215, 248
abiding, 81
abomination, 192, 199
abortion, 124, 158
Abraham, 48
Absalom, 191
abundant life, 162
Adam, 179
admonition, 274–75
adoration, 297
adultery, 188, 197, 221–22
Akiba, 66, 73
allegorical method, 74, 232, 239, 296
altar, 84
Alter, Yehuda Aryeh Leib, 101
Ambrose, 71n2, 91–92, 190n4, 223
anakephalaiōsis, 87, 265, 285, 288–89
Ananias and Sapphira, 66
anathema, 262
anger, 183, 184
animals, 41, 46–47, 114–16, 179
   orders of, 107
   reconciliation among, 114
   right treatment of, 184
Annas, 54
annihilationism, 297
Anselm, 69
Anthony of Padua, 121n2
anthropology, 205–6
anti-Semitism, 98

"any man", 37–39, 46, 48, 54, 56,
61, 90
Arianism, 23, 109n2
Arius, 228
Arminius, 195
asceticism, 23, 25, 198
Athanasius, 173
atonement, 26, 43–44, 58-59, 65, 93,
100, 103, 160, 163, 171, 182,
248, 290–91
   and childbirth, 125, 128–29
   for leprosy, 168
Augustine, 21–22, 23, 44, 50, 103,
114–15, 184, 243, 248n8, 252,
255n14
   on bestiality, 198
   on body fluids, 158
   on good Samaritan, 74
   on intercourse with menstruating
woman, 151
   on language, 296
   on law, 194–95
   on lying, 213
   on monogamy, 190
   on Sabbath, 241–42
   on sacrifice, 288, 289, 292, 294
Azazel, 167–68

Baal Shem Tov, 208
Babylonian Talmud, 24n5, 52, 90,
125, 126, 133, 153, 166n5, 167,
194, 212, 217n3, 260, 261, 282
Balthasar, Hans Urs von, 130n4,
155n9
banquet, 51–52
Barabbas, 164
Barker, Margaret, 166n5, 167n7
Barthes, Roland, 57

Barth, Karl, 71
Bataille, Georges, 181n7
Bathsheba, 192
Baudrillard, Jean, 109n2
beasts, 108, 114–16, 122. *See also*
animals
beatitudes, 275, 278
Beauchamp, Paul, 109n2, 160n1
Bede, 25, 46, 48, 154, 164
bees, 115
Behemoth, 115
belt, 162
Bérulle, Pierre de, 72, 109n2, 169,
253–54, 296, 297
bestiality, 188, 191, 198
bestiary, 46–47, 116
betrayal, 66
Bible, blinding and enlightening, 21
birth control, 158
blasphemy, 184, 257, 258, 259
   of Jesus' death, 262–64
blessing, 50, 82, 274–75, 277
blind, blindness, 63–64, 213
blood, 43, 55, 124–26, 129, 132–33,
172, 174–85, 292–93
   as life, 177, 179
   and procreation, 190
   shedding of, 151–52, 174–75, 179,
182
   of woman, 149–56, 158
Bockmuehl, Markus, 196
body, 136, 158–59, 295–96
body fluids, 148–49, 156, 158, 192
body of Christ, 26, 40, 76–77, 91,
113–14, 118, 251–53, 294
Book of Common Prayer, 143
Bouyer, Louis, 298

306

SCRIPTURE INDEX

*damage noted.
Ink + highlighter pp 9-18
ok Nov. 27 / 17 ck
Ok Jan 6, 2020 AHT*